Presidents' Wives

Presidents' Wives
The Lives of 44 American Women of Strength

by
Carole Chandler Waldrup

McFarland & Company, Inc., Publishers
Jefferson, North Carolina, and London

British Library Cataloguing-in-Publication data available

Library of Congress Cataloguing-in-Publication Data

Waldrup, Carole Chandler, 1925–
    Presidents' wives : the lives of 44 American women of strength
/ by Carole Chandler Waldrup.
      p.   cm.
    Bibliography: p. 373.
    Includes index.
    ISBN 0-89950-393-4 (lib. bdg. : 50# alk. paper) ∞
    1. Presidents—United States—Wives—Biography.   I. Title.
E176.2.W35   1989
973'.09'92—dc19
    [B]   89-42572
                                                                          CIP

Printed in the United States of America.

McFarland & Company, Inc., Publishers
  Box 611, Jefferson, North Carolina 28640

To Vester, Charles, Nancy, Allison, Brian,
and my mother.

Table of Contents

Introduction

This book came to be written because of my strong belief that the wives of the Presidents are not receiving fair treatment in the media — or in history.

The Presidents' wives through the years have encouraged their husbands to discuss problems with them, been protective of their husbands when they are ill, and defended and encouraged their children. These are traits and actions common to many women. Most had individual pursuits and enjoyments as well, from painting to politics. I want my readers to get acquainted with each woman *as* a woman, and as an individual.

First ladies are expected to devote most of their time and efforts for at least four years to making the White House a symbol of American pride in home and family. They receive no salary for their labors, yet their position requires executive-level management decisions and organization. They are on display many hours most days, and constantly under pressure to do and say the correct thing, for fear that a slip of the tongue could be tomorrow's headline.

It's a tough life. They have been loyal wives who assisted their husbands by entertaining the right people, acting as secretaries and counselors, actively campaigning, or contributing their own money to aid their husbands when needed. Yet they are mentioned briefly or not at all in encyclopedias and history books.

All have risen nobly to the occasion of their position. Even if they are not the Chief Executives in the Oval Office, they also serve.

1. Martha Dandridge Custis Washington

Martha Dandridge was born on June 21, 1731, to a well-respected, somewhat noteworthy family, on a plantation near Williamsburg, Virginia, then the capital of the colonies. Her great-grandfather, the Reverend Rowland Jones, immigrated to the Virginia Colony in 1633. He was a graduate of Oxford University in England and served as minister of Bruton Parish in Williamsburg for fourteen years. Her grandfather served in the House of Burgesses as a representative from their county. Her father was a successful planter.

Martha grew up in a moderately wealthy home called Chestnut Grove in New Kent County, Virginia. She was a short, dark-haired little girl and all her life was plump. She was good-natured and radiated cheerfulness.

She learned early to ride horses and rode well. Another hobby she always enjoyed greatly was gardening. For some wealthy women this meant merely directing servants, but it was a hands-on experience for Martha and her own hands got grubby. She sewed well, played the spinet, and was a good dancer with natural talent.

Martha's father insisted that she receive a fundamental education in reading, writing, and basic arithmetic. Many of the women of the period received no such training, as only boys were routinely educated.

When she was eighteen years old, Martha married wealthy, handsome Daniel Parke Custis, twenty years her senior. She settled down happily into married life and always described herself as an "old-fashioned Virginia housekeeper." For well-to-do colonial wives housekeeping was more a matter of training and directing the activities of slaves than doing the actual work.

Custis was proud of his young pretty wife, and he pampered her. She bought freely from London markets and had the finest of clothes. Martha and her husband had four children born to them, two of whom died in infancy.

The Custis family led a happy and peaceful life for eight years on the Custis plantation at Williamsburg, which was a large estate of 17,438

Martha Washington. (Artist: Rembrandt Peale. Courtesy National Portrait Gallery, Smithsonian Institution. Gift of anonymous donor.)

acres. Then, in July 1757, Custis died after a brief illness, leaving Martha a widow with two young children. Her daughter, named Martha but called Patsy, was less than a year old, and John Parke, called Jacky, was almost three.

Since Custis died without leaving a will, Martha administered the large estate. She did well and proved very capable, due in part to her early education. The responsibility for the two children was entirely hers, but she consulted trustworthy lawyers on points of law. She patiently wrote and rewrote business letters until she felt they conveyed her wishes. Mr. Custis had had a good business manager, who stayed on to help Martha.

Although she was on good terms with her many relatives and there were visits back and forth, Martha became lonely. She was only twenty-six years old, and she had no intimate ear to hear her problems and concerns.

George and Martha met at a cotillion in Williamsburg. When they began their romance, he was a colonel in the Virginia militia and had fought in the French and Indian War for the British. He had always wanted a military career and hoped the British would make him a commissioned officer in the Royal Army, but the British had a low regard for the colonists and their abilities and never even considered it.

George and Martha found they had much in common. His father had been educated in England, as had some of her male relatives, and George had had to assume control and management of his family's large estate at Mt. Vernon when his brothers became ill and were unable to continue the work.

Martha fell in love with the tall, handsome soldier, who was a few months younger than she. Probably George was not in love with Martha for a time, as he had lost his heart at age sixteen to a neighbor's wife, Sally Fairfax. This infatuation was almost entirely on his part, so nothing had ever come of the attraction, and George felt it was time he married.

Martha was attractive, and he thought she would be a suitable wife for him. Her good disposition and inherited wealth were added incentives to the match and would change George from an ordinary planter to a man of substantial wealth.

On January 6, 1759, George and Martha were married. Not having received a commission in the regular British army, George had resigned from the militia the year before, so the newlyweds went to Mt. Vernon to live. He had enlarged and remodeled the house in preparation for his new family. Jacky was now four and Patsy was two years old.

They all settled down happily in their changed circumstances, and visited back and forth with the neighbors, including the Fairfaxes. Since Martha was certainly not foolish, apparently George paid Mrs. Fairfax no undue attention now.

Martha was, in fact, blessed with abundant common sense, except where her children were concerned. She indulged and pampered them, bought them expensive gifts and tried to fulfill their every wish. George had assumed control of the Custis estate at the time of their marriage, but if he protested any expenditure, she insisted that the children not be denied. He was a conscientious guardian of the children's money and maintained strict accounts in their behalf.

Both Washingtons enjoyed spending money, and they lived well. At first there was plenty of money, but a few bad crop years left their finances in a decline. Nevertheless, George probably felt an obligation to continue Martha's standard of living on the same level as Custis had provided, and he allowed her the same luxuries she had enjoyed in her first marriage. But the decline deepened, and even before England decided to levy a tax on the colonists in 1765, the Washingtons knew they needed to cut back on buying expensive items for Mt. Vernon.

Another drain on the Washington family finances was the care and feeding of a never-ending stream of guests at Mt. Vernon. Between 1768 and 1775, they entertained about two thousand people. Some were relatives or good friends, others just passing by. It was good that Martha and George both enjoyed having a full house and dinner table; in fact, they fretted when the family was alone.

A tutor was hired for the children when Patsy was six and Jacky eight. His name was Walter Magowan. He would be the only teacher Patsy ever had, as she had an epileptic seizure at age twelve, and her condition would worsen steadily, making study impossible.

Mr. Magowan decided to return to England and study for the clergy when Patsy's illness began, so Jacky was sent to the Boucher School, located first in Caroline County, and later moved to Annapolis in 1770. Mr. Boucher found Jacky to be a difficult student, uninterested in school work. Jacky was skilled in fox hunting and playing a fiddle, but little else. Mr. Boucher wrote Washington he had never before seen a youth so lazy and indifferent. George and Martha worried about him, as he also seemed to have little judgment in the choice of his companions, and they cautioned Mr. Boucher to keep Jacky close to him.

After Jacky had been at the Boucher school for about four years, he had progressed little past the lessons he had learned from Mr. Magowan. Mr. Boucher thought a trip to Europe might help Jacky settle down, but George vetoed this idea. He didn't consider Jacky mature enough to profit from a European tour, and Jacky's inheritance account could not stand this expenditure.

Jacky was enrolled in King's College in New York instead. There he met and became engaged to Eleanor "Nelly" Calvert, a member of an old and wealthy family. The Washingtons were in favor of the match, hoping Jacky would settle down at last.

Just after Jacky moved to New York, Patsy died at the age of seventeen. Martha was extremely distraught. Jacky wrote his mother a surprisingly sympathetic letter when he learned of his sister's death, reminding Martha to call on her own faith in God, telling her he shared her grief and depression, and offering to come home.

Martha thought it would be best for him to stay in school, but in December of that year, he requested permission to return home and marry Nelly. On February 3, 1774, he and Nelly were wed.

Patsy's inheritance from her father came to Martha when Patsy died. The eight thousand pounds in cash eased the financial burden for the

Washingtons for a time, and George paid some debts he owed to businesses in England. He even owed money to the British firm which handled the sale of his farm products and managed their accounts abroad.

During this period of time, the colonists were becoming more and more vocal in their protests against British rule. They felt a Parliamentary decision to levy a direct tax on the colonies constituted taxation without representation. The tax was repealed because of the outraged protest, but Parliament asserted its right to tax at any time and ignore any colonial law that might prohibit such taxation. To show their displeasure with the colonies, they imposed heavy tariffs on products the colonists bought from England.

Among the many guests at Mt. Vernon through the years had been patriots of the stature of Thomas Jefferson, James Madison, and Alexander Hamilton. These men, along with George, felt they were being pushed by England into making a desperate move to ease the burdens imposed by the King and Parliament. George was urged to assume a role of leadership to their struggles, and he felt it was his duty to do so.

Martha was torn in her loyalties. She was too far removed from England to feel any personal loyalty to the Crown, but she saw the conflict between neighbors and family members on the subject. Her interests and talents had always lain in the human relationships in her life, and these were being seriously disrupted. Jacky's wife's parents were fierce loyalists to the Crown, as were the Fairfaxes and many others. Martha had an Uncle Francis Dandridge living in England, of whom she was very fond.

The colonists were openly arming for war, however, and someone must lead. George accepted the responsibility to recruit, train and lead an armed force, if necessary, against the British, and did not tell Martha of his decision for three days. As he would be away from home for at least weeks at a time, he urged Jacky and Nelly to live at Mt. Vernon while he was gone, and they agreed to do this. Martha was sick at heart at the thought of war and George's involvement in the struggle, but she trusted George to make the right decision and supported him in it.

By Christmas of 1775, George Washington had been made Commander-in-Chief of the entire Colonial army and was leading troops at Cambridge, Massachusetts. Martha, Jacky, Nelly and a few friends decided to visit him there, and they set out on the long journey. Jacky carried funds for the troops as the official bearer from Fairfax County.

Martha, who had led a sheltered life until now, proved herself a woman of courage on this trip. The party traveled a week to reach Philadelphia. Martha was impressed by her cordial reception in the city "as if I had been a very great somebody."

It was another week of travel before they reached George in Cambridge. Since it was late November the weather was bitterly cold and snowy. Despite the weather, the British troops were fighting with the colonists, and Martha could hear the sound of cannon fire at George's quarters. She shuddered when she thought of the lives being lost and the men injured. The others returned to Virginia after Christmas, but Martha stayed with George until the end of June 1776.

On July 4, 1776, with the approval of the Continental Congress of the Declaration of Independence, the colonies formally broke all ties with England. The new country would be forced to stand on its own, if they could drive out the British troops.

By Christmas time the Revolutionary War raged fiercely, and Martha could not be with George. She was frantic with worry at Mr. Vernon, but she made the best she could of a bad situation. In March, 1777, George became ill and was sick for ten days, partly because of exhaustion and bad living conditions. He was now in Morristown, New Jersey, and Martha joined him there for two months. When the fighting got closer, George sent her back to Mt. Vernon.

Back at home, she decided to get all her relatives inoculated for smallpox, which was a killer of many people of all ages. A person was inoculated by an injection of smallpox germs in a small scratch on his arm. This would give him a case of smallpox that, with luck, would be milder than if he had caught it in an epidemic. Inoculation was chancy, as some people contracted a bad case of the disease and died anyway. Martha brought her sister's two sons from Elthem (near Williamsburg) to stay two weeks until they had recovered, as well as other nieces and nephews. This helped the time pass while George fought in the war.

George and Martha did not see each other again until she reached Valley Forge in February 1778. She had meant to join him for Christmas, but because she had to take several detours to avoid battle lines, she did not reach him in time for the holidays. George had been sick again, and once again Martha spent several weeks with him until he felt better.

A few other officers' wives were visiting their husbands at Valley Forge, and they and Martha tried to provide some small entertainment for the officers by having dinner parties and card parties. The enlisted men had no entertainment except what they could find in nearby towns.

By 1780 there was open rebellion in the ranks of the army George was leading. Everyone was becoming worn out by the conflict. George had not been back to Mt. Vernon for six years!

At Mt. Vernon Jacky became restless at not being a part of the action, and decided to volunteer as an aide to his stepfather. He had not been with Washington for many days when he became a victim of "camp fever" and died on November 5, 1781.

Martha was overwhelmed with grief at the loss of her last child. She wanted to visit George at Christmas, but he told her to stay home with

Nelly and her grandchildren—Jacky was father to three girls and a boy when he died. The youngest, the boy, was less than a year old.

As soon as Christmas was over and Martha felt the family had somewhat recovered from Jacky's death, she joined George in Newburgh, New York. They lived in a small stone cottage near the Hudson River from March 1782 until August 1783. Martha had little to do there, and no friends or relatives near. It was a long and tedious time for her. Financial woes continued to plague them, due in part to George's generosity in lending money to the Revolutionary War cause. Martha slipped away for four months during that time to Mt. Vernon to take care of family business affairs.

In August they moved to Rocky Hill, New Jersey, near Princeton. The war was at last winding down, and when the peace treaty was finally signed in November 1783, Martha left for Mt. Vernon with six wagonloads of household goods and George's papers. Martha expected to spend the rest of her life keeping house at Mt. Vernon, which was what she wanted more than anything else.

On Christmas Eve George happily returned to Mt. Vernon. He and Martha were excited and pleased to be spending Christmas together in their own home at last. He had not forgotten the grandchildren. He had carried children's books, a whirligig, a fiddle and a locket in his saddlebags.

The next year Nelly remarried and took her two older children with her to her new home. She allowed the Washingtons to keep her youngest daughter, also called Nelly, and her little son, named George Washington Custis and called Wash, at Mt. Vernon. Martha was pleased to have the children live with them, and in Nelly she could see Patsy, whom she had never forgotten for a moment. Nelly looked much like Patsy had at the same age.

Martha happily resumed her household duties and the care of the grandchildren. She visited the sick, both young and old. She reveled in the return of small luxuries, ordering fine handkerchiefs and dimity muslin from ships in port. Guests again crowded Mt. Vernon, sleeping three or four to a room. The guests were fed three substantial meals a day: a hearty breakfast, dinner in mid-afternoon, and an elegant supper later in the evening. George had begun building a two-story banquet hall before he went to war, and he worked now to finish it. Over their meals and late into the night, the visitors at Mt. Vernon discussed a new government for the country and the form it should take.

All the activity became too much for Martha. Her mother and brother died in 1785, and she became quite ill and was sick for several weeks. George hired a young man named Tobias Lear who would serve both as a tutor for the grandchildren and a secretary for George. This gave Martha a little free time for herself.

In May 1787, George went to Philadelphia for the Constitutional

Convention. The leading American statesmen and patriots had agreed this meeting should be held to revise the Articles of Confederation, which had been in effect for governing the nation since 1781. The individual states had intense rivalry among themselves, and did not abide well by the Articles. The various patriots felt a document for a central government was necessary. They admitted they knew little of other states than their own. Through much discussion and argument, the Constitution was written based on an ancient Greek concept of a nation ruled by its citizens with officials elected by the people.

Many of the provisions of the Constitution were based on the persons in charge at that time, and the scope of the powers given to the President indicate the high regard the delegates felt for George Washington, whom they had named president of the Convention. Even before the Constitution was ratified, he was being urged to accept the position of first President of the United States.

George returned to Mt. Vernon in September of that year full of enthusiasm for the delegates' efforts. He did not agree with all the provisions, but he was the first to sign the document, and he hoped all the states would adopt it.

By the beginning of 1789, George and Martha realized he would be the first President, even though neither of them wanted to leave Mt. Vernon again. He did not actively seek the Presidency, but he felt it was his duty to serve if the Electoral College chose him.

In April of 1789, George was elected unanimously by the Electoral College to be the first President. Unhappily, George and Martha applied for a loan to finance their move to New York, which had been selected to be the temporary capital of the new country.

George went on ahead alone to New York and his inauguration. The first inaugural ball was held before Martha arrived. It was an elaborate affair. As a souvenir, each lady present received a fan decorated with Washington's portrait on a medallion.

Washington was pleased with the honor accorded him as he assumed his new office. He wrote Martha about all the fanfare involved, and about the many dinners and receptions given in his honor. Martha was proud of George and glad that he was happy, but she dreaded changing her placid rural life for such a hectic one. Nevertheless, she and the slaves packed their household goods and other belongings in barrels and began the long horse-drawn wagon trip to New York in May.

As they traveled, Martha and the two grandchildren were hailed by crowds of people with fireworks, parades and bands. She was amazed that she was receiving more attention as the President's wife than she had when he was a general. She had not yet fully grasped the importance of his new position and hers.

Poor Martha! She had barely gotten her family settled in their new home at the corner of Queen and Cherry streets in New York when all her new duties became evident to her. In addition to running her own household, she now had to arrange formal dinners and receptions, and custom dictated she return all formal calls within three days. She felt somewhat overwhelmed and complained she never went to any public place.

In addition, Martha worried about George. She felt he did not look well, and believed all his feverish activities in establishing the new country had taken their toll on his health.

In time they established a routine. George had his levees (as receptions were called) on Tuesday afternoons. These were open to any clean, respectable male without invitation. Official dinners were held on Thursdays at 4:00 P.M. Martha held her levees on Friday evenings; both men and women were invited. George liked these events best.

Each Sunday was reserved as a family day. George and Martha attended church regularly at St. Paul's on Broadway. On Sunday afternoons they sometimes went for a ride with the grandchildren in their new imported English coach.

Martha tried to make the best of her new circumstances and never indicated dissatisfaction to anyone. Her formal dinners were reserved and dignified, but were noted for the graciousness of the hostess and the interesting conversation.

Abigail Adams, wife of Vice President John Adams, understood Martha's obligations and stressful life more than almost anyone else. She admired Martha greatly for her poise and said Martha's unassuming ease of manner created "love and esteem."

During the next year the First Family moved twice. In February they moved to a larger house, called Mansion House, on lower Broadway in New York. Martha had more room to entertain here, but they moved again in November to Philadelphia, which Congress had designated the new capital while a permanent location was being prepared near Georgetown on the Potomac by 1800.

Martha enjoyed Philadelphia more than New York. Many old friends lived nearby and sometimes attended parties, balls and the theatre with them.

Their much-beloved grandchildren were growing up. Tobias Lear had accompanied the Washingtons to New York and Philadelphia, and he still served as tutor and secretary. Apparently neither George nor Martha had learned from the mistakes they had made with Martha's children, and they showered Nelly and Wash with fine gifts and privileges.

Nelly was now grown-up in appearance and described herself as "harum-scarum." She was a delight under any and all conditions. Wash was lovable and lazy, just as his father, Jacky, had been. He hated school work with the same intensity as Jacky had.

Martha was beginning to feel old and tired. She was counting the days until they could all move back to Mt. Vernon. George's health was not good, and he was aging. It had been a long four years for them both.

However, the time to retire had not yet come. Because of serious differences in viewpoint between Thomas Jefferson, Secretary of State, and Alexander Hamilton, Secretary of Treasury, other patriots were afraid the new government would collapse if Washington left the Presidency. Washington realized this was a strong possibility, and he agreed reluctantly to serve another term, if elected. The Electoral College elected him to a second term since he had not notified them he was not a candidate. Martha sighed and braced herself for another four years away from Mt. Vernon.

Washington's second term began fairly uneventfully, but the next year war broke out between England and France. Washington felt the new government of the United States should remain neutral, but Jefferson thought aid should be given to France. In the dispute, Jefferson resigned as Secretary of State, and Hamilton threatened to resign.

Martha was furious. George no longer enjoyed being President, but Jefferson, Hamilton and others had persuaded him to accept another term. Now they deserted him!

A plague of yellow fever swept over Philadelphia in August, and more than four thousand people died. George, Martha and the grandchildren returned to Mt. Vernon for several weeks until cold weather brought an end to the epidemic. Philadelphia was a city in distress from the epidemic, and George made a large anonymous donation to the needy there.

Martha's daily life did not change much from George's first term to his second. Her tea parties continued to be held on Friday evenings, and the ladies continued to dress in their finest silks and satins to attend them, since these were the only official social events held to which they were invited.

With Jefferson's resignation, however, Washington became a less effective President as men who opposed his policies took over. The country was beginning to develop political parties to accommodate the varying beliefs of its voting men.

On March 4, 1797, George made his farewell speech to Congress. John Adams became the new President. The new government had survived a change in power at the top without collapse, despite the fears of so many.

The Washingtons were heartily glad to go home to Mt. Vernon. Wash was now a student at College of New Jersey at Princeton. He was sixteen. He had behavior problems similar to those of his father many years before, and George had to reprimand him sharply. Apparently, Wash didn't resent George's admonitions. He grew up to be a likable, responsible man, devoted to the memory of his grandfather.

Martha's granddaughter, Nelly, fell in love with George's nephew, Lawrence Lewis, and they were married on George's sixty-seventh birthday. They lived at Mt. Vernon with the Washingtons.

George continued to have health problems, especially fevers. On December 12, 1799, he caught a heavy cold after riding over his estate for more than five hours on horseback. A sleety storm began before he could get back home. Two days later he died.

Martha was stunned. They had had less than three years together back at Mt. Vernon. She was so deeply grieved she could not cry. She heard the salute of the guns being fired in his honor. She visualized the funeral procession in her mind, but she shed no tears. Only when she read condolence letters from President John Adams and his wife, Abigail, did she weep.

George's will had ordered that half of his three hundred slaves be freed at his death, except those too old to work or children too young. The elderly ones would be supported as long as they lived, and the children he hoped would be apprenticed to learn a trade as white children were. He had hoped to educate these black people, but Virginia passed a law forbidding their education, so this part of his will could not be carried out.

Lawrence and Nelly continued to live with Martha at Mt. Vernon. In December 1800, Abigail Adams visited Martha and reported the great estate was in deteriorating condition. Although George's will had specified that half the slaves would remain slaves until Martha's death, Martha freed them all at the end of 1800 in an effort to cut her expenses. (Many of them were unable to live successfully away from Mt. Vernon and came back.) A nephew of George's named Bushrod Washington would inherit Mt. Vernon at Martha's death.

Martha's health was failing. Perhaps feeling a premonition, she made her will in March 1802. Afterward she burned all the letters she and George had written to each other except for two. She spent most of her time in her room now. On May 22 of the same year, she died of "severe fever" with her beloved Nelly at her side.

Both George and Martha are entombed at Mt. Vernon, as George had planned years before.

2. *Abigail Smith Adams*

Abigail Smith was born in Weymouth, Massachusetts, on November 11, 1744. Her father, William Smith, was a Congregationalist minister, educated at Harvard. Abigail's mother was a Quincy and a member of a well-respected family in the Bay Colony in Massachusetts.

Girls customarily received little formal education in those days, but Abigail and her sisters were fortunate in this regard. They were tutored by their father and received a fundamental education in reading, writing, and simple arithmetic. All her life Abigail was keenly aware of her lack of formal education, which is evident in her spelling and grammar in the letters she wrote. (Despite these problems, her letters are intensely interesting.)

While growing up, Abigail was quiet and rather reserved at home, but she felt no reserve with her Grandmother Quincy, whom she loved with all her heart. Her grandmother enjoyed Abigail's company, and recognized that her spirited interest in life and her surroundings was a trait to be encouraged. "Wild colts make the best horses," her grandmother said firmly.

Small and frail as a child, Abigail early developed a love for reading, and when not busy with household chores, she read Shakespeare, Pope and Locke. Her efficient mother taught her household skills, but Abigail's greatest interest was the world of literature. She became one of the most informed readers of her time.

She would never be much taller than five feet, but her fierce determination and strong personality made her seem taller. She was small-boned with dark hair and dark brown eyes.

When John Adams first met Abigail at a party in Boston, she was a novelty to him. She was then fifteen years old, delicate-looking, with a slender figure. While John thought she was pretty, it was her conversational ability, her knowledge of subjects in which he was interested and her freely expressed opinions that attracted him to her.

John was twenty-three, a graduate of Harvard and just beginning a law practice in Braintree, Massachusetts, several miles away. He had found girls in general to be giggly and more interested in clothes than in him. John

Abigail Adams. (Courtesy Library of Congress.)

was quite short, a little chubby and a little too talkative. None of these features bothered Abigail; she decided he was just what she had been looking for.

Even if they had considered marriage at this time, John was in no position to support a family, so they had to pursue their romance by writing to each other. They had an ardent, lively correspondence (much of which survives today), which served to make them better acquainted, and their love grew.

After a five-year courtship, Abigail and John were married on October 25, 1764, in a ceremony performed by her father. They went to live in a small cottage John had inherited from his father. John's law practice was going well, and the future looked bright.

A daughter, also named Abigail but called Nabby, was born in July the next year. Their first son, John Quincy, was born two years later, followed by sons Charles and Thomas. Another little daughter, named Suzanna, died at the age of fourteen months.

Early in their marriage, John decided to move his family to Boston. His law practice was still growing, and he was becoming interested in political activities in the colonies. When England passed the Stamp Act, which was viewed by the colonists as taxation without representation, John wrote his first important political assessment of the situation. This essay was published in the *Boston Gazette* in 1765.

When Bostonians dumped British tea in the harbor at Boston in 1773, rather than pay what they considered an unfair tax on it, John realized troubled times lay ahead for the colonists. To safeguard his family, he bought his father's old farm from his brother and moved Abigail and the children back to Braintree early in 1774. Again Abigail and John corresponded almost daily, she telling him news of the children and their neighbors, and he telling her of the activities in the larger world. Politics had always been a source of much interest to Abigail. She told John she foresaw the eventual war between England and the colonies if Parliament did not temper its demands on the colonists. The colonists converted to drinking coffee so completely, John wrote Abigail he could not even buy a cup of tea in Boston.

When John was elected a delegate to the First Continental Congress to be held in Philadelphia in 1774, Abigail had no objections, even though it meant she would be left for months to manage all the family's affairs on her own.

Tensions were increasing throughout the colonies, and it was painful for John and Abigail to see relatives and friends beginning to take sides in the dispute, with some remaining fiercely loyal to English rule and others feeling the colonies could better run their own affairs. The Adamses hoped the conflict could be settled before there was open war.

John went to Philadelphia, and in letters back home to Abigail, he made it plain he wished he were home and farming. About the Congressional deliberations he had little or no progress to report. Abigail wrote him encouraging letters full of homey details so he would feel a part of their lives.

John returned home after several weeks, discouraged and disheartened. Abigail was delighted to have him home. Inflation was making it more difficult for her to manage their household on their limited income.

John was elected a delegate to the second Continental Congress, and he returned to Philadelphia in 1775 with the firm belief that matters would now be settled. Instead the Congress initiated the establishment of an army, arranged for its administration and appointed George Washington to be Commander-in-Chief. Private citizens were also arming themselves.

Meanwhile, the British army was trying to squelch the insurrection, then fought with colonists at Bunker Hill, and much of Charlestown was burned. Families fled Boston in terror, and Abigail housed what people she could in her home.

In July 1775, George Washington and his army came to Massachusetts, and Abigail was much impressed with him — more, she wrote John, than she had expected to be. Earlier, when John had written her that the Virginia colony would send militia to Massachusetts to defend the colonists, Abigail said she doubted they would fight as well as colonists from the North. She felt their passion for liberty could not be too strong when they held fellow men in slavery. The Adamses had household help, but no slaves.

With John now away for weeks on end, Abigail was in charge of all the family business affairs and care of their children. She arranged for farm laborers, collected rents, and took over more and more of the duties normally assigned to men of the family. She had no choice, but she also had no hesitancy, believing firmly in her own capabilities.

She was well in control of her children, and fostered in them an independent spirit. This caused them to resist her somewhat overwhelming influence in their lives, particularly after they became adults. Despite her emphatic personal views, Abigail was a loving and generous woman, intensely concerned for the welfare of her loved ones and friends, and they loved her unreservedly.

Independence from English rule was declared on July 4, 1776, and the conflict with England increased. John was gone from home most of the time, and Abigail faced the birth of their sixth child in 1777 without him. Her baby girl was stillborn. Abigail was deeply grieved by her loss. Her grief was not lessened when she learned John had been elected by the Congress to go to Paris as a delegate with Benjamin Franklin and Arthur Lee in attempt to gain peace in the United States.

She wanted to take their children and go with him. John convinced her this course was unwise. Travel was indeed hazardous, and Abigail would not have liked it at all. But she missed John greatly, and wrote him long and frequent letters, whenever she could find someone who could carry them to him.

During these troubled days, Abigail began to envision a dynasty of Adams men as heads of state. With this in view, she took John Quincy, her oldest son, to Bunker Hill to view the site of the battle and to impress on his mind the sacrifices and obligations that liberty might call for. She encouraged him to study ancient history to learn statesmanship and to instill in him a sense of public duty.

John missed his family, and in February 1778, after a short visit home, he took John Quincy back with him to France. The trip from Boston to Bordeaux took six weeks. Poor Abigail was frantic with worry until she heard they had arrived safely.

While John and John Quincy were in France, Abigail began corresponding with James Lovell, a casual acquaintance of hers and John's, and John Thaxter, a family friend. Mr. Lovell was a newly elected delegate to the Continental Congress from Massachusetts, and Thaxter was serving as Secretary to the Congress. By writing to these men, Abigail hoped to learn how events proceeded on the official level and how John was faring in France. Thaxter wrote factually, and she gained valuable information from him. Lovell engaged in what Abigail considered flirtation by mail. She professed outrage at his attitude, but she continued to write to him.

Meantime, John's negotiations in France were not progressing as well as he had hoped. He and Benjamin Franklin did not like each other, and Franklin wanted John relieved of his duties, arguing that he could do better alone. John wrote Abigail that Franklin let French women kiss him whenever they wanted, and he told Franklin he was going to tell Congress about his actions when he returned home. Franklin considered John too rigid in his thinking for the mission; the French minister could not get along with John either.

When John indicated an admiration for French women and their accomplishments, Abigail replied angrily that French women had more opportunities than the women in the colonies. "But in this country you need not be told how much female Education is neglected, nor how fashionable it has been to ridicule Female learning, tho I acknowledge it my happiness to be connected with a person of a more generous mind and liberal Sentiments," she wrote.

Abigail continued to handle all the family's business affairs. When she asked John's advice, he made it clear he did not want to be bothered. This led to her firm belief that women deserved more respect for their role in daily life and their efforts in caring for their families. John knew how she felt, and it made him a little uneasy, but he had learned it was better not to disagree with her.

Benjamin Franklin got his way with Congress, and John was called home from France. He and John Quincy came home in August 1779. After they had been home only two months, in a turnaround decision, Congress voted to return John to France as the only Minister Plenipotentiary to negotiate peace treaties and arrange commerce with Great Britain. This time he took both John Quincy and Charles with him to France.

As the war dragged on, prices continued to rise drastically, and Abigail feared they would lose everything they owned. John began sending home luxury items from France, such as handkerchiefs, muffs, laces, and tea, which Abigail sold at a profit. She used the money she made to support the family and feed their livestock.

Throughout 1780 and into 1781, the Revolution seemed to be going in favor of England. Most of the heavy fighting had moved further South, but Abigail's nerves were beginning to fray and she felt overwhelmed by her burdens. She suffered illnesses and deaths of family members without John to help or comfort her. She began to long for a quiet place where they could escape from all the problems.

In 1782, she bought 1,620 acres of undeveloped land in Vermont to further her dream. As soon as he received the news, John wrote her, "Don't meddle any more with Vermont."

Abigail was not the only one worrying with financial problems. The colonies, too, were struggling to find money with which to wage the war. John obtained a large loan from the Netherlands in 1782 to help finance the army. A peace treaty with England was finally signed in January 1783, and the United States of America was recognized as an independent country.

From home, Abigail wrote John that it was "difficult to get Gentlemen of abilities and Integrity to serve in congress, few are willing to sacrifice their Interest as others have done before them."

John Quincy, now age fourteen, left France and went to Russia with Francis Dana, who had received an appointment as Minister to the court of Catherine the Great. John Quincy spoke French fluently, and would serve as Mr. Dana's secretary and translator, as Mr. Dana spoke little French. Charles returned to America, to his mother's delight.

John Quincy was ever mindful of his mother's ambitions for him, and in letters to her, he assured her he wanted to be "a good boy" and become the man she desired.

Back home, Nabby had become seriously infatuated with a young man named Royall Tyler. John had never liked Tyler, and both parents considered Nabby too young to marry. When John became ill in Europe and expressed the wish they could be together, Abigail sent Charles and Thomas to live with her sisters and their families, and she and Nabby left for France by way of London.

For the first few days, Abigail, Nabby and their two servants were violently seasick. As soon as she was able to look around, Abigail was disgusted with the condition of their cabin, and ordered one of the manservants to scrub it.

Abigail and Nabby stayed in London for three weeks before going on to France and John. Abigail thoroughly enjoyed her stay in England, and even Nabby forgot her romantic interest briefly in the company of the ship's doctor. Abigail was impressed with the style and graciousness of British entertaining.

Abigail was appalled at conditions in France. She said Paris was the dirtiest place she had ever seen, and she refused to live there, which caused some coolness with the French government. John rented a house in Auteuill, and there they lived. She did do some sightseeing in France, and she learned to enjoy French theater and dances, but she never warmed to the nation in general. The free and easy manners of French women shocked her Puritan soul, and being Abigail, she did not hesitate to say so. She also considered French servants lazy, and complained it cost more to run a household as she had to hire eight servants here to do the work of two or three at home, and she had even taken the two servants with her from America.

The French citizens and English diplomats were equally unimpressed with the Adamses. As their new country was still a collection of state governments, with no central authority, there was no money for entertaining. This distressed John and Abigail as they realized dignitaries in foreign countries were expected to entertain, and they feared their inability to do so lowered the esteem felt for America.

Before long, they moved to London when John was appointed Minister Plenipotentiary to England by Congress. To her dismay, Abigail discovered prices were even higher in London than in France.

Nabby's romance with Tyler had ended some time before, when he failed to answer her letters. She soon fell in love with William Smith, who was the American Legation secretary. This romance had a happy ending, and he and Nabby were married in London in June 1786. Abigail was happy for her daughter, but felt sad that their former closeness would change.

In typical Abigail fashion, she did not spend much time fretting about her loneliness. Instead she turned her attentions back to her sons and her sisters in America. She had always paid her sisters, Elizabeth and Mary, for her sons' care, but now she began sending them silk for dresses, ribbons, bonnets and shoes from Europe. She knew no one else would have given her children the loving care they had, and she appreciated it.

The state governments in America were not getting along, and it was becoming more evident that some central government must be formed. Deep depression was everywhere. Abigail wondered why people were disgruntled, since they had won the war with England. She had forgotten her own fearful economic struggles.

John had been reading and studying diligently to get ideas for shaping the new government. He studied ancient forms as well as the ones in place at the time. He communicated some of his ideas to other patriots. When a national convention was organized in 1787 to write a constitution of laws, John felt they should return home. In July 1788, they reached Boston and went on to a large house and farm near Braintree, which had been bought for them by their good friend Cotton Tufts.

The new Constitution had been ratified by the states, and a new government was taking shape under the constitutional rules. As the new government required both a President and a Vice President. John felt strongly he should be named Vice President. He knew George Washington would be President.

The vote for Washington for President was unanimous in the Congressional caucus, but John became Vice President by a narrow margin. He was disliked by some patriots, who voted against him. James Madison, for one, considered John arrogant and obnoxious in his attempts to create an aristocratic government. John had been vocal in his beliefs that government belonged in the hands of the wealthier, better-educated citizens.

Abigail was thrilled with John's election to the Vice Presidency, but she dreaded leaving the farm again and moving to New York, the city designated to be the temporary capital of the new government. Within a short time they would move to Philadelphia, the next temporary capital. She fretted so much that she made herself sick.

When she pulled herself together and made the second move, she found she liked living in Philadelphia better than she had expected. She was most impressed with Martha Washington, and made herself useful in any way possible in entertaining. Like John, she had few official duties, and she was restless. They were more social than they had been in several years.

John was totally unimpressed with his job as Vice President and told Abigail, "My country in its wisdom contrived for me the most insignificant office that ever the invention of man contrived or his imagination conceived." He accepted the second term as Vice President only because he wanted to be President.

Abigail's health was not good, and from 1791 until John was elected President in 1796, she spent a lot of time in Braintree. She maintained contacts with her friends in that area, and she was happier there.

When John realized his dream of being inaugurated as President, Abigail rejoined him in Philadelphia. She employed the style of Martha Washington in entertaining, with strict etiquette observed. The new government wanted to show the other governments they knew the proper way to do things.

John was a rather controversial President. He advocated the Federal government's rights over states' rights, held a running conflict with France, whom he viewed with deep distrust, and was viewed by many as attempting to use English common law as the rule of government rather than the Constitution. The Alien and Sedition acts supported by him and passed in the summer of 1798 gave the Federal government broad powers in the apprehension and deportation of aliens on suspicion of opposition to the government. Thomas Jefferson and James Madison both felt this law violated a person's right to free speech as guaranteed by the First Amendment.

Fines or jail terms were imposed for scandalous or false writings about any government official. A man from Newark was fined $100 when he expressed the fervent wish that cannon-wadding would land in President Adams' back end. Campaign statements made by opponents of government officials in elections were subject to punishment.

In November 1800, the Executive Mansion on the banks of the Potomac was at last ready for occupancy, making Abigail and John the first Presidential family to occupy the White House.

Living conditions in Washington were deplorable, with muddy streets and few or no trees around buildings, which were mostly unattractive wooden structures. Abigail was unimpressed with her new home and wrote Nabby:

> My dear child:
> I arrived here on Sunday last, and without meeting with any accident worth noticing, except losing ourselves when we left Baltimore, and going eight or nine miles on the Frederick road by which means we were obliged to go the other eight through woods, where we wandered two hours without finding a guide or the path. . . .
> The house is made habitable, but there is not a single apartment finished, and all withinside, except the plastering has been done since Briesler came. We have not the least fence, yard or other convenience without, and the great unfinished audience room I made a drying room of, to hang up the clothes in. The principal stairs are not up, and will not be this winter.
>   Affectionately your mother,
>   A. Adams

A New Year's reception, the first in the White House, was held in 1801. Abigail duly continued dinners and receptions until John's term of office expired on March 3, 1801.

In the election of 1800, John Adams had sought reelection and was a candidate of the Federalist party. Thomas Jefferson, a candidate of the Democratic-Republican party, defeated him.

John was disappointed about his defeat and refused to attend Jefferson's inauguration, leaving for Braintree (now named Quincy) by stagecoach early in the morning of Inauguration Day. He felt very sorry for himself and told a friend mournfully it might be just as well he was defeated, that he didn't think he had long to live. He was then sixty-six years old and would live to be ninety.

After their return to the farm, Abigail and John saw a steady parade of children, grandchildren and other relatives come to visit them. Abigail especially enjoyed all the activity. She continued to handle family business matters as John still did not want to be bothered with them.

John Quincy had been in diplomatic service in the Netherlands and Prussia, and on his return to the United States he served as a United States

Senator. He married beautiful Louisa Johnson while in Europe, and he brought her proudly back with him to meet his family.

Abigail had decided, sight unseen, that Louisa was a fragile, impractical "lady," too delicate to be a good wife for John Quincy. Louisa was actually the perfect wife for John Quincy, since she was sophisticated, spoke French and was wise in the ways of society in foreign capitals. John Quincy spent a number of years abroad, and she helped him immeasurably.

John Quincy had always tried to be deferential to his mother's wishes, but he defied her and married Louisa because he loved her. Abigail loved their children, and later kept them so they could attend school in America when John Quincy and Louisa were reassigned to Russia and England.

Thomas and Charles were not so respectful and invited her to butt out of their affairs on more than one occasion. Nabby ran her own household and cared for her own children, but since her husband never seemed to get a really good financial start, they often needed money.

In 1814 Nabby died of cancer, and Abigail also lost several close friends as well as her sister, Elizabeth. She began to worry that she might never see John Quincy again, as he was now serving as Minister to England. But when James Monroe was elected President, he appointed John Quincy Secretary of State, and he and Louisa reached New York in August 1817. They went to Massachusetts, where they spent about a month with John and Abigail.

In August the next year, they visited again. A few days after they left, Abigail developed typhoid fever. She had been in declining health for several months, and this disease was too much for her weakened system. She died in October without pain.

Abigail had gotten her wish to see John Quincy one more time, but she did not live to see him elected President. John did survive, and on that great day he must have grieved anew for Abigail and wished she could have seen her son's inauguration. He died July 4, 1826, a few hours after the death of Thomas Jefferson.

3. Martha Wayles Skelton Jefferson

Martha Wayles was born in Charles City County, Virginia, on her father's plantation ("The Forest"), on October 19, 1748. She grew up in the luxury of a wealthy home, but without her mother, who died when Martha was very young. Mr. Wayles remarried twice, and Martha never did get along with either of her stepmothers.

Martha married Bathhurst Skelton on November 20, 1766, when she was barely eighteen years old. Martha's then-stepmother was the widow of Bathhurst's brother, making her both Martha's stepmother and her sister-in-law.

Martha and Bathhurst had a little son born to them the next year, whom they named John. She, her husband and her baby lived happily on Bathhurst's large estate at Williamsburg, Virginia, where Martha learned to be a mother and the mistress of a household. Their happiness was short-lived, however, as Bathhurst died in September 1768, when John was less than a year old.

Since Martha was not yet twenty, she took her little son and went back to live in her father's household. Following a decent interval of mourning her loss, Martha went into Williamsburg for a part of the social season of dinner parties, balls and theater. It was there she met Thomas Jefferson, who had recently begun a law practice in Williamsburg.

Martha and Thomas were immediately attracted to each other. Thomas had been a schoolmate of Martha's late husband. Both he and Martha loved music, and both were lonely. Jefferson had recently had an unfortunate romantic involvement with a friend's wife, which he and the lady had broken off by mutual agreement.

Martha was enough to interest any man, with her auburn hair, hazel eyes and exquisite complexion. She had received some formal education and had above-average intelligence. In addition, she was wealthy. Thomas was not her only suitor, but he quickly became her favorite.

Martha's father, John Wayles, was reluctant to give his consent for Martha to marry Thomas. Wayles had emigrated from England and had a large legal practice in addition to his extensive land holdings. Thomas liked Wayles, but he was in no way awed by his education or legal abilities. Thomas considered himself equal to Mr. Wayles. This probably bothered Wayles quite a bit. Another reason Wayles hated to have Martha leave his home was that she kept plantation accounts for her father.

Mr. Wayles was also unimpressed with what Thomas had to offer Martha in the way of a house or other property. Thomas owned a plantation of five thousand acres, but the family home had burned to the ground about two years before. Thomas had drawn up plans for a magnificent home to be built on a mountain on that property, but so far he had only completed one room. It was to this one-room brick cottage he proposed to take his new bride. He promised he would add to the cottage, but he had not yet found time to do so. His law practice was bringing in a substantial income, so money was available.

Mr. Wayles insisted that Martha be provided a better home, and Thomas realized his demand was somewhat valid. Thomas then hired a builder to help him enlarge his new home, which he named Monticello. He ordered a pianoforte for his bride-to-be and some wedding finery for himself, such as a green silk umbrella and some stockings.

On January 1, 1772, Martha and Thomas were married. Thomas looked forward eagerly to being a father to little John, Martha's son, but in this he was disappointed. The child died a few months before their wedding.

The newlyweds spent two weeks at The Forest, then visited with other relatives for a few days, reaching Monticello before the end of January. Three feet of snow lay on the ground when they arrived, and they managed to get two months of uninterrupted privacy before the outside world intruded on their happiness.

Thomas had earlier been elected to the House of Burgesses, the governing body in the Virginia colony. Though the February meeting of 1772 was minus a member as Martha and Thomas honeymooned, Thomas was on the way to becoming a respected, influential citizen of the Virginia colony.

In September that year the Jeffersons' first child, a girl, was born. She was named Martha for her mother, but was generally called Patsy. Even though she had a touch-and-go infancy with several health problems, she did survive.

Though it was rare in that time for a wife and mother to pursue her own interests, Thomas encouraged Martha to do so. He engaged an Italian musician named Alberti to give Martha music lessons on violin and piano. Alberti also gave Thomas instructions on the violin, and the two men became good friends.

About the time a second daughter was born eighteen months later, Martha's father died, and Martha inherited more than eleven thousand acres of land as well as a large number of slaves. At the time of his death, John Wayles owed a sizable debt to a mercantile company in England so Thomas sold some of the land Martha had inherited to pay the debt.

Meantime Thomas bought the property on which the Natural Bridge was located. The Jeffersons always lived well, often beyond their means.

In the larger world the spirit of rebellion again British rule was growing among the colonists, who were beginning to wonder why they should not form a government of their own.

Thomas stayed home with his family and out of politics for about two years after he and Martha were married. The House of Burgesses did not meet for a year on orders from Governor Dunmore of Virginia, who was an official appointed by the British government. When Governor Dunmore learned of the colonists' talk of rebellion against the Crown, he did not simply postpone a meeting of the House of Burgesses — he dissolved the group.

Thomas was then elected a member of the Continental Congress, meeting in Philadelphia, which hoped to draft a document to establish governing rules for the colonies. Thomas had not been gone from home long before the Jefferson's second child died. Martha was distraught with grief, and Thomas left for home to be with her. He stayed home until May 1776.

As the year of 1776 had begun, Governor Dunmore had ordered that the city of Norfolk be bombarded by British naval guns, and this served to further stiffen the colonists' resistance to British rule. Fortunately, Monticello was a long way from the bombardment, and Thomas and his family were safe for the moment.

But something had to be done. When Thomas returned to Philadelphia in May to attend the ongoing Second Continental Congress, he helped John Adams, Benjamin Franklin, Roger Sherman and Robert R. Livingston write the Declaration of Independence, by which the colonists were to be freed from British domination. In June that year the colony of Virginia adopted a constitution for a new government. The Revolution against England was beginning.

Thomas missed his wife and little Patsy during these troubled days. One of his fellow delegates had brought his wife with him to Philadelphia, and he urged Thomas to bring Martha to be with him. Thomas was sad, knowing Martha was not physically able to make the trip. She was not even able to attend balls held in Williamsburg, in which she had formerly delighted.

With Thomas away from home so much, Martha decided to help him by keeping careful household accounts. Her pen sketches in the page margins of little birds sitting on leafy branches revealed her boredom with her job.

The Declaration of Independence was approved by the Continental Congress and made public on July 4, 1776. Thomas had done the actual writing of the document, although he was assisted by other delegates, and he included in the original document a condemnation of slavery, which was about five hundred words long. The delegates to the Congress expunged this passage before they approved the Declaration, to Thomas's bitter disappointment.

In October that year Thomas had been back home with Martha and Patsy for about a month when he was asked to go to France as a Commissioner with Benjamin Franklin and Silas Deane. This was an honor he declined with genuine regret, but he could not possibly go so far away from Martha, and she was not able to go with him.

On October 27, 1776, he accepted a post as a member of the Virginia House of Delegates, which met in Williamsburg and Richmond. He continued to hold this post for the next three years. Martha came to be with him in 1777 in Williamsburg for a few weeks, but returned to Monticello to give birth to their only son, who died three weeks later.

So far only Patsy had survived, but the next year (1778) another little girl born to Martha would reach adulthood. They named her Maria, but she was generally called Polly.

Thomas had more work done at Monticello during his year at home, and had many fruit trees planted. Martha enjoyed all the beauty surrounding her, but she resented Thomas's being gone from home so much. She began to plead with him not to leave.

Meanwhile, fellow patriots were criticizing Thomas severely for staying close to his home and not taking a more active part in the country's political upheaval. The truth was he was afraid to go far or stay long because of Martha's poor health, although he was passionately interested in the Revolution.

Virginia was now considered a state and was led by a Governor appointed by two legislative branches of the Assembly. On June 1, 1779, Thomas was elected Governor of Virginia. Martha had taken their two little girls to visit relatives at The Forest, and Thomas was forced to spend most of his time in Williamsburg. Soon Martha and Thomas moved their family into the Palace, the official residence in Williamsburg for the Governor.

Thomas was not successful as Governor, and was eventually accused of failing to provide an adequate militia to protect the citizens when the British army invaded Virginia. An investigation was launched, and Thomas left office.

When the British army advanced to Monticello in June 1781, Thomas and Martha were forced to flee with their children to Richmond. While they were living there, Martha gave birth to another little daughter, who died within a few days. Martha was so overcome with grief that Thomas could not leave her for even a few minutes.

There is no evidence to indicate Martha ever had any influence on Thomas's political thinking. She was a sweet, amiable, loving wife and mother, whose chief interest was her home and children.

Martha's last child was born in May 1782, reportedly weighing sixteen pounds. The birth of such a large child completely exhausted the already frail Martha, and she never recovered her health. The baby died after a few weeks.

Martha's health declined steadily until her own death four months later on September 6, 1782, probably from diabetes. No picture of her is known to exist. She was buried at Monticello.

Thomas now had two little daughters to rear without a wife to help him. Martha had made him promise before her death he would never remarry, as she did not want her daughters to have a stepmother. Thomas never did remarry.

When Thomas became the third President of the United States in 1801, he named James Madison to be his Secretary of State, and he asked Dolley Madison, James's wife, to serve as his official hostess in the White House or Executive Mansion. As his daughters grew older they also served on occasion.

Thomas served as President for two terms. During his administrations he urged Congress to approve the Louisiana Purchase, which added greatly to the land area of the United States. This territory was bought from the French government for fifteen million dollars, which amounted to three cents per acre.

In his retirement years, Thomas founded the University of Virginia at Charlottesville to further the education of young male Americans. He donated his extensive library to Congress to serve as the beginning of a new national library. The Library of Congress was destroyed completely when the British army burned Washington during the War of 1812.

Thomas died on July 4, 1826, the fiftieth anniversary of the Declaration of Independence. He is buried beside Martha at Monticello. His old friend and rival, John Adams, who had helped Thomas draft the Declaration and served as second President of the United States, died the same day.

4. Dorothea (Dolley) Payne Todd Madison

Dolley Payne was born to parents of the Quaker faith in Guilford County, North Carolina, on May 20, 1768. The Payne family did not stay long in the small North Carolina farming community. When Dolley was a year old, her father, John Payne, moved his family to Virginia, where they lived for a time at Scotchtown, a plantation Patrick Henry had once owned. Henry was a cousin of Dolley's mother. The main house on the plantation was one hundred feet long.

The plantation was prosperous, but John Payne could not enjoy his prosperity because he obtained it by slave labor and he did not approve of slavery. He and other Quakers urged the Virginia legislature to abolish slavery in their 1776 Declaration of Rights. He refused to serve in the Revolutionary War as he did not approve of violence either. When slave owners in Virginia were allowed to grant freedom to slaves in 1782, he set all his slaves free and sold the plantation.

Possibly feeling the sting of criticism from less generous neighbors, Payne then moved to Philadelphia. He had no way to earn money when he arrived in Philadelphia, so he became a starch-maker.

Dolley loved living in Philadelphia, where life was more exciting than any she had known before. She attended Quaker gatherings, and young Quaker men were not unaware that she was developing into an unusually pretty, vivacious, friendly young woman. At age sixteen she was a black-haired, blue-eyed and full-figured beauty. She wore the Quaker garb, which she privately considered drab and unappealing, to please her parents. She lived by Quaker discipline, but admired two girl friends who married men outside the faith, "the choice of their hearts." She had received an education from Quaker teachers as the Quakers believed in education for women.

John Payne, who had always worked as a farm manager, was unsuccessful in starch-making, and by 1789 he was bankrupt. Quakers were expected to pay all their just debts, and solvency was considered godly; so sadly, John Payne was expelled from the Pine Street Meeting. He went to

Dolley Madison. (Artist: William S. Elwell. Courtesy National Portrait Gallery, Smithsonian Institution.)

his bedroom and stayed there, broken and discouraged, until his death two years later.

During this sad time, Dolley had fallen in love with a young Quaker lawyer named John Todd, whom she married on January 7, 1790. The Pine Street Meeting was so pleased by this marriage that eighty of them attended the wedding. The Paynes, too, heartily approved of Dolley's choice, who had stood loyally by them during the bankruptcy proceedings.

The Todds had a happy marriage, and by 1793 they had two little sons. They lived in a fine house in Philadelphia at the corner of Fourth and

Walnut streets (now restored and open to visitors). Todd's law practice grew.

During the yellow fever epidemic that occurred that fall, Dolley and her two children went with Dolley's widowed mother and Mrs. Payne's three small children to the country for a time in an effort to avoid the disease. John Todd stayed in Philadelphia, where both his parents died in the epidemic, as well as many other Philadelphians. Dolley came back in October, only to have her husband and baby son die the same day from the fever. She became critically ill herself.

At last frost and cold weather stopped the terrible epidemic. Dolley recovered slowly and found herself a widow at age twenty-five with a two-year-old son to rear and nineteen dollars to her name. However, her husband had been a wealthy man, so in a short time she had more cash. Aaron Burr, who was a family friend, helped her with her financial affairs, and it was through him that she met James Madison.

Dolley continued to live in her own home, and her sister Anna came to live with her. Dolley's mother and her other two children went to live in Virginia with Dolley's sister Lucy, who had married George Washington's nephew a few months before.

As a widow Dolley was much admired by the men of Philadelphia. In addition to her obvious beauty and pleasing personality, she had inherited a sizeable amount of money.

From the beginning James Madison admired Dolley for her looks and for her social graces, which he lacked. Her money was probably secondary to him. He loved Dolley's style in clothes and her ready charm, tact and kindliness. There was not a mean bone in Dolley.

Their romance was swift and ardent. James had been surrounded for years by the interests of his large family of brothers and sisters, as well as his parents, and had been preoccupied by his own intense interest in politics. He was well known in Philadelphia, especially by all men in government, as he had played a major role in the drafting of the Constitution for the new country. He was now forty-three years old, very proper in his conduct, and most of his friends had considered him to be a confirmed bachelor. They were completely surprised by the marriage.

James was madly in love with Dolley despite his outward reserve. As a male friend wrote her in a letter, "At night he Dreames of you and Starts in his Sleep aCalling on you to relieve his Flame for he Burns to such an excess that he will be shortly consumed...he has consented to everything that I have wrote about him with Sparkling Eyes."

On September 15, 1794, James and Dolley were married at Harewood, Lucy's home in the Shenandoah Valley of Virginia, in the presence of members of both immediate families. Dolley realized she was breaking with Quaker beliefs by marrying James, and that her life would be greatly altered by this marriage. Still she felt it was the right thing for her to do. A few weeks later she was expelled from the Pine Street Meeting for marrying a non–Quaker.

On the advice of her lawyer, Dolley made a generous property arrangement for her son from the inheritance from her first husband, partly to protect Madison from gossip that he had married her for her money. Madison was not a wealthy man.

James and Dolley went to live in a house in Philadelphia recently vacated by James Monroe and his wife when they left for Paris, where Monroe would serve as Minister to France. Monroe was supposed to return some of the furniture, and after a wait of more than two years, it finally arrived—watersoaked. The furniture was welcomed by Dolley all the same, as it gave the Madison home a modified French decor, much admired by Americans at this time.

Dolley's and James's younger sisters kept the household lively with parties, courtships and talk of French fashions. Dolley adopted the French styles—clothing that disgusted outspoken Abigail Adams, who called it "an outrage upon all decency." Dolley was severely criticized because she did not always conceal her cleavage with a handkerchief.

James was delighted with his new wife (and her clothes). If he heard the criticism of her, he ignored it, for he knew Dolley meant no harm. Whether Abigail's opinions played a part or not, James never liked John Adams, Abigail's husband, even though they had mutual friends and interests in the new government. He stayed strictly out of political activities while John Adams was President. He retired from his Congressional seat and stayed home with Dolley. He spent his days managing the family plantation in Orange County and overseeing the remodeling of the mansion at Montpelier. However, Dolley never made nor attempted to make any change in his political beliefs or activities.

Dolley enjoyed her new role as the hostess of a plantation, but then Dolley tended to enjoy her life wherever she found herself to be. She and James paid frequent visits to various relatives and friends throughout Virginia.

James Monroe returned from his post in France in 1797 and built a home a few miles from Monticello, the home of Thomas Jefferson. Since Dolley and James had been visiting Thomas Jefferson and his family at least twice each year, they were glad to have the Monroes living in the same vicinity.

When Thomas Jefferson was elected President in 1801, he asked James to serve as Secretary of State in his Cabinet. Dolley became President Jefferson's unofficial hostess, as President Jefferson was a widower. A British diplomat, Sir Augustus John Foster, when he visited the White House found Dolley to be "a very handsome woman and though an uncultivated mind and fond of gossiping, was so perfectly good tempered and good humored that she rendered her husband's house as far as depended on her agreeable to all parties."

James and Dolley had lived briefly in the unfinished "President's House" before moving to a three-story brick home two blocks East of the White House. The Federalists charged that President Jefferson had charged the Madisons rent while they lived with him, which all parties involved denied.

When the President's House was finished, President Jefferson asked Dolley to decorate it for him. Congress, being not unappreciative of Dolley's charming manner and hostessing abilities, voted six thousand dollars for this furnishing and decorating. The architect, Benjamin Latrobe, assisted Dolley in her choices. Dolley selected yellow satin sofas and chairs for the Oval Dining Room. Damask drapes were hung at the windows, large mirrors on the walls. Another of Dolley's purchases was a set of table china costing five hundred and sixty dollars.

Dolley staged lavish entertainments in the completed mansion. She hired extra waiters for dinner parties, enough for each guest to be served by his own waiter. These men received thirty-five cents for their evening's work.

Dolley brought gaiety and informality to official entertaining in Washington, which suited President Jefferson. He allowed French food to be served, but he refused to hold receptions (or levees, as they were called).

Dolley did the shopping in the food markets herself, and talked with the people she encountered there. These acquaintances enjoying hearing her reports of the elegant parties held in the President's house. Even the society ladies in Washington were impressed by Dolley and her hostessing skills, as well as her good nature.

The subject of fashion arose again when Betsy Patterson, a good friend of Dolley's from Baltimore, married Jerome Bonaparte, brother of French leader Napoleon Bonaparte. Betsy's uncle, who was President Jefferson's Secretary of the Navy, gave a ball for the happy couple, and the good ladies of Washington were scandalized when they saw Betsy's evening gown. She was described as being almost naked, with her back, arms, and much of her bosom uncovered. Some of the ladies vowed they would not attend parties with Betsy Bonaparte if she didn't promise to wear more clothes. Their husbands' reactions to the sight of Betsy were not recorded.

Dolley was undoubtedly amused by the flap Betsy had caused with her gown. Possibly it was a reaction to the drab clothes she was required to wear as a Quaker child, but Dolley had a special fondness for bright colors and pretty dresses.

James found satisfaction in his job as Secretary of State. He and President Jefferson successfully negotiated the Louisiana Purchase from France, which nearly doubled the amount of land within the boundaries of the United States. Lavish celebrations of this accomplishment were held all over Washington.

During President Jefferson's second term, Dolley developed a tumor near one of her knees. It was a serious problem, and there was fear for a time she might never walk again. She went to Philadelphia for treatment and spent the summer of 1805 there. Many old friends came to visit her, and she found her stay a pleasant one despite her discomfort. She recovered and returned to Washington, and James, in November of that year.

Payne Todd, Dolley's son, was now fourteen. He entered St. John's School in Baltimore, where he would learn to speak French and be educated as a gentleman.

When President Jefferson's second term was ending, he began to urge James to seek the office of President himself. James was already called the "Father of the Constitution" because of his scholarly studies to learn what elements the new government needed and his willingness to promote compromises to get new legislation approved. He was a logical candidate for President in Jefferson's opinion.

James won the election. On March 4, 1809, he was inaugurated the fourth President of the United States. George Clinton was elected Vice President. A huge celebration was held in Washington to commemorate the event. The Madisons held an open-house reception at their home on F Street. Dolley looked "extremely beautiful, all dignity, grace and affability" in a cambric dress with a long train. On her black curls, Dolley wore a purple velvet bonnet trimmed in white satin and decorated with white plumes.

Now that she was actually a President's wife, Dolley's parties became more lavish, and Washington society was dazzled by the splendor of her official dinner parties and the gaiety of the private ones.

On May 31, 1809, Dolley held the first of her Wednesday evening levees. These parties assumed political importance in a short space of time. From this time on the Madisons' home in the President's House became the center for social informalities in the nation's capital. Author Washington Irving described Dolley during this period as a "fine portly, buxom dame, who has a smile and a pleasant word for everybody...."

Dolley again busied herself refurbishing the Executive Mansion. This time a pianoforte, which Dolley had yearned for, was added to the furnishings at a cost of four hundred and fifty-eight dollars.

Dolley was credited by Washington politicians as being a positive force in James' Presidency. James was unusually small physically, only five feet and four inches tall. He only weighed about one hundred pounds. He was shy and retiring, and exuberant, energetic Dolley overshadowed him socially, but she caused officials to view him in a more favorable light.

The new country of the United States did well until Napoleon's defeat in France in 1814. The War of 1812 between England and the United States had been in progress, but there had been no major victories by British forces. Now that Britain no longer had to contend with the French armies, they turned their full attention on the conflict with the United States.

The conflict centered around the British navy's practice of boarding American ships at will, often carrying off the crews to serve on British vessels. Britain insisted they were within their rights. Military operations for the United States were largely uncoordinated, and President Madison had not appointed a commander to lead them. He felt strongly that Britain was wrong and should be stopped from aggressive behavior toward American shipping, and the war came to be known as "Mr. Madison's War."

Even though Washington had been threatened, many American government officials found it impossible to believe British forces would really invade the city. President Madison did not share their optimism, and he had government documents of all sorts taken out of the city to a safe hiding place. Baltimore's defenses had been increased to help keep the British out of Washington.

On August 24, 1814, James went to the navy yards to a meeting. Before he could return, the British army marched on Washington. Dolley had been anxiously watching through a spyglass, trying to wait until James got back so they could leave. However, a servant brought word of the advance of the British, and Dolley began making hurried preparations to leave. She had the portrait of George Washington by Gilbert Stuart stripped from its frame, and she loaded silver and other valuables on a wagon and left barely ahead of the invasion.

She left behind in the White House completed preparations for a dinner for forty guests. Plates were left warming on the hearth, and wine was cooling on the sideboard. The British soldiers who stormed the White House ate the food, drank a toast to President Madison in his absence with the wine, then burned the White House down.

The White House and all other public buildings, including the Capitol, were burned. Only the Patent Office was spared.

Dolley found refuge in Virginia with the Richard Hendry Love family, who had earlier been guests of the Madisons in the White House.

James saw Washington burning when he tried to get back to the White House. He was frantic with anxiety about Dolley but could find no one who could tell him where she was. He did not dare go on to the White House for fear of capture, and he spent the next four days searching for his wife or someone who knew about her. One day he spent twenty hours in the saddle without rest.

Alexandria, Virginia, avoided Washington's fate by turning over all their army and navy supplies, ships and private merchandise on board the ships to the British. The supplies confiscated by the British filled seventy-one ships, which had also been seized.

The American public, particularly those citizens in the New England area, called for President Madison's resignation. They had been supporters of the British against the French, and they were contemptuous of President Madison's conduct of the war.

Dolley returned to find all the finery in the White House ruined, the mansion destroyed and their personal belongings gone or burned. She and James found a temporary dwelling, and she resumed giving her dinners and parties as before.

Payne Todd was becoming a problem to his mother and stepfather. Before the War of 1812 started, he was known to spend much of his time in taverns, often gambling heavily. He borrowed money from anyone who would lend it to him. He entered the military service, but he spent so much energy trying to get back to Washington on leave that President Madison ordered Payne's commanding officer not to grant leave without Madison's written orders.

President Madison then sent Payne to Europe with a commission seeking a peace agreement between England and the United States. In Europe Payne continued his high living and wild life on the money he had inherited from his father. He spent all he had, and President Madison had to sanction a draft for over six thousand dollars to pay Payne's debts and finance his passage back home.

The peace commission was successful, and the war ended officially on February 17, 1815. Neither side had gained anything, and neither conceded anything. The British forces had inflicted heavy property damage in the United States, but the new country's forces could not be decisively defeated by the British.

James Monroe was elected to be the new President, and was inaugurated in March 1817. James Madison was leaving office with the country at peace again, and the nation had gained new respect from European heads of state. The United States had demonstrated they would not allow American shipping to be terrorized by outside forces.

For the entire next month James and Dolley were wined and dined by Washington hostesses at balls and dinners before their retirement to Montpelier. They finally left Washington on April 6, 1817, and they never went back to Washington for the seventeen years James had yet to live.

At home at Montpelier the Madisons continued to have problems. The Madison farm had always been a profitable venture before, but a series of rainless summers, followed by heavy downpours which destroyed crops, combined with heavy insect infestation, almost brought an end to James's farming career.

Richard Cutts, Anna Payne's husband, had squandered twelve thousand dollars James had given him for safekeeping while the Madisons were living in Washington. James took a house Richard owned in Washington in settlement of the debt.

Payne Todd, now in his thirties, spent his time roaming throughout the East, running up gambling debts he could not pay. James felt obligated to pay the debts made by Dolley's son. When Payne was repeatedly sent to debtors' prison, James paid for his release each time at Dolley's tearful urging.

James finally began keeping a record of Payne's bills, which from that time amounted to more than twenty thousand dollars. He told a friend that the amount represented about half of what he had paid for Payne, and when James died, the friend gave the record to Dolley.

James did not lose his interest in the political arena when he left Washington. He continued to stay informed about national and world events. Even though he was urged, he refused to endorse candidates for President.

Thomas Jefferson had been working toward establishing a university for Virginia. In 1819 he asked James to help him. This was a project James could really enjoy, and he accepted gladly.

Both men felt a glow of pride when the University of Virginia first opened its doors to students in September 1825. They had disagreed, however, about the matter of rules for student behavior, with Madison urging sternness and Jefferson feeling these young adults were interested in learning and would cause no trouble.

Within a few weeks there were student riots, supposedly in protest against having European professors. Jefferson was forced to allow harsh discipline to be imposed, and several leading agitators were expelled.

These events led to Jefferson's severe financial difficulties and hastened his death. Realizing his health was failing, Jefferson asked James to succeed him as Rector of the University and a member of the Executive Committee. Jefferson died the next year on July 4.

James's mother, Nelly, lived with James and Dolley when they returned to Montpelier. She was in her eighties and very proud of James and his accomplishments. She loved Dolley, who catered to her whims and made every effort to make her comfortable. She told Dolley it seemed as if the daughter-in-law had become the mother. She retained her mental acuity all her life and had few health problems except for some deafness. She died at age ninety-seven.

James's health began to fail, and by 1831 he was bedfast. He suffered acutely from rheumatism, which crippled his arms and legs. He stayed cheerful and accepted his condition as a part of old age. Dolley spent her days taking care of the two invalids, and she had no time to conduct business affairs. She asked her brother, John Payne, to come live with them at Montpelier and help her.

It appeared at this time that Dolley's son, Payne Todd, had begun to change his ways. He was now embarked on a study of geology.

The slavery question was becoming more hotly debated, and James fastened his interest on that subject. He thought a colony of former slaves should be formed in Africa. This project was carried out on a small scale, but it was never widely accepted. James feared the United States government would collapse if a permanent solution to the problem could not be found. Southern leaders, including those in Virginia, were beginning even now to threaten to secede and form their own government.

Friends all over the United States and Europe came to visit James and Dolley at Montpelier, where Dolley made them as welcome as she had at the President's House. All this lavish entertaining was expensive, and James's small financial reserves were soon exhausted.

By 1836 James was plainly dying. He had been forced to resign his post at the University of Virginia two years before. Now he had been honored to have a biography of Thomas Jefferson dedicated to him. He told Dolley on June 26 he wanted to write the author, George Tucker, and thank him for the dedication. Dolley could see he was worse, but he told her "to be composed if not cheerful." Next morning he was unable to swallow his breakfast, and he died on June 28. He was buried at Montpelier.

Dolley decided she would return to Washington to live. She had friends there, and she would leave Montpelier in her son's hands to manage. Congress bought James's *Notes of Debates* for thirty thousand dollars, but after bequests in James's will were paid, Dolley only had nine thousand dollars left on which to live.

She moved into the house James had taken from her brother-in-law, Richard Cutts, and again started giving parties. She was now sixty-five.

The House of Representatives in a rare move awarded Dolley a seat on the floor of the House, the first time any woman had been so honored. Dolley had always enjoyed attending Congressional debates, and she wondered why other women were not interested.

Back in Virginia, Payne Todd was mismanaging Montpelier, and he caused Dolley to lose all income from the estate. James's will had not freed their slaves because he knew Dolley would need someone to work on the land and she would have no money to hire help. His will stipulated, however, that slave families were to be kept as an intact unit and that old slaves were to be supported for their lifetimes. Dolley was forced to sell Montpelier at a low price because of all these imposed conditions.

Martin Van Buren became the new President the year Dolley returned to Washington. When she called at the White House and saw there was no resident hostess, she sent for one of her nieces in South Carolina to come to visit her. The niece, Angelica Singleton, went with her Aunt Dolley to visit the widower President and his bachelor sons. Abraham Van Buren, the President's oldest son, fell in love with the beautiful Angelica, and they were married within a few months' time. Angelica served as hostess as long as her father-in-law was President.

When Priscilla Tyler, daughter-in-law of President John Tyler, was forced to assume the role as hostess during the illness of the elder Mrs. Tyler, Priscilla asked Dolley to advise her. Dolley knew Washington society like the back of her own hand, and she was delighted to help Priscilla.

From an account left by one of the Tylers, Dolley was a "jolly, buxom woman who dipped snuff and rouged her face like a Paris streetwalker, but she was much loved by the Tylers."

James Madison bequeathed his library to the University of Virginia, but Payne Todd sold the books and spent the money. Congress made an offer to Dolley for some of her husband's correspondence to give her some financial aid, but before she could get the papers to Congress, Payne sold a large portion of them to a James C. McGuire.

At last Payne had rendered his mother penniless. She had her pride and memories, but little else. Friends had to give her assistance carefully to keep from offending her.

While James Polk was President, Dolley's parties were livelier and better attended than the ones given at the White House. In January, 1848, she went to her last party, which was held in honor of President Polk. She died on July 12, 1849, and is also buried at Montpelier beside James.

5. Elizabeth Kortright Monroe

Elizabeth Kortright was born in New York City on June 3, 1768. Her father, Captain Lawrence Kortright, was a former officer in the British army who became a New York merchant in the West Indies trade following his discharge. His business prospered, and the family lived on the upper levels of society until the Revolutionary War.

The war almost destroyed the Kortright fortune, but Captain Kortright continued to be highly respected by his accquaintances. In 1770 he helped found the New York City Chamber of Commerce.

Elizabeth developed an aristocratic hauteur from her background of wealth and privilege, and as a result of her own imperious personality. When Elizabeth became engaged to James Monroe, a Virginia lawyer, in the 1785–1786 winter season, the favorite topic of conversation among her friends was how the marriage would work out.

James came from a more ordinary family, just as respectable as Elizabeth's, but not nearly as wealthy. His father owned the land which he farmed, but he only managed to earn a modest income for his efforts.

James was presently engaged in helping to form a new government in the colonies, and was as unpretentious and affable as Elizabeth was vain and commanding. People were often awed by Elizabeth's presence, even though she was only seventeen.

Elizabeth's family encouraged her marriage to James as it would leave one less dependent on their dwindling family fortune. On February 16, 1786, Elizabeth became Mrs. James Monroe in a New York City ceremony in the presence of their families and friends.

The extent of Elizabeth's education is not certain, but she was almost certainly literate, having probably had a private tutor in childhood.

James was well educated. In his earlier days he was a student at William and Mary College in Williamsburg, Virginia. His father's death forced him to leave college, and shortly afterward he joined the Continental army as the colonies struggled to gain their independence from England.

James spent three years in military service, returning home in 1779. He began studying law with Thomas Jefferson, who was then Governor of Virginia. James had already been elected as a Virginia assemblyman in 1782

Elizabeth Monroe. (Courtesy Library of Congress.)

and to the Continental Congress a year later. By the time of his marriage to Elizabeth, his interest in politics and government affairs was far advanced.

After their marriage, James opened a law practice in Fredericksburg, Virginia, but he also continued his political activities. They bought property at Albemarle and settled down to married life.

The next year, on July 27, 1787, James wrote Thomas Jefferson, "Mrs. Monroe hath added a daughter to our society who though noisy, contributes greatly to its amusement." The new daughter was named Eliza.

After he became a member of the Virginia Convention of 1788, James found he did not approve of the far-reaching powers that would be granted to the federal government by the Constitution, and he urged changes be made before its adoption.

In 1790 James was elected to serve in the United States Senate. One reason he had sought election was to be able to move his family to Philadelphia, the national capital at that time. From Philadelphia, Elizabeth could visit her family in New York more frequently. She had not been back home since their marriage, and she missed all her relatives badly. Messages to and fro were uncertain at best, as letters had to be hand-carried by travelers visiting between cities.

In 1794 President George Washington appointed James to be the American Minister to France. This was an opportunity to serve his country in an outstanding way, and James accepted. He and Elizabeth moved their household to Paris.

During the civil uprisings and revolution in France before the Monroes' arrival, the Marquis de Lafayette and his wife had been imprisoned. Lafayette had long been a supporter and friend of the colonists as they struggled to gain self-government, and he and Madame Lafayette had visited frequently in the homes of various American statesmen.

James learned that Madame Lafayette was being threatened with execution, and he decided some action must be taken to save her life. The American government was officially neutral, and he could not intervene in his post as Minister. Instead he ordered a handsome carriage with liveried coachmen and footmen to take Elizabeth to visit poor Madame Lafayette in prison. He felt no one could criticize a woman for visiting her friend.

Elizabeth set out bravely, although her own reception by prison authorities was by no means certain. Shortly before Elizabeth arrived at the prison, Madame Lafayette's mother and grandmother had been removed from their cells and beheaded.

When Madame Lafayette was called out of her cell, she became hysterical, thinking she would also be beheaded. It was a tremendous relief and joy to her when she found Elizabeth waiting to offer her friendship and comfort. The people watching the meeting between the two friends wept along with them.

Elizabeth's visit attracted much attention from the moment her carriage neared the prison. Crowds gathered to see who was riding in the carriage. What did it mean that the wife of the American Minister to France should come to visit poor Madame Lafayette? The news of the visit raced throughout Paris.

Apparently feeling the weight of public opinion and the uneasiness occasioned by this evidence of American concern about Madame Lafayette, the French government freed her a short while later. The grateful French people called Elizabeth "la belle Americaine."

A few months later James secured the release of Thomas Paine, an American writer and philosopher, from a French prison. Paine had been sent to prison for opposing the execution of the King of France. Only a few days after his release, Paine launched a verbal attack on President Washington for insisting that America maintain neutrality in the war in France.

President Washington decided Paine was a chronic troublemaker who might have profited from a prison term, so James's efforts at securing the release of a prisoner were not as admired as Elizabeth's had been.

The Monroe family quickly adopted the language, manners and mores of the French people during their years of living in France. Eliza Monroe, now eight years old, was enrolled in the most fashionable school for girls in France, the St. Germaine-en-Laye School operated by Madame Campan. Here aristocratic little girls developed inflated ideas of their own importance and often became insufferable snobs. Eliza was no exception.

Among Eliza's classmates was a girl named Hortense Eugenie Beauharnis, who was stepdaughter of the French Emperor, Napoleon. As long as Hortense was a member of the student body at the school, Napoleon would not allow harm to come to the school. Elizabeth Monroe was comforted by the fact that Eliza was attending the most protected school in France during these turbulent times. Eliza's friend, Hortense, would grow up to become the Queen of Holland.

President Washington began to wonder if James were not too friendly with the French government officials for the good of America, so he recalled James in December 1796. The Monroes traveled through Holland before they left for home.

Back in the United States, James discovered he was now in disfavor because of his reasonable, evenhanded diplomacy with French officials. He became wary of expressing his views to friends in letters, fearing charges of treason might be lodged against him. President Washington was still angry with James, feeling James had failed to uphold the American government's policy of neutrality in France.

Since he was no longer serving the government, James had construction begun on a home for his family on land near Monticello, Thomas Jefferson's home. The Monroe home was known as Ash Lawn, and its proximity to Monticello allowed frequent visits to and from Thomas Jefferson, and well as James and Dolley Madison, who had always spent time with the Jeffersons.

In 1799 James was elected Governor of Virginia, in which office he served for the next four years. The same year Elizabeth gave birth to their only son, who died when only a few months old. Elizabeth was deeply grieved by the child's death, and it required several months for her to recover from their loss.

When Thomas Jefferson succeeded John Adams as President, James felt he had a friend in the White House. James's term as Virginia's Governor ended in 1803, and President Jefferson decided he would use James's talents again in France.

James did not really want to return to France. He had meant to devote more time to his law practice to improve their poor financial condition. He hated to refuse if he could be of service, but the hard fact was that the United States government did not pay its emissaries enough money on which to live comfortably in Europe. James still owed a large debt from their previous stay in France, but he reluctantly agreed to give diplomacy another try.

Elizabeth, James and Eliza arrived in France in April 1803. Eliza again enrolled at Madame Campan's school, and life gradually assumed its former pattern.

One reason James had been sent back to France was to try to arrange for the United States to purchase the Louisiana Territory from the French government. Shortly after his return, he learned that Napoleon had agreed to sell the area to the United States, and James saw an excellent opportunity to redeem himself in diplomatic circles by arranging the negotiation. France sold the Louisiana Territory to the United States for fifteen million dollars. The acquisition doubled the land area of the United States, as it extended from the Gulf of Mexico on the South, to what is now Minnesota on the North, and from the Mississippi River west to the Rocky Mountains.

In the summer of 1803 James was transferred to London. This move was most unwelcome to both Elizabeth and Eliza. None of them liked living in England, with its cold, damp climate, and they missed their French friends. Elizabeth developed rheumatism, which made her miserable at times. She was also pregnant again, and the Monroes were hoping this child would be healthy and survive the perils of childhood. To add to Elizabeth's unhappiness, the calls she made on ladies of the court in England were not returned.

Maria Monroe was born the next year, and helped to brighten the lives of all the Monroes. They were more family-oriented in England than they had been in France, as they found English government officials rude and abrupt in the contacts they had with them. Plainly the English people resented these colonists who had rebelled against English rule. When James was sent on to Madrid in sunny Spain the next year, he welcomed the change.

James was unsuccessful in his attempt to persuade Spain to sell the territory of Florida to the United States. Later, when he negotiated a treaty with England which failed to guarantee American sailors would be in no danger of seizure on the high seas by English ships, President Jefferson felt it might be wiser to bring James back to the United States. He offered James the post of Governor of the Louisiana Territory, but James refused the offer.

On his return to the United States in 1808, James became a candidate for President against his old friend, James Madison. Madison won the election and generously named James Monroe his Secretary of State. During the War of 1812 Monroe was named Secretary of War. These two Cabinet posts were a better showcase for James's talents than the diplomatic field had been, so when he again ran for President in 1816, he won the election!

Washington was a dusty, unpaved town filled with ugly brick buildings and dilapidated slave quarters when the new President and his family arrived there to make their home. In windy times citizens choked on dust, while rain turned all the dust into a thick, sticky mud. It was not a town that many people viewed as a desirable home.

James and Elizabeth had lived in a Pennsylvania Avenue house in the capital during his years in President Madison's Cabinet. Since the repairs to the White House had not been completed since it was burned by the British in 1814, Elizabeth decided to keep their household where it was until they moved into the Executive Mansion. They did not like living in Washington, but they had grown somewhat accustomed to it.

President Madison and Dolley, his wife, had been living in a house known as the Tayloe House. The Monroes could have moved in there when the Madisons returned to their home in Virginia, but Elizabeth wanted more distinctive surroundings.

After his inauguration in March 1817, James left on a goodwill tour through thirteen states. Elizabeth went back to their home in Virginia for a few weeks until the White House could be made ready for them.

On her return, Elizabeth set Washington tongues wagging by her refusal to call on any of the society ladies in Washington first. She clung to the French custom of staying home and expecting the ladies to call on her.

Even though they gossiped about her, the ladies did call on Elizabeth, partly to see the furniture the Monroes had bought at auction in France, which had once belonged to the deposed Queen Marie Antoinette. Later, when Congress appropriated money for furnishings, the Monroes took their own furniture to their home in Virginia and ordered a few items from France for the White House.

Eliza Monroe had married a lawyer, George Hay, not long after she and her parents returned from Europe. Mr. Hay was about twenty years older than Eliza. They had a little daughter named Hortensia, who was the pride and joy of both James and Elizabeth. The Hays moved into the White House to live while James served as President.

The Monroes hosted a gala reception on New Year's Eve of 1818, to let the diplomatic families see the renovated White House. Elizabeth reportedly spent fifteen hundred dollars for her dress for the occasion, which was an elegant Paris original creation. Again Washington tongues were busy gossiping.

Elizabeth was a private person by nature, and she calmly ignored the criticism. She loved dressing in pretty clothes and she considered it no ones' business other than hers and James's. However, Louisa Adams, wife of President Monroe's Secretary of State, John Quincy Adams, said "tastes differ and Dear Dolley was much more popular," referring to Dolley Madison, whom Louisa admired.

Each Wednesday evening Elizabeth and James held a formal reception in the White House, when they solemnly made welcome anyone who was connected with politics. Their dinner parties were outstandingly dull affairs, as Elizabeth rarely attended, and by custom this prevented any other women from attending. Dinner guests arrived, were introduced, sat down in chairs placed in order around the walls, and after a few uncomfortable minutes, marched silently in to dine in the State Dining Room.

James and Elizabeth accepted no invitations to political dinners outside the White House. Elizabeth's health, never good, became worse during their years as First Family, and Eliza had to serve as official hostess for her father on many occasions.

Eliza still kept the snobbish airs she had acquired in the French school she attended as a girl, and she reminisced frequently in public about various famous aristocratic classmates she had had. She was a beautiful, stylish young woman, but she had a razor-sharp tongue. One evening a guest asked Eliza where her husband was, and she replied vaguely. When he persisted in his questioning, she snapped, "He's dead and buried! Now don't ask me anything more about him!" Perhaps it was such remarks that caused Louisa Adams to note that Eliza had "such a love for scandal no reputation is safe in her hands."

Despite their ready criticism of Elizabeth and the members of the Monroe household, the women of Washington never missed an opportunity to see the First Lady. Elizabeth was elegant in her appearance, which was that of a well-bred aristocrat, and any time she was present at gatherings, throngs attended. She made no attempt to be jovial like Dolley Madison. She was just herself.

Elizabeth was an unusually attractive matron who looked younger than her age. The gossips speculated: Did she rouge her cheeks? Was that why she looked so well? Rouging was done only by women of bad reputation, but who knew what outlandish habits Elizabeth had acquired while living in Europe?

When Maria Hester Monroe, the youngest Monroe daughter, married her cousin, Samuel L. Gouverneur, in the White House in 1820, Elizabeth and Eliza caused another flurry of controversy. They persuaded Maria to have a "New York style" wedding, very select and private, with only relatives and a few close friends attending.

The Washington society ladies were outraged! This was the first wedding ever held in the White House, and the public had a right to be included, they felt. When the Russian Minister asked how he might honor the bride, Eliza icily informed him that he should just ignore the wedding. John Quincy Adams said Eliza was "an obstinate little firebrand" engaged in a "senseless war of etiquette."

Maria had a sweeter nature than Eliza, and the two sisters were never close. Maria was only sixteen when she married, and almost from the beginning she and her husband had financial problems. They had three children born to them through the years, the eldest being a deaf-mute. The Monroe parents always had to be ready to assist them with money to pay their living expenses.

There was no expense allowance for White House living and maintenance, and by 1822 James owed more than thirty-five thousand dollars. His annual salary was only twenty-five thousand, and the only solution he could see was to curtain entertainment, which they did during the last two years they lived in the White House.

James was elected to serve a second term, despite the fact that the Bank of the United States failed and caused a financial panic. In fact, his administration came to be known as the Era of Good Feeling.

Despite his attempts to save money, by the time he left office, James owed seventy-five thousand dollars. He felt strongly that the government of the United States owed him money to repay what he had spent while serving in various official capacities. He would devote the rest of his life trying to secure repayment, and finally collect thirty thousand. He would also give land he owned which was valued at twenty-five thousand to a bank to apply to his debts.

Before his second term ended, James had construction started on an elegant mansion near Leesburg, Virginia, which would serve in retirement for Elizabeth and himself. The new home would be called Oak Hill.

The house was built on the site of an old cottage, which was torn down. Thomas Jefferson drew the house plans, and the man who was in charge of constructing the White House, James Hoban, built the mansion for James Monroe.

A grateful Marquis de Lafayette, remembering the role Elizabeth had played in gaining his wife's freedom, gave them two marble mantelpieces to be used in the house. When they returned to Oak Hill to live, Lafayette came to visit his American friends, and Elizabeth and James held a banquet in his honor on August 9, 1825.

Both Elizabeth and James were happy to be settled at Oak Hill after leading such busy, eventful lives for the last several years. Elizabeth felt well enough to pay an extended visit to Maria and her family in New York City, but her improvement in health did not last. She had suffered from convulsions for many years, and in 1826 she fell into an open fireplace, apparently while having a convulsion, and was badly burned.

Eliza Hay and her family then moved to Oak Hill to care for her aging parents. James continued to enjoy good health for his age, but Elizabeth was declining steadily.

In the summer of 1830, Eliza's husband, George Hay, became ill, requiring him to go to Washington to receive medical treatment. Eliza went with him, but before she could return to Oak Hill, her daughter, Hortensia, had a new baby and developed scarlet fever. Hortensia was then living in nearby Baltimore with her husband, Nicholas Lloyd Rogers. Eliza went on to Baltimore from Washington and was forced to spend several weeks with Hortensia and care for the new baby.

Poor Eliza! Trouble piled on trouble. George died on September 21 of that year, and Eliza's mother died two days later. Eliza and James sadly laid Elizabeth to rest at Oak Hill. They both then went to live with Maria and her family in New York.

James continued to live in New York until his death on July 4, 1831. He was buried in the Gouverneur vault in a New York cemetery, but his body was returned to Hollywood Cemetery in Richmond, Virginia, in 1858. In 1903 the bodies of Elizabeth and Maria, who died in 1850, were moved to lie beside him.

Eliza Hay returned to her beloved Europe a few years after the death of her father. She remained there for the rest of her life, living in a Catholic convent.

6. Louisa Catherine Johnson Adams

Louisa Catherine Johnson, who would become the wife of the sixth President of the United States, was born in London, England, on February 12, 1775. Her mother, Catherine Nuth Johnson, was an English native, but Louisa's father, Joshua, was from Maryland and was a mercantile trader. During the Revolutionary War he remained neutral so as to not offend his English friends and customers.

Louisa grew up in a wealthy home, somewhat pampered. She had musical talent and played both harp and pianoforte. She also had a good singing voice, could dance and write poetry.

Louisa's childhood was peaceful, well-ordered and secure. Her father was head of the household and made all decisions for his family. Louisa loved him dearly, but she dreaded his outbursts of temper — a temper she inherited.

In 1778 the Johnson family became uncomfortable living in England since the Americans and British were at war, so they moved to France. Louisa was three years old. She and her sisters learned to speak French fluently, an accomplishment she would find useful all her life.

The Johnson children were tutored while they were very young, but when they were older they were sent to a Roman Catholic convent school. Louisa became a devout Catholic and attended Mass every Sunday.

Louisa was a beautiful young woman, but extremely shy. Her parents discouraged her from pursuing educational interests too far, as much education was considered unwomanly. However, her interest in "masculine" subjects such as science and Greek had been aroused by one of her teachers at the convent, Miss Young. This teacher encouraged Louisa in the discussion of books and ideas, and from her Louisa learned to think for herself and form her own opinions.

European women in this period of time were expected to be primarily ornamental and subservient to their husbands, so Louisa's development was following a radical course for an English gentlewoman. American women were generally more self-reliant through necessity, but they usually had little education.

Louisa and her sister, Nancy, were so close in age that they were

Louisa Adams. (Courtesy Library of Congress.)

presented to society at the same time. Their father's brother in Maryland wrote saying he thought his nieces should be encouraged to marry American men. Joshua admired his brother and his opinions, so he decreed his daughters would only be allowed to have American suitors. Both girls already had European admirers and were unhappy with their father's decision, but they did nothing to defy him.

American John Quincy Adams, had been assigned to diplomatic service in the Netherlands by the United States government, and was in England on a diplomatic errand when he first met Louisa. When he first visited in the Johnson's home, everyone there assumed he was attracted to

Nancy, who was considered to be the family beauty. It was a great surprise to everyone, especially Nancy, when John Quincy made it plain that shy Louisa was his choice. Louisa was small and graceful with auburn hair, hazel eyes and a lovely, fair British complexion. Louisa had had other suitors, but she had never developed any serious attachment to any of them.

John Quincy had grown up in a much poorer home than had Louisa, but his parents encouraged him to make the most of any opportunities which came his way. Moreover, as the son of America's second President, he was reared to believe he was destined for greatness, and would one day become President himself. His mother, Abigail Adams, envisioned an Adams dynasty in American government.

John Quincy and Louisa had a six-month courtship, after which he proposed in May 1796. He felt six months was long enough to spend on romantic efforts. He had to return to his post, but assured Louisa he would be back for her in a year.

John Quincy had been in love with a girl named Mary Frazier before he left America. Abigail Adams had derailed this romance, feeling Mary was unworthy to marry her son. Abigail told John Quincy he was not ready for marriage, since she and his father were still assisting him financially. She told him they could not possibly increase this assistance. So John Quincy ended his romance with Mary, but never forgot her nor his love for her.

By the time he met Louisa, John Quincy was twenty-nine and lonely. He was also determined to marry. When the Adamses raised objections to Louisa's British background and her family's wealthy lifestyle, John Quincy wrote them he intended to marry Louisa whether they approved or not. He said, with some justification, that if he waited until he found a girl of whom everyone approved, he would die celibate!

But despite his show of defiance to his parents, when John Quincy got back to his post in the Netherlands, he began dragging his feet about settling details for his wedding to Louisa. Louisa tried to pin him down, and finally even her father offered to make arrangements so they could marry. After several postponements and continual refusals to commit himself to specifics, at last John Quincy decided when and where they would take their vows.

Louisa was hurt and bewildered by John Quincy's attitude. She felt uneasy about marrying him but did not quite know why. When Louisa suggested as tactfully as she could that John Quincy should dress more fashionably, they quarreled so bitterly that she told him to feel free to marry someone else. She was often aware of his disapproval, but seldom understood it.

But John Quincy was really quite settled on Louisa from the first.

Perhaps he felt pressured by her and her father and became balky about completing arrangements as a way of protesting. At last, on July 26, 1797, the two were married in a ceremony in the Church of All Hallows Barking, Tower Hill, London. Of John Quincy's relatives, only his brother, Thomas, was present, serving as best man.

John Quincy had been told before he married that he would be assigned to a new post in Portugal, and he sent his personal belongings on to Lisbon. About the time of the wedding, his father, who was now President John Adams of the United States, told John Quincy he would be named Minister Plenipotentiary to Berlin in Germany, or Prussia, instead. He "hoped he would not be inconvenienced by the change."

John Quincy was hurt and furious, feeling that his parents were still trying to run his life. He began his honeymoon with Louisa in a bad mood.

Since Louisa was now settled in a marriage, the Johnsons decided to go to the United States to live. Mr. Johnson had become uneasy about some of his business interests there and thought he should take care of some problems. Louisa had never before been away from home or her family, and she was distressed that her family was moving so far away. She knew it would be months or possibly even years before she saw any of them again, and she was unhappy. She also knew John Quincy's parents questioned the suitability of an English girl as John Quincy's wife. She, too, departed for the honeymoon in a less than optimistic frame of mind.

For their honeymoon, the newlyweds, accompanied by John Quincy's brother, Thomas, went on a tour of England. Louisa had a maidservant who accompanied them also. It was customary at this time to take other people along on honeymoons as chaperones.

Louisa and John Quincy had only been married for a few weeks when she learned her father's business had collapsed and he had suffered severe financial reverses. There would be no money for Louisa's dowry.

Louisa felt guilty and ashamed. She wondered if their friends and acquaintances would think she had tricked John Quincy into marriage. John Quincy worried about the effect her father's misfortunes would have on his political career.

Mr. Johnson's creditors began demanding payment from John Quincy for his father-in-law's debts. John Quincy wrote Mr. Johnson an angry letter demanding that he pay his own creditors promptly.

Louisa was humiliated by the open hostility John Quincy felt for her father, and she wondered if he might also be angry about receiving no dowry from her. Certainly he offered Louisa no sympathy during her family's troubles.

In November 1797, John Quincy, Louisa and Thomas left for John Quincy's new post in Berlin. By the time they reached Berlin, Louisa had suffered a miscarriage and had been quite ill. She would suffer a total of seven miscarriages during their marriage. For three months Louisa was sick, unhappy, lonely — and neglected by her new husband.

Because of John Quincy's diplomatic status, Countess Pauline Neale came to call on Louisa. She was a member of the Royal Court in Prussia, and she found Louisa both beautiful and charming. She insisted that the lonely little bride attend the theater with her. Louisa was delighted with her invitation and happy to find a friend. Louisa's fluency in French was a distinct asset, as French was a second language for many Europeans.

Louisa became a member of Berlin society, where Thomas served as her escort to balls and dinners. They associated with all members of the royal court and were presented to King Frederick III of Prussia and his Queen, Louisa of Mecklenberg-Strelitz. John Quincy, however, was unimpressed with Berlin and its royal society functions. He found it to be "little more than a nation of soldiery."

Berlin was certainly a city of indulgence, and parties were frequent and elaborate. Because of her close friendship with the Countess Neale, Louisa learned royal secrets and gossip. She danced often with King Frederick. John Quincy said he himself did not care for the "sea of dissipation."

John Quincy's and Louisa's family financial condition was very poor. John Quincy had expected Louisa's dowry to make their lives more pleasant. Instead they were forced to live on his small salary, and it was extremely difficult to present a good image as American Ambassador with so little money.

Louisa found it incredible that John Quincy's government would expect them to be members of a royal society and not finance it. She sewed her own dresses and felt deprived because she had no jewels. They kept a bare minimum of servants, drove a secondhand carriage and bought the cheapest furniture they could find for their rented apartment.

Louisa and John Quincy had a major disagreement about her use of rouge. Queen Louisa told Louisa at a ball one night that she looked pale and would be prettier with some color in her cheeks. The Queen may have guessed Louisa could not afford to buy rouge, and she gave Louisa some. John Quincy told Louisa she could not use rouge, and he washed it from her face one evening when she refused to remove it as she prepared for a party.

Louisa's inherited temper came boiling to the surface, and she informed John Quincy coldly that she had had enough of male domination. She angrily insisted she had a right to use rouge if and when she wanted.

John Quincy was astonished by her defiance, when she had previously been so compliant, that he rushed out to his carriage and attended the royal gathering alone. John Quincy had been defied few, if any, times in his life, especially by a female.

To be fair, John Quincy's deplorable financial condition was not entirely due to lack of Louisa's dowry. John Adams had given his son a fairly large sum of money when John Quincy first entered diplomatic service. John Quincy entrusted the money to his brother, Charles, to invest for him. John Quincy was unaware that Charles was becoming an alcoholic and had bad judgment. Charles and Colonel William Stephens Smith, who was the husband of John Quincy's sister Nabby, lost all John Quincy's money through bad investments.

Louisa was pregnant each of the four years the Adamses spent in Berlin. By the time they had been married for thirteen years, Louisa had been pregnant eleven times. Her twelfth and last pregnancy occurred when she was forty-two years old.

All this procreative activity caused Louisa's health to suffer, and John Quincy was forced to take her on trips to mineral bath spas to try to restore her vitality while they were in Berlin. She did not carry a child to term until her sixth pregnancy, when she gave birth to a son, who had long been desired by both Louisa and John Quincy. The little boy was named George Washington Adams.

During his Berlin assignment, John Quincy sent his father, President Adams, detailed reports about the French Revolution, which helped the President keep peace with France during these trying times. President Adams was defeated in his bid for a second term by Thomas Jefferson, so he recalled John Quincy in January 1801 before he left office. He did not want his successor to have the privilege of recalling John Quincy.

The recall came just before the birth of little George Washington Adams, and Louisa and John Quincy had to delay their trip to America because of Louisa's health. When they did leave, Louisa was unable to walk and could stand only when supported. Thomas Adams met them when their ship docked in New York, and he was shocked to see Louisa so pale.

Louisa's father had been appointed to a job in the Stamp Office in Washington by President Adams, and the Johnson family lived there. Louisa decided to go visit her family for a few weeks while John Quincy went to Massachusetts alone to visit his relatives.

Louisa and the baby had a long, tiring journey by stagecoach to Washington. She wrote John Quincy that when she was ready to leave Washington, she expected him to come for them and go with them to see his family in Massachusetts, which he did.

When John Quincy and Louisa arrived in Massachusetts, Louisa and her father-in-law immediately liked each other, a feeling that never changed for either of them. Abigail still feared Louisa was too aristocratic and frail in health to be a suitable wife for John Quincy. Since Louisa's health problems at least partially stemmed from her almost perpetual pregnancies, Abigail might have considered that John Quincy had shared in Louisa's poor health, but apparently this never occurred to Abigail.

Louisa was profoundly shocked from the time she and John Quincy first landed in New York at what she considered the coarseness of the American people. The deplorable roads and primitive living conditions depressed her when she remembered the glittering cities in Europe. She was unfavorably impressed by John Quincy's own family, considering them only unrefined replicas of gentlefolk. She was repelled by being forced to worship with "hereticks" in church.

Abigail tried to please her new daughter-in-law, or possibly to please John Quincy, by preparing special dainty food. But the more trouble Abigail took, the more isolated Louisa felt. Abigail offered much advice and counsel on the care and feeding of John Quincy as well as other domestic matters, causing Louisa to describe Abigail as being "equal to every occasion in life." She felt all thumbs around Abigail, even in the simplest of tasks.

It was while Louisa was visiting with John Quincy's family that her own father died, and her mother was reduced to living in abject poverty. Louise began to question the role of women in a man's world when she saw that a good wife and mother like Mrs. Johnson could be left in such a pitiable financial condition.

John Quincy was himself now unemployed, so he began to campaign for a United States Senate seat from Massachusetts on the Federalist ticket. He was elected in 1803, and the family moved to Washington to live. Another Adams son was born, whom they named John, and Louisa settled down to child rearing and housekeeping.

In 1803 Washington was an unfinished wilderness settlement for the most part. There were about six hundred wooden buildings, and two magnificent structures — the Capitol and the President's House.

Louisa and John Quincy moved in with Louisa's sister and brother-in-law, Nancy and Walter Hellen, five miles away from Washington. John Quincy walked the five miles every day both ways, regardless of weather. He contracted many colds and flu from this exposure, and as soon as Abigail learned he had been sick again, she began sending Louisa messages about taking better care of him.

Louisa still found her new country unappealing — even the food seemed unappetizing. She especially despised the new President, Thomas Jefferson. She called him ugly and common and viewed him as the reason for much unhappiness in her own life. Her father had lost his job in the Stamp Office when President Jefferson took office. Louisa felt her father's anxiety about financial matters probably led indirectly to his early death. President Jefferson had also defeated her beloved father-in-law, and he had been the reason John Quincy and Louisa left Europe. Nevertheless, John Quincy admired President Jefferson greatly, and considered him almost his second father.

In 1805 in another visit to Massachusetts, John Quincy insisted on leaving their two little sons in the care of his parents, where they could further their education. A pattern of living first with their parents, then with the Adams grandparents, and back again with their parents would continue all through George's and John's childhood, to Louisa's dismay. A third son, Charles, was born in 1807, and Louisa insisted on keeping him with her in Washington.

In 1808 James Madison was elected President, and John Quincy was dumped by the Federalists in his bid for reelection to the Senate. President Madison offered John Quincy a post as the first United States Minister Plenipotentiary to Russia. Would he go?

John Quincy accepted gratefully without asking Louisa's opinion. Since he lacked the courage to tell her what he had done, he sent his brother Thomas to tell her: the good news was that John Quincy had a job, but the bad news was the job was in Russia. Further bad news was that she could take only their youngest son, Charles, and her younger sister, Catherine, with them. George and John would remain with their grandparents in Massachusetts to be educated.

Louisa was sick at heart at the thought that her sons were growing up without her, and wildly furious with John Quincy. "In this agony of agonies," Louisa wrote, "can ambition replay such sacrifices? Never!!"

In order to reach Russia, the Adamses had to supply their own food, drinks, beds and clothing, as well as medicines. They packed their household furnishings in special sea trunks for the long ocean voyage.

They finally arrived in St. Petersburg, Russia, where they would live. They found it to be a city of beautiful palaces, many cathedrals, wide boulevards and open squares.

Czar Alexander received John Quincy a week after he arrived, and again John Quincy and Louisa were welcomed into wealthy society circles. Yet, as before when they lived in Prussia, they were extremely poor. Louisa and Catherine had to sew their own clothes, and Louisa continued to resent the fact that other ambassadors from other countries had money to spend lavishly while the Adamses had so little.

Finally Louisa flatly refused to attend the Czar's birthday ball because she had only one ball-gown and she had worn it to several other functions. The Czar's mother came to see her and reprimanded her sharply for failing to attend. The Czar's mother told Louisa that if she ever refused to attend another court gathering, she would not be invited in the future.

Strangely enough, the Adamses and Catherine were not snubbed for their poverty. Possibly the wealthy considered it charming.

Louisa and Catherine were social assets to John Quincy, as the Czar found both women enticing, especially Catherine. He ordered that Catherine be invited to all royal balls, which startled society as Catherine held no official position. Louisa discouraged this friendship as much as she could in talking with Catherine, as Louisa feared the Czar intended a relationship with her sister which would not include marriage.

John Quincy and the Czar also developed a real friendship as they both took long walks in the same area for exercise. This closeness proved valuable to John Quincy in his official capacity.

Since the Adamses had last been in Europe, Napoleon and his armies had conquered a great deal of territory, and conditions had altered greatly. American ships were seized frequently by various countries, and one of John Quincy's assigned duties was to keep shipping open for the Americans. When Denmark seized fifty-two American ships in 1809, the Czar used his influence and got them released. He also won the release of twenty-three American ships that were being held in Russian ports on suspicion of carrying British cargoes.

In 1811 Louisa finally gave birth to a little daughter, which she had always wanted. She named her Louisa Catherine, and enjoyed every moment she spent caring for the child. When the baby died at thirteen months of severe dysentery, it was almost more than Louisa could bear. She went into deep mourning. She tried to end her depression by reading, and in the winter of 1812–13 she read fifty-two books. John Quincy insisted she attend official dinners and court affairs, but her heart was not in them.

Catherine settled the matter of her own romantic preferences in the year of 1813 by marrying John Quincy's private secretary, a young man named William Steuben Smith, with the Czar's blessing.

The next year Napoleon was decisively defeated, and John Quincy was sent to Paris to aid other American officials there in formulating a peace treaty to end hostilities between the Americans and the British, as well as those between the French and the Russians. The British were being routed by the Americans, and there was hope that peace might be brought about.

Catherine and her new husband returned to America, John Quincy went to Paris, and Louisa and Charles remained in Russia.

In January 1815, John Quincy sent word to Louisa that he wanted her to move their household from Russia to France, a distance of eighteen hundred miles.

Louisa was now forty years old, and should have questioned John Quincy's judgment about taking such a trip in the middle of winter, but she did not. Instead, she and Charles, accompanied only by her French maid, left Russia on Febraury 12 in an unheated carriage.

The entire trip across the frozen landscape was like a nightmare. Their carriage was fitted with ski-like runners, but despite these they mired frequently in the deep snow. All their provisions froze solid, even the wine. At one point they came dangerously close to going through the ice on a river.

Later, near Poland, wheels replaced the runners on the carriage, but one wheel broke. They reached Poland, where a crude wheel was fitted so they could press on to France. They were forced to spend a week in Berlin while repairs were made to the carriage.

Somehow the rumor sprang up, as they traveled, that Louisa was Napoleon's sister. This smoothed the way for them at times, and Louisa, who needed all the help she could get, did not deny the rumor.

After two months in Paris, John Quincy was sent on to England as minister to that country. Louisa found a nice English country cottage for her family's home, and their two sons from Massachusetts joined them.

The Adamses had a real family life for the next two years, as John Quincy had few official duties in England. It was the happiest time they ever had with all their children.

Louisa guessed that Abigail and John missed the two boys, and she wrote long letters about the changes in England since the time Abigail and John had lived there. These letters were important to Abigail and John, as they were both failing in health, and they enjoyed Louisa's newsy correspondence.

In 1817 John Quincy was appointed Secretary of State in President James Monroe's Cabinet. On their return home, John Quincy and Louisa first took their children to visit his parents in Massachusetts and again left George and John to continue their education.

On arriving in Washington, John Quincy found the State Department in disarray, and he felt he needed to organize it. Louisa worked as his secretary, and they both worked long, hard hours before he felt everything was in satisfactory order.

As President Monroe's second term neared the end, Louisa began entertaining political guests in their Washington home every Tuesday evening with dinner and dancing. She took every opportunity to tell important dignitaries what a good President her husband would make. She is credited with being the major factor in his subsequent election, as John Quincy was too proud to actively seek the nomination. He expected his talents to be so apparent that he would be automatically chosen by the Democratic-Republican party, which had formerly been known as the Federalist party.

During the campaign John Quincy bought a three-story home for his family on F Street. This house remained in possession of an Adams family member until 1884.

Here in her new home, Louisa was able to entertain in what she considered a proper manner. Realizing that General Andrew Jackson, who led American forces in the decisive defeat of the British at New Orleans, was a formidable opponent in John Quincy's race for the Presidency, she decided to give a ball in honor of the General. Nine hundred invitations were issued, and the whole family was involved in the preparations.

Louisa's Jackson Ball was most successful from both a social and political standpoint, probably the largest and best of the next ten years. The dancing continued until one o'clock in the morning. General Jackson left early to attend another ball in his honor, but it was sparsely attended. All the important people were at the Adamses' home.

In the election, General Jackson, John Quincy and Henry Clay, as well as a man named W. H. Crawford from Georgia, were candidates, none running under party labels. General Jackson received more popular votes, but John Quincy was elected President by the Electoral College.

The average voter believed that General Jackson's victory over the British at New Orleans had won the War of 1812. They rarely considered the role of John Quincy's peace negotiations in France. Thus John Quincy never received credit for what he had done to end the war, a controversy that caused a split in the Democratic-Republican party. John Quincy's faction after the split was known as the Whigs.

John Quincy's pride was hurt when he failed to win the popular vote. He noted that "perhaps two-thirds of the whole people [were] adverse to the actual result." However, popular vote or no, his dream of being President was realized at last.

John Quincy hoped to unify the nation during his administration, but the states felt they already had too much big government and were in the mood for less, not more. John Quincy wanted to build roads and canals, establish a national university, increase scientific exploration and bring uniformity to weights and measures. One by one Congress rejected all his proposals, feeling these projects would infringe on states' rights.

During the last half of his term, voters packed Congress with candidates of the opposition party, and John Quincy was rendered totally ineffective.

In the President's House, John Quincy and Louisa lived quietly, as they were both often sick. Former President Monroe had taken much of the White House furniture with him, and Congress appropriated fourteen thousand dollars to furnish the Executive Mansion. There was no indoor plumbing, and there were no shade trees on the lawns. Louisa began to feel imprisoned in her new role as the President's wife. The couple hosted dinners weekly for dignitaries, held receptions every two weeks and gave an occasional ball — yet they rarely went *out* socially. Louisa occupied her spare time writing letters, stories, poems and plays. Such writing was considered an appropriate pastime for a lady. Louisa was losing her militant insistence on her rights as a person, as she realized she had little or no hope of overcoming traditional male dominance and achieving her goal.

Louisa began to find comfort in eating chocolate. When John Quincy or her sons went anywhere on trips, her one request was that they bring her more chocolate treats.

To add to her distress, her oldest son, George, was beginning a downward slide toward alcoholism. John Quincy had always expected his children to be outstanding achievers, and he constantly berated them for what he perceived to be their failings. Louisa and John Quincy separated for a time because of disagreements about how to deal with George and his problems. Louise felt he needed love and understanding, while John Quincy insisted his nervous symptoms were an excuse to avoid work.

George's feelings of unworthiness finally culminated in his apparent suicide. He could never achieve the greatness his father had expected of him. Possibly George inherited Louisa's sensitivity without also inheriting her backbone of steel which resisted John Quincy's unreasonableness.

In his bid for a second term, John Quincy was defeated by Andrew Jackson. The defeat, plus George's death, caused John Quincy much emotional pain, and he returned to Massachusetts for a time to take measure of his own life. Louisa joined him some weeks later, anticipating a peaceful retirement.

Again without consulting Louisa, John Quincy sought a seat in Congress in 1830 to represent Massachusetts, which he won. Louisa was intensely angry with him, and vowed she would not go back to Washington to live. Their second son, John, wrote and asked her to go with his father. This only made her more angry. She told John indignantly she had suffered enough for John Quincy's career — that her only reward had been loss, tragedy and ill health. But since John Quincy's income could not pay the expenses of two homes, she was forced to return.

John Adams, Louisa's son, had been put in charge of a large wheat and corn grinding and milling operation in Washington. John wanted desperately to succeed in the enterprise, and he worked long hours. Like his brother, he became an alcoholic. He died from the combined effects of overwork and neglect of his health at age thirty, convinced that he, too, was a failure.

The loss of their second son left both John Quincy and Louisa stunned with grief. John Quincy's solution to his intense despair was to immerse himself in his job in Congress. Louisa became involved in the women's movement to abolish slavery.

For the first time in American history, women were making public speeches. John Quincy declared in a speech to Congress that women had a right to be heard. Needless to say, John Quincy had mellowed considerably with age. Louisa collected petitions from women in several states urging Congressmen to vote to end slavery in America. Through her efforts with this movement, Louisa began slowly to regain some of her own self-esteem.

Louisa and John Quincy returned frequently to Quincy, Massachusetts, where their several grandchildren lived. They both doted on their amazing grandchildren, in the manner of all grandparents, and even enjoyed their mischievous behavior. Each summer their house was overrun with relatives.

In 1847, Louisa and John Quincy quietly celebrated their fiftieth wedding anniversary in Quincy before returning to Washington and a new social season. After being married to Louisa for fifty years, John Quincy said he thought marriage was preferable to celibacy. Louisa said she thought "that hanging and marriage were strongly assimilated."

When they got back to Washington, they gave an elaborate New Year's Eve party at their home, during which their grandchildren and the grandchildren's friends entertained guests with Swiss songs accompanied by guitars, which were "tuned to the highest pitch of discord," as Louisa described it later.

John Quincy continued to serve as a member of Congress for the next eighteen years, until his sudden death from an apparent stroke on February 21, 1848.

Louisa was ill almost continuously after his death, but she was fairly well fixed financially. She received income from the grain mill they still owned in Washington, as well as rentals from real estate holdings.

In April 1849, she had a stroke and spent the next three years quietly. She died in their Washington home on F Street on May 15, 1852. Of her children, only Charles survived her.

Louisa and John Quincy lie side by side in the First Parish Church in Quincy, Massachusetts.

7. Rachel Donelson Robards Jackson

Rachel Donelson was born June 15, 1767, in Halifax County, Virginia, but she did not grow up a Virginia belle. When she was thirteen, her father, Colonel John Donelson, led a party of sixty women and children, with a thirty-man guard, down the Tennessee River to the site where the city of Nashville would be established. It was planned as the first white colony in the Cumberland River area and was considered a part of western North Carolina, as the state of Tennessee had not yet been formed.

The pioneers left Fort Patrick Henry on December 22, 1779, and would join a group of men who had left early in November to blaze a trail through the wilderness and fight any hostile Indians along the way.

The men's group was led by James Robertson and was composed of the husbands and fathers of the women and children in Colonel Donelson's party. They considered the river passage safer than the overland route.

The Donelson party encountered many hardships along the way, however. Their boats were hurled against rocks when they were caught in whirling eddies, and one ship sank. Extremely cold, snowy weather forced them to stay in a makeshift camp on the riverbank for almost a month. Their ammunition supply dwindled; they had to trap rabbits and deer for food, which was also in short supply.

Rachel and the other children who had accompanied Colonel Donelson matured rapidly in the wilderness as they survived Indian sneak attacks and learned to watch over one another. Many of the party became ill from exposure in the dreary, patched-together camp.

At last the weather broke and the Donelson group pushed on to the Cumberland. None of them had seen it, and no one had any idea what to expect.

When they reached the area, all their food was gone. Some of the men went buffalo-hunting, while Rachel helped her mother and some of the other women in the party gather herbs for Shawnee salad. The settlers lived on stringy buffalo meat and herbs until they finally reached the men's party and food supplies on April 24, 1780.

Rachel Jackson. (Courtesy Library of Congress.)

Colonel Donelson and his brood, like the other families, set to work to build a homestead. The Donelsons cut trees, trimmed them and notched the logs to build their cabin by a spring. Rachel helped her mother pack mud and moss in the cracks between the logs to make the cabin air tight. Colonel Donelson swapped work with the other men so they would help him move large rocks to build a sturdy fireplace for heating and cooking.

Soon the cabin was home, and the Donelsons began involving themselves in community activities. The men helped each other with house-building, barn-raising, and clearing land for crops. The women met for quilting bees and clothes-making.

Rachel enjoyed living in the new settlement. She liked square dancing with young men at parties as the fiddler played familiar tunes and called the moves to be made.

The corn supply dwindled in 1785 as more settlers came to live in the new community, and it was several months before a new crop could be harvested. Rachel went with her father back to Kentucky to buy corn, and while they were there, Rachel met Lewis Robards.

Rachel was seventeen, with long dark hair and laughing eyes. She moved with an easy grace that captivated Robards from the first time he saw her. On March 1, 1785, they were married in Kentucky.

The marriage was unhappy from the beginning. Robards was wildly jealous of the fun-loving, story-telling, horseback-riding Rachel. He loved her deeply, but he felt she was far too free with her interest in and attentions to other men.

Rachel was bewildered by his attitude. She had not changed since her marriage — she was just being herself. On the frontier everyone was friendly with everyone else.

It is not certain, but Robards may have tried to whip her into submission. At any rate, after a few months Robards wrote Rachel's mother that he wanted Rachel to leave as he could not live with her. Rachel's brother Samuel took her back to Nashville.

Just after Rachel married Robards, Colonel Donelson had been found murdered, and Rachel's mother was now a widow. When a young lawyer named Andrew Jackson arrived in Nashville needing lodging, he asked Mrs. Donelson if he could board with her. She was glad to have him stay in her home, both for the income, which she needed, and the protection he offered from Indians, who still attacked with discouraging frequency.

Andrew had been sent to the area as part of a law enforcement team at the request of the North Carolina Governor. The Cumberland River area settlers had formed a new state and named it Franklin. North Carolina still claimed the Cumberland territory as its own and viewed their actions as treasonous. Andrew and others had been sent to thwart the settlers' efforts.

Rachel was still living with her mother, and she and Andrew were immediately attracted to each other. They were better suited than she and Robards had been, since both were products of the frontier and its hardships. Also they were similar in temperament. Both enjoyed a rousing good time; both told lively, interesting stories of adventures; and both were fond of horseback riding and the great outdoors.

But Rachel was still a married woman. Her husband had decided they should try to make a go of their marriage, and he bought some property to build a home for them only five miles from where her mother lived. Indian unrest forced them to live with Mrs. Donelson until the Indians were better controlled.

Robards spent his time watching Rachel closely for any evidence of misconduct, and he especially watched for any sign that she might be interested in Andrew. It was not a happy household.

According to others in the household and community gossips, Robards slipped out at night to visit women slaves. Since he was guilty of adultery, he believed Rachel was guilty too. When Andrew attempted to tell Robards his suspicions of Rachel were without foundation, Robards only became more abusive in his remarks. There seemed no way Rachel could satisfy her jealous husband, and everyone was sorry for her.

John Overton, another lawyer boarding at Mrs. Donelson's, persuaded Andrew to go with him to live somewhere else. He felt Rachel was being tormented beyond endurance. After the lawyers had moved out, Robards left Rachel and went back to Kentucky.

Andrew was very successful in his law career in the Cumberland. He began to accumulate enough wealth to enable him to marry — and he wanted to marry Rachel.

In 1790 Rachel heard a rumor that Robards planned to come to Nashville and take her back to Kentucky with him by whatever means required. Rachel became terrified when she heard of his plans, and she decided to go to Natchez, located on the Mississippi River and still under Spanish control. She left Nashville in the company of an old family friend, Colonel Robert Stark and his family . . . and Andrew Jackson.

The story was that the two men went along for protection, but Rachel had a number of male relatives who could have gone with her instead of Andrew. It was as if she and Andrew hoped to force Robards to make his move.

Andrew saw Rachel safely settled in Natchez and then he returned to Nashville. About the same time, he and some of Rachel's relatives heard Robards had divorced Rachel. The rumor was untrue, as Robards only received permission to sue Rachel for a divorce.

Andrew made no attempt to learn whether the divorce rumor was true or not. He left for Natchez as soon as he could, and he and Rachel were married in the summer of 1791, or so they claimed. There is no official record of the marriage.

In the fall they came back to Nashville and settled down to married life on a small plantation called Poplar Grove. They were both well liked by their neighbors, and everyone considered them a happy, respectable couple.

Two years later Rachel received a summons to appear in court in the Kentucky territory to answer to a charge of adultery in a divorce action by Robards. Why Robards had waited so long to actually obtain the divorce is not known, unless he wanted revenge.

Andrew's friend, Overton, urged Andrew to marry Rachel again immediately, as it was evident their first marriage was illegal. Andrew argued this would indicate guilt on their part and he insisted they were innocent. He did not understand they had already been found guilty in court by openly living together while Rachel was still married to Robards. There was no way she could prove she thought she was divorced.

Overton finally persuaded Andrew this was the best way to settle the argument, so on January 17, 1794, they were married again in Davidson County.

Possibly no one living in today's world could ever understand the shame and humiliation Rachel felt from Robards' accusations of her. The events had a subduing effect on Andrew, but Rachel became deeply religious, with a piety approaching fanaticism. None of their friends, neighbors or relatives criticized them for their personal problems, but Rachel felt she needed to atone. Happily, Andrew and Rachel truly loved each other, and their marriage was all her first marriage had not been.

Andrew was elected to Congress in 1796 when Tennessee became one of the United States. He was elected to the United States Senate the next year. He went to Philadelphia, then the capital, without Rachel, leaving her sobbing hysterically. He resigned the following year to serve as a justice on the State Supreme Court in Tennessee, which paid a salary of six hundred dollars a year.

For the next few years Andrew tried to make a living through land speculation, but he used little judgment or common sense in his deals, always lost money, and ended up in debt.

In May 1806, Andrew killed a young lawyer from Nashville in a duel. The young lawyer, Charles Dickinson, had made an unflattering comment about Rachel's virtue, and Andrew reacted furiously at the insult to his wife's character.

Andrew was severely criticized by the citizens of Nashville for the killing, even though Dickinson had shot first and hit Andrew in the chest. The bullet lodged so near Andrew's heart that it could never be removed, and the wound never healed properly as long as he lived. Andrew suffered much pain from it.

In 1809 Rachel and Andrew adopted one of Rachel's nephews. The child was named Andrew Jackson, Jr., and was one of twins born to Rachel's brother, Severn, and his wife, Elizabeth. Elizabeth's health was poor and she felt she could not care for two babies. She gave the little boy to Rachel when he was only three days old, and he was the only child Rachel and Andrew ever had.

Rachel and Andrew extended the hospitality of their home to many people during these happy years. Aaron Burr visited and tried to involve Andrew in a treasonous plot against the new United States government, but Andrew refused to become involved. They also entertained all the important politicians in Tennessee, and Andrew almost unwittingly built a base for his own future political activity.

The War of 1812 made Andrew Jackson an American hero. He gained the nickname of "Old Hickory" for his toughness in hardship from the men in his command, who loved and respected him. During his time in the army he became a general. He was the leader of the men who decisively defeated the British at New Orleans, the last major battle of the War of 1812.

Rachel and Andrew, Jr., went to New Orleans to be with Andrew when the war was over. He had asked them to come, and he was delighted to see them. Rachel had been managing their plantation, The Hermitage, in his absence, and she was deeply tanned from the time she had necessarily spent in the sun. Unfortunately for Rachel, a deep tan was considered unladylike in the early eighteen hundreds. Only field hands were tanned, while ladies always had delicate pink and white complexions.

Rachel had also become overweight during Andrew's absence. She looked countrified in her clothes and sounded the same way when she talked. Andrew told her gently that he wanted her to improve her appearance. "You must recollect that you are now a Major General's lady — in the service of the United States, and as such you must appear, elegant and plain, not extravagant — but in such style as strangers expect to see you," he told her.

Andrew's aide's wife, Mrs. Edward Livingston, undertook to help Rachel learn about proper clothes and bring her up to date on social behavior overall. Rachel, for her part, admitted her ignorance. She was intimidated by the elegance of the local Creole women, and told Mrs. Livingston she had never been to a city bigger than Nashville. Even though she tried to improve her appearance for Andrew's sake, Rachel did not really approve of all of the delights of New Orleans, considering it to be a city given to total dissipation.

At first the stylish New Orleans ladies were slyly amused by the country manners and appearance of Rachel, but her kindness and gentleness won them over. They demonstrated their affection for her by giving her a set of topaz jewelry. They gave Andrew an expensive diamond pin.

At one of the most elaborate balls given in their honor, Andrew and Rachel danced for the guests country style. "To see these two figures, the General, a long haggard man, with limbs like a skeleton, and Madame la Generale, a short, fat dumpling, bobbing opposite each other like half-drunken Indians, to the wild melody "Possum up de Gum Tree" and endeavoring to make a spring into the air, was very remarkable," according to one of the guests at the ball.

Little Andrew enjoyed being with his father again, even though he was awed by him and his obvious importance. There were greetings from the crowds of people on the streets of New Orleans, and the soldiers saluted snappily whenever they met the Jacksons. Andrew began indulging the little boy with extravagant gifts during this visit, and he continued the practice all his life.

Rachel's management of the plantation was more successful than Andrew's management had been, and it was now a profitable enterprise. He returned home gratefully, exhausted by all his exploits. His salary also helped raise their standard of living.

Andrew's health was poor for the next four years from all the deprivation he had suffered in military service, but Rachel willingly provided him with the nursing care he needed. He retained his army commission.

In 1819 when he finally began feeling better, Andrew decided to build a brick mansion for Rachel on their one thousand acre estate. The home they were presently using was an old blockhouse. The new house would be ninety feet across and one hundred feet deep, two stories high. Andrew had elaborate flower gardens designed to surround the mansion with paths and hedges. He had recently had a brick Presbyterian Church built on the property.

There were always crowds of visitors in the mansion when it was completed. Visiting relatives with their children, as well as politicians, military dignitaries and ministers of all denominations were among Rachel's and Andrew's guests. Rachel loved the church Andrew had built for her more than any other gift he had ever given her, and she talked for hours with the clergymen, discussing religious questions.

Various military aides of Andrew's lived with the family from time to time, as well as Ralph Earl, an artist and portrait painter. He married Rachel's niece, Jane Caffery, who died a short time after their wedding. Rachel considered Ralph very talented and hired him to be Andrew's resident portrait painter. Ralph was not a great artist, but he did manage to capture on canvas some of Andrew's fierce determination and courage.

Florida territory was acquired from the Spanish government in 1803, and President Monroe asked Andrew to be Governor of the territory. Actually, with the reduction in the army which had recently been ordered by Congress, either Andrew or Major General Jacob Brown would have to be demoted. President Monroe always avoided a fight whenever possible, and he knew both men were going to fiercely resist demotion; hence the offer to Andrew.

Andrew resigned his army commission and accepted the post as Territorial Governor. Yet Andrew continued to issue orders to troops stationed in Florida, and the troops obeyed the orders. President Monroe and some Cabinet members felt Andrew was exceeding his authority, but John Quincy Adams, Secretary of State, insisted Andrew needed the authority to govern effectively, and there the matter ended.

Rachel and little Andrew went with General Jackson to Florida. They stopped in New Orleans, and Rachel was appalled at the sights and events there. She felt the crowd was making an idol of her husband when they placed a crown of laurel leaves on his head and yelled, "Vive Jackson!"

When they reached Florida, Andrew set out to reform the territory by establishing a Board of Health, requiring registration of all persons who wanted to be United States citizens, stopping gambling and ordering all shops be closed and noise stopped on Sundays. "Failure to keep the Sabbath holy" carried a penalty of a two hundred dollar fine and required a bond of five hundred dollars be posted, guaranteeing good behavior.

Rachel was thrilled with Andrew's reform measures and rejoiced in the changes she observed. Her religious fervor was increasing steadily.

The Florida territory had many citizens who were either Indian or Spanish, and Andrew admired neither group. For this reason, he was unhappy in his position as Governor. The Spaniards considered Andrew strange and a little wild with his outbursts of yelling and motioning, none of which they understood.

Andrew remained in Florida for only about eleven weeks. President Monroe was relieved when Andrew decided to resign and go back home to Tennessee. There had been a fair amount of turmoil and misunderstanding while Andrew was in charge, and Monroe hoped Florida's problem would lessen with Andrew gone.

When they got back home to The Hermitage in late fall of 1821, they had come home to stay, or so Rachel believed. She had not been home long before she began having chest pain and apparent heart problems. She began breathing with short wheezes, and her doctor prescribed that she smoke a pipe.

When she was not rushing around in their large house directing household activities, she sat on the front porch in her rocker and smoked the pipe. By now she was known affectionately to all as "Aunt Rachel."

Andrew jeered at the suggestion that he run for President when he was first approached. He said he knew his limitations and he was not fit to be President, but he was obviously flattered.

In 1822 Andrew ran for a seat in the United States Senate and was elected. When Rachel went to Washington to be with Andrew, there was much speculation as to how she would be received by Washington society. The stories about her first marriage were widely known. People called in droves. "How I shall get through this bustle...from fifty to one hundred persons calling in a day," she wrote to a neighbor.

The Democratic leaders considered Andrew a natural, since he had become such a national hero to the American public, to be their next candidate for President. John Quincy Adams, the incumbent, was not well liked. When Andrew had campaigned against John Quincy in 1824, he lost when Henry Clay switched his vote to Adams. Andrew had more popular votes.

Despite Rachel's vehement objections, Andrew resigned his Senate seat and began an intensive campaign for President in 1828 — and was elected.

With Andrew's new position, all the old stories about improper conduct on the part of Rachel and Andrew resurfaced, and became more and more vitriolic.

Rachel realized she would need more formal dresses for wear in the nation's capital than she owned, so she went shopping in Nashville. She wanted Andrew to be proud of her. While shopping, she picked up a political pamphlet which had been discarded, and for the first time she learned the extent of the slanderous allegations that had been made against her.

She was completely devastated by the blow. The entire time since the scandal first erupted she had spent in penance, and still the talk continued.

Rachel's physical and mental states deteriorated rapidly. She spent much of her time simply sitting and staring into empty space.

On December 22, 1828, she died from an apparent heart attack — perhaps in reality from a broken heart because she was never forgiven by the public. She was buried in her beloved flower garden at The Hermitage.

Andrew was inaugurated ten weeks later. He was dressed completely in black and, according to reports, appeared thin and pale. He never remarried.

8. Hannah Hoes Van Buren

Hannah Hoes was born March 8, 1783, in Kinderhook, New York. Her father was John Hoes and her mother Maria Quackenboss Hoes. Hannah's family was a part of a Dutch Reformed religious community in which church affiliation and church activities played a major role in the lives of the members.

Hannah grew up in a village that ice-skated in winter and went on picnics in summer for recreation. Everyone worked hard, and leisure time was valued.

Hannah was a pretty little girl with reddish-brown, naturally curly hair, hazel eyes and a sweet face. One of her childhood playmates was her cousin, Martin Van Buren, also a member of the Dutch Reformed religious group. Martin was about four months older than Hannah. Martin's father was a local tavern keeper, and Martin frequently helped out in the tavern as he grew up.

Hannah attended Vrouw Lange's classes with the other girls in Kinderhook. Here they learned basic educational skills of reading and writing, in lessons containing moral themes and religious overtones. Kindness and thoughtfulness to others was stressed, and obligation to duty was emphasized, whatever duty might be.

Martin attended a separate academy for boys until he was fourteen. At the academy he also received a basic education, but he found himself dissatisfied, and he left school.

He went to work as a janitor, copy-boy and general handyman in a law office, where he began studying law. His employer was a member of the Federalist political party, but Martin discovered he preferred the beliefs of the Republican party. When his employer became irritated by Martin's political leanings, Martin left Kinderhook and went to live in New York City. There he continued to study law while he worked for Attorney William P. Van Ness, who had the same political philosophy as Martin.

Martin felt he was capable of supporting a wife and family by the time he was twenty-four, so he proposed to Hannah, whom he called Jannetje. On February 21, 1807, they rode over the snow in a sleigh to the nearby village of Catskill, New York, where they were married.

Hannah Van Buren. (Courtesy Library of Congress.)

Apparently their marriage was happy, although no written account exists of their life together. According to their church's teachings, it was shameful to mention a lady's name in any public account, and Martin did not even mention Hannah's name in his own autobiography.

They had a total of five sons born to them, four of whom reached adulthood. Martin served as Columbia County surrogate in Hudson, New York, from 1808 to 1812, and three of their sons were born while they lived there.

In 1812 Martin was elected to serve in the New York State Senate, but they did not move to Albany until he became New York's Attorney General in 1816.

In Albany both Martin and Hannah lived busy lives. In addition to having their four young sons to care for, the Van Burens also had Martin's law partner and at various times three law apprentices living with them. For recreation, their families lived near enough so Martin and Hannah could visit often, and their families visited them.

Letters referring to Hannah from other sources indicate she enjoyed her sociable, active life.

By the winter of 1818, Hannah began to suffer from poor health, probably tuberculosis. She died the next year on February 5, 1819. In a newspaper account of her death in the Albany Argus, she was called "an ornament of the Christian faith." She was buried in Kinderhook Cemetery in Kinderhook, New York.

Martin never remarried. When he became President of the United States in 1837, he and his four bachelor sons moved into the White House together. The next year his oldest son, Abraham, married Angelica Singleton from South Carolina, a relative of Dolley Madison's by marriage. Dolley had introduced pretty Angelica to the Van Buren men when she saw the White House had no woman to act as official hostess.

Abraham and Angelica honeymooned in Europe, and when they returned, Angelica served as her father-in-law's official hostess as long as he was in the White House.

Martin lived to age seventy-nine, dying on July 24, 1862. He is buried beside his Jannetje in Kinderhook Cemetery.

9. Anna Tuthill Symmes Harrison

Anna Tuthill Symmes was born in Flatbrook, New Jersey, on July 25, 1773. Her father, Colonel John Cleves Symmes, would later buy a million acres of land in the northwestern part of Ohio known as the Northwest Territory, and he would figure prominently in that area's politics.

Anna's mother died when Anna was a few months old, just about the time the Revolutionary War moved into New Jersey. Colonel Symmes donned a British army uniform, put his baby girl in the saddle with him and rode through enemy lines to take Anna to live with her grandparents, Henry and Phebe Tuthill, on Long Island, New York.

Anna and an older sister, Maria, grew up in the home of their grandparents and attended schools in the New York area. Anna attended Clinton Academy at East Hampton, Long Island.

Maria married when she finished school. Her husband was Major Peyton Short. They went to live in Lexington, Kentucky, and it was on a visit to Maria that Anna first met Lieutenant William Henry Harrison.

Anna was dark-haired, dark-eyed, and of a serene nature. William Harrison, who had recently been involved in arranging treaties with various Indian tribes, was impressed by Anna when they met. They only had a few meetings before he had to return to his duties for about three months.

Mr. Symmes, now a judge in the Northwest Territory, took Anna and her stepmother to North Bend, Ohio, to live. William Henry located Anna's new home, came to court her, and proposed marriage. She accepted immediately, but Judge Symmes was unhappy with her choice.

His first objection was that William was only a Lieutenant; his second was that there had been some rumors that Lieutenant Harrison was rowdy in his behavior. The rumors were untrue. Ironically, they sprang from Lieutenant Harrison's arrest of two drunk army powder and ball makers on the orders of his commanding officer, General Wilkinson. The two angry drunks then swore out a warrant for William's own arrest, which resulted in some resentment on William's part. William knocked down the deputy sheriff who came to take him to jail. General Wilkinson straightened out the matter and described William as "one of the best disposed and most promising young gentlemen in the army."

Anna Harrison. (Courtesy Library of Congress.)

Anna knew her fiance was brave and not unruly, but Judge Symmes expressly forbade her to see William. Anna could not let William go out of her life, so they eloped and were married by one of her father's tenants, a justice of the peace, on November 25, 1795. The justice was Dr. Stephen Wood, who lived in a log cabin on Judge Symmes's farm.

The couple's first home was at Fort Washington in Cincinnati, Ohio. There their first child, Betsey Bassett Harrison, was born. William did not plan to stay in military service indefinitely, so he bought a four-room cabin on one hundred and sixty acres of land at North Bend.

William was promoted to captain just before he decided to leave the army. He was half-owner of a whiskey distillery in North Bend and had an income. He was offered the Land Office Registrar job in the area, but he got a much better offer from President John Adams, who appointed William Secretary of the Northwest Territory.

Anna was glad to move to North Bend, where she would be nearer her relatives and away from army camp life, which was primitive, rough and rowdy. She had been reared in a genteel atmosphere with a finishing school education, and she must have wondered at times if her life would ever again be so pleasant with a few of the finer touches she had taken for granted before. She loved William, but she was not in love with his army career.

The next year William was elected to Congress from the Northwest Territory, and the year after that he became the Governor of the Indiana Territory. This last change meant Anna and the children would be moving from North Bend to Vincennes, Indiana, as soon as the Harrisons' third child was born.

Lucy Singleton Harrison was born in September 1800, and a few weeks later William and Anna left by stagecoach for Lexington, Kentucky, where they would spend Christmas with Maria and her family. Since Anna's children were so young, Maria and her husband insisted that they and Anna spend the rest of the winter in Lexington with them. William left for Vincennes alone after the holidays.

The town of Vincennes was the capital of an area that extended from Northwestern Ohio to Wisconsin. It was a beautiful countryside, and when Anna and the children arrived in May, fruit trees were in bloom and the fields were red with strawberries.

The beauty of the scenery was diminished by the many disputes between various Indian tribes living in the area and the French and American settlers. Many Indians sold rights to land they owned, infuriating their tribal chiefs, who realized the lands belonging to the Indians were dwindling. White hunters killed the game the Indians needed for food, and laws were applied more harshly to Indian offenders than to white settlers who committed the same crimes.

Anna and the children had to become accustomed to turning around and finding one or more Indians standing silently, almost at their elbows, wanting to make a complaint to William. William was considered Superintendent of Indian Affairs as well as Governor of the territory.

William felt sorry for the Indians and worked hard to improve their affairs. He urged them strongly to become farmers, as game for hunting was becoming more scarce and many Indians were starving. He pointed out that the Cherokee and Creek tribes in the South were now raising both good crops and cattle. William even offered to ask Washington to send advisors to help them get started, but the Indians could not come to any agreement about such a radical change.

As the Indians hesitated, President Thomas Jefferson notified William that the United States government needed all the land east of the Mississippi River for settlers, and asked William to do all he could to bring this about. President Jefferson even granted William the power to make treaties with the Indians.

Anna wanted a better house to live in than the second-class dwellings they had been using ever since they married, so William built a brick house for his family. It was the first brick house that was built for miles around. It was an elegant home with beautiful black walnut paneling, hand-carved mantels for the many fireplaces, and window glass imported from England. Slits were built in the outer walls where rifle barrels could be aimed at intruders, and there was a good supply of gunpowder in the basement in a heavily constructed room. Shrubbery, fruit and shade trees surrounded the thirteen-room mansion, which Anna and William named Grouseland.

As soon as his family was settled in this fine new home, William set out to make land trades with the Indians throughout the territory. Most of the tribes agreed to the various annuities and other benefits William offered them, but the Shawnee warrior Tecumseh and his brother hated white men and set out to influence the other tribes to break the treaties to which they had previously agreed.

William notified Washington that troops should be sent immediately so that trouble could be put down if it started. A regiment was sent reluctantly, and it was to be firmly understood all the soldiers would be used only "if indispensably required," with only one company coming to Vincennes. The other soldiers remained in Cincinnati.

The Indians went on the warpath with a vengeance at Tippecanoe in 1811, and if William had not called volunteers and reserves into readiness when Washington vacillated, there would have been many battles and much bloodshed. As it turned out, their defeat in this battle convinced the Indians the treaties had to stand. The Indians insisted that British settlers from Canada had incited them to fight, which later appeared to be true.

Anna was coping at home alone with the children as best she could. There were raids and massacres of neighbors by Indian warriors, but neither she nor any of the children were hurt. However, they lived in fear for their lives daily.

When the fighting subsided, William thought the War Department in Washington should send a minimum of six companies to Vincennes for frontier protection, but only one was assigned. Since the horrors of the uprising were so close to his own home, he sent Anna and the children to Kentucky and on to Cincinnati for safety.

The British realized their support of the Indians would cause all-out war with the United States Government, so they backed off. With their lessening support, the Indians had too few supplies to continue fighting.

When war with England broke out the next year, William, who was perceived as a great hero by the American public, was named Supreme Commander in the Northwest Territory. He rented a house for his wife and (by now) eight children in Cincinnati so the children could attend school and learn more about cultural subjects.

Anna's ninth child, Anna Tuthill, was born in Cincinnati on October 26, 1813, while William was fighting British forces in the Great Lakes area. The war was called the War of 1812 by this time. Some of the resentful Indians had joined forces and were fighting with the British army.

Secretary of War John Armstrong, of President James Madison's Cabinet, decided he would diminish William's popularity, so Armstrong took over the direction of the war effort. It would have been an abysmal failure if the decisive battles had not already been fought. As it was, William became irritated about orders given by Secretary Armstrong to the various officers in William's command, and William resigned from the army.

Anna was glad and relieved that her husband would be coming home. She had recently given birth to their tenth child, James Findlay, who was not thriving well. The little boy died not long after William reached Cincinnati.

Betsey Bassett, the Harrisons' oldest child, had married a cousin, John Cleves Short, in 1814, and their little girl died just before William came home. With many family members there were many troubles.

Being a war hero made the former General Harrison a natural for political success. In 1816 he was elected to the United States Congress and in 1819 to the Ohio State Senate.

Anna had done her job as wife and mother well. As the Harrison children became adults, they were highly regarded by all who knew them and had developed into responsible citizens. One son became a receiver in the Land Office in Vincennes; another was in medical school for a time. When William Henry urged a third son, William, Jr., to continue with his college studies and promised financial support, Anna added a cautionary note against reckless spending: "Money is very scarce and hard to be got." This son went on to become a lawyer.

Possibly due to the fact that they were educating so many children at the same time, Anna and William were having large financial difficulties. William had to mortgage some of his property in order to pay for the children's education and other obligations.

In 1825 William was elected to the United States Senate. He introduced legislation there to improve morale among soldiers by improving their pay and other benefits, rather than by imposing harsher discipline as some had advocated. This proposed legislation, plus William's successful military career, caused Henry Clay and some other leading statesmen to fear that

William might become a candidate for Vice President in the next election. Clay urged President James Monroe to send William to Colombia as a minister to remove him from the national scene.

President Monroe took Clay's advice, and William was appointed Minister to Colombia. William took his seventeen-year-old son, Carter Bassett, as his attache as well as Edward Taylor to be his secretary in Colombia.

William found his mission interesting, but it became controversial when William supported dictator Bolivar's efforts in the region. Bolivar insisted he only wanted to restore peace to the area, after which his dictatorship would end. This support of Bolivar was contrary to American foreign policy, so William was recalled.

At home, Anna was worried about her sons. William, Jr., had abandoned his law practice and moved his family to the Harrisons' former home, the North Bend Cabin. William, Jr., had become an alcoholic and could no longer support his family in town. Another son, Symmes, encountered financial problems in his Land Office job and was heavily in debt.

When William reached home, he told Anna there was not much he could do to help his sons as he was also strapped financially. To help cheer her, he brought some South American plants for her flower garden and a macaw, a brightly feathered tropical bird.

William decided a solution might be found to his and Anna's money problems, as well as those of his sons, if he sold some of the land they owned. He was in the process of negotiating a sale when Symmes died unexpectedly of typhoid fever, leaving a widow and six children.

Anna and William had lost a daughter, Lucy, some years before as well as their young son James, but the death of Symmes was more devastating to both of them because of Symmes's profound unhappiness before his death. Congress voted to allow the Harrison family eighteen years to repay Symmes's debt without interest, which relieved that financial emergency.

The other Harrison children were doing better. Benjamin was now a medical doctor; Carter was entering Miami of Ohio University to study law; one daughter, Mary, had married a Virginia doctor; and Betsey and her husband were farming.

William's health began to suffer from all the stress and strain, and Anna had many anxious hours as he alternated between illness and health. He was now almost sixty years old.

Anna was honestly dismayed when William was nominated to be the Whig party's candidate for President in 1836. Since William was clearly pleased and flattered by the honor, she wisely held her tongue, but she breathed a sigh of relief when he was defeated by Martin Van Buren, the Democrats' candidate.

Anna's and William's next four years were spent in peaceful surroundings with children and grandchildren to enliven their days, as well as many visitors. The splendid macaw flew screaming among the trees as a colorful reminder of William's mission to Colombia.

Anna was a kindly matriarch, who observed the Sabbath strictly and expected all around her to do so. William would not even discuss politics on Sundays in deference to her wishes.

In 1840 the Whig party found itself with no surefire winning candidate for President, and they begged William to run again. Despite Anna's pleas to the contrary, William began a long, exhausting campaign. He was now sixty-eight, and Anna knew his health was not good.

In addition to the asset of a distinguished military career in his background, William had also voiced the firm opinion that slavery could not be legally abolished in any state unless that state government specifically requested it. Since this was what the Southern states' citizens wanted to hear, William won the election this time, defeating incumbent Van Buren.

Anna received the news of William's election with mixed emotions. She was happy for him to win since he was pleased, but she noted privately, "I wish my husband's friends had left him where he is, happy and contented in retirement."

When William left in March 1841, Anna was too ill to go with him. Another son, Benjamin, had died unexpectedly the summer before, and Anna's health had been poor ever since. Anna's and William's daughter-in-law, Jane Findlay Harrison, would serve as hostess for William in the White House until Anna could join him in May.

When he reached Washington, William set out to mend fences with former President Van Buren after their bitter campaign. Van Buren felt sorry for the old man, who looked so tired, and he offered to move out of the White House early so William could get some rest. William refused the kind offer, and went to stay in Virginia with his daughter, Mary, and her family.

On March 4, 1841, a cold wind blew as William delivered his inaugural address, which lasted almost two hours. He was bareheaded and wore neither coat nor gloves. It was unfortunate Anna was not there, for she would have probably insisted that he dress more warmly.

In the days following, William was besieged by office and job seekers on every side, and got little rest day or night. Three weeks after his inauguration, he attended St. John's Episcopal Church and told the Rector he planned to join the church as a communicant. After church, he walked home in a cold spring rain which was mixed with sleet. By the next day, William had developed pneumonia.

After he had spent several days in bed, William appeared to rally, but a sudden relapse caused his death on April 4, 1841, in the White House. He had been President only one month and was the first President to die in office. He was buried in North Bend, Ohio. Anna never got an opportunity to serve as First Lady. She was packing to go when she heard the news.

William had turned over the management of the Harrison family farm to a son, John Scott Harrison, when he was assigned as Minister to Colombia. John was an excellent manager, so he continued in this job most of his life, leaving only long enough to serve two terms in the United States Congress as a representative from Ohio. In gratitude William deeded John a large plot of land on which he could build a house for his own family.

Anna was shocked and deeply grieved by her loss, but she accepted it with grace and dignity. She remained in her own home at North Bend, only five miles from John's home, which was known as The Point.

One of John's sons was Benjamin Harrison, namesake of his great-grandfather. Benjamin was a favorite grandchild of Anna's and he grew up under her watchful eye. She gave him stern admonitions always to bring honor through his actions to the family name. Benjamin would become the twenty-third President of the United States, but Anna would not live to see this.

Anna and Benjamin had a very close, loving relationship. He often brought his grandmother squirrels or birds he had shot on hunting trips as a special treat for her Sunday dinners.

Anna attended church regularly with John and his family, after which they all went to her house for Sunday dinner. William Henry had frequently invited the entire church congregation to eat with him and Anna while he lived, so Anna continued the practice. Usually there were more than fifty people dining at her table on Sundays. If she served a hunting gift Benjamin brought her, she made a point of telling her guests proudly.

Anna lived a peaceful, contented life among her relatives and friends until her death on February 25, 1863, as the Civil War raged. Benjamin was greatly saddened by his beloved grandmother's death, but was unable to attend her funeral as he was helping guard the railroad near Nashville, Tennessee, and could not be spared.

Anna was buried at North Bend beside her husband of forty-five years, William Henry Harrison.

10. Letitia Christian Tyler

Letitia Christian and John Tyler were a well-matched couple. Both were born of aristocratic parents, spent their early years on Virginia plantations, and shared similar ideas and beliefs.

Letitia's family had more money, however, than John's did. Letitia was born November 12, 1790, in New Kent County, Virginia, on her family's large plantation known as Cedar Grove. She was a member of a large, extended family, well respected and politically important in the newly formed government of the United States.

Letitia was sweet-natured, even as a child. Growing up on the plantation she received little formal education, other than learning to read and write. She learned to sew, to knit, to organize and to run household matters efficiently, and these tasks were perceived to be the chief importance in a woman's education during this period of time. Her hobby was flower-gardening.

John Tyler began studying at William and Mary College at age twelve, graduating with honors at age seventeen. He returned to his home at Charles City, Virginia, to begin a study of law. His father and a cousin served as his tutors until his father was elected Governor of Virginia in 1809. After that, John went to study in Richmond in the law offices of Edmund Randolph, former United States Attorney General during George Washington's presidency.

In 1811 John won election to the Virginia House of Delegates. He began immediately to introduce motions and resolutions on various subjects, and was pleased when they were passed by the House of Delegates, although some were altered before passage.

Governor Tyler, John's father, died in January 1813, leaving John an inheritance of part of the Greenway estate and some slaves. With his legal career progressing nicely and his political interests growing, John felt he was ready to marry.

Letitia Christian was his choice. She was slender, slightly built and unusually pretty, with sparkling black eyes. More important to John, she always projected an aura of serenity that was restful.

John proposed to Letitia, although he worried because she came from

Letitia Tyler. (Courtesy Library of Congress.)

a wealthier background. He told her in a letter that since she accepted his proposal, he was glad he was not wealthy after all — that he might have doubted her reason for accepting him if he were. "If I had been wealthy, the idea of your being actuated by prudential considerations in accepting my suit, would have eternally tortured me," he said.

Letitia had not allowed economic considerations to cross her mind. She loved John, she wanted to marry him, and in her life there had always been money available when it was needed. She wanted a husband, a home and children.

With her reserved, dignified manner and her outstanding beauty,

Letitia could have had her choice among her admirers. Her wealth added to her desirability, and John was fortunate that Letitia chose him.

Letitia was devoutly religious, and their courtship was very proper. John wrote her some poems, they exchanged books they had read and enjoyed, and that was the extent of their passionate encounters. Three weeks before their wedding, John had not dared even to kiss her hand!

As strange as this type of courtship may seem in today's society, both John and Letitia were content with this mild approach, and anything stronger would have been a little frightening. Their marriage endured for more than twenty-nine years and they had eight children, so waiting until after they were married for passionate embraces did not hinder them from enjoying their relationship.

Shortly after their wedding on March 29, 1813, both of Letitia's parents died, leaving her a sizable inheritance. This assured their marriage of a firm financial footing, and Letitia settled down willingly to providing a comfortable home for her husband while he pursued a political career. If Letitia had political opinions of her own, they were never expressed.

The newlyweds went to live on the five hundred acre estate John had inherited from his father, which they named Mons-Sacer. They had barely moved in when John was called to military service in the War of 1812 against the British. The British invasion forces had landed at Hampton, Virginia, and all the area was threatened. John joined a local militia company and was commissioned as a captain.

His fellow soldiers in the company were local farmers and unskilled in military activities. One night while they were all sleeping in their second-floor quarters at William and Mary College, word came that British soldiers were approaching. John's company, which had feared an imminent attack, panicked and rushed for the stairs. They fell headlong to the floor below, and landed in a heap of arms, legs and bodies at the foot of the steps.

The rumor was false, no British soldiers appeared, and the farmer-soldiers were allowed to return to their homes, convinced they had saved the countryside by their heroic efforts. John often joked later about his "distinguished military services during the War of 1812."

John was elected to serve in the United States House of Representatives in 1816 from the Richmond district. Since he was from a prominent Virginia family and married to a member of another, he was accepted immediately into Washington's elite society. Yet he lived in a boardinghouse where the food ranged from barely edible to potentially dangerous. He became quite ill on one occasion from eating bad fish.

President James Madison and his wife, Dolley, invited John to dine with them at the White House. Dolley loved highly spiced French-type food and champagne, and she served these to her guests. John wrote to Letitia that the food at the White House was too "flum-flummery" for his taste, and for his part, he would rather eat at home. But at least Dolley didn't serve him food that made him sick.

Letitia was content to stay home with their growing family while John served two terms in Congress. At this time, the city of Washington was a mudhole with cows and pigs wandering about in the roads. There was no sewer system, and malaria was rampant among the inhabitants. The Tyler home in Virginia, by contrast, was a pleasant, clean place to live, and Letitia had no desire to change. John came home during Congressional recesses.

In 1825 John was elected Governor of Virginia, as his father had been many years earlier. The Tyler family moved to Richmond. In Richmond they entertained government officials and notables of Virginia society on a regular basis, but John was not given any money to pay for official entertaining. Letitia tried to keep expenses as low as possible, but they generally spent more than his income. Many of John's later difficulties with finances began during this period.

John urged the Virginia legislature to increase the salary of the Governor, as he pointed out how expensive the duties of the office were, but they refused. At one banquet the Tylers hosted, the members of the legislature were served only Virginia ham and pones of cornbread, washed down with cheap whiskey.

The legislative members may have been amused at John's attempt to make a point, but they still refused to increase his salary. After two years as Governor and wife, John and Letitia were experiencing a serious cash-flow problem.

In 1827 John was elected a United States Senator. Again he spent many months each year living in a Washington boarding house, while Letitia remained at their home at Mons-Sacer.

John and Letitia now had six children to support, as well as a number of slaves. To get money to support himself and his household while he served as Senator, John was forced to sell a woman slave named Ann Eliza. He really hated to do this, and he begged his friends to buy her so he would know she had a good home, but most of the other plantation owners were land-poor themselves, and had little cash money.

John had a habit of lending money freely and indiscriminately to relatives and friends, which added further to his money problems. Letitia closely supervised all the cooking, food preserving, clothes making and other household duties in an effort to keep them financially solvent.

During his Senate years, John's main interests were focused back home in Virginia on his family. He waited eagerly for Letitia's letters to him telling what the children were doing, and he made an effort to take an active part in their upbringing. He hired tutors to educate both his sons and daughters.

He wrote his daughter, Mary, "Your resolution to attend to your studies and not to be led away by the vanities of the world affords me sincere pleasure. Without intellectual improvement, the most beautiful of the sex is but a figure of wax work."

One little Tyler girl died at the age of three months, but another daughter, Alice, and a son, Tazewell, were born not long after. Letitia and John loved them all sincerely, and tried to teach them Christian principles on which they should base their conduct.

Although John was a member of the Senate for nine years, Letitia rarely went to Washington. She spent one winter (1828–1829) there, and the Washington citizens commented on her "beauty of person and eloquence of manner."

After his defeat in a bid to be elected Vice President in 1836, John moved his law practice and his family to Williamsburg, Virginia. Letitia had always enjoyed being in Williamsburg, and she and John felt their children would gain social advantages from their participation in the balls and other social gatherings there, as well as in those in Richmond. John was especially certain that "polish and shape to manners which constitute one-half the concern in our journey through life" would be theirs. In addition, John advised his children, "I have known persons possessing only ordinary capacities getting on better than others who were in intellect greatly superior, simply for force of manners."

In 1839, while they still lived in Williamsburg, Letitia suffered a stroke, from which she never fully recovered. When her son, Robert, married actress Priscilla Cooper in September of that year, Letitia was unable to attend the wedding in Bristol, Virginia. Both Letitia and John were fond of Priscilla and had no objections to the marriage, although Priscilla came from an impoverished family. Robert proudly assured Priscilla that "my mother is more glad that I shall marry you than anyone else in the world."

After their honeymoon, Robert and Priscilla came to make their home with John and Letitia in Williamsburg. Robert was a graduate of William and Mary College, and was practicing law.

Business was not very brisk for the new attorney, however, and Priscilla wrote her sister, "At present the situation is anything but comfortable. Robert has nothing to do scarcely in Williamsburg, and his father won't send him away. The family are very extravagant. The governor [referring to John Tyler] is pressed for money."

To help save money, Priscilla tried to sew her own dresses. She said when she got finished they reminded her of the French towns, Toulon (too long) and Toulouse (too loose).

Priscilla fitted admirably into the Tyler family, and everyone loved her for her cheerfulness and willingness to do whatever she could to help. Priscilla especially loved Letitia, and had great pity for Letitia's disability at age forty-nine. Letitia's unselfish attitude impressed Priscilla greatly.

In 1840 John was again a candidate for Vice President on the Whig ticket, with William Henry Harrison the Presidential candidate. This time the Whigs won the election.

John and Letitia were preparing to move to Washington when a messenger arrived at their Williamsburg home on April 5, 1841, to tell John that the newly inaugurated President Harrison had died most unexpectedly. John was now President of the United States! He was inaugurated on April 6, 1841, one month after President Harrison had been inaugurated.

Since this was the first time a United States President had died while in office, no one was quite sure John Tyler was supposed to be President. Was he only an acting President or actual President? John determined in his own mind to be a President in fact.

Neither Letitia nor John had had time to give any thought to the social and ceremonial duties required of a President and his wife. Letitia decided she would leave for Washington immediately to be with John, but she asked Priscilla to go along to assume the duties as official White House hostess in her place. Letitia's two older daughters were married and living in Virginia with their own families, and eighteen-year-old Elizabeth and thirteen-year-old Alice were too young for such a responsibility.

Priscilla proved to be a capable, charming hostess. Dolley Madison offered her assistance, and was extremely helpful to Priscilla. All the Tylers came to love Dolley — even if she did dip snuff and use too much rouge on her face.

Even while living in the White House, the Tylers lived in a perpetual state of genteel poverty because of exorbitant expenses for entertaining.

Letitia was installed in a second-floor bedroom, too weak to serve in any official capacity. When her daughter, Elizabeth, was married to William N. Waller in January 1842, Letitia did come downstairs for the reception and wedding. It was the only public appearance she made as First Lady.

On September 10, 1842, Letitia gave up her long struggle with illness and died quietly in her bedroom. When she was discovered by her family, she was holding in her hand a damask rose, which she had apparently taken from a vase beside her bed.

All the Tyler family members were deeply grieved by her unexpected death. She was taken back to the Virginia plantation of her family for burial.

John Tyler would remarry later, and an account of his second marriage follows this chapter.

11. Julia Gardiner Tyler

President John Tyler's second wife, Julia Gardiner, burst on the Washington social scene like a flaming meteor, so beautiful and exciting. Julia was an exuberant bride, with reactions often bigger than life. President Tyler's daughters were less excited by their father's second marriage so soon after the death of their mother, but in time they came to accept her, if not love her. The Tyler sons gave Julia no difficulty — indeed, Julia rarely encountered difficulty with any men in her life.

Julia was the daughter of a New York state Senator named David Gardiner, who traced his lineage back to sixteenth century England and his wealth to the first English settler in New York in 1635. This ancestor, Lion Gardiner, wisely acquired a thirty-three hundred acre island, which he named for himself, in Block Island Sound, just off Long Island to the East. He bought the property from the Montauk Indians, but to be on the safe side, he also got a deed from the British government during the reign of Charles I.

Julia's mother was descended from a Scotsman, Michael McLachlan, who also had the foresight to buy several parcels of land in New York City in the eighteenth century. The beauteous Julia (born May 4, 1820, on Gardiner's Island) was a product of families with "old money."

John Tyler's lineage, while not as enhanced by wealth and property as Julia's, went directly back to Henry Tyler from England who first came to Williamsburg, Virginia, in 1653. His family tended to be more interested in politics and government service, and John's father had been a Governor of Virginia.

Background and breeding were important to both Julia and John, but John was so impressed with lovely, self-assured, vivacious Julia that he would have probably married her if she had been the daughter of his tenant farmer.

John's friends and associates were truly amazed that so level-headed a man could so completely lose his common sense and caution in his admiration for Julia. Only four months after the death of his wife of twenty-seven years and the mother of his eight children, John behaved as one bewitched. He could not be with Julia enough, he could not stop talking

Julia Tyler. (Courtesy Library of Congress.)

about how wonderful she was, and he did not care how many tongues wagged about them in Washington and elsewhere.

Julia was educated at Chegary Institute, an exclusive finishing school in New York City. She was a member of elite society groups in both the city and state of New York. She and her pretty sister, Margaret, gave their parents anxious moments during their teenage years with suitors, who were ardent and numerous, but not always suitable. When Julia was twenty, her parents took both girls to Europe for an extended period to prevent them making an unsuitable marriage at too young an age.

The year before she went to Europe, Julia had given permission to a fashionable cloth and clothing firm in New York to use her photograph in their advertising brochure. Her relatives were horrified that Julia would use such poor judgment. People at their level in society just did not *do* such things!

Julia's father decided his daughters' education was lacking, particularly in more practical directions. After their return from Europe, Mr. and Mrs. Gardiner decided to spend some time in Washington with their daughters so they could learn about the government in their own country.

The Gardiner family was welcomed immediately into Washington's most elite groups, and received invitations to attend all important social events of the season of 1841.

When Julia went on her first visit to the White House, Letitia Tyler was still living, although confined to her bedroom on the second floor by the effects of an earlier stroke. John Tyler behaved as the courtly Virginia gentleman that he was on this occasion, but Julia heard something more. She told her mother his "thousand compliments" were so enthusiastic that the people who overheard him "looked and listened in perfect amazement."

Julia was younger than her years in some ways, having been reared in such a protected environment, and she was possibly a little bit "in love with love" rather than with a person, but it is also possible that she told the complete truth about her first meeting with John Tyler. Certainly John's subsequent behavior lent weight to her story.

After a two-months stay in Washington, the Gardiners went home. Julia found life in her East Hampton, New York, home excruciatingly boring after the excitement of European capitals and Washington. Early in 1842 she began begging her father to take their family to Newport or Saratoga Springs for a vacation. Then, as if suddenly struck with inspiration, she suggested a return visit to Washington, to which her father finally agreed.

Letitia Tyler, President Tyler's ailing wife, died in September, 1842, just before the Gardiner family's return to the capital in December for the 1843 winter social season.

Money was often tight for the Gardiners, despite their elevated social standing, and David Gardiner rather hoped either Julia or Margaret, or both, might meet an eligible young man in Washington and marry.

Both girls flirted and played the field of young and old men, but with the frequent invitations of both Robert and Priscilla Tyler, as well as Robert's brother, John, Jr., to visit the White House, the Gardiner girls discouraged serious attentions by anyone else. John, Jr., was especially smitten by Julia. He wrote her poetry, which he included in boxes of candy made in the White House kitchen. Julia knew very well that John, Jr., was married but separated from his wife, so she did not allow herself to be too impressed by his ardor.

Julia's father called on President Tyler just ten days before Christmas to pay his respects, which led to a dinner invitation for the entire Gardiner family to spend Christmas Eve with the Tyler family at the White House. President Tyler had been expelled recently from the Whig political party when he vetoed important Whig legislation, and he needed friends. Since Julia's father was prominent in conservative politics in New York state, the White House dinner invitation may have been dictated as much by political consideration as by a personal interest in the Gardiner daughters.

Regardless of the motives behind the invitation, the Gardiners and Tylers spent a most pleasant evening, and Julia met many of the Tyler relatives.

By the next February, in 1843, it was becoming apparent to even the most casual observer that President John Tyler was extremely interested in Julia, and that she returned his admiration. On February 7, 1843, he invited the Gardiners to dinner once again, along with other New York politicians. It was on this occasion that President Tyler indicated his overwhelming fascination with Julia, for she "flew down the stairs with the President after her around chairs and tables until at last he caught her," to quote Julia's sister, Margaret.

John Tyler had been almost sick with loneliness and grief since his wife had died, and it was easy to understand why sparkling Julia was like a breath of fresh air to him. He embarked on a relentless pursuit of her, with tongues all over town working overtime on the juicy gossip.

At the Washington Birthday Ball two weeks later, John asked Julia to marry him. Julia was most impressed to receive a proposal from the President of the United States, but she declined at first.

Julia's brother, Alexander, saw an opportunity to use his sister's conquest to gain an appointment as a Collector for the Port of New York. In the middle of February, he wrote a glowing letter of praise of President Tyler to the *New York Post*. On the advice of his father, Alexander followed the letter by arriving in Washington two weeks later. He set out to cultivate the friendship of men who were still close to President Tyler, but Alexander still could not accomplish his goal.

Before the Gardiner family left Washington in March to return to their East Hampton home, there was a definite understanding between Julia and President Tyler that they would be married. He wanted the wedding to be in November, but Julia's mother begged Julia to give the matter more thought since Tyler was thirty years older than Julia.

In August, when the Gardiners went on vacation to Saratoga, New York, Julia was pleased to discover she had attracted the envious notice of the elite in New York society by her romance with President Tyler. As soon as summer ended, Tyler began pleading with Julia to return to Washington.

Apparently Julia's father was not sure how he felt about the possibility of Julia marrying President Tyler. Mr. Gardiner leased an apartment in New York City for his family, so the girls would be nearer the scene of social activities and in closer proximity to eligible young men. Because of the move, the Gardiners did not return to Washington until February, 1844, where President Tyler welcomed them back in a fine mood.

Three days later, President Tyler, Julia, her father, and Margaret Gardiner, along with some two hundred other guests, went on board the steam frigate *Princeton* for the test firing of a new naval gun, said to be the world's largest. The gun had been fired several times previously, but on this day the breech exploded, killing several government officials and Julia's father.

Julia was totally overwhelmed by grief and had nightmares for weeks after the accident. President Tyler was so understanding and sympathetic during her ordeal, she decided there was no reason to delay their marriage.

On June 26, 1844, Julia and President John Tyler were married in New York City in the Episcopal Church of the Ascension on Fifth Avenue. It was a small wedding since the Gardiners were still in mourning. Julia's mother, sister and brothers attended from her family and John Tyler, Jr., was present from the President's family. There were a few non-family guests also present.

Julia wore a simple white dress, but no jewelry, for the ceremony. Thereafter, for the next year, she wore black dresses or white lace over black ornamented by onyx jewelry.

Alexander Gardiner plunged wholeheartedly into a campaign to make his new brother-in-law the candidate of the independent Democrats for reelection to the Presidency. Since John had been expelled from the Whig party earlier, he would not be their candidate this time.

Julia and John had not been back long in the White House before Margaret Gardiner reported to her mother that Julia was demanding so much of John's time, he could not get his work done. Mrs. Gardiner wrote Julia to "let your husband work during all business hours. Business should take the precedence of caressing."

Mrs. Gardiner told Julia to apply herself to cleaning the filthy White House. "You know how I detest a dirty house," she wrote. "Commence at once to look around and see that all things are orderly and tidy. This will amuse and occupy you. . . ."

After Margaret had returned to New York, she wrote Julia to remember that Alexander expected Julia to "make hay for him while the Sun shines."

Julia chose to turn her attention to more practical matters. A spiteful Congress had not voted any money for the cleaning or refurbishing of the White House while John Tyler was President. The rugs and draperies were worn out, the house needed painting inside and outside, and the beautiful white pillars had tobacco juice stains all over them.

Julia was neither a whiner nor a quitter. She bought new French furniture, had the walls papered tastefully, bought rugs and chandeliers, as well as many decorating accessories, all with her own money. Some of these items the Tylers could take with them when John retired to Sherwood Forest, a home John had bought for his retirement years in Virginia, after Letitia died. He had named it while in a whimsical mood because of his own outlaw status with the Whig political party.

A queen must have a royal setting, and Julia meant to reign as a queen of Washington society in John's final months as President. She had the male White House servants dressed in black livery, and she ordered an Italian greyhound for a pet.

Julia presided over one of the brightest, liveliest social seasons that winter that Washington had ever seen. In addition to her sister Margaret, Julia invited two young female first cousins to stay at the White House as members of her "Court." John's youngest daughter, Alice Tyler, was now eighteen, and she joined Julia's entourage with enthusiasm.

Alice was not at all pretty, and Julia did not like her at first, but Mrs. Gardiner advised Julia to give the girl a chance, and they became good friends.

Whatever beauty Alice lacked, Julia more than compensated. Attending one of her first White House balls as hostess, an Ohio Congressman from Columbus was struck speechless by Julia's beauty in an embroidered black lace and white satin dress with a tasteful array of diamond jewelry.

"Well," the Congressman said to a friend after several silent moments, "Now I'll go home and tell all about her." It was likely Columbus, Ohio, did not have a resident to equal Julia!

When John decided not to seek reelection, Julia began planning one magnificent, monumental ball for their departure. She invited two thousand guests and three thousand came. By this time Julia's parties were famous. Wine and champagne flowed freely, thousands of candles lit the scene, and the food at the buffet was elegant and plentiful. For this occasion, Julia was dressed in a white ensemble with silver embroidery.

John Tyler was pleased by the success of Julia's final effort as White House hostess. When he began receiving letters from angry citizens complaining of excesses in dancing and gaiety, he told them all politely to get lost. He had no reason to fear criticism now. One hundred and sixteen years would go by before another White House hostess would be seen as an equal to Julia; that would be Jacqueline Kennedy.

Julia and John made every effort to be hospitable and helpful to James and Sarah Polk, who would be replacing them in the White House. When they finally got all their furniture and belongings moved back to Sherwood Forest, they had a good feeling of accomplishment under trying circumstances.

Life at Sherwood Forest was peaceful, but so is a graveyard. John tried his hand at farming, which was fairly successful. Julia had recurrent difficulties with her stepdaughters, and she missed all the praise and admiration she had received in Washington society. Stark reality was beginning to enter Julia's fairy-tale life.

Margaret Gardiner had not married, so John decided maybe a visit with Margaret and the rest of her family would help cheer Julia. Julia went to visit and did enjoy it, but she found she attracted less attention and excited less envy among her friends as an ex–First Lady than she had while living in the White House.

Julia was also pregnant for the first time, and the change in her physical appearance was depressing to her. With each successive child she worried about her change in appearance. Mrs. Gardiner told Julia she felt that one child was enough for them since John had other children, but Julia refused to listen to her. Julia wanted a large family, and she had seven children before she was through.

Before her pregnancy, Julia had run her brother, Alexander, ragged buying clothes, hats, gloves and jewelry for her in New York City. Now she asked him to buy baby clothes and other baby needs. Alexander could never resist Julia's requests, and he continued to shop for larger sizes as the children grew.

The Tylers' neighbors at Sherwood Forest were almost uniformly members of the Whig party, so they tended to avoid contact with John and Julia as much as possible. Thinking they would heap embarrassment on John, they made him District Overseer of the roads. They thought he would refuse such a lowly job after being President of the United States, but he didn't. As overseer he could say when and where the local residents would do allotted work on the roads. He picked days in harvest time and all holidays!

Before long the officials were begging John to resign, but he refused. He was enjoying turning the tables on his tormentors.

As time passed, Julia and John took their children on visits to relatives and to fashionable resorts. These vacations never lasted long, however, and they were glad to return home.

John was disturbed by reports that President Polk had replaced most of the men John had given official jobs. Julia was pleased to hear how dull the social seasons were in the White House with Sarah Polk as hostess.

Alexander Gardiner and Robert Tyler encouraged John to keep his political hopes alive with the idea he might once again be a Presidential candidate. When the slavery issue reached the boiling point in the nation, it seemed John might indeed win the nomination as a Southern conservative, but Abraham Lincoln was nominated instead.

John agreed with secession from the Union and was elected a member of the Confederate government's House of Representatives. He had served only one week when he was stricken by a heart attack in Richmond on January 12, 1862. He died six days later and was buried in Hollywood Cemetery in Richmond, Virginia. The Union government made no official mention of his death.

Julia was profoundly shaken by her loss of John. She had always had a man to tell her what to do, and now there was no one. She was forty-one years old, had seven children to rear and a large estate to manage, and a war had started which moved closer to Sherwood Forest every day.

Mrs. Gardiner felt Julia and the children would be safer living on Staten Island in New York with the rest of the Gardiner family than where they were at present. When the young male slaves began leaving Sherwood Forest, Julia became frightened and took the children with her to join her mother.

David Gardiner, another brother of Julia's, had brought his family to live with Mrs. Gardiner also. David and Julia disagreed frequently and bitterly about the war, with Julia a Southern sympathizer and David for the North. Unfortunately for Julia, most all the other relatives, except Mrs. Gardiner, agreed with David.

After a few weeks Julia left her children in the care of her mother and went back to check on Sherwood Forest. She meant to sell it, but she was unable to find a buyer. She was having financial difficulties since her money was tied up in the Southern banks, and she decided to sail to Bermuda on a blockade runner with bales of cotton from the plantation she hoped to sell. Julia managed to sell the cotton for a good price, but had to stay in Bermuda for about two months before she could get back to Staten Island.

When she returned, David became so abusive to both Julia and her children that she told her mother it seemed she would be forced to leave. Instead, Julia angrily ordered David and his family to leave after he knocked her down during an argument, and he never had any contact with Julia again.

Julia became involved with subversive, so-called copperhead activities against the Union. She sent money and clothes to Confederate forces, bought Confederate war bonds and distributed pamphlets for peace. She had supreme confidence that Confederate forces would win the war, although all information she received both publicly and privately indicated the South was fighting a losing cause.

In May 1864, as the war was winding down, Union forces occupied Sherwood Forest. They destroyed everything possible in the surrounding countryside, but spared the Tyler plantation for a time. But soon, looting men carried away or destroyed all furnishings at Sherwood Forest and took all the livestock. The only thing left of value was the house itself, and it was now being used to house an integrated school.

Mrs. Gardiner died that year in October, and Julia and David spent years in court fighting over their mother's will. Since Mrs. Gardiner had left Castleton Hill on Staten Island to Julia, Julia meant to live on the estate and rear the children she had remaining at home. Two sons were now grown up.

David was angry about the terms of his mother's will and hired a gang of three thugs to break into Castleton Hill and vandalize it, scaring Julia half to death.

Both Margaret and Alexander Gardiner had died during the war years, and Julia had no reason to remain in the North after the war ended. She decided to return to Sherwood Forest and salvage it, if possible. There were no schools operating in the South, so she sent her two older sons to school in Germany.

Throughout the late 1860s and early 1870s, Julia was sued by various people for debts, taxes and other claims. She stayed only one step ahead of her creditors. One of her sons, Gardie, had moved into Sherwood Forest and was working to restore it.

When one of Julia's daughters, recently married, died giving birth to her first child, Julia took the little girl, whom she called Baby Spencer and reared as her own. She moved to Georgetown and put her two children still at home in Catholic schools there, while she again became a member of the Washington social circle. In time, Julia converted to the Roman Catholic faith.

Julia turned her attention to campaigning for a government pension to be given to all living widows of Presidents. After months of disappointment, in March 1882 Congress awarded Julia, Sarah Polk, Mary Lincoln and Lucretia Garfield each an annual pension of five thousand dollars. As the nation's economy grew, Julia's rents increased from her mother's real estate holdings and other property, and Julia's outlook on life improved.

Julia gained a lot of weight as she grew older, and her health began to fail. In 1882 she moved to Richmond, where she lived for the rest of her life. She visited her son from time to time at the now restored Sherwood Forest, but she had no desire to return there to live.

On July 10, 1889, Julia felt ill and asked Baby Spencer to get a doctor. They had been staying in the Exchange Hotel for a few days before leaving for a visit to Sherwood Forest. The eighteen-year-old girl returned to find her grandmother dying from a stroke. In a strange twist of fate, Julia died in a room only a few doors down from the one where John died years before.

Julia was also buried in Hollywood Cemetery beside John, in the company of such famous people as President James Monroe and other august personages, as she probably would have wanted.

12. Sarah Childress Polk

Sarah Childress was born on September 4, 1803, in Murfreesboro, Tennessee, the daughter of wealthy Tennessee plantation owner Joel Childress. Mr. Childress took an avid interest in politics, and the Childresses' beautifully furnished home was often the site of parties and dinners for politicians and other prominent Tennessee citizens. President Andrew Johnson was a family friend and visited often.

The Childress family were devout members of the Presbyterian Church. Sarah and the other children in the family were required to observe the Sabbath strictly, and were expected to excel in their school work.

When Sarah and her sister, Susan, were little girls, there were no good schools for them to attend. Their brother, Anderson, was enrolled in Bradley Academy, a boys' school in Murfreesboro. Believing his daughters would profit from an education as well as his son, Mr. Childress requested permission from the officials at Bradley to allow his two daughters to receive private instruction in the afternoons after regular classes had ended for the day. The permission was granted.

Mrs. Childress usually accompanied her daughters to their afternoon classes, and one day Anderson waited to see them so he could introduce his good friend, James Polk, to his family. They all liked James, and Mrs. Childress invited him to dine with them that evening. At this time, Sarah was only eleven years old and James was nineteen, so theirs was not to be a romance at first sight.

When the school year ended in 1815, James graduated at the head of his class, and Sarah and Susan were busy making plans to attend Mr. Abercrombie's private School for Young Ladies in Nashville, Tennessee.

James entered the University of North Carolina in Chapel Hill, where he studied for three years. Following his graduation, he went to work in the Tennessee House of Representatives as a chief clerk. In 1820 he was admitted to the bar to practice law in Columbia, Tennessee.

After Sarah graduated from the school in Nashville, she went to the Moravian Female Academy at Salem, North Carolina. Here she broadened her musical and artistic skills in addition to taking college-level

Sarah Polk. (Courtesy Library of Congress.)

academic courses. Sadly, Mr. Childress died while Sarah was attending the academy, and she was forced to leave without graduating.

When James encountered Sarah again in 1822 at a Governor's reception in Murfreesboro, he found she was now an elegantly dressed, cultured, well-educated and interesting young woman. He had liked the little girl Sarah, and he fell deeply in love with pretty, dark-haired, grown-up Sarah.

Sarah's sister, Susan, was married to Dr. William Rucker, and they both approved of Sarah's candidate for her hand in marriage, as did Sarah's mother. Mrs. Childress's fondest hope for her pretty daughter was to see her settled in a marriage and life of her own.

Before James could marry Sarah, however, he felt he should improve his financial standing. His family was only moderately wealthy, and his job with the Tennessee Congress did not pay enough to support a wife. With Sarah's encouragement, he became a candidate to serve in the state Congress himself in 1823.

James was elected, after an arduous campaign that kept him continuously on the go for weeks, during which time Sarah hardly saw him.

On January 1, 1824, Sarah and James were married in the home of her mother. While James had been campaigning, Sarah had spent her time getting her wedding clothes made and arranging the wedding, which was country style. A seven-course wedding supper followed the ceremony. Background music was played all evening by a black musicians' group. All in all, the wedding celebration lasted for a week! During all this time James and Sarah had no opportunity to be alone together. When the festivities finally ended, they went home to a two-room house belonging to the Polk family, located near the Polk family home. Slave quarters were in back of the cottage.

Jane Polk, James's mother, visited the newlyweds frequently, and found herself impressed by Sarah's diligent efforts to make the little house homey with bright rugs, quilts and other decorative accessories. She took the opportunity to plead with Sarah to use her influence to get James to join a church, which he had never done, although the Polks were also devout Presbyterians. James had been presented for baptism as an infant, at which time his father, Samuel Polk, became involved in a heated argument with the preacher. The christening was not completed, and now as an adult, James was not a member of any church.

Sarah sympathized with the older woman, but she told Mrs. Polk as gently as she could that James needed to make such a decision for himself for it to be worthwhile. She knew Mrs. Polk was distressed about James's seeming indifference to religion, and she promised she would do all she could to get him to attend.

In 1824 James was elected to serve in the United States Congress. He would serve in this body for the next fifteen years, becoming Speaker of the House in 1835. His nickname was "Young Hickory" among his fellow Congressmen because of his loyal support of President Andrew Jackson's policies.

At first Sarah did not go with James to Washington. Instead, she remained in Murfreesboro with her mother to save money. Both James and Sarah soon discovered they were miserable apart, and they decided the savings were not worth their unhappiness.

When she moved to Washington, Sarah and James shared a home with other families for reasons of economy, commonplace practice at the time.

Sarah was young and attractive, and she soon found herself involved in the Washington social whirl. She enjoyed these events and would have continued, but James reminded her sharply that they had come to Washington to work, not to run around!

Sarah decided she should respect his wishes in the matter, and in return she asked that he respect her wishes by attending church with her. On Sunday mornings Sarah always attended services at the First Presbyterian, and James consented to go with her.

Each Sunday morning thereafter, even if James was conferring with colleagues, Sarah brought his hat and cane as she started to leave for church. His companions knew she meant for him to go with her, and they would end their conference. Sarah was keeping her promise to James's mother.

As time passed, Sarah became more and more involved with James's career in politics, and he formed the habit of discussing political dilemmas with her. He found her opinions helped him reach better decisions about what course of action to take. Sarah read newspapers and magazines from various sections of the United States and condensed the political comments for James, so he could keep current with public thinking.

When James was nominated to run for Governor of Tennessee in 1839, Sarah found to her surprise she was reluctant to leave Washington. James admitted he had also enjoyed being a part of the nation's capital scene.

James and Sarah both worked hard during his campaign for Governor. The voters of that day took a keen interest in campaigns for public office and would tolerate long speeches if the candidate made a point of launching a personal attack on his opponent. The gatherings were usually picnic-type events, and the lengthy speeches were followed by plenty of food and drink. Sarah helped arrange such events for James, which must have been effective, for James was elected Governor of Tennessee.

James saved the state of Tennessee from almost certain bankruptcy during his term as Governor by limiting the amount of currency banks could issue. However, he was defeated in his next two bids for reelection. He was unfortunate to be caught in the backlash of discontent with Democrats at a national level, with a Whig President sweeping other Whigs into office with him.

By 1844 President John Tyler was so unpopular with his own Whig party members, he was not nominated as their candidate in the Presidential election. Instead, they chose Henry Clay.

Clay felt sure the Democrats would nominate former President Martin Van Buren, and was dismayed when James Polk was nominated.

James got the news of his nomination by reading a newspaper article at his home in Tennessee. He was lying in a hammock, taking life easy for the moment, when he read it. Both he and Sarah were delighted. Now they would get to go back to Washington to live.

James won the election by a narrow margin, due in part to the fact that Henry Clay was better known nationally. His Tennessee neighbors were thrilled that one of their own would once again be President. They were excited that Sarah would be the President's Lady, since their former Tennessean in the White House had been a widower.

The neighbor ladies asked Sarah what she would wear while she lived in the White House. Would she sew her own dresses? On an even more practical level, would she have to churn her own butter?

If these eager, innocent questions amused Sarah, she gave no indication. She reassured their friends she and James could hire some household help in the White House as Congress always appropriated money to pay for servants.

James was inaugurated on March 4, 1845. For the two inaugural balls in his honor, Sarah wore a Worth designer gown of pink satin trimmed with lace to the first ball, and a blue velvet dress with a deeply fringed cape to the second.

As mistress of the White House, Sarah did not attempt to redecorate the mansion to her liking, saying, that if the living quarters had satisfied Mrs. Tyler, they would be fine for her, too.

Sarah's religious convictions led to a ban on dancing in the White House, and no alcoholic drinks were served while James was President. Society leaders and some politicians were very unhappy with this turn of events, but the general public approved Sarah's stand.

Sarah held two receptions each week at which both she and James received guests. In addition, there were numerous state dinners and luncheons for important guests. An elegant dinner party was held every two or three weeks during the winter season.

Former First Lady Dolley Madison was a frequent, welcome White House visitor. Dolley's cheerful disposition and jolly nature brightened many White House gatherings. Both of the Polks were very fond of Dolley.

Pleasant, kindly Sarah was more admired in Washington than James. He was perceived as a hard-working, narrow-minded, stubborn man determined to do things his way. Henry Clay told Sarah, "A general approbation has been expressed of your administration . . . but there is some difference of opinion about your husband's administration."

James entered the office as President determined to bring the territories of Texas and Oregon into the Union. He was also casting wishful eyes toward California. Mexico took a dim view of his aims since they claimed ownership of Texas, and when James pushed the annexation, Mexico declared war on the United States in 1846.

Great Britain owned a part of Oregon, and James was able to work out a compromise with them. Later a compromise was also reached with the Mexicans for both Texas and California territory, for which the United

States paid the Mexican government fifteen million dollars. Later James was criticized for his aggressive actions toward Mexico, but no one objected while the conflict raged, and it was financed by money willingly appropriated by Congress.

Since Sarah Polk never had any children of her own, she invited young relatives and friends to visit often in the White House. Martha Johnson, the daughter of fellow Tennessean, politician Andrew Johnson, was an especial favorite of Sarah. Martha's father was a member of Congress, and Martha was attending school in the Washington area. She gladly helped Sarah with some of the housekeeping details in the White House, as she had helped her own mother back home in Tennessee.

Sarah's niece, Joanna Rucker, came to live with them at the White House for a time. Another young niece and two nephews brought life and laughter to the stately mansion.

Sarah and James accepted few invitations, dining out only once during the first ten months he was President. They did attend an occasional ball, but James was a true workaholic. He begrudged time spent away from his duties.

Sarah continued her earlier habit of marking and condensing news articles for his later reading. Any letters he wrote had to be written by hand, and she sometimes helped with these. He had an official male secretary, but the young man could only do so much, as there were no typewriters or word processors then. Sarah enjoyed helping James when she had time.

Office seekers bothered James more than any other problem he faced as President. He was shocked to find he was expected to appoint people to jobs because good party members wanted him to do so, whether or not the job applicant was qualified. ". . . Will the pressure for office never cease! I have no offices to bestow without turning out better men than a large majority of those who seek their places," he said in despair.

James had announced at the time he first became President that he would serve only one term. As time went on, he found himself looking forward more and more to the day when he and Sarah could go home to Tennessee to stay. James sold the home they had bought earlier in Columbia, Tennessee, and now he bought a fine Nashville home, which had been the residence of the late Senator Grundy from Tennessee. He and Sarah would make this new place their retirement home.

After the Mexican War had ended and the announcement had been made to Congress that gold had been discovered in California, James began taking short holiday trips to visit areas he wanted to see before he returned to Tennessee. While he traveled through New England, Sarah went back to Nashville to visit both their mothers in the area and to make preparations for their return home. She measured windows and room sizes in their new home so she could buy drapes and rugs to bring back with her when they left Washington.

James had seriously damaged his health with his devotion to duty. He was feeble in his movements, and his hair was completely gray. He had suffered with chronic diarrhea the entire time they had lived in the White House.

They attended the inauguration of the new President, General Zachary Taylor, on March 5, 1849, before leaving for Nashville. The long trip home aggravated the health problems from which James had been suffering. He had an acute attack and was seriously ill for several days after they reached Nashville.

James and Sarah renamed the Grundy house, calling it Polk Place. James was happy with all the improvements Sarah had made, and he threw his energies into arranging his books in his new library.

The effort was too much for him. He collapsed, and it soon became evident to all around him that he was dying. His mother came from her home to get him to be baptized. He told her he had long ago promised a Methodist minister, the Reverend McFerren, that he would let him baptize him when he was ready. The Reverend McFerren was called, and he baptized James on his deathbed.

James said he was now prepared "to meet the great event." He died on June 15, 1849, only three months after leaving the White House. He was buried in the Polk Place garden.

Sarah felt lost without James. He had been the center of her attentions and affections for so many years. How could she ever enjoy life again without him?

To help ease her sorrow and to gain a new interest in life, she took her brother's orphaned granddaughter to rear as her own child. The little girl's name was also Sarah.

Sarah delighted in talking about James if a visitor mentioned him, but she did not dwell on her loss. She kept her lively interest in world and national events. Many people from their past visited her, but she refused invitations to visit the Philadelphia Centennial and the White House and would not attend the wedding of her nephew. She dressed in mourning for the rest of her life.

When the Civil War began, Sarah told friends she was glad James had not lived to see the conflict. She insisted she had no idea with whom his sympathies would have been. She refused to leave her home even as the Union army neared Nashville.

The Union leader, General Buell, came to call on Sarah. He asked Sarah's black manservant, Elias, how he felt about the war. Elias said briefly he was for the South.

Several other Union generals also visited Sarah, and by special orders her Nashville home was not damaged. She welcomed each visitor, whether Northerner or Southerner, with dignity and kindliness.

Her home was spared, but plantation property she and James had owned in Mississippi was destroyed. All the buildings and crops were burned, and the workers left upon their emancipation. She sold the land for a small amount so she would have money to pay her expenses at Polk Place.

Crippled badly with rheumatism, Sarah was almost completely without any money for the next nineteen years. In 1882 Congress finally approved a five thousand dollar annual pension for her.

Sarah died on August 14, 1891, of natural causes. She was eighty-eight. She was buried beside James in the garden at Polk Place. In 1893, their tomb, which resembles a Greek temple in design, was moved to the State Capitol grounds in Nashville, Tennessee, where it remains today.

13. Margaret Mackall Smith Taylor

Margaret Mackall Smith was born in Calvert County, Maryland, on September 21, 1788. Her father, Walter, was a successful planter, and she traced her heritage back to Richard Smith, who emigrated from England in 1649 and became Attorney General of the Maryland province. Margaret's father served in the Revolutionary War under George Washington's command.

Margaret was by all accounts a pretty little girl who grew into a stately, attractive woman of medium height and slender build. She was reared in a genteel home, where she learned etiquette and household management and developed firm religious convictions which would remain with her all her life.

In spring of 1810 Margaret went to visit her sister, Mrs. Samuel Chew, in Kentucky. While there she met a young neighbor of the Chews named Zachary Taylor.

Zachary was home from his first assignment in the army to recover from yellow fever. He was feeling better and attending a social evening in the Chews' home when he met Margaret.

Even though Zachary lived most of his childhood in Kentucky frontier country, he was no country bumpkin. He was a son of parents from Virginia aristocracy and was related to President James Madison. His father was a descendant of wealthy plantation owners, and his mother had received her education from European tutors.

As he entered his early twenties, Zachary decided he wanted to leave the farm and join the army. He had only been in Louisiana for a short time when he contracted yellow fever.

Zachary and Margaret were instantly attracted to each other, and in about three months' time, on June 21, 1810, they were married at the Taylor farmhouse in Jefferson County, Kentucky.

Theirs was a marriage of equals in breeding, background and tastes. It was a happy marriage which would last more than forty years. No one in either family had opposed the match.

Zachary was ordered back to the Ohio River region to help fight Indians shortly after their marriage. While he was away, Margaret, remaining on the family farm near Louisville, Kentucky, gave birth to their first child — a daughter they named Anne Margaret.

When the War of 1812 with the British began, Zachary continued his army service while his family stayed in Kentucky. Again he was stationed in Louisiana. Many New Englanders hoped the British, with whom they sympathized, would overrun Louisiana, as they had not wanted that area in the Union in the first place, but United States forces were victorious in the Battle of New Orleans. When the war ended, Louisiana was welcomed as a state by the Republican party, while the Federalists feared their power would be diminished in Congress by its entry into the Union.

One result of the end of the War of 1812 was the reduction in the armed forces of the United States. Zachary was offered a commission if he would stay in the army, but he decided he would go home to Kentucky in 1815.

The Taylor family stayed there farming for almost a year, working steadily. Zachary and his slaves raised a corn crop using oxen to pull the plow, and their wheat crop had to be mowed by hand with a sickle. He used no fertilizer. When the land became worn out from use, more fields would be cleared.

Life was no easier for Margaret. On Mondays the family wash was done in a nearby creek. On other days she sewed, ran the spinning wheel and wove cloth for their clothes. Slaves cooked and cleaned.

They visited with neighbors and felt they were settling into married life. Another daughter, Sarah Knox (called Knox), was born in 1814, and a third, Octavia in 1816.

Also in 1816, Zachary returned to the army as a major with the Third Infantry. From this time on he continued his army career for thirty-three years. Margaret and the children went with him from one army post to another. Margaret was cheerful and uncomplaining as she cared for their children, many times in primitive surroundings. Army posts were frequently in wilderness locations, had few or no conveniences, and the environment was rough and unsuitable for young children.

A total of five daughters and a son were born to the couple during their marriage, with two of the daughters dying in childhood. Margaret's source of comfort in life's many trials was her faith in God. She was an Episcopalian. Zachary was not a member of a church, although he was a generous contributor to Sarah's. He raised no objections when she arranged for church services to be held at the various forts where he was the commanding officer. She fiercely resisted the evil and weakness around her and tried to rear her children to be law-abiding, God-fearing and respectable.

As the family moved around, the children began to grow up. They went to stay with relatives in Kentucky or Maryland to be educated.

When the eldest Taylor daughter, Anne, was eighteen, she fell in love with Dr. Robert Crooke Wood, a surgeon at Fort Snelling where the Taylor family lived at the time. Zachary liked the young doctor, and he and Margaret approved the match. The young people were married in September 1829.

Zachary was reassigned to Fort Crawford, Prairie du Chien, Wisconsin, near St. Paul, Minnesota, in 1832. Here their second daughter, Sarah Knox, met and fell in love with Lt. Jefferson Davis, who would someday become President of the Confederacy. Zachary and Margaret both opposed this romance as they felt Lt. Davis was not of good moral character. Lt. Davis was feeling his oats as a recent graduate of West Point and had a smart mouth. Otherwise his character was excellent. He did take an occasional alcoholic drink, which the Taylors abhorred. Zachary neither drank nor smoked, but he chewed tobacco.

To put distance between him and their daughter, Zachary had Lt. Davis sent to another army post. He was gone for two years, but he and Knox wrote each other faithfully. When he got back he still wanted to marry Knox, and Zachary was still firmly set against it.

Knox was unhappy with her father's attitude, but she loved Lt. Davis and she was determined to marry him. Knowing of the family squabble, an aunt invited Knox to visit her in Kentucky. Knox accepted gratefully and married Lt. Davis there in June, 1835, with her sister Anne the only family member present.

These newlyweds were on their honeymoon in Vicksburg, Mississippi, when they both contracted malaria, but they were not aware of their illness. When Margaret wrote Knox that she feared for her health in Vicksburg, the couple went on to Lt. Davis's sister's plantation in Louisiana. Knox died there after a few days from the fever her mother had feared. She had been married for three months.

Lt. Davis was bitter and distraught by her unexpected death, so much so that he lived in virtual seclusion for the next eight years.

Not until after Knox died did Margaret receive a letter she had written the day of her wedding, thanking Zachary for the money he had sent her and telling her parents she would always love them. Margaret was overcome with grief at the loss of her beautiful daughter. To assuage her grief, she visited the wounded and sick soldiers in camp hospitals, taking them flowers and trying to cheer them.

After heroic military action by Zachary against the Seminole Indians in Florida, he was named commander of military operations in the whole Southwest. His duty was to improve defenses in this wilderness territory and make friends with the Indians living there. His headquarters were at Baton Rouge, Louisiana. Margaret was delighted to find old friends at this new location as many of Zachary's old regiment were stationed here.

Margaret and the two children still living at home, Mary Elizabeth
(called Betty) and their one son, Richard, set out to find living quarters for
the family. There were new brick buildings, well-equipped, which were the
officer's quarters, but Margaret did not choose any of these. These could
never really belong to her and Zachary.

She found a four-room cottage nearby, needing major repairs, but
located on the banks of the Mississippi River. It had been built by Spanish
forces for their commanding officer about forty years earlier. From
Margaret's point of view it had great potential. It had wide verandas on all
four sides, so there was always a shady porch. The house overlooked the
river, and it was some distance from the post. Even better, the price was
right. Zachary raised no objections as he respected Margaret's judgment in
such matters, so the house became theirs.

Margaret and Betty went to work, enlisting aid from two servants and
some recuperating soldiers. In a short time the cottage was transformed
into a most pleasant home. There were tall trees around the house, a large
yard which Margaret decorated with brightly blooming flower beds, and
space for a vegetable garden in back.

Zachary was impressed with Margaret's choice, and he bought an ad-
joining field to use as pasture for their cows. He realized Margaret had
finally found the home she had been silently longing for during the years
they had moved around.

Margaret was happy. She could now attend church regularly, which
she could never do before. She and some of the other army wives mounted
a campaign to build an Episcopal chapel. They got their chapel built at last,
and it formed the beginning of a church still active in Baton Rouge.

Not only did Zachary again contribute generously to the building of
the chapel, but he attended services there each week with his family, adding
to Margaret's contentment.

Before many months had passed, Zachary was ordered to Fort Jesup
near the Louisiana-Texas border, then on to Fort Gibson in Indian territory. He gained his nickname of "Old Rough and Ready" while dealing
with Indian affairs at Fort Gibson.

The Taylor family lived back and forth between Fort Smith on the
Arkansas River, near Fort Gibson, and their real home in Baton Rouge.
Fort Smith offered better living conditions than Fort Gibson. Army families
never knew where they would live next.

To Margaret's horror, war broke out in 1846 between the United States
and Mexico, and Zachary was in the thick of the battles. Their former son-
in-law, Jefferson Davis, had rejoined the army and was fighting with
Zachary. The two men reconciled when they found they would be serving
together. Each realized how much the other had loved Knox.

Margaret was greatly upset to have Zachary in the middle of a fierce war. She vowed if he lived to return home, she would never go out into society or try to dress fashionably again. She was terribly distraught, fearing he would never be home again. She was also having health problems, which added to her mental distress.

Betty Taylor wrote faithfully to her father, telling him news and gossip and reporting on her mother's health. Betty also began paying household expenses for her mother. Betty had been well educated as was possible during the time and was very capable in business matters.

Richard Taylor graduated from Yale at age nineteen. He did not choose to enter military service, partly because he suffered greatly from rheumatoid arthritis and was not able to stand life in the field.

Realizing he might not survive the war, Zachary made it clear in a letter that he wanted Richard to assume control and management of Cypress Grove, a cotton plantation Zachary had bought shortly before the Mexican War broke out. It was also located on the Mississippi River about forty miles north of Natchez. Richard was trustworthy, and his hard work and serious attention to his task made his parents proud of him.

Zachary did survive the war, despite his and Margaret's misgivings, and during his service became General Zachary Taylor. Margaret did not care about his title — she was thrilled and happy to have her husband home with her when the war ended. Their happy reunion and joy at being together was evident to all. Now they could look forward to a peaceful retirement.

Zachary was glad to be home. As he visited with relatives and friends who came to see them in their Baton Rouge cottage, he was reveling in the idea of a future filled with leisure and contentment. His faithful horse, Old Whitey, who had carried him through the Mexican War, grazed contentedly in the nearby pasture.

But Zachary had come home a hero. Neither he nor Margaret guessed that this fact would cause their newfound happiness to be short-lived.

The nation's mood had turned against professional politicians who kept their place in the public eye. The citizens now wanted a simple, capable fellow who was genuine in his opinions and not really a part of the political scene to lead them. In short, they wanted a man like Zachary Taylor.

The Whig party did not have a candidate they felt could be elected — unless Zachary would be that candidate. Would he?

Zachary was flattered by their request and felt it was his soldierly duty to help if he could. All the attention he received did embarrass him, however. Margaret was vehemently opposed to the idea as she felt sure he would be elected and she wanted to live only in their cottage for the rest of her life. She felt strongly that Zachary deserved a rest after all his stressful years, and she was worried about his health.

When the Whigs sent him official notice that he had been nominated to run for President on the Whig ticket, he refused to pay postage due on the letter and so did not receive it for a time until it had been returned to the Whigs and remailed. Later as Margaret had feared, Zachary was elected.

So Margaret Taylor had to move her household again, this time to the White House in Washington. With Zachary and Margaret came a new son-in-law. In December 1848, before her father's inauguration, Betty Taylor married Brevet Lt. Col. William Wallace Smith Bliss, her father's adjutant in the Mexican War. Betty was a lighthearted, beautiful girl with a winning smile who had many of the lieutenants competing for her attention. She waited until her father had come home before she chose, and she selected the best one. He was nine years older, but he was extremely intelligent and a graduate of West Point. Most important of all, General Taylor was as fond of him as if he were one of his own children.

Colonel Bliss resigned from the army so he and Betty could live with the new President and Margaret. Betty would serve as her father's official hostess since her mother was not physically able. Margaret may have also feared she would be inadequate since she had spent so much of her life in the wilderness and had not kept up with the changes in customs and manners of society.

Snow was falling in Washington the night of Zachary's three inaugural balls. He and Millard Fillmore, his Vice President, attended all three. The most expensively dressed, most jewel-bedecked ladies attended the last and most official ball at City Hall that evening, but no one was more outstanding in her vivacious personality or attracted more admiring looks than Betty Taylor Bliss in her simple white dress, wearing one flower in her hair.

Although Betty was the public hostess for her father, Margaret was also a vital part of the daily life in the White House. Margaret stayed in her sitting room much of the time, but she always had laughing, talking, noisy relatives and friends around her. The corridors rang with the sound of children's voices and running feet. All the family's relatives on both sides, nieces, nephews and cousins, as well as friends came for visits of several days, which Margaret and Zachary both enjoyed. There were the usual official receptions and dinners, but there were also children's parties for the Taylor grandchildren and their friends, and even teen-age dances.

Jefferson Davis had remarried, and he and his wife, Varina, visited often. Varina admired Margaret for her refinement and gentle nature. Varina was an aristocratic Mississippi belle, and she recognized a gentlewoman in Margaret. Margaret loved her.

One of Margaret's grandsons complained his grandmother was too strict, but the grandson was the most mischievous one and undoubtedly needed scolding. His grandmother probably had a twinkle in her eye.

While the Taylors lived in the White House, gas chandeliers were installed for the first time. Otherwise the tired old house was showing its age. When the Taylors moved in it needed painting, new gutters and a furnace. In addition, the roof leaked. Zachary had the house painted and put in good order while he and his family lived there.

Betty proved to be a lively official hostess who presided twice a week at dinners as elegant as any ever held in the White House.

As President, Zachary had firm opinions, which he stuck to when challenged. He thought California and New Mexico should be admitted as free states without Congress deciding on the matter. This did not sit well with his Southern supporters. When they began muttering about secession from the Union, Zachary told them he would personally take command of the army to quell the rebellion. He said firmly, "Disunion is treason."

In the spring of 1850, Zachary was shocked when three of his Cabinet officers were accused of using knowledge gained in their government duties for making money for themselves, which is illegal even today. President Taylor spent sleepless nights worrying about it. Margaret knew how upset he was, but did not know how to comfort him.

A few weeks later, he made a speech at the Washington Monument as part of the Independence Day celebration. The weather was extremely hot and humid, and he complained of feeling a little dizzy when he got up to speak. He then sat unprotected in the hot sun through other long speeches. Afterward he complained that neither Mexico nor Florida was any hotter than Washington in summer, and he drank several glasses of ice water.

When he returned to the White House, he ate an unusually large amount of cherries, followed by iced milk. His family warned him he should not overdo in drinking cold fluids.

Within an hour, Zachary had developed severe abdominal cramps, which continued until his death five days later on July 9.

An official funeral was held in Washington. Behind the funeral carriage in the parade to the Congressional Cemetery three miles away, Old Whitey, Zachary's faithful horse, walked with an empty saddle. Abraham Lincoln gave the eulogy. Zachary's body was sent to Jefferson County, Kentucky, for burial.

Margaret's grief knew no bounds. The night of Zachary's funeral she moved to Baltimore. After remaining there for three months, she and her daughters, Betty and Anne, joined Richard in Louisiana.

Margaret lived for two more years, no day passing without a mention of Zachary. She never mentioned Washington again as long as she lived. Betty and her husband moved in with her to make their home.

Zachary left a total estate of about one hundred thirty thousand dollars, so Margaret had enough to pay her living expenses. She died on August 18, 1852, in Louisiana. No picture of her has ever been found.

14. *Abigail Powers Fillmore*

Abigail Powers was born on March 13, 1798, in Stillwater, New York, a small village in Saratoga County. The town was an outpost of the settled area of New York State at the time, and the uncharted wilderness was only a short distance away.

Despite this, when Abigail's father, the Reverend Lemuel Powers, died while Abigail was still very young, her mother gathered her children and household belongings together to move further west. She had little money and felt they could live better on less in the country.

Although he left little savings, Abigail's father did leave an extensive library for the times. He had bought and used some of the books to prepare sermons for the Baptist congregations he had served.

Mrs. Powers also valued learning for its own sake, and she set out to give Abigail and Abigail's older brother a decent education by herself during their childhood, as there were no schools nearby.

As the children grew older, Abigail's brother became a judge and Abigail entered an academy at nearby New Hope, New York, to study to become a schoolteacher. She was now twenty-one years old, a striking tall girl with long black hair and lovely dark eyes.

When a classmate, Millard Fillmore, saw Abigail for the first time, he thought she was the most beautiful woman he had ever seen. Before he came to the school, Millard had spent all of his nineteen years helping his father scratch out a bare living as a tenant farmer. His father hoped his son could have a better life than his own, and encouraged Millard to attend the academy with this in mind.

Millard was six feet tall, unusually tall, for a nineteenth century man, and was always considered handsome. He and Abigail were together as often as their studies allowed during the winter of 1819, and they fell deeply in love.

Millard realized his humble beginnings were not equal even to Abigail's, and he lacked confidence in his ability to rise higher in the world than his parents had managed to do. Abigail encouraged him endlessly, spurred his ambition and brought out his best abilities. With Abigail by his side, Millard felt he could move mountains.

Abigail Fillmore. (Courtesy National Portrait Gallery, Smithsonian Institution.)

While Abigail's and Millard's courtship continued, Millard's father decided to become a tenant farmer for County Judge Walter Wood, whose farm was about twelve miles away at Montville. Millard's father then asked his new landlord if he would let Millard clerk in his law office for two months to see if he might enjoy legal work.

Judge Wood agreed to the proposal, and Millard left the academy to work for the judge. He and Abigail parted tearfully, but Millard promised they would be married as soon as he could save some money.

Millard's new employer was a strict, sometimes harsh, taskmaster, and after working for him almost two years, Millard decided to look further afield for another job. He was earning very little and saved almost no money. He could never marry Abigail at this rate. He also felt strongly that Judge Wood enjoyed keeping him subservient, and would always do so if allowed.

Millard had found he did like legal work, so he went to Buffalo, New York, where he found a job as clerk in a law firm with much better working conditions. Millard's new associates were impressed by his good judgment and dedication, so they helped him get admitted to the bar. Now he could practice law on his own.

Despite all these events, Millard's self-doubts continued. He wanted to avoid competing with older, more experienced lawyers in Buffalo, so he went to East Aurora to set up a practice. After only two years he was secure enough financially to marry. He rode back in style by stagecoach to Moravia, where he and Abigail were joyfully reunited. This was the first time he had seen her since being admitted to the bar two years earlier.

Abigail was still the loving, beautiful woman he remembered. She had been teaching school for most of the time they had been apart. She told Millard she would not mind continuing to teach for a while after they married to help him get a firm financial footing.

Abigail and Millard were married on February 5, 1826, in Moravia. They went immediately to East Aurora to begin their new life together.

Abigail got a teaching job, which probably aroused comment among their acquaintances, as women did not customarily work outside their homes after marriage. Millard decided he would improve his knowledge of law. He bought many law books during the next year and studied earnestly. Soon he was qualified to be admitted as a counselor to the New York State Supreme Court.

With his appearances as counselor in the higher court, Millard's reputation was enhanced. His law practice increased to the point that he hired a young man to assist him. Millard felt he was beginning to attain his goals in the legal profession. One Buffalo lawyer, soon to become a judge, suggested to Millard that they form a partnership, but Millard did not feel the time was right for him to leave East Aurora.

The year 1828 was an important year in the life of the Fillmores. Their first child, a son also named Millard, was born, and Millard was elected to the New York State Assembly from his district. He had been a candidate on the Antimason ticket, which political party he had helped form two years earlier when rumors began circulating that a New York bricklayer had been murdered for revealing Masonic secrets.

For the next three years, Millard was frequently traveling back and forth to Albany, while Abigail stayed home and cared for little Millard Powers.

In Albany Millard became friends with Thurlow Reed, editor of a leading newspaper in the state capital, who was also a political boss. Mr. Reed encouraged Millard to continue his involvement in the political process.

In 1830 Millard decided the time had come to move his family to Buffalo, which Abigail was glad to do. By today's standards, Buffalo was a primitive town with unpaved streets, few sidewalks, freely roaming cows and pigs throughout the city and a dilapidated-looking waterfront area. There was more to Buffalo than these external features, however. It was also a city with genteel, well-educated, social-minded citizens, who welcomed Abigail and Millard to their midst.

The Fillmores had been so busy getting started in their marriage and professional lives, they had had little time for socializing before. Now in Buffalo, where frozen rivers prevented navigation for about four months each winter, there was much visiting, partying and gaiety.

Abigail and Millard joined enthusiastically into this new way of life, and for the rest of their lives would consider it ideal. They attended formal dinners, music recitals of various types, dances, the theater, and lectures.

For the first time Abigail and Millard had enough money to buy books, which they both read avidly. Millard rarely returned from a trip without bringing back several books, and Abigail increased the bookshelves as needed.

They joined a Unitarian church, despite their family backgrounds of membership in other denominations. Millard found he could accept the Unitarian belief in the inner worth of mankind and the elevation of one's consciousness through self-effort better than a doctrine of faith and good works. This was no temporary aberration on the Fillmores' part. They remained Unitarians all their lives and were faithful in the support of Unitarian causes.

In early spring of 1832, Mary Abigail Fillmore was born. Just after her birth, an epidemic of Asiatic cholera began in Buffalo, having first begun among immigrants landing in Quebec in Canada. Along with many other citizens in Buffalo, Abigail and Millard took their children and left town. They returned to East Aurora for the summer. They enjoyed their stay there, but were glad to go back home when cold weather brought an end to the cholera epidemic.

Millard had recently been elected to serve in the United States Congress, and he soon had to return to Washington. He worked hard for the interests of his constituents of the Buffalo area, and they rewarded him by reelecting him four times to serve them in Congress. In 1840 he became Chairman of the House Ways and Means Committee.

Millard's friends and supporters were astonished when he declined to seek reelection in 1842. Millard had secret hopes he could be elected to the United States Senate in 1844, but instead his editor friend, Thurlow Weed, told Millard he thought Millard could be elected Governor of New York State.

In his campaign for Governor, Millard was decisively defeated for the first time in his political career. He tried to be philosophical in defeat, saying he would have more time to spend with his wife and children now.

Young Millard Powers was now sixteen, and his father hired him to work in his law office as a clerk. Mary Abigail, now twelve, was talented in music especially.

Abigail was glad to have her husband become a real part of the family again. Millard still treated Abigail with tenderness and respect, as few of the men of their acquaintance did their wives. After eighteen years of marriage, Abigail and Millard were still in love.

Millard had devoted much time to the establishment of a university at Buffalo before he was defeated in his Senate race. Since he was free of political obligation, he accepted the post as chancellor of the new university, which at present consisted only of a medical school as the first department.

Millard watched national events unhappily as the new President of the United States, James K. Polk, managed to get duties reduced on imports in a new Tariff Act. The tariff law Millard and fellow Whigs had passed while he was in the Senate was scrapped. This old law protected manufacturers and businessmen in the United States from unfair foreign trade competition. If only Millard could be a part of the national government again!

He got his opportunity sooner than he expected. He was asked to be a candidate for Vice President on the Whig ticket of 1848, with Zachary Taylor the Presidential candidate. This unlikely combination of military Southern slave owner and New York lawyer won the election.

Abigail and Millard moved to Washington, where he began his duties, such as they were. Millard had been the target of jealous fellow Whigs for some time, and he did not have enough influence even to get his choice appointed Port Collector in Buffalo. He presided over the Senate and watched as tempers waxed ever hotter over the slavery question.

Neither of the Fillmore children was at home. Millard Powers was a student in Harvard, receiving the college education his father had never had. Mary Abigail attended a finishing school in Massachusetts.

Abigail's health began to fail. In the summer of 1850 she and Mary Abigail went to Buffalo to spend a few weeks away from the terrible Washington heat. They were still in Buffalo when they learned of President Taylor's death on July 9, 1850. Millard was now President of the United States.

They hurried back to Washington as soon as they could get ready, but they missed Millard's inauguration. Millard was glad to see them when they did arrive. He needed their moral support as he faced his monumental task as President. He had not slept at all the night before his inauguration, as all his old insecurities came flooding back.

Abigail's health continued to be poor. Often Mary Abigail was required to act as official hostess for her father, as her mother was not up to the activity.

Abigail stayed busy as much as she could. She had been amazed when they moved into the White House to find there were no books at all in the Executive Mansion, not even a Bible. She approached Congress with the problem, and an appropriation was made to buy books. Abigail then set about happily establishing the first White House library.

There were other improvements made in the White House by the Fillmores. In the kitchen a cast-iron cookstove replaced the open fireplace which had previously been used by the cooks to cook meals for the First Families and their guests. In the Presidential bathroom, the first bathtub with running water was installed. Millard and Abigail liked their comfort.

In carrying out his Presidential duties, Millard supported a compromise bill in an attempt to settle the increasingly tempestuous issue of slavery. The bill was passed, but it only served to fan the flames of discord on both sides of the question. He also supported a Fugitive Slave Act, which set out the punishment to be imposed on anyone who harbored or in any way aided a runaway slave. This particular law was not only passed, it was strictly enforced.

The Fugitive Slave Act led to Millard's failure to be the Whig party candidate for election in his own right in the next election.

Millard's family provided his only comfort during these trying, turbulent days. Abigail's eyes still shone with pride and admiration when she looked at her husband. She knew he was trying to be a good President to all the American people. They often discussed current events in private, and how it might be best to handle various problems.

Millard Powers was now a licensed attorney, and he took the post of his father's private secretary. He was a credit to his parents, with his willingness to work hard, and he had a sincere devotion to duty.

Mary Abigail was a beautiful, gracious White House hostess, obviously cultured, and displaying a maturity beyond her years. She had become an accomplished musician.

The Southerners were so vehement in their insistence that slavery should not be abolished, Millard decided that maybe he did not fully understand the problem, and began to map out an itinerary for an extensive tour of the South when he left office. There would be political contacts, no doubt, but there would also be sightseeing and relaxation for both him and Abigail.

Privately, Millard was worried about how he would provide for his family in retirement. He had bought property and had saved some money, but he realized no one could be sure of what the future might be. He felt their simple frame house in Buffalo would not be suitable for a home for an ex–President.

He looked at some houses he considered more appropriate under his changed circumstances, but he could not afford to buy any of these larger homes. It appeared they would have to continue living in their two-story white frame home after all.

Millard's ex-partner in the law practice in Buffalo convinced Millard he should return to practicing law in higher courts when he left the White House, which would bring in much-needed income.

The Fillmores' clothes and household belongings had been moved back to Buffalo before the inauguration of the new President, Franklin Pierce. Millard and Abigail attended the inauguration ceremony, which was held at the front of the Senate Chamber.

It was a raw, cold, windy day, and the snow falling turned to slush a few minutes after it fell. Millard shivered as the cold wind chilled him, and he noticed Abigail's lips were blue with the cold.

By the next morning Abigail had developed a severe cold, and they were forced to remain in Washington until she could get better. She then developed pneumonia, and after a three-week illness, Abigail died in Washington on March 30, 1853. She was buried in Buffalo in Forest Lawn Cemetery.

Millard was heartbroken. All his previous worries about retirement seemed foolish. Without Abigail by his side, he no longer cared where he lived. Mary Abigail would live with him and be a companion of sorts, but she was young and had her own friends and other interests. Retirement would be lonely for Millard.

Later he would remarry, and the account of his life with his second wife follows this chapter.

15. Caroline Carmichael McIntosh Fillmore

Millard Fillmore continued his interest in politics after leaving the Presidency as a way to assuage his grief after the death of his first wife. He had his daughter, Mary Abigail, living with him and running his household, which helped. But while Mary Abigail was visiting her grandfather in July 1854, she died after a very brief illness, leaving Millard in a state of shock and disbelief.

Since his personal life was already in a shambles, Millard decided to seek another term as President as a candidate of the "Know Nothing" or American party, but was defeated in the 1856 election.

Retiring in disgust from the arena of national politics, Millard married Mrs. Caroline McIntosh on February 10, 1858, in Albany, New York.

Caroline Carmichael was born October 21, 1813, in Norristown, New Jersey. Her father was Charles Carmichael and her mother was Temperance Blachley. Little is known of Caroline's earliest years, but she was from a wealthy family and attended a finishing school in her teens. She was a lifelong art enthusiast.

Caroline's first husband was Ezekiel C. McIntosh of Albany, New York. He was engaged in business in Troy, New York, as a merchant before his death. He was also wealthy, and Caroline was left financially secure after he died.

As his Presidency ended, Millard had been seriously concerned about his return to the modest home he and Abigail had shared in Buffalo for twenty-six years. With his new marriage, Millard was now the administrator of his wife's large inheritance, out of which they bought a large mansion on Niagara Square, which was impressively elegant and would serve nicely as a suitable home for any ex–President. It was built in the Gothic style with towers and parapets outside, and decorated in ornate Victorian style inside.

The second Mrs. Fillmore was fifty-two years old, fragile-looking, and had an air of tragedy about her. She had no children.

She was thrilled to be the wife of a man who had once served as

Caroline Fillmore. (Courtesy Library of Congress.)

President of the United States. She invested heavily in portraits and
sculpted busts of Millard, which she displayed throughout their mansion.
Young people of their acquaintance tended to laugh at such open admiration of the aging Millard, but Millard's own circle of friends thought it was
sweet for Caroline to be so devoted. They welcomed her as a new friend.

Caroline set about making their Buffalo home a gracious center of
hospitality. Among their distinguished guests through the years was
Abraham Lincoln (who stopped by on his way to Washington), Japanese
Ambassador Tomomi Iwakuar and Prince Arthur of England.

As tensions heightened between the North and South over the issue of slavery, Millard feared the continuation of the democratic form of government in the United States might be in serious jeopardy. He urged Northern friends and colleagues to try to understand the viewpoint of Southerners. He begged Southern supporters not to secede from the Union, so the nation would not fall.

Because of his efforts to effect a settlement, in 1860 Millard was asked by leading New York politicians to go to South Carolina to beg officials there to delay taking any action until a solution could be found. Millard refused to go, saying it would do no good. He felt members of the Republican party were responsible for pushing abolition on the South and had caused much of the bitterness between the two regions.

When the Civil War began, Millard recruited men to join the Union army. He led fund-raising drives for the war effort, but as the war continued and more and more lives were lost, he began openly criticizing the Lincoln administration.

When Lincoln's body was brought through Buffalo after his assassination, Millard led the citizens' committee that provided an escort from Batavia to Buffalo.

Because Millard had voiced earlier criticism of Lincoln in his seeming determination to end slavery whatever the cost, Millard became the butt of the ill-will and insults of the citizens in Buffalo and surrounding areas. Caroline's love sustained Millard during these trying days and gave him courage to state his opinions as he saw fit.

After the Civil War was over, Millard once again could involve himself in the activities he most enjoyed. His chief interest was the Historical Society of Buffalo. He spent many hours alone and with other members collecting and organizing records pertaining to Buffalo history.

Caroline's interest in art had never waned. Both she and Millard were active in the establishment of a Fine Arts Academy for the city. When the academy held its first exhibition in December 1862, Buffalo joined Philadelphia and Boston as one of the only cities in the United States with permanent art galleries.

Caroline's health began to fail, and in 1866 she and Millard took a trip to Europe in an attempt to improve her condition. She became an invalid, but Millard remained in excellent health until two weeks before his death from a stroke on March 8, 1874. He was buried in Forest Lawn Cemetery in Buffalo.

Caroline continued in her invalid state until her death on August 11, 1881, in Buffalo.

16. Jane Means Appleton Pierce

Jane Means Appleton was born to a Congregationalist minister and his wife on March 12, 1806, in Hampton, New Hampshire. Jane's father, the Reverend Jesse Appleton, also served as President of Bowdoin College in Maine before his death in 1819. Jane was thirteen years old when her father died.

Jane's mother, Elizabeth Means, was a member of an aristocratic, wealthy New England family, and when the Reverend Appleton died, Jane and her mother went to live in the Means mansion at Amherst, New Hampshire.

Jane soon found her grandmother expected perfect, even prim behavior from her granddaughter, as befitted a member of a cultured, pious family with a Puritan background. Madame Means had no cause for distress. Jane was a shy, frail child who wanted to please her elders.

As Jane matured, she took wealth for granted and enjoyed having servants to do all the work. She learned no household skills, and filled her time with church-related social events, the weddings of friends and relatives, and other genteel pursuits. She had no strong personal interests other than religion.

Franklin Pierce was a sharp contrast to any man Jane had ever met. Buoyant, vain and sociable, Franklin had previously been a student at Bowdoin, which gave them a common topic of conversation when they met. One of Jane's relatives had been an instructor of Franklin's at Bowdoin, and it was through this young man the two became acquainted.

Franklin was so handsome, he fairly took Jane's breath away. He had dark curly hair and dark brown eyes, and he swept shy, retiring Jane away in a cloud of love. Her stiff-necked female relatives did not consider Franklin a suitable match for her, but Jane ignored them all. Franklin was equally charmed by the elegantly attractive, adoring, quiet Jane, who also had dark hair and eyes.

Franklin's background was entirely different from Jane's, and this only seemed to lend enchantment to their romance. His father, Benjamin Pierce, had served as a General in the Revolutionary War, owned a tavern for a time, served in the New Hampshire State House of Representatives for

Jane Pierce. (Courtesy Library of Congress.)

twelve years, and became Governor of New Hampshire in 1827. For most of his life, Franklin had heard political discussions, had seen his father involved in campaigns for public office, and as a result, Franklin had developed an intense interest of his own in politics. He was now serving his first term in the United States Congress as a representative from New Hampshire. He and Jane were from two different New England society levels.

Undoubtedly, her mother and grandmother brought all these differences to Jane's attention, but Jane insisted she loved Franklin and nothing else mattered.

On November 19, 1834, Jane and Franklin were married in the parlor of the Means mansion, with only relatives and a few friends attending. Only General Benjamin Pierce attended from Franklin's family.

The newlyweds spent their honeymoon in Washington, while Franklin served as Congressman. Meanwhile, General Pierce was occupied in overseeing repairs on a house in Hillsborough, New Hampshire, which Franklin had bought two years earlier and to which he planned to bring his new bride when Congress adjourned.

The couple moved to Hillsborough on May 27, 1835, to the refurbished house. Franklin returned to his law practice with his former partner, Albert Baker, brother of Mary Baker Eddy, founder of the First Church of Christ, Scientist.

With Franklin fully occupied with his law practice, Jane was left to amuse herself. Since Jane had few interests or skills in cultural pursuits, she found her life boring. The couple who had previously rented their house agreed to stay on as servants, so Jane had no household duties to occupy her time. She made no attempt to become a part of village life and did not like the people who lived in the village.

When Franklin prepared to return to his Congressional duties that fall, Jane told him she thought if might be better if she returned to Amherst for the winter. Since she was pregnant with their first child and really did not appear to feel well, Franklin raised no objections. He wrote her daily loving letters from Washington.

A railroad now operated in Washington, as Franklin found when he got there. The noisy rattle from the trains changed the previously peaceful and placid atmosphere of the capital to one of hustle and bustle. The slavery question continued to occupy the minds of legislators on both sides of the issue, with charges and countercharges hurled like weapons.

On February 3, 1836, Franklin Pierce, Jr., was born, only to die three days later. Franklin learned of these events only through letters, but he grieved deeply for the baby son he never saw. He worried about Jane, who was recovering too slowly from the birth and the loss of the baby.

As his mother had done throughout his own childhood, Franklin sought comfort in alcohol. He drank more and more until one night he was involved in a brawl with two friends at a theater. Subsequently, he had a severe bout of pleurisy, and he decided to change his habits.

When summer came, he brought Jane from Amherst to their home in Hillsborough. Jane pleaded with him to sell the house, and he tried, but failed, to find a buyer. She wanted to move to Concord.

Franklin was elected to the United States Senate that fall, but Jane was unimpressed with his political success. She went with him to Washington in 1837, but she stayed in their rooms at the boarding house and moped.

"Oh, how I wish he was out of political life!" she wrote. "How much better it would be for him on every account!"

Jane had her own methods for gaining her desires. When the summer of 1838 came, she spent the whole month of June in bed. In August they moved to Concord, where Franklin had entered a new law partnership with Asa Fowler.

When their second son, Frank Robert, was born in 1839, Franklin began to worry about their financial circumstances. Since 1833 when he first was elected to serve in Congress, he had little time to practice law and had accumulated little money. Their life-style was expensive, since Jane now refused to live with him in Washington, preferring instead to stay in their Concord home or with relatives. With two households to pay for, Franklin was finding his financial future bleak.

Two years later, in April 1841, a third son, Benjamin, was born. Franklin decided to resign his Senate seat, since New Hampshire law prohibited his reelection.

Franklin settled down to his Concord law practice, determined to ignore politics. Jane was more cheerful than she had been in some time. With their two little boys to care for, and a new way of life, she felt they would now be much happier in their marriage. They joined Concord's South Congregational Church.

Concord was a thriving town, and the railroad had recently begun operation there. Franklin found that in the excitement of the growing town, he could not remain long indifferent to the political scene, any more than Jane could have turned her back on religion. He decided he would pursue his political interests on a local level and was soon a party "boss" in New Hampshire.

Little Frank Pierce, now four years old, died in 1843 from typhus fever, again plunging both his parents into shock and depression. Jane again took to her bed for a time. She suffered from tuberculosis, and this added to her weakness and depression. Only the presence of little Benjamin and the necessity of his care forced Jane to return to a more normal daily life.

James Polk was elected President of the United States in 1845, and he asked Franklin to be the United States District Attorney in New Hampshire. The next year he invited Franklin to join his Cabinet as Attorney General, but Franklin declined because of the state of Jane's health.

When the Mexican War began, President Polk gave Franklin a commission as Colonel of the Volunteer Ninth Regiment. A month later Franklin was a Brigadier General! He had a good army service record and made new friends everywhere he went. He and his regiment were a part of the drive on Mexico City, led by General Winfield Scott, during which Franklin was thrown from his horse and painfully, though not seriously, injured.

Probably Jane really missed Franklin, as he brightened her life with his friendliness and involvement with community activities. She may have assumed his political career had ended with his entry into the Mexican War. Their Concord home was sold while he was gone to war, and when he came back, the family went to live in a boarding house, operated by Mr. and Mrs. Willard Williams. Little Bennie may have not liked the arrangement as much as he would have in their own house, but it was ideal for Jane as she did not have to do housework or cook their meals. Franklin refused to accept nomination for Governor that year.

The next four years were the happiest the Pierces would have together. Jane's health improved, but she still suffered from bouts of "nerves." Little Bennie and his father were patient when she was irritable, gave her affection which she found difficult to give them, and tried to meet her exacting standards.

Bennie was the core of their family, and both of his parents were firmly convinced he was the most wonderful child ever. He was a sensitive, good-natured little boy, who had the same eagerness to please as both his parents.

Jane began teaching little Bennie about the Bible, to which Franklin did not object. Bennie already knew about God from having attended church most of his life. He was now developing a strong, vivid faith approximating Jane's. They had family worship each day, and he always said his prayers.

Franklin's law practice became increasingly profitable as he devoted more of his attention and time to it. For the first time their financial picture was bright.

Franklin was a good trial lawyer, with a persuasive power that converted juries to his way of thinking. He won a well-publicized slander case against a woman defendant, which again brought him national political attention. Some of the leaders in the Democratic party besieged him with pleas to be their candidate for President in the election of 1852.

Franklin was not enthusiastic about the idea because he knew Jane would be upset if he accepted. However, he did not refuse outright to consider it. When the convention was held in Baltimore, James Buchanan and Lewis Cass were the leading contenders for the nomination, but neither could get enough delegate votes to be nominated. After the thirty-fifth ballot, Franklin's name was submitted and he won the nomination.

Jane fainted when she heard the news. Bennie knew how opposed his mother was to his father's political activities, and while Jane and Franklin vacationed in Cambridge, he wrote her from home, "Edward brought the news...that Father is a candidate for the Presidency. I hope he won't be elected for I should not like to be at Washington and I know you would not either." Franklin assured Jane he had not actively sought the nomination.

Franklin won the election and would be the next President of the United States. While most women would be ecstatic at the idea of their husband being President, Jane was filled with deep gloom at the thought of living in Washington, even if she would be living in the White House. Her older sister, Mary Aiken, and her young aunt, Abby Means, tried to cheer Jane about her future, but she said sadly, "the expectation seems too heavy to be borne."

Franklin refused to allow Jane's feelings to cast a shadow on his own high hopes and great plans for his administration. He hoped to keep the Union strong and reunite the nation on the slavery question. He hoped to accomplish peaceful expansion of the borders of the United States, and he planned to make every effort to heal the rifts in the Democratic party.

On January 6, 1853, Franklin, Jane and Bennie boarded a train in Andover, Massachusetts, to go to Concord and pack in preparation for their move to Washington. The train had traveled about a mile when the coupling on the car in which they were riding broke. The car rolled down an embankment and turned over. Franklin and Jane were uninjured, but Bennie was killed instantly.

Bennie dead in an instant! Their only son gone now! Jane's mind was almost deranged by grief. She told Franklin she thought the Lord had taken Bennie from them so Franklin could give all his attention to running the country. She felt he had traded the life of their beloved little son for the Presidency.

Franklin was horrified by her accusations, as he had loved Bennie deeply also, and would have never wished any harm to come to him.

Jane's attitude completely unnerved Franklin, and his mind and heart were no longer involved with his coming inauguration. Bennie had been his real hope for the future, and Franklin no longer cared at all about being President.

However, he had been elected, and he was forced to proceed with his duties. When he went to Washington in February 1853, Jane did not go with him. The Fillmores moved out of the White House early, but as Abigail Fillmore's health was poor during the last months of her husband's administration, no preparations had been made for the incoming President.

Franklin was alone in his moment of glory, as Jane refused to attend his inauguration. There was no inaugural ball held, but he did arrange for a large reception at the White House in the afternoon after he was inaugurated.

When Franklin and his secretary, Sidney Webster, went upstairs to retire for the night after the long, tiring day, they found no beds were ready and they had to make them up themselves.

It was on inauguration day that Jane learned for the first time from a cousin that Franklin had actually worked long and hard to secure the nomination. She felt betrayed and bitter in her terrible grief. She waited about two weeks before she joined Franklin in the White House. Her young aunt, Abby Kent Means, went with Jane and planned to act as official hostess until Jane felt better.

Jane did not have much chance of feeling better as she had made up her mind beforehand that she would go to Washington but would not like it. She kept to herself, totally immersed in melancholia from which she made no attempt to escape. She wrote endless pathetic letters to her dead son. When anyone tried to engage her in conversation, she projected such an air of martyred sadness that her companions soon abandoned all efforts to talk with her. She always wore unrelieved black.

The noted author Nathaniel Hawthorne had been a good friend of Franklin's since they had attended college together many years before. He came to visit the Pierces in the White House, and Jane would talk to him a little. She also attended church on occasions and asked the servants to attend each Sunday. During one of his visits, Nathaniel Hawthorne wrote a friend, ". . . of all dismally dull and heavy domestic circles, poor Frank's is certainly the most intolerable. It is too bad that the nation should be compelled to see such a death's head in the pre-eminent place among American women."

The atmosphere in the White House was prevailingly gloomy, and the death of the Vice President, William R. King, a month after inauguration did nothing to dispel the gloom. Franklin tried to fulfill his social obligations with the aid of Abby Means, but it was an uphill struggle. Jane made only an occasional, reluctant public appearance.

Congress was in a generous mood during Franklin's administration, and the White House was extensively renovated and refurbished. Indoor plumbing was installed for the first time, as well as central heating. New draperies, carpets, furniture, and table accessories of china, crystal goblets and silverware were purchased.

During his years as President, Franklin found it difficult to realize his dreams. He never did like the abolitionists, as he considered them troublemakers. He promised to uphold the Compromise of 1850 as a hopeful attempt to please everyone. Instead, he pleased no one.

There was no end to the burning slavery issue. It permeated all discussions and other matters that arose. Since the question was so divisive, Franklin was thwarted in his hopes to reunite the splintered Democratic party.

In his third summer as President, both Franklin and Jane were seriously debilitated from grief, heat and endless disappointments. Franklin decided he would not openly seek a second term, but would accept it if nominated and elected. However, James Buchanan, a contender in the previous election, was elected President on the Democratic ticket.

The Pierces had saved money while living in the White House, so they took a trip to Europe that lasted about two years. They went to Madeira and the West Indies, in a vain attempt to restore Jane's physical and mental health. They met Nathaniel Hawthorne and his family in Rome and spent some time with them. From Rome they went on to Venice. Nathaniel Hawthorne thought Franklin showed "the marks of care and coming age."

Jane carried Bennie's Bible with her everywhere. She could not let go of the past.

On their return to Concord, Franklin and Jane bought the boarding house formerly operated by the Williamses for their home. They had been happy while they lived there years before, and they hoped to regain peace and comfort there now.

Franklin became an open, outspoken foe of President Abraham Lincoln, after Lincoln was elected to succeed President Buchanan. Franklin felt Lincoln had not made enough effort to preserve the Union when the Civil War started. He became a pariah among his neighbors for his stand on Lincoln.

Jane's tired body and exhausted mind gave up the struggle on December 2, 1863. She was buried near Bennie in Old North Cemetery in Concord. Her death was caused by complications of a long-term tubercular infection.

Nathaniel Hawthorne came and stayed for several days with Franklin so he would not have to be alone in his sorrow. The next spring Nathaniel also died while he and Franklin were on a vacation trip.

Because of Franklin's criticism of abolitionist policies and the Civil War, he was not even asked by the Hawthorne family to be a pallbearer for his old friend. Nathaniel had agreed with many of Franklin's views, but the Hawthorne relatives and close friends did not.

Franklin survived six years more, a broken, dejected, lonely man. He died on October 8, 1869, from heart failure and was buried beside Jane in Concord, New Hampshire.

17. Mary Todd Lincoln

Mary Todd was born on December 13, 1818, in Lexington, Kentucky, to a wealthy banking family. She was the fourth of seven children in the family. She was a pretty little girl, much loved by all her relatives, especially her mother. Mary had a sensitive nature, and her mother's death, which occurred when Mary was only six years old, caused her emotional devastation for a time. In later years she described these trying days and months as desolate.

Her father remarried, and Mary and her stepmother did not get along well with each other. There were nine more children born to her father and stepmother, causing Mary to feel neglected and overlooked in such a large group. Perhaps as a way of attracting her father's attention, she developed a habit of weeping uncontrollably when thwarted. She also began having temper tantrums that were outstanding in their ferocity and well known to all her family and friends.

Mary was impulsive and passionate in her reactions, with a pronounced stubborn streak. She was given to making cutting, sarcastic remarks as a girl, which served to alienate those she sought to attract. Her one real interest in life was pretty clothes. She never had enough clothes to suit her, and this obsession would cause her trouble all her life.

Following the death of her mother, the love of Mary's life was her father, Robert Smith Todd, a prominent banker in Lexington, Kentucky, and a member of the Whig political party. Mary learned early from him that power bestowed privilege, and she came to admire the power of political achievement. She circulated socially with Governors, members of Congress and other dignitaries. Since women of the period were not even allowed to vote, there was no hope Mary might gain a political office herself. However, if she married the right man, who could tell what the result might be?

Mary received her education at John Ward's academy and Madame Mentelle's school in Lexington, where she learned to read French and made a study of English literature. She was considered well trained for marriage and her place in society at age seventeen, so she received no more formal education.

Mary Lincoln. (Courtesy Library of Congress.)

After her graduation from finishing school, Mary went to live for a time with her sister and brother-in-law, Elizabeth and Ninian Edwards, in their mansion in Springfield, Illinois. It was during these months that Mary met Abe Lincoln for the first time.

Abraham was now thirty-one years old, a lawyer with a well-established practice in Springfield, who had begun to think about marriage. He was fascinated by the stylish, witty, vivacious Mary who loved poetry as much as he, and who could converse intelligently about politics. Even more important, in his judgment, she was not snobbish and indicated an interest in him.

Abe had developed a little sensitiveness about his humble background, and felt it could not compare with Mary's society upbringing. (This feeling never left him; he never took his wife and children to visit his father and did not even attend his father's funeral in later years.)

Abe was tall and gangly, not a handsome man. When Mary's relatives indicated strong opposition to their courtship, Abe was plunged into deep despair. Mary soon made it plain to him he was the man she wanted to marry, and her family could approve or not, as they chose. She apparently sensed the burning ambition in Lincoln which was as strong as her own.

Mary chose January 1, 1841, as their wedding date. Abe reportedly left her waiting at the altar, dressed in her wedding gown and veil, and never came to the house at all. He had a complete nervous collapse and was out of sight for several months.

After this episode, Mary's relatives were at a loss to understand why she continued to be interested in him, but Mary found Abe to be loving, understanding and protective.

Despite her sister's open hostility to the match, Mary and Abe were married in Elizabeth's mansion on November 4, 1842, by an Episcopal minister. Mary had informed her family of the wedding plans only the day before, and only a few friends and relatives attended. None of the Lincoln family was invited.

Following their wedding, Mary and Abe went to live in a single room at the Globe Tavern in Springfield. Apparently Mary had failed to grasp the extent of Abe's poverty. She became upset with their living conditions and feared her friends were laughing at them behind her back. She chose to continue to live with him, however, and on August 1, 1843, they had a son, Robert Todd Lincoln, born to their union.

With the baby's birth, their one-room living situation went from bad to deplorable. In January 1844, Abe bought a one-and-one-half story house and lot for his family. Mary was relieved to begin to live like other families, and Bobby, as the new baby was called, would have a yard in which he could play. Two years later a second son, Edward, was born.

Mary was dismayed by the amount of housework she was required to do in her new life. She must have felt she had entered another world at times. She had always before lived in a wealthy home with plenty of servants to keep the household running smoothly. Now she had to clean house, cook meals, do laundry and take care of the children, all on a very limited budget. Her finishing school education had prepared her for marriage, but not a marriage like this.

Since he had always been poor, Abe did not fully understand her difficulties, and he did little to help her. He loved his little sons dearly and enjoyed playing with them, but he never disciplined them. Mary was the disciplinarian. Abe was intensely proud of his family.

Lincoln was a moody and often depressed individual, which caused Mary to feel shut out of his life at these times. He avoided all confrontations and efforts to get him to discuss difficulties. He would just walk away. Her own insecurity caused Mary to become obsessed with money, and even when their fortunes improved in later years, she was unable to enjoy the pretty clothes she bought, as she was convinced her extravagances would plunge them back into the poverty they suffered during the early days of their marriage.

Mary had other unreasonable fears. She was exceedingly terrified of thunderstorms. She was an overly protective mother who went into a panic if one of her children wandered out of sight.

Despite all these problems, the Lincolns loved each other and had a stable marriage. Even Mary's relatives thought they seemed happy.

Lincoln was in law practice with a partner named William (called Bill) Herndon. Herndon and Mary disliked each other intensely, and during all the years he and Lincoln were law partners, Mary never entertained Herndon in her home. Abe irritated Herndon, also, by reading aloud from his newspaper and allowing the Lincoln children to run and play freely in the law offices.

In later years, it was Herndon who painted a vivid picture of Mary to the newspapers as a half-mad, raging harridan who made Lincoln's life miserable. All these allegations about Mary were untrue, and she often asked others piteously why Herndon wished to destroy her.

In 1846, Lincoln was elected to Congress, and thus began his political career on the national level. Mary and the boys moved to Washington, D.C., with him, but Mary disliked living there. After three months, she packed up, and she and the boys went back home to Springfield while Abe stayed on alone in Washington.

Lincoln had become sensitive to the plight of slaves several years before when he saw slaves in irons on a steamboat. Now, in Washington, he walked by the auction blocks where slaves were sold. From the Capitol building he could see the "Georgia pen" where he noted ". . . droves of Negroes were collected, temporarily kept, and finally taken to Southern markets, precisely like droves of horses." Mary considered slavery a necessary evil, and tried to tell him slaves would be unable to take care of themselves if they had no master.

Lincoln's beliefs about slavery were unpopular in his own state of Illinois, and he was defeated in his bid for election to the United States Senate in 1855 and again in 1858.

Shortly after Abe's first term in Congress had ended and he was back in Springfield with his family, four-year-old Eddie Lincoln died after a two-month illness. Mary was shocked and distraught, but found solace in her religion at the First Presbyterian Church. Abe was not a church member.

The next year, William Wallace Lincoln was born, followed in 1853 by a fourth son named Thomas, called Tad. The Lincolns recovered slowly from their grief over the loss of Eddie. Robert was sent to a private school in Springfield and later to one in Jacksonville to prepare him for college.

The Southern and Northern politicians were becoming more and more bitter in their denunciation of each other's views about slavery, and in the struggle, the Whig party disintegrated. A new political party, called Republican, was formed by Northerners who took an anti-slavery stance. Because of his well-known outspoken opinions concerning the evils of slavery, Lincoln was chosen to run as the new Republican party's candidate for President — and elected. From the time Abe told Mary triumphantly, "Mary, we're elected!" and they left for Washington, Abe never returned to Springfield.

Mary was thrilled and excited by the victory, but Abe's enthusiasm was tempered by the open hostility shown him by bitter Southerners. The day after his election, the talk of secession by Southern states grew loud. Seven states in the Deep South seceded shortly after and had formed the beginning of the Confederacy by the time Lincoln was inaugurated. The Civil War began a few weeks later on April 12, 1861, when Confederate forces fired on Fort Sumter with its resident garrison of Federal troops in Charleston, South Carolina.

In the White House, Mary began an extensive renovation of their living quarters and public rooms. She had realized all her dreams, and she lost no time in her efforts to impress Washington society and the nation with Abe's importance and her own taste and refinement. She went on shopping trips to Philadelphia and New York, where she ordered and bought imported draperies, custom-made carpets, carved furniture, beautifully cut glassware and china. Congress had appropriated twenty thousand dollars for the renovation, but she spent almost twenty-seven thousand.

Abe lost his temper when he found out how much she had spent. Throughout their marriage her lavish spending had been a source of controversy, but now she wanted him to ask Congress for more money. He told her he refused to ask for more money for "flub-dubs for this damned old house," especially since Union soldiers did not even have blankets to keep them warm at night.

Despite his opposition, Congress paid the bills for Mary, as they included extra money in the budget for the next year for the White House.

Mary's attempts to become popular in Washington society were largely unsuccessful. She was obsessed with surpassing the wealthy aristocrats, and she tried to do so by outdressing them. Her dresses were finer, more stylish and often more expensive than theirs. To get money to pay the debts she made buying her finery, she made plans to sell manure from White House stables. Abe turned thumbs down on this idea.

Not long after he became President, Abe and Mary hosted an official dinner honoring General John C. Fremont. Mary had a total of eighty invitations returned with regrets. The guests who did attend showered the Fremonts with attention and largely ignored the Lincolns. This was agony for Mary, who felt insulted by the guests' attitude.

Washington society buzzed with tales about Mary's extravagant spending, causing her to become more insecure and Abe to become furiously angry. Mary reacted to their marital spats by jealously keeping close to his side at social affairs.

Next Mary tried to become a leader in Washington's social scene by being a gracious hostess, at which she worked valiantly. She dressed in her beautiful clothes and determined to show the nation she was well suited to the position as the President's wife. Some found her charming, but Lincoln was so unpopular because of the war raging in the country that Washington's social leaders reviled Mary. They even accused her of being a spy sympathetic to the Confederacy because she had close relatives serving with Confederate forces. Her brother, George Rogers Clark Todd, was a surgeon in the Confederate army, and she had three half-brothers-in-law who served. Truly Mary must have felt torn to her loyalties at times, but publicly she supported Lincoln in all his policies.

The one bright spot in the turmoil surrounding the Lincolns were their two young sons, Willie and Tad. The little boys ran happily through White House halls, kept various pets, and kept servants busy by ringing bells all at the same time. Tad once drove a pair of pet goats through the East Room. Their oldest son, Robert, was now grown up and a student at Harvard.

Sadly, twelve-year-old Willie died in 1862. Mary was overwhelmed by grief. She remained isolated in her room for three months, begging Willie to return. Mediums held seances in the White House.

Mary tried to regain her mental stability by visiting the wounded soldiers and taking them flowers. She began to work at finding jobs for blacks, who were now coming to Washington in great numbers from the plantations in the South. Robert begged his mother to let him leave Harvard and join the army, so he could do his share. After much hesitation, she finally agreed.

Mary's confidante was a black woman, Elizabeth Keckley, who sewed for Mary. She consoled Mary as best she could, and Mary revealed many of her innermost thoughts and problems to Elizabeth.

Mary began to spend money even more wildly as her troubles increased. In one four-month period she purchased three hundred pairs of gloves.

As the war dragged on, social functions dwindled, giving Mary less to do. Her spending for clothes became a matter of real concern when she learned that while Abe had been campaigning for a second term, she had overspent her budget by twenty-seven thousand dollars. This terrified her, and she had a dread of Abe finding out.

Despite fierce opposition to his views on slavery and other issues, Abe was reelected. His issuance of the Emancipation Proclamation and his suspension of the writ of habeas corpus, under which citizens must be given the reason for their arrest, had been seen by his supporters as obstacles to his being reelected. The Emancipation Proclamation did lead to total abolition of slavery later when the Thirteenth Amendment was added to the Constitution.

Abe complained of not feeling well as the time for his inauguration for a second term approached. Mary told Elizabeth Keckley she feared Abe might "leave me too," referring to his possible death. During these dark days Mary became close friends with Senator Charles Sumner. Sumner was already a good friend of Abe, and he came often to the White House, where he and Mary held long conversations.

More and more young men on both sides were killed in the bloody battles of the war, and Lincoln decided it must be ended by whatever means. He ordered General William T. Sherman to join forces with General U. S. Grant and move to bring an end to the terrible conflict. Sherman's solution was to burn his way South, across Virginia and the Carolinas and into Georgia, ending with the burning of the city of Atlanta. In addition to the widespread devastation caused by the raging fires, the soldiers killed livestock and chickens, confiscated food and any valuables they came across. They tore up railroads and destroyed crops in the fields.

Within five months the war had ended, with an embittered South forced back into the Union. Lincoln prepared a reconstruction plan which would teach the rebellious Southerners a lesson. The plan included stringent qualifications for voting, a resident army to enforce the end of slavery, and state government officials appointed by the Union to preside over the reconstructed Southern state governments.

Mary had watched Abe with growing concern as he battled with these and other problems. He suffered from nightmares and had premonitions of disaster. She still loved him deeply, but was at a loss as to how to help him. Therefore, she welcomed his suggestion that they attend Ford's Theater on April 14, 1865. They planned to see *Our American Cousin*. Ulysses Grant and his wife, Julia, had been invited to go with them.

Robert Lincoln was home from service and ate breakfast with his parents that morning. He told them he planned to return to Harvard in the fall since the war had ended. At last it seemed their lives, as well as those of their countrymen, might be getting back on a normal track.

At a Cabinet meeting later that morning, General Grant told Abe that he and Julia would be unable to attend the play that evening with the Lincolns. He did not tell President Lincoln that Julia had flatly refused to consider the invitation because of her intense dislike for Mary Lincoln. Mary had earlier humiliated and insulted Julia before several other people when she expressed her displeasure at having Julia sit down beside her without being asked.

The gas street lights glowed in the evening fog as Mary and Abe left for the theater in their carriage. They were a little late. Accompanying them were Major Henry Rathbone and his fiancee, Clara Harris. Mary wore a gray silk dress, and she and Abe seemed happier than they had been in some time. They sat holding hands, and during the play, President Lincoln was heard to laugh at various funny scenes.

The third act was well underway, when John Wilkes Booth crept into the Presidential box and shot President Lincoln at close range. Major Rathbone tried to restrain Booth, who slashed Rathbone's arm with a knife. Booth had considered himself a Southern sympathizer for some months and felt he would be honored for this terrible crime.

There was total pandemonium in the theater. "Help, somebody, help! The President is shot!" one person is reported to have yelled.

An attempt was made to revive Abe, but the bullet had destroyed his brain. He was carried across the street to a boarding house bed, where he died the next morning.

Mary was shattered by the tragedy and sank into deep despair. She was unable to attend the funeral. She lay for the next entire month in her White House bedroom, moaning and begging Abe to take her with him. As she grieved, looters carted away many of the new White House furnishings and accessories Mary had chosen with such care only a few months before. Later a hostile public would accuse Mary of stealing some of these items herself.

At last Mary regained control enough to move out of the White House. On June 9, 1865, she left Washington with her two sons and Elizabeth Keckley to move to a hotel in Chicago. She could not bear to even think about returning to Springfield and their former home there.

President Lincoln left an estate of eighty-five thousand dollars, which went in equal portions to Mary, Robert and Tad. In addition, Mary received twenty-five thousand dollars, which was one year's salary for Abe, in December of that year. Her income would be fifteen hundred to eighteen hundred dollars annually in interest from investments made for her by one of Abe's friends.

In characteristic impulsive fashion, Mary spent a large part of her inheritance on an expensive home in Chicago. Two years later, unable to maintain it, she was forced to sell it.

In 1867, Bill Herndon's book was published, painting Mary in an unflattering, almost vicious light.

Mary's debts continued to plague her, and she decided to take her expensive clothes from her White House years to a broker for sale. She requested anonymity for the sale, but the broker not only told whose clothes they were, he even sent them on a tour across the country.

Mary was humiliated and horrified by this latest unexpected blow. Would these problems never end?

In 1868 Elizabeth Keckley, her friend, wrote a book entitled *Behind the Scenes: Thirty Years a Slave and Four Years in the White House.* She was no longer employed by Mary as a seamstress. She had meant to defend Mary in her writing, but she included many details of Mary's spending and even quoted from letters Mary had written her in confidence. Thus the nation was again swept with whispers of Mary and her excesses.

Mary was deeply hurt and furiously angry with Elizabeth for her betrayal, and for making confidential matters public. Ever after, Mary scornfully referred to Elizabeth as "the colored historian."

In October Mary and Tad went to Europe to live. Tad was enrolled in a German school in Frankfurt. They stayed there a year and a half before Mary decided to move to England, where she hired a tutor for Tad. Her headaches and depression rarely left her now.

The Congress of the United States finally voted Mary a three thousand dollar annual pension in 1870, after many delays and much string-pulling on her part. She needed the money desperately, but she was bitter that she received so little, when Abe had been killed serving his country.

With her health continuing to suffer, Mary wondered if American doctors could do more to restore her health, so she and Tad came back to the United States in 1871. They went to visit with Robert and his family while they hunted a place to live. Robert was now a successful Chicago attorney, and he was glad to have his mother and brother near him again.

They had only visited about six weeks when Tad died after a few days' illness from the complications of a chest cold he had taken on the voyage home from Europe.

Mary managed to attend his funeral, but her slender hold on reality slipped badly. Robert tried to care for her in a Chicago hotel, but her bizarre behavior forced him to have her committed to a sanatorium for treatment. She had been spending her money wildly and foolishly, wandering in hotel halls in a state of partial nudity, and feared people were hunting her. She said she felt "an Indian" was pulling wires out of her eyes.

Despite all these evidences of instability, she was highly indignant with Robert for taking her for treatment. She accused him of trying to steal from her. After less than four months in the hospital, she went to live again with her sister and brother-in-law in Springfield.

That arrangement did not work out either, and she went back to Europe a year later. She broke her back in a fall in France, and at last returned to her own home in Springfield.

Robert and his daughter, also named Mary, visited her in Springfield, and Robert begged her to forgive him. She assured him he was forgiven.

Mary spent her remaining months in debilitating pain and seclusion. Her confusion deepened, and public criticism no longer registered with her or hurt her now.

Mary died at home on July 16, 1882, and is buried beside Abe in Oak Ridge Cemetery in Springfield.

18. Eliza McCardle Johnson

Eliza McCardle, born on October 4, 1810, in Greeneville, Tennessee, learned early in life that if she wanted to eat, she must work. Eliza's father was a shoemaker who died when Eliza was very young. Eliza and her mother began making quilts and fashioning a type of cloth sandals to support themselves in a meager existence.

Eliza was a pretty girl with light brown hair and hazel eyes that sparkled with intelligence. She and her mother were proud people, and despite her poverty, she was always clean and neatly dressed. She learned reading and writing, as well as basic arithmetic, probably from her mother.

Eliza first met Andrew Johnson in Greeneville, where he had come looking for a better life. Eliza happened to be walking on the main street in the fall of 1826 when Andrew, his mother and his stepfather first got to town. They had all their worldly possessions piled on an old dilapidated wagon, pulled by a blind mule.

Andrew asked Eliza if she knew where he and his parents might find a place to live. She took Andrew to a local merchant, who rented the Johnsons a cottage. The family only stayed in Greeneville for six weeks before they moved on to Rutledge, Tennessee, forty miles away, but Andrew could not forget pretty Eliza.

The next spring Andrew came back to Greeneville and Eliza. The local tailor had left town, and Andrew felt he could operate a successful tailor shop there.

Eliza learned that Andrew and his family had moved to Tennessee from Raleigh, North Carolina. Andrew was born in Raleigh and lived the first seventeen years of his life there. Andrew's father had died when Andrew was a young child, and Andrew had been apprenticed to a tailor to learn the trade. Although Andrew's father was born in England, Andrew's family did not belong to the aristocratic, early settler-descended society in the Raleigh area, and Andrew was never comfortable living there.

Andrew's mother chose a shiftless man when she remarried, and the family lived in abject poverty. When Andrew got into trouble for throwing rocks at a house, he decided to head for eastern Tennessee, where his older

Eliza Johnson. (Courtesy Library of Congress.)

brother, William, had recently found work. He deserted his apprenticeship, but he had learned enough to operate a shop of his own.

Two months after his return to Greeneville, Eliza and Andrew were married in a civil ceremony at the courthouse in Greene County, Tennessee. It was May of 1827, a time when spring had come to the South and young hearts were singing.

Andrew and Eliza were happy in their marriage. When she learned he knew only the alphabet and could read only a little, she set out to teach him to read fluently and to write. Later he would also learn arithmetic from his loving teacher.

What small education Andrew had received previously had come to him in the Raleigh tailor shop where he had worked as an apprentice. The owner and others, often customers, read to the apprentices as they worked. One educated man, who had often read to all the men in the shop, took special interest in Andrew and helped him begin reading. He gave Andrew a book of his own when he saw Andrew had put all his energy into his efforts to learn.

Now that Andrew had set up his own shop, he had a young man to come in and read to his apprentices. The young man was a paid reader. Business was brisk in the tailor shop, and Andrew could afford to hire a reader for the journeyman tailors who worked with him. These young tailors also stayed with Andrew and Eliza from time to time in their home, paying the Johnsons room and board of one dollar and fifty cents each week.

Andrew felt at home in Greeneville. Here the leading townspeople often worked with their hands, as he did, and there were few social pretensions among the citizens.

As was the custom then, there were often groups gathered in the tailor shop discussing news, gossip and politics. They also gathered in the general stores and barbershops.

Among Andrew's customers and acquaintances were students and teachers from two nearby colleges. Andrew heard of debating activities at both Greeneville and Tusculum colleges, and he asked if he might join the groups, which permission was granted. Since many of the debated topics were the political issues of the period, Andrew's interest in politics was aroused, and his interest deepened with time.

Eliza and Andrew had four children, two daughters and two sons, born to their marriage within a six-year period. Eliza stayed busy with her children and home duties while Andrew went politicking.

Some of the Greeneville businessmen were fed up with the Town Council seats remaining year after year in the hands of the same clique, and they urged Andrew to enter the next campaign. So, in 1829, Andrew and two fellow craftsmen entered the race for Town Council, and all three won. In only two more years, Andrew was elected mayor.

Eliza was a good mother and manager. Since she was better educated than Andrew, he asked her to handle their family money matters. Before long she had saved enough extra money that Andrew was able to buy a small farm in the country for his mother and her husband.

Andrew's political ambitions were growing, and in 1835 he was elected to serve in the Tennessee Legislature. He worked hard in this job, and Eliza continued to work hard at home.

Andrew loyally supported Governor James K. Polk's ideas and vetoes, but Polk never liked Andrew very well. Andrew continued to serve in the

Legislature for eight years, at which time he became a United States Representative from Tennessee in Congress.

Both Eliza and Andrew believed in a good education for their children. When Andrew arrived in Washington to begin his work in Congress, his daughter Martha was already there to greet him. She had been a student in Female Seminary at Georgetown University for the past year.

Andrew served in the House of Representatives for five terms. He lived in various boarding houses in Washington, while Eliza stayed home in Tennessee. The younger children attended the local schools there, and Eliza was busy managing the family business affairs in Andrew's absence.

James Polk was elected President in 1844, and Mrs. Polk invited Andrew's daughter Martha to visit her in the White House often. Mrs. Polk had no children of her own, and she asked Martha to help her select White House fabrics, furniture, and the like to redecorate. Possibly it was because Martha was also from Tennessee, but Sarah Polk really seemed to enjoy the young girl's company. She gave Martha a pair of onyx earrings as a gift for helping her, and Martha treasured them as long as she lived.

Andrew made an honest effort to assist Eliza in rearing their children, even if it had to be from a distance. He wrote Mary, another daughter, then a student at Rogersville Female Academy in Tennessee: "In School sustain yourself as honorable and highminded — be guilty of no low and vulgar acts or expressions even with your associates, for there is the place to make a good character, and to induce others to form a high opinion of you."

To his sons, Charles and Robert, he wrote, "You and him have talents enough, nature has done her part if you will but do yours." Both young men had alcohol problems, and neither seemed able to settle down to work.

In 1852 Eliza's and Andrew's fifth and last child, a son, was born. They named him Andrew for his father, but he was always called Frank. Frank was twenty years younger than the next-youngest child, Robert. Eliza developed tuberculosis during this last pregnancy, which left her a semi-invalid. Robert had also developed lung difficulties with hemorrhages.

In the same year Frank was born, Andrew lost his job in Congress when the Whigs gerrymandered the state and rearranged the voting districts. The plan backfired on the Whigs, for Andrew then entered the race for Governor of Tennessee and was elected. It was under his guidance that the public school system in Tennessee was established.

Eliza was now mistress of a nice brick home in Greeneville. They had sold their old frame house. Eliza's health required her to allow her daughter Martha to assume more and more of the household duties. Martha lived nearby with her new husband, David Patterson, a circuit judge and a political friend of Andrew.

Eliza remained in Greeneville while Andrew was Governor. There was no Governor's Mansion, and Andrew boarded in hotels. He first went to live at the Nashville Inn, but it burned in 1856. Andrew lost all his belongings in the fire, including two thousand dollars in cash.

After being Governor for five years, Andrew was elected to the United States Senate in 1857. He could not resist the excitement of seeking public office, even though he enjoyed being home and dearly loved his family.

Eliza went with Andrew to Washington, but she did not stay long. The slavery question was reaching white-hot levels, and Andrew strongly felt that she and their little son, Frank, would be safer in Tennessee. Eliza gave him no argument. She was glad to go home.

Andrew was for the Union, first, last and always. Most of the Johnsons' neighbors and relatives in east Tennessee agreed with him that the government must stand, but the rest of Tennessee was strongly secessionist. Few people in Andrew's home area had slaves, so they did not feel the threat to their livelihood that the plantation owners felt further West toward Nashville and Memphis.

Early in 1861 Andrew returned to Greeneville to beseech his fellow Tennesseans not to vote for secession. After the battle at Fort Sumter, South Carolina, in April of that year, Tennessee ignored Andrew's pleadings and joined the other states of the Confederacy.

Now considered a traitor in his home state, Andrew fled to Kentucky with Charles and Robert and Mary's husband, Daniel Stover, where the three young men joined the Union army. The whole area was in such turmoil, neither Andrew nor Eliza heard from any of them for over six months.

As the war became more widespread, Eliza, Mary and little Frank left Greeneville to go to Carter County, where they thought they would be safer. Their home in Greeneville had been confiscated by Confederate soldiers and turned into a Rebel hospital, so they could not possibly remain there.

After General Ulysses Grant captured part of Tennessee for the Union, Andrew was appointed military governor of Tennessee, but was unable to establish any form of civilian government that would protect citizens who were pro–Union in their sympathies.

In March 1863, Andrew went to Nashville, where he pleaded with Confederate officials to reconsider the secession from the Union, and begged them to rejoin the United States. For an answer, Confederate officials notified Eliza they wanted her to leave the state. They hoped to expel all the Johnsons from Tennessee. But Eliza sent back word that she was in poor health and unable to go anywhere. Meanwhile, Martha and her family were marooned in Greeneville, unable to leave, and neither Eliza nor Andrew could visit them.

It was late in 1863 before all Confederate troops had been driven out of Tennessee, and Andrew was able to set up a provisional government in Nashville. Eliza joined him there.

Andrew had been commissioned as a brigadier general in his establishment of a military government. About the same time, Charles Johnson was thrown from his horse and killed. Robert's alcoholic problems had intensified, and he resigned his army commission.

Andrew and Eliza were still living in Nashville when he learned he had been nominated to run for Vice President with President Abraham Lincoln, who was seeking reelection. The choice of Andrew was an effort by the Republicans, now calling themselves the National Union party, to bring Southern Union supporters into the fold with a Southern candidate.

Citizens of the eleven Southern states that had seceded did not vote in the 1864 election. Lincoln was reelected, and humble Andrew Johnson from Greeneville, Tennessee, had become Vice President of the United States.

All the tension and stresses brought on by the Civil War, the death of Charles, the election campaign, and the bitter enmity shown him by former friends led Andrew to brace himself for the inauguration with alcohol. When he made his inauguration speech, he was clearly drunk. He rambled on and on incoherently, causing dismay among his supporters, who were confused by his condition. Andrew was rarely known to drink at all.

When President Lincoln was assassinated about six weeks later, many people wondered what sort of man they now had to lead them as the new President. Was he even capable of leading the country?

Eliza was Andrew's strongest friend and supporter now, as even he wondered privately if he were qualified to be President. She reassured him she was confident he would do a good job, and as long as he acted in what he considered the country's best interest, everything would be all right. She knew how much faith he had in the Constitution and what it represented.

The Johnsons were unable to move into the White House for more than a month, while poor, bereaved Mary Lincoln grieved and tried to regain her composure. Mary finally left on June 9, 1865.

The Johnsons' two married daughters and their families came to live with Eliza and Andrew when they finally moved into the Executive Mansion. Both Martha and Mary worked long hours in an effort to restore the White House to its previous grandeur. While Mary Lincoln had been immersed in her grief, vandals had almost destroyed the first floor. The carpets had been slashed, as had upholstered sofas and chairs. Wallpaper hung in tatters, and many White House accessories, such as pictures and china, had been stolen during Mary's emotional collapse.

Andrew plunged headlong into his Presidential duties, and his family began to fear he would shorten his life by working too hard, as his fellow Tennessean President James K. Polk had done several years before.

Eliza's health was very poor now, and she spent most of her time in her second floor bedroom in the White House. There was no lack of spirit and gaiety in the big house, however, with all the grandchildren living there. They invited playmates in, who sometimes ate snacks with the President, rode ponies in Rock Creek Park, and went on picnics. A friend of Andrew's often entertained them during lunch with exciting tales of piracy on the high seas.

Andrew formed the habit of going with the children on some of their adventures, and he discovered the time away from his desk helped him gain new perspectives and make better decisions.

Each morning without fail, Andrew visited Eliza in her bedroom and asked her opinion about what public reaction would be to various ideas and proposals he had for Reconstruction. She would tell him honestly what she thought, and never failed to reassure him he was doing a good job. Often her comments would help him reach a firm conclusion about the best course to pursue in his difficult task.

Andrew was not Eliza's only visitor by any means. The Johnson grandchildren, as well as other family members, were in and out all during the day, for Eliza had a lively interest in all the activities that transpired.

On January 1, 1866, Andrew held his first official reception at the White House, with his daughters serving as hostesses. Eliza was too sick to make an appearance, but Martha and Mary were capable, and this reception, like all the official social functions that would follow, was done correctly and well. Since Martha had visited frequently in the White House when Sarah Polk was First Lady, she felt at ease in her own role as hostess.

Martha's husband had been elected to the United States Senate, so living in the White House was convenient for him. Mary's husband had seriously weakened his health by serving as a guerilla fighter for Union forces in the Civil War, and he died during the time he and his family were White House residents.

The radical members in government were determined that Southern citizens should pay a high price for their secession and for the lives of Union soldiers lost during the war. Andrew knew the South was as sincere in their firm belief that they should be allowed to own slaves as the North had been in believing that slaves should be set free. He tried to bring reason to the discussions about Reconstruction, such as returning voting rights to Southern citizens. About all he managed to do was get caught in the middle of the two factions, with both sides becoming furious with him.

Feelings ran so high against Andrew that he was impeached by Congress in 1868 and made to stand trial on various charges concerning his official conduct. Gideon Welles, Secretary of the Navy in Andrew's Cabinet, termed the charges against Andrew to be "a mountain of words, but not even a mouse of impeachment material. . . . Those who may vote to convict . . . would as readily vote to impeach the President had he been accused of stepping on a dog's tail."

Andrew was acquitted of charges by one vote and was restored to office. Eliza told him she had never doubted the outcome, as she knew he had done nothing wrong.

Andrew hoped the Democrats would nominate him to run on his own as President, since he had not been elected in his own right. He felt this would completely vindicate him in the eyes of the public, but he did not get his wish. The Democrats nominated Horatio Seymour, who was defeated by General Ulysses S. Grant when the election was held.

Neither Andrew nor Eliza was sorry to leave Washington and go home. They had never sought the Presidency for Andrew, and they felt much sadness when they remembered the treatment he had received at the hands of his friends, or people he had thought were his friends.

As one last gesture, the Johnsons decided to hold a lavish children's ball to celebrate Andrew's sixtieth birthday. Eliza came downstairs to help Andrew receive his young guests. There were about three hundred present, children of dignitaries and of White House servants. Andrew and Eliza were the only adults present. Andrew kissed the little children, and shook hands with the older ones.

The ball was a formal affair, with the State Dining Room open and music provided by the Marine Band. The children all had a glorious time as they feasted on ice cream, cake and other delicacies. The affair was so enjoyed by the children that it became an annual feature of Washington society.

Mary and her children, accompanied by her brother, Robert, left Washington early to get Andrew's and Eliza's home ready for their return to Greeneville. Martha admitted she would also be glad to leave the White House. "Mother is not able to enjoy these entertainments, Belle [Martha's daughter] is too young, and I am indifferent to them, so it is well they are almost over," she said.

In one of his last official acts as President, Andrew granted a Presidential pardon to everyone who had been involved in secession, fully restoring all rights under the Constitution to Southern citizens.

On their return home to Tennessee, Eliza was a complete invalid. Andrew cared for her himself, in addition to making a garden and puttering around the house. He was always pleased to have visitors, especially the ones he and Eliza had known in their younger days. He sometimes found Greeneville a trifle dull after their exciting life in Washington.

Each election year Andrew would hit the campaign trail for his favorite candidates, and in 1875 he won his own campaign for a United States Senate seat, but he served only a short time.

In July 1875, Andrew and Eliza went to visit Mary and her family in Carter County, Tennessee. While there, Andrew suffered a stroke and died on July 31. He was buried in Greeneville on a hilltop just outside town.

Eliza returned to Greene County and their home, sadly broken in health and spirit. She survived Andrew by only six months in a totally bed-fast condition. She died on January 15, 1876, and was buried beside Andrew, her "beau," as she had termed him so many years ago, after funeral services in the Methodist Church where she had been a member most of her life.

19. Julia Boggs Dent Grant

Julia Boggs Dent was born January 26, 1826, in St. Louis, Missouri. Her father, Frederick Fayette Dent, was a plantation owner and farmer. He was given the courtesy title of "Colonel" by acquaintances, which was the custom. Julia's mother, the former Ellen Wrenshall, had been born in England, but came to live in America with her parents when she was still a young child.

Julia enjoyed her carefree childhood days living on the plantation. She and her sister, Nellie, were especially close, and they spent many happy hours playing under the shade trees near their home. Little black girls, children of slaves, also played dolls with them.

Julia had four brothers, and she admired their courage and energy more than she did her own or Nellie's. Julia was powerfully built, stocky and short. She enjoyed fishing more than any other sport, but she rode horses well also. Any outdoor activity was more interesting to her than staying indoors.

Julia was not pretty, and she knew it. Her right eye wandered independently of her left eye due to a malfunctioning muscle. Her vision was never good because of this defect, and she had difficulty in school. What Julia lacked in beauty she made up for in willfulness and determination. Her family referred to her as "the boss."

When Julia was almost eleven, her parents sent her to a boarding school in St. Louis, the Academy for Young Ladies operated by the Misses Mauros. Julia was not impressed with either the courses taught or the discipline. Her teachers tried to make Julia an eager student, but Julia only wanted to read. She had a total lack of interest in mathematics, grammar, science or studies of governments. She did fairly good work in mythology and ancient history.

Despite her lack of enthusiasm, Julia attended the academy for seven years. Many of her academic problems probably were related to her poor eyesight. This may be why her teachers hesitated to force her to make up work and allowed her to study independently and learn what she would. Due to her stubborn nature, Julia did not try hard to learn unless she liked the subject she was studying.

Julia Grant. (Courtesy Library of Congress.)

Fred Dent, Julia's brother, graduated from West Point Academy in 1843, the same year Julia left boarding school. Since Fred was interested in the military life, he made friends with young officers at Jefferson Barracks, an army post near their home. It was through him that Julia met Lieutenant Ulysses Grant.

Ulysses had graduated from West Point with Fred, and was temporarily assigned to Jefferson Barracks. He had accepted an appointment to West Point with reluctance, mostly because his father insisted it was a good opportunity to get an education.

Ulysses hated military discipline and was an indifferent scholar. He preferred taking his horse over high jumps to spending time studying. In fact, in this area of horsemanship, he set a West Point record which endured twenty-five years. (In true army fashion, he would be refused a commission in the cavalry when he graduated.)

Within a few weeks' time, Julia and Ulysses were deeply in love. Both were romantics, loved poetry and admired beauty in their surroundings. Soon Ulysses asked Julia to marry him. She was only eighteen and did not feel ready for marriage, but she agreed to an engagement.

Ulysses was assigned almost immediately to Camp Salubrity in Louisiana. For the next several months the young people were forced to conduct their romance by correspondence. When he got leave at last, Ulysses came back to St. Louis and asked Colonel Dent's permission to marry Julia. Colonel Dent did not like the idea at all, as he said Julia was unsuited to live the roving life required of an army wife.

Ulysses said he had been offered a professorship in an Ohio college, which he would leave the army and accept if he could marry Julia. Colonel Dent did not like this idea either. He felt Ulysses should pursue the career for which he had trained.

When he saw Julia and Ulysses were committed to their relationship, Colonel Dent gave permission to Julia to continue writing to Ulysses, but he wanted her to give some serious consideration to the sacrifices she would be required to make as the wife of a soldier. If she did not change her mind after a year or two of contemplation, they could marry.

Ulysses had barely returned to his post in Louisiana when he was transferred to New Orleans. He and Julia did not get to see each other again for more than four years. He went on to fight in the Mexican War and stayed in Mexico most of the time they were apart.

When Ulysses left Mexico in 1848 and returned to St. Louis, neither Julia nor he would tolerate any more delay. They were married on August 22, 1848, in the Dent family home in a ceremony attended only by her family and closest friends.

They then took a long honeymoon trip to visit the Grant relatives in Kentucky, and friends of Ulysses. Julia liked her in-laws, especially her mother-in-law.

In October, after a brief visit with Julia's parents, they went to Ulysses's new post at Sacketts Harbor, New York. At their new home Julia had servants, and was surprised to learn she had to direct their activities. She had assumed servants knew what to do. When she tried to have their cook prepare food to taste like the meals served on the plantation, it was a disaster. She was forced to allow the cook to do things her own way.

In spring of 1849, Ulysses was sent to Detroit. Julia and Ulysses both enjoyed living in Michigan and made many friends. To add to their happiness, their first child, Frederick Dent, was born there in 1850.

Ulysses was sent to California on his next assignment. Since Julia was expecting their second child to be born momentarily, Ulysses told her it would be better if she went to her parents to stay for a time. She dreaded being parted from him, but she was in no condition to travel. Only three weeks after he left, their second son, also named Ulysses, was born.

Ulysses was as miserable in California without his family as they were back East without him. For the first time in his life, he began drinking heavily. After a two-year stay in California, during which time he became more and more depressed, he resigned from the army so he could rejoin his family. He had never even seen his newest son, who was now almost two years old!

Julia was overjoyed to have him back with her and the children again. Before long, though, his joy of reunion turned to a concern of how he would support his family.

Julia's father gave her a one-hundred acre tract of land, and Ulysses decided to try his hand at farming. His father considered him addled even to think of resigning his army commission as a captain. Ulysses did not argue with his father, but Julia resented the older man's interference. If Ulysses wanted to farm, then that was what Julia wanted, too.

Ulysses built a log house for his family on the farm, and there they lived for three years. Julia hated the house, which they had named Hardscrabble. She described it as "crude and homely." She refused to be friendly with any of the other farm families, but Ulysses found friends wherever he went.

Julia was always a fiercely proud woman, and their present manner of living on the ragged edge of disaster, with little or no income, got on her nerves. For the first time in their marriage they had no steady source of money. To increase their financial burdens, two more children were born to them—a little girl named Ellen, called Nellie, and a son named Jesse.

Their finances continued to worsen, and for almost the whole winter of 1856–1857, Ulysses cut firewood and sold it in St. Louis to get money for their support. He received an average of forty-eight dollars a month for his efforts.

In 1858 they decided to give up the struggle. They sold their farm and livestock, and went to live with Julia's now widowed father in St. Louis. Here their growing children could attend school, and life should be easier.

Julia looked after the children, and took the responsibility of running the household, while Ulysses worked as a rent collector for one of Julia's cousins, Harry Boggs. As Julia said at a later time, "I cannot imagine how my dear husband ever thought of going into such a business, as he could never collect a penny that was owed to him.... He always felt sorry for them [the debtors] and never pressed them again."

This job did not work out for Ulysses either. Mr. Grant suggested to his son that they move to Galena, Illinois, where Ulysses could work with his brothers as a leather merchant. Two younger brothers were successfully managing the profitable enterprise and were glad to have Ulysses join them. Ulysses could have become a partner in the family business if he had been more interested and willing to work harder, but Ulysses was miserable doing this type of work.

Julia liked living in Galena, where they could visit frequently with Grant family members and old friends. The children were doing well, and she had realized her fondest ambition of living in a brick house.

When the North began preparing for civil war, Ulysses gladly entered a volunteer company of Galena residents. He was a colonel in 1861 when Julia and the children were allowed to join him at headquarters in Cairo, Illinois. Ulysses was frequently gone from home as the company to which he was attached engaged in battle in other locations.

Later that year Ulysses had progressed in rank to General. As the war came closer, he urged Julia to take the children and go to Kentucky to stay with his parents for a time. As Julia wrote, however, "Mr. and Mrs. Grant were very kind to the children and became very fond of them, but I was not at all happy there. . . ."

From time to time Julia visited Ulysses at various field locations during the next three years, while their children remained in Kentucky with their grandparents.

Julia tended to take credit for General Grant's battle successes. In her autobiography, she claimed to have asked her husband, "Why do you not move on Vicksburg at once? . . . Move upon Vicksburg and you will take it." She wrote that General Grant then asked, "Do you have a plan of action to propose?"

"Of course, I had," she said. "Mass your troops in a solid phalanx at a point north of the fortress, rush upon it, and they will be obliged to surrender."

Apparently Ulysses did make honest efforts to have her join him whenever possible, whether he sought her battle advice or not. As the war wound down, Julia returned to St. Louis, where the three older children were now living with Julia's relatives and attending school.

"I was happy to be at home again, busied myself putting my house in order, and hoped soon to have the pleasure of a visit from my husband," Julia wrote in her autobiography.

When the summer ended, Julia moved their family to Burlington, New Jersey. Apparently her Missouri neighbors had not been overly thrilled to have the Union General's family in their midst. Julia was indignant when some of the Missouri citizens asked her if she had studied the Constitution regarding secession. As she wrote later, "No, I have not. I would not know where to look for it even if I wished to read it, and, besides, the Northern people think and say it is unconstitutional for any of the states to secede. I really was much grieved at my ignorance of these matters. . . ."

At last the Civil War ended, and Ulysses returned home to a hero's welcome. Mary Lincoln, wife of President Lincoln, was distressed to see how popular Ulysses had become with the general public. When Julia and Ulysses accompanied the Lincolns on a boating trip, Mary took the opportunity to reprimand Julia in the presence of other people for sitting down beside her without her permission. It was this snub and Mary's imperious attitude toward her that caused Julia to flatly refuse to go with the Lincolns to Ford's Theater the night President Lincoln was assassinated.

There were financial rewards attached to the new popularity Ulysses enjoyed. The town of Galena built a house for the General and his family, the city of New York gave him one hundred and five thousand dollars in cash and the city of Philadelphia gave them a mansion.

Andrew Johnson had become President when Abraham Lincoln was assassinated, but he was unpopular and was impeached by Congress and made to stand trial on various charges of official misconduct. He was not put out of office, but his Democratic party felt he was not a good choice to be their candidate for President in 1868. They nominated Horatio Seymour, and the Republicans nominated Ulysses Grant. Ulysses won the election and became the nation's President on March 4, 1869.

Julia was absolutely ecstatic with the honor shown her beloved Ulysses. She felt she would burst with pride as she heard Ulysses take the oath of office.

For some unknown reason, Ulysses's mother did not attend his inauguration, but his father did. Several weeks before, the elder Mr. Grant had asked Julia's brother to help him and other relatives to find a place where they could stay in Washington, as "Ulysses said his house would be too full," his father said. Although Julia had been friendly with Ulysses's father since he had interfered years before in their affairs, she may have still angry with him. She apparently made no effort to include Ulysses's own family in any of the festivities of the occasion.

Julia enjoyed the eight years they lived in the White House. She felt as much at home there as she had at the old Missouri farm. As First Lady, she held lavish, expensive receptions and dinners, and she bought the finest of clothes to wear.

One happy event that occurred during the Grants' White House years was the wedding of their daughter, Nellie, to Algernon Charles Frederick Sartoris on May 21, 1874, in the White House. Mr. Sartoris was a member of the British legation, and the newlyweds returned to England to live.

The next year, a son, Fred, brought his new bride to live with his parents in the White House. Both Ulysses and Julia were excited and pleased by the birth of their little granddaughter, Julia Grant, in the

Executive Mansion on June 7, 1876. Julia was especially flattered that the child was named for her.

Ulysses was not outstanding in his role as President. Corruption and graft were widespread in the government during his two terms, and inflation and financial panic gripped the country in 1873. He blamed many of the problems on his lack of experience in government affairs, and accepted responsibility for the bad choices he made in filling various positions of power.

Even though he had loyal supporters who urged him to seek a third term, Ulysses was not disappointed when the House of Representatives declared an attempt to serve a third term would be "unwise, unpatriotic and fraught with peril to our free institutions."

Julia was extremely overwrought when the time came for them to leave the White House. She wrote that "in an abandonment of grief," she flung herself on a sofa in her room "and wept, wept, oh, so bitterly." Julia tended to be somewhat dramatic in her reactions, but she had thoroughly enjoyed being in the limelight as First Lady, and she was undoubtedly sad when it ended.

In May 1877, Julia, Ulysses, their son Jesse and Julia's maid sailed for England to visit Nellie and her family. After their visit there had ended, they wandered all over the world, with no particular pattern to their travel. Everywhere they went they received a welcome befitting a President of the United States. There were receptions, parades and banquets for them in England, Germany, Japan, Egypt, China and India.

When they finally returned home, they found the public dissatisfaction with Ulysses's administrations had largely faded, and he was once again perceived to be a national hero.

They bought a mansion in New York with some of the money the city had given them earlier. Ulysses borrowed one hundred fifty thousand dollars from William H. Vanderbilt to invest in a banking firm, in which his son, Ulysses, Jr., called Buck, was a partner. The firm went bankrupt in 1884 when the leader, Ferdinand Ward, was sent to prison as a swindler.

The Grants had lost all their money, and their financial condition was nearly as bad as it had been long before Ulysses became President. Ulysses insisted that Vanderbilt take all the property they owned to apply to the debt they owed him. Congress voted to restore Ulysses to the rank of general with full pay, which helped, but did not solve, their financial plight.

Julia and Ulysses went sadly to their little summer home at Long Branch, New Jersey, to decide how they could get their monetary affairs in order. While there, Ulysses developed throat cancer.

Ulysses decided he would write his memoirs to get money, and they returned to New York. His health was failing rapidly, and he was confined to his bedroom. He spent the final months of his life racing to complete his book, which he hoped would bring in enough money to pay his debts and support Julia after his death. He completed his book on July 19, 1885, and died four days later.

Julia lived seventeen more years. She gave up the house in New York and went to Washington to live. The book Ulysses wrote was an outstanding success, and Julia never had to worry about having enough money to live on again. Mark Twain was Ulysses's publicity agent, and he gave five hundred thousand dollars to Julia in profits. She also received a pension of five thousand dollars annually as the widow of a President.

In 1897 she attended the dedication of Grant's Tomb in New York City, built as a monument to Ulysses. She lived quietly and contentedly in Washington, where she received frequent visits from her children and grandchildren. Nellie's marriage ended in divorce, and she was left with three young children to rear. She returned to America to be with her mother and attended Alice Roosevelt Longworth's wedding, also in the White House.

Julia wrote her own memoirs, but these were not published until 1975. During her lifetime she could never come to terms with an interested publisher, as each contact she made felt she wanted too much money for her book.

When Julia died of congestive heart failure on December 14, 1902, the *New York Times* headlines referred to her as "a wealthy woman." This description would have pleased her. It was also an honest description as she left assets of about a quarter of a million dollars.

Julia was buried beside Ulysses in the Grant's Tomb Monument in New York City.

20. Lucy Ware Webb Hayes

Lucy Ware Webb was born in Chillicothe, Ohio, on August 28, 1831. Her father, James Webb, was a doctor. When Lucy was two years old, her father died, and she, her mother and two older brothers went to live with her grandfather, Isaac Cook, on his Chillicothe farm.

Lucy enjoyed her childhood years on the farm. She often rode her pony through the fields, or played with her brothers and cousins.

She attended the Chillicothe Female School, where she had difficulty with mathematics. She did good work in her other subjects, but she had to try extra hard to learn arithmetic.

A lecture by a reformed alcoholic, given at her school when she was entering her teens, impressed Lucy profoundly. Her grandfather, who had recently been converted to Methodist beliefs, reinforced her views on the subject of temperance with lectures of his own. Young Lucy grew up with an ingrained hatred of drinking alcohol in any form.

In 1844 Mrs. Webb moved her family to Delaware, Ohio, to enable Lucy's two brothers, Joseph and James, to attend Ohio Wesleyan University, recently established there by the Methodist Church. Lucy was also allowed to attend preparatory classes at the university, although no females were admitted officially at that time. The university awarded her a few credits for her work.

Lucy was fifteen years old, dark-eyed and friendly, when Rutherford Hayes saw her for the first time. She and some girlfriends had a habit of meeting at the sulphur springs on the campus of the university in the afternoons after school. Rutherford was in Delaware to attend a temperance convention and was taking a stroll near the springs when he heard a girl laughing. She sounded so merry he went over to the group and managed to be introduced to Lucy, whom he found very pretty as well as fun-loving.

Rutherford's mother had met Lucy herself on an earlier visit to Delaware and was impressed with the young lady. Lucy's mother and Mrs. Hayes formed a conspiratorial friendship to encourage a romance between their son and daughter, so Rutherford had already been given much information about Lucy before they met.

Rutherford was surprised at how young Lucy was, and he was baffled

Lucy Hayes. (Courtesy Library of Congress.)

as to why his mother was encouraging a meeting so enthusiastically. He considered Lucy just "a bright sunny-hearted little girl not quite old enough to fall in love with—and so I didn't."

Lucy had not been waiting around for Rutherford or any other man at this happy time in her life. She had her own plans for the future, and just now a man was not included. When she reached sixteen, she entered Wesleyan Female College in Cincinnati, also a Methodist school.

Rutherford's mother told her son that Lucy had been sent away to school because her mother was afraid Lucy was "too great a favorite among the students" in her hometown. "She will do well if she can keep from being carried off by a Methodist minister till she is of age," Rutherford's mother told him solemnly, in an attempt to pique his interest.

Mrs. Hayes may have had some of her own interest in mind in her attempts to work up a romance between Rutherford and Lucy. "Lucy knows how to treat old people," she said on one occasion, ". . . a rare and excellent trait of character."

Rutherford's sister, Fanny, also began praising Lucy, although not as insistently as their mother.

While the Hayes ladies were busy trying to arrange Lucy's future for her, Lucy was enjoying her years in school. She made many friends and never lacked a male escort to any event requiring one. She even seriously considered becoming engaged to one young admirer.

Rutherford went to Cincinnati to open a law practice the year Lucy graduated from college. He went to her college campus to renew their acquaintance before the school year ended in 1850. He found a more mature, even more attractive Lucy, a charmer who had developed an interest in the larger world. She read her essay entitled "The Influence of Christianity on National Prosperity" at commencement exercises to an audience which included Rutherford.

They began a courtship, which was characterized by a mutual lack of enthusiasm for letter-writing. When they were separated and Lucy hesitated to name a wedding date, Rutherford worried and fretted when he received no communication from her. He had not written either, but he thought that was a different matter.

When she celebrated her twenty-first birthday in August, 1852, Lucy decided it was time to get serious. They were married on December 30, 1852, in her mother's home in Cincinnati. Lucy's wedding dress was made of white-on-white patterned satin with a fitted bodice and a pleated skirt. Her floor-length veil was decorated with orange blossoms. About forty people were present, including Lucy's mother and brothers, as well as Rutherford's sister, now Fanny Platt. His mother was ill and unable to attend.

The couple spent their honeymoon, which lasted a month, on a visit with his sister, Fanny, and her family in Columbus, Ohio. There they attended various teas, dinner parties, lectures, concerts and church gatherings. Lucy enjoyed the opportunity to dress up in her trousseau finery and be escorted around town by her handsome husband. She loved the Platt children and enjoyed playing with them.

Lucy could see no cloud on the horizon of their life together. If the Northern politicians argued with Southern politicians about slavery, so what? It didn't affect Lucy or Rutherford in any way.

Their first child, a little son, was born at Lucy's mother's home in November 1853. They delayed naming the baby until Rutherford's mother and sister told him they felt the baby deserved a better name than "Puds," which he was being called at the moment. He was finally named Birchard Austin, called Birch.

Later that year Fanny Platt invited Lucy to go with her to hear a lecture on women's rights by activist Lucy Stone. Fanny was an ardent supporter of emancipation of women and felt they should be given the right to vote.

Lucy found herself more impressed than she expected by the logic shown in the lecture, and she told Rutherford when she got back home that she felt women deserved to be better paid for jobs they did in the workplace. Lucy might have gone on to become a real advocate of the women's rights movement if Fanny had not died two years later from childbirth complications. After this sad event, Lucy turned all her attention back to her home and family.

Within the next five years, Lucy gave birth to two more sons. Again, with each birth she and Rutherford waited for a name to overtake the child. Their second son eventually became Webb Cook, and the third was named Rutherford Platt, called Rud.

Lucy and Rutherford had lived with Mrs. Webb for several years, but with the increase in their family, Rutherford bought a house. Lucy's mother then moved in with them, as well as Lucy's brother, James, who was now a doctor. (Joseph Webb, also a doctor, lived elsewhere.) All these in-laws seemed happy living together, and Rutherford's law practice grew.

In 1856 Lucy and Rutherford began to take an interest in politics when General John C. Fremont was the Republican candidate for President. Lucy was impressed with the anti-slavery views expressed by members of the Republican party. Her father's family from Louisville, Kentucky, freed their slaves long before the Civil War because they became convinced slavery was wrong. Their Southern Methodist church based these opinions on religious rather than economic grounds.

Lucy was proud of her heritage, and she had formed her own firm opinions about slavery. Rutherford tended to see some right on both sides of the question, and Lucy did not antagonize him. She just gently led him over to her way of thinking.

Lucy's allegiance to the temperance movement was also total and unyielding. She was severely disappointed when General Fremont was defeated. Encouraged by Lucy's evident political involvement, Rutherford accepted a post as Cincinnati's City Solicitor in 1858.

About this same time, the slavery issue was reaching fever pitch at the national level. Since the Hayes family lived in Ohio, almost on the Mason-Dixon line dividing slave and free states, they saw firsthand how escaping slaves were beaten and run down like animals on city streets. Rutherford became so enraged at the spectacle that he offered free legal representation to any fugitive slave.

When the first shot of the Civil War was fired on April 12, 1861, at Fort Sumter in Charleston, South Carolina, Lucy and Rutherford knew there would be no peaceful settlement to the conflict. The next month Rutherford went into service for the war.

Lucy was completely supportive of Rutherford's actions. She felt the war was a necessary evil, and expressed a wish that she could have led a female garrison at Fort Sumter. She was convinced surrender there by Union forces could have been prevented if she had been on hand.

Rutherford's mother was unhappy about his decision to go into the army. She wondered out loud "why any man with a happy home wanted to leave it." Lucy considered this remark to be in poor taste and resented it.

As time passed, however, Lucy lost some of her own intense fervor for the conflict as she learned that war was more often dreary, sad and unbelievably lonely than it was enthusiastically patriotic. With Rutherford in the Union army, first as a colonel, then a major general, for four years, it was up to Lucy to rear their sons and maintain their home. She and Rutherford seldom saw each other, although he did write her fairly often.

Adding to her sense of loss and devastation were the deaths of two little sons born during the war, neither of whom survived to reach his first birthday. Lucy's young son Rud wished his "papa would get a little wounded—then he would come home again and we would keep him."

In 1864 although still an active member of the Union army, Rutherford was nominated as an Ohio Representative to the United States Congress. He was elected, despite his firm refusal to leave his duties to campaign. He took his seat in the Thirty-ninth Congress just before President Lincoln was assassinated.

The Hayes family had a little daughter born to them in 1867, whom they named Fanny. The arrival of this little girl helped Lucy regain her old enthusiasm for life, which had diminished after the deaths of her two infant sons, as well as the deaths of her mother and Rutherford's mother the year before.

Lucy did not like the idea of living in Washington, so Rutherford lived in boarding houses while he served two terms in Congress. Again their lives were shared chiefly through occasional visits and correspondence.

Rutherford was then elected Governor of Ohio, which suited both Lucy and Rutherford better. Rutherford did not at all agree with President Andrew Johnson's policies for Reconstruction in the Southern states, believing the President was being too soft with the Southern rebels. Lucy was glad she and Rutherford could be together again.

Lucy had no regrets when they moved from Cincinnati to Columbus, Ohio's capital. They would be living in a rented house that held no memories of the sons who had died or her deceased mother. Little Rud, now nine years old, and baby Fanny went with their parents to Columbus, while the two older boys stayed in Fremont, Ohio, with Rutherford's Uncle Joe and attended school.

As the Governor's wife, Lucy felt it was safe to support such causes as orphanages, prison reform and support for veterans, as these were not controversial. She hesitated to espouse women's right to vote, and it is uncertain whether she believed all women should be allowed to vote.

Two of her mother's sisters felt emphatically that women should be given this right and urged Rutherford to help bring this about. Rutherford put them off by saying he felt women were too busy at home to know much about politics.

Scott Russell Hayes was born on February 8, 1871, and baby Fanny was reportedly glad to have a "little boy sister."

Both older sons were doing well in school at Uncle Joe's, but little Rud was carefree and offhand in his attitude toward his schoolwork. He irritated Lucy by getting good grades with little apparent effort.

Lucy and Rutherford entertained often. Rutherford teased Lucy that she "exceeded the statute of limitations on cobwebs" with her vigorous, energetic cleaning when she was preparing for these social events.

In June 1870, they held an elegant reception in honor of Civil War General William T. Sherman. In 1872, as Rutherford prepared to step down as Ohio's Governor, their guests at a New Year's Day reception numbered over one hundred.

Rutherford had not sought a third term as Governor, preferring to campaign again for a seat in Congress. This time he was defeated. Lucy and Rutherford were disappointed, but their older sons rejoiced. "We will now have a home somewhere," they wrote from college.

Rutherford's uncle, Sardis Birchard, offered them his home at Spiegel Grove in Fremont, but Lucy wanted to return to Cincinnati. She finally agreed to the move, and they went to Spiegel Grove on May 1, 1873. In August that year their eighth and last child, a little boy, was born. He, too, died while an infant.

The Hayes family found they enjoyed living at Spiegel Grove more than they had expected. They set about making improvements to both the house and the lawns. Rutherford inherited the property in 1874.

In 1875, Rud, now sixteen years old, entered a new agricultural college in East Lansing, Michigan. Birch, the eldest son, had recently graduated from Cornell University in Ithaca, New York, which Webb had also attended for a while before coming home to care for the family estate while Rutherford campaigned again for Governor.

Rutherford was elected Governor by a narrow margin, and the Hayes family was once again center stage in politics. Rutherford wrote Birch that Lucy "enjoys our return to public life more than I do." Lucy admitted she was glad to be back in Columbus where they had "true, sincere friends."

Reconstruction efforts had floundered under the guidance of President Ulysses Grant. In seeking a stronger leader, the Republicans turned to Rutherford, and they nominated him to run for President in 1876. New York Governor Samuel Tilden was his opponent.

Tilden received two hundred and fifty thousand more votes than Rutherford, but Rutherford won the election by Electoral College votes. There were many bad feelings generated by such a close contest, and for many years the Democrats insisted the election had been stolen. Rutherford's life was threatened, and someone actually shot into their home in Columbus. He and Lucy were sitting on the ragged edge for weeks before the controversy was settled.

Lucy was the first President's wife to be referred to as "First Lady" in print. Before these women had been either "the President's wife" or "Mrs." With her college education and her demonstrated interest in social welfare, women hoped Lucy would advance the cause of women's rights in the nation. Temperance advocates were pleased to have one of their own serving in the White House.

Both Rutherford and Lucy breathed a sigh of relief when his inauguration was completed without incident. It was only a few months since President Lincoln had been assassinated, and Rutherford feared the same fate.

Simplicity marked the Hayeses years in the White House. They held official receptions and dinners, and their table was bountiful, but little or no alcohol in any form was served. Many Washington socialites muttered the Hayeses were too stingy to buy whiskey or other alcoholic beverages, but this was an unfair charge. Both Rutherford and Lucy were teetotalers. Wits gave Lucy the nickname of "Lemonade Lucy" because of the mildness of the refreshments, but Rutherford insisted it was he who banned alcohol.

Webb Hayes, now twenty-one, served as his father's private secretary. Lucy invited various nieces, cousins and friends to assist her since there was no official staff for the First Lady's use.

The younger children, six-year-old Scott and nine-year-old Fanny, were an integral part of the household, and were the source of amusement and delight to guests and the American public in general. On Scott's seventh birthday he had thirty guests at a party, during which the children played Blind Man's Bluff and ran up and down White House halls. Fanny had two dollhouses she kept in the hall, and she spent much of her play time there. Scott was especially thrilled by a visit by Red Cloud, a Sioux Indian chief, who called Scott a "young brave."

Other visitors to the White House included Mr. and Mrs. John Herron, longtime friends of the Hayes family. Their seven-week-old daughter was christened Lucy Hayes Herron during their visit. They were accompanied by an older daughter, Helen, who would one day also be a First Lady when her husband, William Taft, became President.

Lucy asked former First Lady Julia Tyler to assist her at a reception, which pleased Julia and all the Tylers greatly. The Tylers had been ostracized since former President John Tyler had accepted a post in the Confederate government during the Civil War. When he died, the Union government did not even recognize his former service to his country as President. Lucy's gesture of reconciliation was appreciated.

After several months of constant entertainments and public scrutiny, Lucy felt she had to get out of Washington for a few days. She went on a three-week vacation to Ohio, where she visited family and friends. Later she took Fanny on a fishing trip to Saranac Lake, where Lucy caught a fifteen-pound trout!

Congress was hostile to Rutherford's attempts to reform civil service. They also refused to appropriate any money to redecorate or buy new furniture for the White House. Lucy used her own money to buy needed items, as the White House needed refurbishing after eight years of occupation by President and Mrs. Grant and their family. After two years had passed, Congress grudgingly appropriated some money, which Lucy used to have the conservatories enlarged.

The Hayes family attended a nearby Methodist Church on Sundays instead of the fashionable Metropolitan Church. There were daily Bible readings and prayers in the White House. Rutherford never joined any church.

Lucy allowed the annual Easter Egg Roll to be held on White House grounds when Congress closed the grounds of the Capitol. This custom prevails today. In her leisure time, Lucy enjoyed china painting, and songfests with her family and guests around the White House piano.

When government officials continued to complain about the tedium of sitting at dinners and receptions at the White House without alcoholic refreshment, a steward devised a solution. He made a sherbetlike drink with lemon juice, sugar and beaten egg whites, to which (unbeknownst to the Hayeses) he then added a generous portion of St. Croix rum. He first served the mixture in orange cups, then more boldly in glasses. This course became known as the Life-Saving Station. Apparently neither President Hayes nor Lucy ever suspected they had been tricked.

Another bitter controversy arose during the Hayes administration when California wanted laws passed which would restrict the number of Chinese immigrants to that state. President Hayes vetoed the legislation when it came to his desk, and California threatened to secede. Tempers quieted when a compromise bill allowed the United States government to "regulate, limit or suspend" such immigration when national interests were in jeopardy.

Lucy had been troubled with inflammatory rheumatism since her teens. This health problem now was becoming worse, and she had been unable to assume her role as hostess on several recent occasions. Her health, plus Rutherford's own lack of interest in a second term, caused him to decline renomination.

When Lucy and Rutherford returned to live at Spiegel Grove, Lucy was looking forward to peace and quiet. She had begun having frequent headaches and digestive upsets in addition to her rheumatic problems. She did go to meetings of the local temperance group and continued to serve as national president of the missionary society of the Methodists. She taught a Sunday School class for boys, and helped at church social gatherings. Ministers and their families were frequent overnight guests in their home.

The Women's Christian Temperance Union pleaded with Lucy to accept a national office in their organization, but she did not feel she could leave home for the long periods of time required. The suffrage movement also solicited her involvement, or at least an endorsement, but again she declined.

Birch was a lawyer now in Toledo; Webb was living and working for a manufacturer in Cleveland; Rud was studying to be a civil engineer in Boston; and the two younger children attended local schools. Later Fanny graduated from a Cleveland finishing school and Scott went to Cornell University.

Lucy lived to see the birth of two grandchildren born to Birch and his wife, but died from complications of a stroke on June 25, 1889. Lucy's funeral services were conducted by the same minister who had married her to Rutherford, almost thirty-seven years earlier. She was buried at Spiegel Grove.

Rutherford lived three and a half years more, but in failing health. He spent his remaining years working for educational improvements. Fanny lived at home with him, and Rud went with him when he traveled.

Rutherford suffered a heart attack in the railroad station in Cleveland on January 14, 1893, and died three days later. He is buried beside Lucy at Spiegel Grove.

21. Lucretia Rudolph Garfield

Lucretia Rudolph was born to a farming family in Hiram, Ohio, on April 19, 1832. Her father, Zebulon Rudolph, and her mother, Arabella Green Mason, were devout members of the Disciples of Christ, as were most of the other residents of their secluded area called a reserve. Mr. Rudolph was one of the church leaders.

Lucretia grew up learning to work hard and to be kind and considerate of others. She had a genuine love for learning, inherited from her father. The only school available to her was Geauga School and Seminary, operated by the Free Will Baptist denomination.

It was at Geauga that Lucretia first met James Garfield. James was something of a child prodigy, having first attended school at age three at Chagrin Falls, Ohio, then later his village school at Orange. He had a broader education than the other students at Geauga and was a year older than Lucretia and her friends.

James's family were also members of the Disciples of Christ, and James often disagreed with the Baptist teachings at the school. James had left home two years earlier to work on the canal, located not many miles away, and he was more independent in his thinking than the other students. His work at the canal had been so difficult that he suffered a mental and physical breakdown and had to postpone his education for several months. Despite his criticisms of Geauga, he had to admit it was better than canal work.

Lucretia did not know what to make of James. He was handsome and friendly, and he liked girls, but he had a prudish outlook on life which caused him to be extremely critical of his schoolmates. Lucretia decided he was a "strange mortal" and the "drollest genius."

In 1850 James was a teacher in mathematics at Geauga, and he spied on some of his students and reported their misconduct to the school authorities. Four of the students were expelled, and the other students turned against James.

When the Free Will Baptists closed Geauga a little later, James went to teach and live with his mother's relatives at Gaysport. He had never been so far away from the reserve before. He enjoyed seeing new sights and

Lucretia Garfield. (Courtesy Library of Congress.)

hearing new sounds, but as the novelty wore off, he longed for the peace and friendships of the reserve.

Lucretia's father and the other leaders of the Disciples of Christ founded their own school, the Western Reserve Eclectic Institute. Zeb Rudolph was a trustee of the school, which he built literally with his own hands. He felt it was a good school, and he built a house for his family nearby so all four of his children could receive their education at Western Eclectic. Some of the teachers there boarded with the Rudolphs.

In 1853, to Lucretia's delight, James came to teach Greek and Latin classes at the Eclectic. Lucretia was one of his students.

While they had been apart, both had been involved in serious romances with other people and had not really thought that much about each other. They were glad to meet again, however, and they felt a strong mutual attraction this time.

Lucretia was petite, small-boned, with a pretty face, long, dark, shining hair and beautiful black eyes. More important to James, she was demure, reserved and dignified in her demeanor. James disliked aggressive females intensely, and Lucretia was exactly what he thought girls should be. Lucretia was highly intelligent, and while her eyes often sparkled with interest, they could also flash with spirit when she was aroused to anger.

James had become even more handsome as a man, with a charismatic vitality and a number of wide-ranging interests which aroused Lucretia's admiration.

James was no newcomer to the romance field. He had even had a previous involvement with one of his teachers, but from the very beginning of their reunion, he thought of marriage when he thought of Lucretia.

During commencement festivities at the end of the school year, James took the part of King Ahasuerus, while Lucretia was Queen Esther in a play about that unhappy Biblical couple. If James enjoyed pretending the marriage was real, apparently Lucretia never gave it a second thought. Her mind was fastened on a teaching job at a neighboring school, which she would begin in the fall.

When she left for her new job in the fall of 1854, James found he missed Lucretia exceedingly and began corresponding with her. She stayed in the village where she taught during the week, but came home on weekends. Their love might have never had a good chance to develop if Lucretia had not developed pneumonia that winter and been forced to resign in February 1855. She came home to stay, and she and James began an ardent courtship.

As soon as James had managed to get Lucretia to admit she loved him and he had proposed marriage to her, he began to have second thoughts. Lucretia had surprised him by being one of the speakers at the commencement exercises, and James felt this was very bold of her. He did not approve of women making public speeches.

To increase the difficulties, gossip had reached Lucretia that James was again involved with his teacher-lover, Almeda Booth. It was more than idle gossip, unfortunately. It was true.

James was in a fit of indecision. He left Hiram for the summer and decided to enter Williams College in Williamston, Massachusetts. He did not write Lucretia for weeks, and she was in a fever of anxiety about where their love stood. James was working very hard at college, but he was also questioning his feelings for "Crete." (He now referred to his fiancee by this shortened version of her name.)

To help pay his college expenses, James had begun preaching the gospel part-time. The ladies in his congregation found him more attractive than average, and one of the women members deliberately arranged for her best friend, Rebecca Selleck, to entice James into a flaming affair.

James did not resist Rebecca's seduction very enthusiastically. If he couldn't be with the one he loved, he would love the one he was with. Rebecca knew he was officially engaged to Crete, but neither James nor Rebecca allowed this to be a barrier. Rebecca was an exuberant, exciting lover, and James was totally enthralled and confused.

Their affair continued at Williamston all that winter, and they went to spend three glorious weeks together at Rebecca's home near Norwalk, Ohio. James wrote Crete he had a new friend, and he knew she and Rebecca would love each other when they met!

Crete was not stupid by any means. She knew things were not right between her and James, but she hoped that when they saw each other again, all their old love for each other would come flooding back.

With this happy prospect in mind, Crete jumped at the chance to visit with James in the home of Rebecca's conniving friend at Poestenkill, New York. Rebecca's friend, still pushing the relationship, arranged for James and Rebecca to spend a month together before Crete arrived.

The tryst had the effect Rebecca and her friend had hoped. When James and Crete were together again, there was no joy in their reunion. James was distant and offhand with Crete, and Crete knew the problem still existed, but she had no idea what was wrong.

After she returned home Crete wrote James, "How many, many times have I felt that if you would only love me just enough to come and tell me all, I could endure to know the worst; but to see you shrink away from me as though you could not endure my presence, and hide from me the truth, was almost more than I could bear."

As for Rebecca, Lucretia had not liked her at all, and then she felt guilty because James said he wanted Crete to love her "as a sister." Crete had unwisely confided in Rebecca about her anxiety when James was cold and distant to her, never dreaming that Rebecca was the cause and that Rebecca was doing all she could to take James away from Crete.

Why did James not just break off with Crete and marry Rebecca? It was the prudish streak in his personality — the one Crete had noticed many years before — that made him consider his love for Rebecca to be sinful and profane. He felt Crete was the one meant to be his wife.

Another reason he hesitated to dump Crete was that he hoped to become principal of the Eclectic Institute. Mr. Rudolph, Crete's father, still was in a position of great influence at the school, and James knew he might as well forget ever being principal if he did not marry Crete, since he had asked her. So at last he left Rebecca and went with Crete back to Ohio.

Back in Hiram and teaching again at the Eclectic Institute, James was almost constantly in a black mood. He missed Rebecca, he was sorry he had proposed to Crete, and it appeared the present principal of the school had no intention of leaving anytime soon. Crete was teaching school in nearby Ravenna, but he saw her only on weekends.

The principal did finally leave, and James became the top administrator, but not before tales were spread which caused much bitterness about his various love interests. Almeda Booth had reentered his life, and he did nothing to turn her away.

At last James confessed to Crete that he and Rebecca had been much closer than friends while he was in Massachusetts. Crete was stunned by his revelation. She decided to go to Cleveland for awhile, forget James and get on with her life. Romance with James was decidedly more difficult than she had expected, and she was tired of the whole mess. She told James if he wanted to marry Rebecca, he was released from their engagement.

While Crete applied herself to her studies of art and music in Cleveland, James returned to Rebecca for another romantic interlude, but this time it was short-lived. He told her their relationship was over and he planned to marry Crete.

On November 11, 1858, with their families and friends present, Crete married James in her father's home. Following the wedding they went to live in a nearby boarding house — also the home of Almeda Booth! In fact, her room was beside theirs.

James was still serving as principal at the Eclectic Institute, and Almeda was teaching there. They spent much time together through necessity, as Almeda helped James prepare for debates on current topics, one of which was evolution. But if Almeda was a problem for Crete, she became decidedly less so as two changes occurred in the Garfields' life that left little time for worries about outsiders: Crete became pregnant, and James entered politics.

James had always had a talent as a gripping, forceful, interesting speaker, which had helped him in his career as a preacher. Now this same talent helped him win a seat in the Ohio State Legislature, the youngest member ever elected to that governing body. Politics would become James's new mistress, and Crete would never be free of this one. If he ever had any involvement with another woman after he married Crete, there is no record of it.

When James went to Columbus to serve in the state Senate, he roomed with a fellow Senator while Crete stayed reluctantly behind in Hiram. When James later became embroiled in the campaign to secure the Republican nomination for Abraham Lincoln for President, Almeda and another friend from Eclectic days, Harry Rhodes, went with James on a tour of the Great Lakes region while Crete stayed home to care for their newborn daughter, Eliza Arabella Garfield.

James was pleased with his new daughter, and promptly nicknamed her "Trot." The little girl seemed to provide the bonding their marriage needed, and outsiders and their lives had less importance to James. He rejoiced when Lincoln was nominated, and scoffed at the idea that any Southern states would actually secede from the Union.

When the Civil War began (despite James's predictions), he organized a volunteer company to fight for the Union. He was commissioned a colonel, which made his Disciples of Christ brethren unhappy with his actions. He broke some longtime ties of friendship when he spoke at one of their gatherings and endorsed the desirability of fighting to defend the American government from destruction from within. Since the sect was more pacifist than aggressive in beliefs, his arguments failed to persuade them to adopt his viewpoint, and Garfield never preached for them again.

Crete took little Trot back to Hiram to live with her parents when James left to fight. She and Almeda Booth had become good friends. They visited other mutual friends together and pursued their shared interest in painting. They went on frequent excursions through the area to find suitable subjects for their artistic efforts.

James became ill with typhoid fever in the field and was forced to return home to recover. While he was there, he and Crete seemed to fall really in love for the first time. Perhaps it was a combination of his serious illness and long absence from home, but Crete responded to him openly and freely for the first time, as Rebecca had done years before. Before he left again for Washington, Crete was pregnant for the second time, and she felt more secure in their relationship than she ever had.

On his way to Washington, James stopped off to visit Rebecca. Crete was crushed by what she saw as his betrayal of her and of their love, but this time he paid Rebecca only a friendly visit. He was still interested in his old friends and how they were faring in the war.

James was nominated and elected to the United States Congress in 1862, while he was still serving in the Union army. He returned to duty and fought in the battle at Chickamauga. His rank as Brigadier General gave him much personal satisfaction and a badly needed boost to his self-esteem. Bad soldiers did not win promotions, which he knew well.

Since it was uncertain when James would get to come back home, Crete rented a home for the children and her to live in across from the cricket field of Eclectic Institute. It was a humble little two-story house, needing repairs and enlarging, but it was a start. Crete bought furniture and fixed it up as attractively as she could. James got leave to come home at Christmas, and he was so thrilled with their new home that he made arrangements to buy it. For the next nine years the little house was home for the Garfields.

James represented Ohio in the United States Congress for seven years, following the end of the Civil War. He made the annual trip to Washington, leaving Crete and their five children in Hiram at times. At other times they stayed in a boarding house. In 1869 they built a home in Washington.

Their first child, Trot, died of diphtheria just before James began his service in Congress. Crete and James were heartbroken at her death. She had been a sweet child with a lively personality and a fierce independence.

Another daughter, Mary, was born as time passed, as well as five sons, one of whom also died when young. Three of the boys were born in their new home in Washington. The children were lively and often in trouble for misdeeds, but interesting and perfectly normal.

Garfield was always a strong supporter of educational proposals, but he was adamantly opposed to women being given the right to vote. He had not changed much in his attitude toward women's rights since he had disagreed so sharply with Crete over her public speaking at the commencement at the Eclectic Institute so many years before.

In Washington Crete and James attended literary society meetings, visited with mutual congenial friends and read to their children and each other.

In 1880 James was elected President of the United States. Their move into the White House was made easier with the help of a loyal staff of servants, who had remained from the Hayes administration.

James's mother, Eliza, came to live with the family now. She loved living in Washington. She was eighty years old, and was the first mother of a President to attend her son's inauguration. She was very interested in the government's workings. When she had spent time with James and his family earlier, she had attended the impeachment trial of Andrew Johnson and many sessions in both the House and Senate.

Eliza and Crete loved each other. Crete was always good to her mother-in-law and gave her every consideration.

As James settled into his new job as President, he was appalled by the large number of people who expected to be rewarded with political jobs for their support of him during his campaign.

Crete became seriously ill in May 1881, and for the first time James realized how much he depended on her level-headed assessment of problems. He remarked that she rose "to every new emergency with fine tact and faultless taste."

On July 2, 1881, James left on a trip to the New England area, accompanied by his sons, Jim and Hal. He intended to introduce them to his alma mater, Williams College. Crete was still recuperating in New Jersey, but planned to join them in the afternoon as their train passed through New Jersey.

In the Washington depot, an unhappy lawyer named Charles J. Guiteau shot James in the back as he and his sons waited to board the train for their trip to New England. Guiteau had expected a political appointment for his support of Garfield and had decided that if Vice President Chester Arthur were President, his chances of getting an appointment would be better.

Doctors tried to remove the one bullet which had lodged deeply in James's back, but they could not find it. Sanitation standards were poor, and James developed a serious infection in the wound. Crete read to him daily and tried to help him keep up his spirits, but it was no use. He was never able even to lift his head from his pillow.

Washington was suffering from the usual summer heat, and the doctors decided perhaps James would do better at the seashore in New Jersey. Crete, his mother and the children went with him when he was moved.

He may have been more comfortable, but he was too ill to recover. James died on September 19, 1881, at age forty-nine. He had served only seven months as President. He was buried in Lakeview Cemetery in Cleveland, Ohio.

About five years earlier James had bought a farm in Mentor, Ohio, twenty miles from Cleveland. He and his sons enjoyed the hard work they had done in rebuilding the farm and restoring the run-down farmhouse so it was fit for habitation. Their efforts had been successful, and there was now a comfortable three-story house on the farm. It was to this house that Crete came to live for the rest of her life.

Crete was deeply grieved by her terrible loss, but she found comfort in her religion and maintained her interest in the lives of her children and grandchildren. She led a private but busy life for thirty-six more years after James's death.

At Lakeview Cemetery a memorial honoring James was erected in 1885 at a cost of two hundred twenty-five thousand dollars. As time passed and the excitement caused by the assassination faded from the mind of the American public, Crete felt James and his accomplishments would be lost to future scholars of history, so she set about preserving records of his career.

Crete was justly proud of her children's achievements, too. One son, Harry, was named President of Williams College and served for over ten years. Another son, also named James, served as a conservationist in Theodore Roosevelt's Cabinet. The Garfield daughter, Mary, married her father's presidential secretary, Joseph Stanley Brown.

Congress awarded Crete a lump sum of twenty-five thousand dollars, with an additional pension of five thousand dollars annually. Sympathetic citizens raised about three hundred fifty thousand dollars for her and her children.

Crete died on March 14, 1918, at her home and is buried beside James in Lakeview Cemetery in Cleveland.

22. Ellen Lewis Herndon Arthur

Ellen Lewis Herndon was born into an exciting, adventurous family, most of whom were involved in fascinating pursuits. She was born on August 30, 1837, in a little Virginia town named Culpepper Court House. Her father, William Lewis Herndon, was a lieutenant in the United States Navy at the time. Her mother, Elizabeth Frances Hansbrough, was a domineering, aristocratic Washington socialite.

When Ellen was still a young child, her father was assigned to Washington, D.C., to help Ellen's uncle, Lieutenant Matthew Fontaine Maury, develop the United States Naval Observatory there for the study of oceanography.

Ellen's family was close-knit, with all the members having a strong sense of family. She and her parents made frequent visits to aunts, uncles and cousins as she grew up.

Ellen's father led an Amazon River exploring expedition when Ellen was fourteen, at which time he was gone for several months. When he returned he submitted an extensive report of his findings to the Secretary of the Navy, which was published by Congress.

At age sixteen Ellen was invited by her Uncle Matthew Maury to accompany him, with his two daughters and another cousin on a trip to Europe. Ellen was thrilled with the offer, and she and her cousins enjoyed their trip immensely. Lieutenant Maury attended a naval conference in Brussels, Belgium, while the girls played tourist. Ellen developed a lifelong love for travel from this experience.

While they lived in Washington, Ellen and her parents attended St. John's Episcopal Church on Lafayette Square. There Ellen's lovely contralto singing voice attracted attention, and she was asked to join the choir, which she did.

In 1856 Ellen and her parents moved to New York City. Her father had accepted a position as commander of a mail-carrying steamship, and New York was his home port.

Ellen's cousin, Dabney Herndon, was a frequent visitor in the Herndon home, as he was a medical student in New York. On one of his visits he brought along his friend Chester Arthur, a young New York lawyer.

Ellen Arthur. (Courtesy Library of Congress.)

Ellen and Chester formed a quick attachment to each other. Both were physically attractive, and they made a handsome couple. Ellen was small-boned, dark-haired and sweet-natured. Chester was more than six feet tall, had dark eyes and brown hair. He fully fitted the description of "tall, dark and handsome." Within a year the two were engaged. Ellen was almost twenty, and Chester was twenty-seven.

Before the couple could complete their wedding plans, Ellen's father was killed when his ship sank in a vicious storm off the North Carolina coast at Cape Hatteras. The ship, loaded with mail and passengers, had left Havana in Cuba en route to New York a few days before on September 7,

1857. When the ship ran into the storm, Commander Herndon had all the passengers evacuated in lifeboats. When the crew returned for him, he ordered them to come no closer as the ship was sinking and he was afraid the boat the crew was in would be engulfed by the waves. He was standing on the bridge in full uniform when the ship disappeared into the angry sea. No other lives were lost.

To honor this immensely courageous man, a memorial shaft was erected in Commander Herndon's memory at Annapolis, and Congress ordered a medal struck in his honor. New York City citizens gave Mrs. Herndon a house to live in on West 21st Street. She and Ellen lived there for a time.

Ellen postponed her and Chester's wedding until she and her mother could recover emotionally from their terrible loss. She and Chester were finally married on October 25, 1859, in Calvary Church, which was near their home.

Chester and Ellen went on a two-week honeymoon before returning to live with her mother. Chester was a partner in a struggling law firm with a partner named Henry D. Gardiner. Ellen and Chester lived with Mrs. Herndon until the Civil War started in April 1861.

The year before the war began, Chester joined the militia, comparable to today's National Guard. The Governor of New York expressed a desire to have an official military staff for various state ceremonies, and Chester liked the Governor and wanted to help him achieve his wish. Chester had previously worked in the Governor's campaign for election, so the Governor named him engineer-in-chief of the brigade. During his militia service Chester and Ellen lived in a family hotel, which was well furnished and comfortable.

If it had not been for the Civil War, Chester's militia duties would have been more honorary than tiring. As the war did start, he worked long and hard arranging for housing, food, and transport, for the soldiers from New York State who had been recruited to defend the Union.

Chester wanted to go on active duty, and he requested that he be replaced in his militia post. The Governor told him he was much more valuable where he was and refused to replace him.

Chester's brother, William, was a commissioned officer and was involved in battles for the Union army. Their sister, Malvina, had married a Southerner named Henry Haynesworth, who was a Confederate government official. For part of the war Malvina and her husband lived in Petersburg, Virginia. When General Grant advanced on Richmond, Henry was in danger. Malvina wrote her brother William, "If Grant has got Petersburg mined...I hope you will contrive to let Henry know. I don't want him blown up." In another Malvina said, "I don't care how soon you take Petersburg, but *don't hurt Henry.*"

Ellen Arthur's sympathies were with the Southern states also, although she supported Chester publicly in his efforts. Chester knew well where her loyalties were, and referred lightly to his "little rebel wife."

Both Ellen and Chester were distressed when Dabney Herndon became a prisoner of war at Gettysburg. Ellen visited Dabney in prison, but no publicity was attracted by her kindness to her cousin. Ellen's mother did not hesitate to express her Southern sympathy and spent most of the war years in Europe.

Ellen's and Chester's little son, William Lewis, born just before the Civil War began, died at age three while the family was vacationing in Englewood, New Jersey. Both parents were deeply grieved by the loss of their beloved child, and Ellen found comfort in her religious faith. Chester could not find comfort in this way as he refused to accept any church teaching as authority. The next year, in 1864, another son was born to them, whom they named Chester Alan Arthur.

At last the terrible Civil War ended, and with it came an end to division in families' loyalties. Old wounds and deep resentments gradually were forgotten. Chester's sister Malvina and her Henry stayed with Ellen and Chester for a time in New York while Henry tried to find a job; however, Henry's prior Confederate activities prevented his obtaining a job worthy of his talents.

Dabney Herndon and his wife also visited in the Arthur home. Dabney had been reconciled by the fact Ellen and Chester did all they could for him while he was a prisoner of the Union forces during the "late unpleasantness," as some Southerners referred to the Civil War.

Chester's fortunes continued to improve during Reconstruction. He and his partner, Henry Gardiner, resumed law practice together, and their practice greatly increased. With things going so well, Ellen and Chester moved their household to a better home in a better neighborhood, which more nearly reflected Ellen's ambitions for their future.

Ellen regained her optimism, entered enthusiastically into decorating their new home fashionably, and had elegant parties and dinners for their prominent social and intellectual friends. Christmas was always a time for lavish decorations, expensive toys for little Alan and diamonds from Tiffany's for Ellen.

Ellen was not well educated, and her attention centered chiefly on domestic concerns involving her husband, his career and her children.

Now that the world was returning to normal, as Ellen saw it, she renewed her musical efforts also. She often sang for their guests and for elite society fund-raisers. She joined the new Mendelssohn Glee Club, and sometimes sang with them in their concerts.

Ellen and Chester added a little girl to their family in 1871, and they named her Ellen for her mother. Ellen was delighted to have a little daughter

whom she could dress in the latest fashions for children, and she looked forward to having young Ellen share some of her own interests as the child
grew older. The Arthurs' life was pleasant and happy, although Ellen still
had higher ambitions for her husband than had been realized.

During each summer's heat, the Arthurs left New York and went to
the country, where Chester could fish, Ellen could shop, read and play with
the children, and they could all get a refreshing break from their daily rou-
tines.

Chester accepted a post as Collector of Customs for the Port of New
York while little Ellen was still a baby. It was a political appointment by
a grateful President Grant for Chester's work on behalf of the Republican
political organization in New York City. The new job paid well, and it appeared the future was brighter than it had ever been.

The new position carried heavy responsibility. During the time
Chester served as Collector, over eight hundred and sixty million dollars
was received, and only forty million was spent. Chester was scrupulously
honest and allowed no graft or dipping into the receipts by anyone, which
had not been true of all the previous collectors.

During these years, Chester devoted most of his time and interest to
machine politics, which he felt necessary to keep his well-paying post. As
time passed, this caused some severe problems with his and Ellen's marriage. He rarely got home before two or three o'clock in the morning. Now
they went nowhere together. Occasionally Ellen attended an opera accompanied by an elderly friend, but this was the extent of her recreation. Was
the larger salary and greater prestige worth this drastic change in their
family life?

Chester made enemies along the way, even among fellow Republicans.
When Democrats claimed he was dishonest, Chester was let go after serving
eight years. The charges were later proved to be entirely untrue, but the
damage was done.

Ellen stood loyally by her husband during the dark days of the charges
against his honesty, and was as happy as he when he was cleared of any
wrongdoing. Chester still enjoyed being a part of the political scene, and
hoped to be a candidate for the Senate in the upcoming election in 1880,
when there would be a vacancy.

Chester was in Albany, working on the campaign of a friend who
hoped to be Speaker of the House, when he received a message that Ellen
was critically ill at their home with pneumonia. It was January 11, 1880,
bitterly cold and snowing heavily. Passenger service on trains was curtailed
on Sundays, and he was forced to travel the long way to Ellen's bedside by
milk train.

Chester found Ellen's condition had worsened when he got home. Less
than twenty-four hours later, she died. Chester was profoundly shocked

and deeply grieved. She was only forty-three years old, and they had just begun to rebuild their close relationship.

An Arthur friend said, "Mrs. Arthur was a very ambitious woman. There was no happier woman in the country than she when her husband was made Collector of the Port of New York. Her address book contained the names of New York society's most elite members from Theodore Roosevelt, father of the future President, to William Vanderbilt."

Many prominent people attended Ellen's funeral at the Church of the Heavenly Rest, where she had been a member. The Mendelssohn Glee Club furnished music for the services in her honor, although this was not usually done by the group. She was buried in the Rural Cemetery near Albany, beside Chester's parents and her own baby son.

Chester devoted most of his time for the next few months to politics to help get his mind off his loss. He was astonished when he was asked to be a candidate for Vice President on the national ticket with Presidential candidate James A. Garfield. He accepted the offer, and felt his sadness return as he thought of how pleased Ellen would have been if she could have shared the honor with him. Chester and James Garfield were elected.

After serving only four months as President, James A. Garfield was shot by an assassin and died in September 1881. Chester was inaugurated as the twenty-first President of the United States.

He asked his sister, Mary McElroy, to serve as his official White House hostess. Mary also assumed the care of Chester's and Ellen's ten-year-old daughter. Their son, Alan, was now a student at Princeton.

Chester still grieved for and missed Ellen. He had fresh flowers placed on a table beside her photograph each day while he served as President. He never remarried.

He also gave a stained-glass window to St. John's Church in Washington where Ellen had been a member. The window depicted Resurrection angels, and at night he could see them from the White House when church lights were on.

Chester tried to be a good President and was largely successful. He was instrumental in the passage of the Civil Service Act, which gave job security to government employees when administrations changed. He called a conference which led to the establishment of standard time zones in the United States.

Chester felt the White House needed refurbishing, and he had it redecorated in art nouveau or Victorian style by Louis Tiffany from New York. In the process of his improvements, twenty-four wagonloads of White House furnishings and accessories were sold at auction, some irreplaceable.

He had the unique problem of coping with a large surplus in the National Treasury, which had accumulated through years of heavy taxation by other Presidents. He wanted to cut taxes, but both branches of Congress refused to consider such a move. He suggested that the extra money be used to improve education in the nation by distributing funds to the states to be spent for this purpose. Again Congress refused to approve such a move. He then asked to have the surplus applied to the national debt, and this was done.

Because Chester had angered influential Republican party bosses in New York when he was Customs Collector, the members of his party would not support him in a bid to be elected President in his own right. He had refused to make unwise job appointments at the Port, and this was the Republicans' way of getting even with him. Democratic candidate Grover Cleveland won the election of 1884.

Chester left office in March 1885 and went back to live in New York. The next year he developed both heart and kidney problems, and died on November 17, 1886. He was buried beside his beloved Ellen.

23. Frances Folsom Cleveland

When Frances Folsom was born on July 21, 1864, in Buffalo, New York, her father's law partner, Grover Cleveland, came to see the new baby and bought her a baby carriage as a gift. As little Frances grew from babyhood into a chubby, attractive little girl, Grover Cleveland was an ever-present part of her life.

Frances, now better known as "Frankie," was eleven years old when her father, Oscar Folsom, was killed when he was thrown from the horse-drawn buggy in which he was riding. From that time on, Grover Cleveland assumed a protective role in Frankie's life and that of her mother. He advised Mrs. Folsom on business matters and interested himself in Frankie's education. He was deeply grieved by the death of his good friend, and perhaps this was his way of honoring his law partner by making the life of Folsom's family easier.

Grover always seemed to enjoy little Frankie's company, even before her father died. He baby-sat with his younger sisters when he was growing up, and he apparently liked children. He was very active in a sports club in Buffalo, known as the Beaver Island Club, and members remembered seeing Grover leading chubby little Frankie by her hand on walks through the grounds.

Grover was not a "goody two-shoes," but a tough, hard-drinking, rowdy barroom fighter, especially during his younger years. His father was a minister who died just as Grover reached maturity, leaving Grover the only source of support for his mother and the five younger Cleveland children. Grover supported them all uncomplainingly for many years, and the saloon visits may have been his way of letting off tension. He also did not marry for many years, since he could not support a wife and family as long as he had his mother and his brothers and sisters to care for.

As years passed, a sister asked Grover when he planned to marry. He told her he was "waiting for my wife to grow up." This remark was probably made in jest to quiet a nosy sister, but it was prophetic.

Frankie did well during her years at Central High School in Buffalo, and she entered Wells College in Aurora, New York, after graduation. While she was in college, Grover asked her mother if he could correspond

179

Frances Cleveland. (Artist: Anders Zorn. Courtesy National Portrait Gallery, Smithsonian Institution.)

with Frankie, which led to a frequent exchange of letters between the young college girl and the older man. He often sent Frankie flowers, and he invited her and Mrs. Folsom to visit him in Albany, where he served as Governor of New York from 1882 to 1884.

In 1884 Grover was nominated to run for President of the United States. During the grueling campaign, it was revealed that Grover was the father of an illegitimate ten-year-old son by a barmaid. He was elected despite this revelation and was inaugurated the next year.

Shortly after Grover took office, Frankie and her mother went on a visit to the White House, where Grover's sister, Rose, was serving as his official hostess. They stayed about ten days, as Frankie was on spring break from Wells. It is probable that Frankie and Grover made plans then to marry.

Frankie returned to college the next year and graduated with a Bachelor of Arts degree, while Rose Cleveland continued to serve as White House hostess.

Newspaper reporters had speculated for some time that Mrs. Folsom might be the lady who would end President Cleveland's bachelorhood, as they were about the same age. Grover was now forty-nine and looked it with his portly figure and full mustache. The reporters were amazed when they learned twenty-one-year-old, slender, beautiful Frankie would be Grover's bride!

Frankie first planned to have the wedding ceremony at the home of her grandfather, who could not attend otherwise as he was very ill. Her grandfather died while she was making her plans, so she and Grover agreed then to have the wedding in the White House.

On June 2, 1886, Frankie and Grover were married in the Blue Room in the presence of their families, members of his Cabinet and a few close friends. Frankie was stunning in her ivory satin wedding dress, which had a fifteen-foot train. Lilies, roses, pansies, ferns and palms were clustered in various rooms and halls throughout the house. The Marine Band, led by John Phillip Sousa, furnished the wedding music. The couple entered together, unaccompanied by attendants. Frankie promised to "love, honor and...keep." Their wedding remains to the present time the only wedding of a President in the White House.

News reporters made the Clevelands' honeymoon and early days of marriage miserable with their constant watching, following and questioning. Shortly before the wedding, Grover had bought some country property, on which an old stone house with large rooms stood. This property was located only about three miles from the White House, and it was a refuge for the newlyweds when duties and social activities in Washington became oppressive. Frankie named their retreat Oak View.

Frankie and Grover settled down happily to a life divided between the quietness of Oak View and the activity of the White House. Both enjoyed working with flowers, and at Oak View they happily trimmed rosebushes and weeded beds.

In the White House they enjoyed the social aspect of the Presidency and the entertaining required, as they enjoyed being with people. Frankie's presence had a softening, polishing effect on Grover. Since she had been reared in a level of society that involved attending and hosting dinners, receptions and balls, Frankie fitted easily into her new role as First Lady and hostess of White House affairs.

At one of the first receptions they held after their wedding, Grover was heard to observe proudly, "She'll do," referring to his new wife, and later, "She's pretty level-headed." That Grover loved Frankie dearly was never doubted by anyone. He doted on her. Once, when they had planned a drive and she was slow in getting dressed, he told a friend that he became annoyed, removed his own coat and decided not to go, to teach Frankie a lesson.

"And did you really not go driving?" the friend asked.

"I didn't say a word after all. I just put on my hat and coat and went," Grover admitted, grinning.

In addition to the many official dinners and receptions held for visiting dignitaries, Frankie held two receptions of her own each week. One was usually held on Wednesday, and the other on Saturday afternoon so working women could attend. Frankie was an outstanding favorite with the American public, and they avidly read all reports about her.

Frankie was straightforward and unaffected in her personality. Shopkeepers all praised her shopping skills, noting that she always knew exactly what she wanted. She loved buying and wearing pretty clothes, and had a special passion for gloves, which were always worn on dress-up occasions by women in that era. She preferred pastel shades and had a large collection of gloves.

On the afternoons she could manage to escape White House duties for a few hours, Frankie enjoyed walking or driving in their carriage in the Oak View neighborhood. She carried pennies with her to give to small children who sold her flowers and danced for her. She found these children enchanting.

Frankie enjoyed telling amusing stories of their family life at social gatherings. She told of Grover buying an orange-brown suit, which set her teeth on edge to look at, but which he insisted on wearing. She was desperate until she happened to think of telling him he would lose the Irish vote if he wore it. That ended the suit problem!

Frankie also enjoyed telling about a tour she and Grover made through the North. Grover was scheduled to make a speech and could not because of a sore throat. Frankie had gone along to let the voters see how she looked, and she had to wear a bandage over one eye because of a stye!

It may have been a deliberate attempt to slander Grover before the Democratic National Convention in 1888, but a minister of the Gospel who had attended a convention in Washington earlier that year told a reporter that Grover was mean and abusive to Frankie. He even said Grover locked Frankie up in a room at times. A woman in Worcester, Massachusetts, read the news report and wrote Frankie to ask if it were true. The woman enclosed a clipping of the slanderous article.

Frankie's reply was:

Executive Mansion, Washington
June 3, 1888

Mrs. Nicodomus,

Dear Madam: I can only say in answer to your letter that every statement made by the Reverend C. H. Pendleton in the interview which you sent me is basely false, and I pity the man of his calling who has been made the tool to give circulation to such wicked and heartless lies. I can wish the women of our country no greater blessing than that their homes and their lives may be as happy and that their husbands may be as kind, attentive, considerate and affectionate as mine.

Very truly, Frances F. Cleveland

Cleveland was not perceived by the American public as a strong President, and it is possible that the wife-beating rumor played a part. For whatever reason, he was defeated in his bid for reelection by Benjamin Harrison. The powerful Tammany group in New York City had turned against Grover, partly because he would not replace Republican job holders with Democrats.

When Grover's term ended, he and Frankie moved to New York City, where he joined the law firm of Bangs, Stetson, Tracy and MacVeagh. He was not a partner, but he attracted clients and stayed busy and happy.

During the four years they lived in New York, the Clevelands' first child, a little girl, was born. They named her Ruth, and the well-known candy bar, Baby Ruth, was named for her.

Grover's feelings had been badly bruised by his defeat four years earlier, but when rival forces appeared likely to assume control of the Democrat party in 1892, Grover agreed to accept the nomination for President, if it was offered. The subsequent election of Grover to a second term provided justification for Frankie's remark she made to one of the White House servants as the Clevelands moved out the first time. "I want you to take good care of all the furniture and ornaments in the house...We are coming back just four years from today," she had said. Sure enough, on March 4, 1893, Grover Cleveland was inaugurated for a second term as President.

The Clevelands, now three in number, settled down, glad to be living again in the White House. The servants were glad to have Baby Ruth to play with and provide with treats.

Grover had sold Oak View, so this time they had no country home, but he leased another house in the same neighborhood as Oak View, known as Woodley.

Baby Ruth was taken out on the White House lawn for air, and many women found good reasons to pass by and hug the baby. The crowds grew so large that Frankie was forced to order the gates locked at the south end of the grounds.

A new telephone switchboard system was not the only change in the White House during this term.

On September 9 that year, Ruth was joined by a new sister named Esther, who was the first child born in the White House to an active President and his wife. The two little girls added greatly to Frankie's family duties, but they also added immeasurably to everyone's pleasure.

Frankie resumed her hostess role with grace and dignity. She was young and energetic and managed to cope with the small crises as they arose. Frankie was always sympathetic and considerate to the White House staff, giving them little birthday and Christmas gifts. She always made a point of letting the servants know when she was pleased with their efforts.

One crisis, however, had both Grover and Frankie reeling from shock. Grover discovered a lesion in his mouth just after he returned to the Presidency, which proved to be cancerous. There had been so many adverse news reports about him that Grover elected to keep his illness a secret. He had major facial surgery performed on a yacht in Bellevue Bay in New York, while the public was told he was having some dental work done. All of the left side of his face was removed up to the eye socket, and ever after he had to use a vulcanized rubber mouth prosthesis in order to talk.

Grover faced national financial woes during this administration, which failed to yield to his best efforts. He used force against workers in labor disputes, which earned him their intense enmity, and his attempts at tariff reform failed. His health was less robust since his surgery, and all in all he began to look forward to the time he could leave Washington for good.

The Clevelands' family continued to grow. Another daughter, Marion, was born in 1895, and two little sons were born after his term had ended.

They decided to make the town of Princeton, New Jersey, their new home. One reason was that they received a letter from the University of Princeton while they were living in the White House which urged them "to send your sons to Princeton." Since they only had three little girls at the time, the advice was out of the question as given. On consideration, however, Princeton sounded like such a good idea that the whole family went there to live!

For their new home, Frankie found a large stone and stucco colonial mansion called Westland, which they both liked. Among its attractions were spacious grounds for play area for the children.

Both Frankie and Grover felt at home in Princeton, and Grover was named a trustee of the university. He was flattered immensely by the honor, and discharged his duties faithfully and seriously. He became acquainted with Woodrow Wilson, who was president of Princeton. Later Woodrow would become President of the United States, but at this time he had not yet entered politics. The Clevelands and the Wilsons attended church together.

On January 7, 1904, Baby Ruth Cleveland died of diphtheria. Frankie and Grover were both nearly crushed by their terrible loss. Grover's health began a steady decline, possibly from his grief. He read much of the time now, was often confined to his bed and was forced to curtail active pursuits.

Grover died on June 24, 1908, of heart and kidney failure at his home in Princeton. He was buried in his adopted New Jersey town.

Grover left his family comfortably fixed financially with about three hundred thousand dollars in assets. He had written of his desire to "make everything snug" for Frankie and the children, all of whom he loved deeply.

Frankie remained a widow during the years the children were growing up. In 1913 she married a professor of archeology at Princeton, named Thomas J. Preston, Jr. President and Mrs. William Taft entertained with a dinner in her honor at the White House on January 11, 1913, which she seemed to appreciate and enjoy.

Frankie continued her gracious entertaining on a smaller scale and was a noted Princeton resident until her death on October 29, 1947, at age eighty-four. She was buried in Princeton also.

24. Caroline Lavinia Scott Harrison

Caroline Lavinia Scott, almost always called Carrie, was born October 1, 1832, in Oxford, Ohio. Her parents, Dr. and Mrs. John Witherspoon Scott, believed in rearing their children to be responsible and insisted that both sons and daughters be well educated. Dr. Scott was a Presbyterian minister and deeply involved with education. He was a teacher at Farmers' College in Cincinnati while Carrie was growing up.

One of Dr. Scott's students was a young man named Benjamin Harrison. Benjamin was a serious-minded, hard-working young man, and was well liked by his teachers and fellow students alike.

Benjamin and Carrie were acquainted and became good friends during these years. There was no real romance, but they were each there for the other in times of trial or trouble. When Ben's mother died in his last year at Farmers', Carrie was by his side comforting him.

Ben went on to become a student at the University of Miami of Ohio, in 1850. This school is located in Oxford, Ohio, also the site of Oxford Female College. Dr. Scott became president of the Oxford Female College, also in 1850, and Ben and Carrie found themselves once again in the same neighborhood.

They became aware that their former friendship had blossomed into love. Even though both would be expected to complete their educations before they could marry, Ben and Carrie became engaged.

Their engagement spurred Ben to study harder and more than ever before. He had decided he wanted to be a lawyer, but his father told him sadly he could not afford to keep Ben in school any longer as the family's financial conditions had worsened.

At the end of that school year, Ben began working as an apprentice in a Cincinnati law firm. Carrie was working to complete her education at Oxford Female College, so they had to continue their romance by means of a lively correspondence.

Fate conspired to help the young couple when Ben's father, John Scott Harrison, was elected to serve in the United States House of Represen-

Caroline Harrison. (Courtesy Library of Congress.)

tatives from Hamilton County, Ohio. Ben's grandfather, former President William H. Harrison, would have been pleased to know his son was also interested in politics, if he had lived to see it.

John Harrison did not want to leave his motherless children alone while he served in Congress, so when Ben suggested hopefully that he and Carrie could go ahead with their wedding and then take care of the younger children, his father agreed. Ben and Carrie were married on October 20, 1853, and went to live with Ben's brothers and sisters at The Point, the family home which was located at the merging point of the Ohio and Miami rivers.

Carrie and Ben did not care how many other people were around. They were thrilled to be living together at last. Ben's family loved Carrie, which made life easier. They were charmed by her pleasant nature and her willingness to do the work required to take care of the family. They told her repeatedly they hoped she would never leave. She shunned the question since she did not know where Ben's future as a lawyer might lead them.

The next year Ben was licensed to practice law, and he thought he and Carrie should leave The Point and move to Indianapolis, Indiana, to live. An older brother came to Ben's aid and told their father he would come back and live at The Point so Ben and Carrie would be free to go.

They happily loaded a wagon with boxes of food, cooking utensils and bedclothes and rode to Lawrenceburg, Indiana. There they unloaded the boxes from the wagon onto a railroad car and rode to Indianapolis on the newly built Indiana and Cincinnati Railroad. Despite their excitement at getting to ride on the train, it was a long, exhausting trip, and they were glad when it ended.

Ben found that establishing a new law practice in Indianapolis was slow going. He was young-looking for his age, which did not help inspire prospective clients, and he had no friends or connections to steer people to him. He soon became extremely discouraged as he was earning little money.

Compounding his problems was Carrie's first pregnancy. She was having a difficult time and needed help with the housework. Also her bills for doctors and medicines were mounting faster than Ben's income. When Dr. and Mrs. Scott suggested that Carrie might like to come to Oxford and stay with them until after the baby was born, both Ben and Carrie gladly accepted their offer.

Ben's fortunes in Indianapolis began to improve after Carrie left. He got a job as Crier of Federal Court, which assured him of enough money to pay their bills. With this pressure eased, he began studying to become a trial lawyer.

Ben was working as an assistant to the prosecuting attorney in an important burglary case when he got his big chance. The prosecutor wanted to go to a lecture while the trial was in progress, and he asked Ben to give a summation of the case to the jury. The courtroom light was so dim that Ben could not read the notes he had carefully made, so he had to speak extemporaneously to the jury. All who heard his summation and realized this young man was speaking entirely from memory and his knowledge of the case were impressed by his presentation, and Ben won the decision. From that time on his law practice began to increase.

Ben and Carrie's first child, Russell, a son, was born August 12, 1854. Carrie brought the baby back home to Ben in October. By the beginning of the New Year of 1855, there was a major downturn in the nation's economy, and Ben's law practice again dwindled to almost nothing. Carrie took Baby Russell back to stay with her parents awhile longer.

The little family was reunited in only a few weeks when Ben joined a law firm with the Governor's son, William P. Fishback, as a partner. Mr. Fishback wanted to campaign for the office of County Clerk, and Ben did most of the work of the firm in his partner's absence. He was once again earning enough money to support his wife and child.

After such a rocky financial start, Carrie's and Ben's married life became more settled, and they joined the First Presbyterian Church in Indianapolis. Both were products of Christian homes, and they missed church involvement in their lives. Now they entered gladly into the social activities of the church, and Ben taught a Sunday School class. He soon became involved in working with the Young Men's Christian Association as well.

Ben was elected City Attorney in May 1857, and their income increased once again. Ben began attracting much favorable political attention to himself by working actively in the campaigns of other Republican office seekers.

The next year their second child, a daughter named Mary Scott and called Mamie, was born. Carrie's sister, Elizabeth, had a little girl born almost the same time named Mary Scott Lord. Both girls were named for their Grandmother Scott.

With his family increasing, Ben knew he needed to buy a house. To increase his income, he decided to enter the political race for Supreme Court Reporter. In this job he would issue periodic lengthy publications of Supreme Court decisions, which would then be sold to lawyers, judges and legislators, all over the state. He won the election, but just as he began working at his new job, the Civil War broke out.

At first there were plenty of volunteers in Indiana heeding the call to arms, but by 1862 enthusiasm had lessened. In July 1862, Ben and a former law partner felt obligated to enter the war, and they joined the Union army. Ben had hoped to keep his job as Reporter to support his family, but a Democrat was elected to replace him in his absence.

Ben was away from home for three years, in charge of the Seventieth Indiana Volunteer Infantry, which he had recruited. He returned home a brigadier general and a hero.

At home he found there had been numerous changes. The children were not little any more. Russell was now almost eleven, and Mamie was eight. Ben felt sadly that he had missed an important part of their childhood years. Their city of Indianapolis had also grown considerably, and there was bustling activity and growth everywhere.

Carrie and Ben were delighted that the war had ended and they were back together again. Ben went back to teaching the young men's Sunday

School class, and Carrie was now a teacher of a children's class. They rejoined friends and neighbors in church socials and dinners, as well as occasionally attending the theater or opera. Life for them was resuming a normal, happy pattern.

Ben was reelected to his job as Supreme Court Reporter, he resumed his habit of working diligently in his law practice and he now accepted the many speaking engagements he was offered. After two years of living at top-speed activity, however, his health began to suffer, and he was forced to take a long vacation.

Carrie and Ben took their children to Minnesota, where they spent several weeks living in a cabin by a lake. He had time to become reacquainted with his children, and he and Carrie rediscovered the quiet joy they felt in just being together.

In 1872 Ben toyed with the idea of campaigning for the office of Governor of Indiana, but he knew it would be stressful and he feared another health breakdown. His father flatly advised Ben against trying it.

With this advice reaffirming his own hesitancy, Ben decided it would be better to continue with his now lucrative law practice. When he did run in 1876 for Governor, he was defeated.

The Harrisons built a beautiful, large home in a good residential neighborhood in Indianapolis, Ben's law practice continued to thrive, both children were now college students, and it seemed Ben had it all. However, Ben could never completely put the lure and challenge of seeking a political office from his mind. His father continued to discourage him vehemently from such a course of action.

Although this time Carrie's and Ben's finances had suffered relatively little, the United States as a whole had been in the midst of a severe depression for the past four years.

In June 1877, Carrie and Ben left on a vacation trip East to pick up their son and daughter at their colleges, go on to visit Carrie's sister, Elizabeth, and her family in Honesdale, Pennsylvania, and go on to Washington. Russell was graduating from Lafayette, and Mamie had completed her second year in college.

Since Ben had spent many hours making campaign speeches for President Rutherford B. Hayes, which helped Hayes win the election, the family would visit President and Mrs. Hayes in the White House before their return home.

They had a pleasant, relaxed trip, but returned home to find the state of Indiana in panic because of a widespread railroad strike called by workers, who had had their wages reduced by 10 percent by the various railroads. Indiana Governor Williams, a Democrat, had advocated mobilizing the militia to move against the strikers, which would have probably led to bloodshed. Ben protested such a procedure, saying, "I don't propose to go out and shoot down my neighbors when there is no necessity for it."

Due to Ben's mediation skills and toe-to-toe confrontation with the strikers, the strike was averted. Ben's personal political appeal, as well as the appeal of the Republican party, was enhanced by these events.

Ben spent the next few years urging party reforms and consolidating his position as a leader of the younger Republicans. Carrie was happily engaged in raising strawberries and grapes, taking trips with Mamie, now twenty, and enjoying her increased leisure time. As Mamie told her mother about her various social activities, Carrie relived a little of her own childhood.

Carrie and Mamie had always been close. A few years earlier, Carrie had conspired with some other mothers to arrange for their daughters to learn to dance. The lessons were given by the instructor in various homes. Ben had always indulged Mamie, but he was fiercely determined Mamie should not learn to dance. Carrie was irritated by never-ending ecclesiastical restraint, and she saw nothing wrong with her daughter having dancing lessons, so Mamie learned to dance. If Ben ever knew of Carrie's rebellion against his authority, he never mentioned it.

Carrie went with Ben to Washington when he was elected to serve in the United States Senate, and Mamie came to live with them. They had only been living there a short time when Carrie fell on ice and bruised herself badly. For some time after, her eyes were blackened and she was covered with purple bruises. Ben was alarmed about her at first, but, as she improved, he saw the humorous side. "I have arranged to take the deposition [sworn statement] of the Miller family to prove that it happened away from home," he told a cousin, grinning.

Russell married May Saunders on January 8, 1884, in Omaha, Nebraska. Carrie was too ill to make the trip, but she felt better within a few days. To compensate for her absence at their wedding, Carrie staged an elaborate reception for the newlyweds when they came to Indianapolis on their wedding trip. Mamie married Robert McKee later that same year, in November.

When the Indiana voting districts were rearranged, Ben lost his bid for reelection to the Senate in 1886, so Ben and Carrie soon returned to their home in Indianapolis. Not long after they got home, Mamie presented them with their first grandchild, a little boy named Benjamin Harrison McKee, who would be called Baby McKee for a number of years. This event cheered Ben and Carrie considerably, and they were glad to be back home.

In 1888, the leading Presidential contender for the nomination of the Republicans chose not to run and named Ben as his choice to replace him. Ben won the election in the Electoral College, even though incumbent Grover Cleveland had more popular votes. Ben had conducted a very low-key campaign, referred to as a "front-porch campaign," during which he spoke to prospective voters from his front porch, and allowed the Republican professional politicians to conduct the larger campaign.

Now Carrie and Ben would spend the next four years in the White House. Carrie assumed her position as First Lady as if to the manor born.

Carrie had not lived in the White House long before she decided a new house was needed to replace the Executive Mansion. The White House was in a deplorably run-down condition. Plans were completed and a model constructed for a new house to be built on Sixteenth Street, which was even called "Mrs. Harrison's place," but the newspapers began a campaign against the project, as they considered the present White House an historic landmark.

When sentiment overcame the practicality of the plan, Carrie went to work on improving the old building's livability as much as possible. She had new bathrooms, a new kitchen and new floors put in. Electric lights and service bells were installed for the first time. She also selected the first official china dinnerware for the White House, which began the historical collection of White House china.

Carrie held elegant dinners and receptions, often with Mamie McKee's assistance. Mamie and her family lived in the White House during much of Ben's term.

Carrie became involved with charitable work, and threw her energies into successful fund-raisers for Johns Hopkins University and Medical School, "on the condition it admit women" as students. She also served as the first President General of the organization of the Daughters of the American Revolution.

Carrie's niece, Mary Scott Lord Dimmick, joined the household in 1890 as her Aunt Carrie's secretary and general helper with First Lady duties.

In Ben's fourth year as President, Carrie's health began to fail. Mamie and her family, as well as Mary Dimmick, assumed the household and entertaining duties Carrie could no longer fulfill. Mary Dimmick served now as a part-time nurse for her aunt.

Carrie had tuberculosis. She traveled for a time to the Adirondacks in an attempt to restore her health, but returned to the White House no better for the trip. Ben sat by her bedside night after sleepless night as she declined steadily all summer. She died October 25, 1892, and was buried in Crown Hill Cemetery in Indianapolis.

Grover Cleveland was reelected President in the election held about the time of Carrie's death, defeating Ben in his bid for a second term. Ben was so numbed by the death of his beloved Carrie, he felt no hurt. "Political defeat carries no personal grief," he said.

Ben dreaded going back to Indianapolis without Carrie, but when he arrived, Mamie and her two children were waiting for him. He spent the next three years writing political articles, practicing law part-time, and became an officer for the Presbyterian Church on the national level.

He would remarry later, and the account of the rest of his life, as well as that of his second wife, is found in the following chapter.

25. Mary Scott Lord Dimmick Harrison

Mary Scott Lord was born April 30, 1858, in Honesdale, Pennsylvania. Her father, Russell Farnham Lord, was an engineer and manager of the Delaware and Hudson Canal Company. Her mother, Elizabeth Scott, was a sister of Carrie Harrison, wife of United States President Benjamin F. Harrison.

Mary was born the same year as her cousin, Mamie Harrison. The two little girls were as close in their relationship as the distance between their homes allowed. Mamie Harrison spent her early years in Indiana, while Mary Lord lived in several different states in the Northeast. In summers, the Harrisons visited the Lords. When Benjamin first began his campaigns for public office, the Lords took an active, interested part in his efforts.

As a girl, Mary attended Mrs. Moffatt's School in Princeton, New Jersey, their home for a time. In 1876 there was a huge Centennial celebration in nearby Philadelphia, during which the Lord family entertained many friends and relatives from Indiana, including Benjamin and Carrie Harrison and their children.

In late October of that year, Benjamin was campaigning to be Governor of Indiana and made a speech at the Centennial. Mary, her sister, Lizzy, and Mamie Harrison were in the audience, and every time Benjamin mentioned Indiana, the little girls cheered.

When she finished Mrs. Moffatt's School, Mary went on to Elmira College in Elmira, New York. There she met and married Walter Erskine Dimmick. Mr. Dimmick, a New York lawyer, lived only a short time after their marriage, dying in January 1882. They had no children.

When Benjamin Harrison ran for President in 1888, again his nieces were active in the campaign. In a letter to her mother, Mary Dimmick described the typical campaign events at the Harrison home: "Little Benjamin [Baby McKee, Harrison's grandson] looked all eyes and ears and someone took him where he could see and hear them. Uncle Ben and Aunt Carrie stood by the front door.... After a little while little boys passed through the house shaking hands and little Benjamin held out his hand so

Mary Harrison. (Courtesy Library of Congress.)

many shook hands with him also. Cheers upon cheers went up continuously until Uncle Ben spoke, and then, as always, you could have heard
a pin drop." Mary Dimmick was plainly impressed by Uncle Ben's
popularity.

Ben was elected President, and following his inauguration in 1889,
Mary and Lizzy Lord Parker, her sister, went to Europe on a sightseeing
tour. While they were away, their mother became seriously ill, and Carrie
Harrison and Mamie went to be with her in her home in New York. Mamie
was now Mamie McKee, and had two children.

Ben wrote Mary in Europe that he missed the McKee children badly when they were away. "It is a meager comfort only to hear from them," he said.

In early November 1889, Ben again wrote Mary, "Your Aunt Carrie did not return yesterday as I expected, and I am for another Sunday the sole occupant of this big house [the White House] — about which I wander without any sense of its being a home." Ben was indulging in self-pity after spending a tiring day working on his first annual report to Congress.

Mary's mother died about two weeks later, and Mary came to live in the White House. She had not remarried and was now thirty years old. Carrie Harrison needed help with her correspondence, charity functions and other duties as First Lady, and she felt Mary would be a help to her.

Mary was at loose ends and was happy to accept her Aunt Carrie's invitation. In Washington she found plenty to occupy her time, and she enjoyed being with her family. The Chief Usher in the White House at that time, Ike Hoover, said Mary often accompanied her Uncle Ben on long afternoon walks into Washington suburbs.

In Ben's last year as President, Carrie developed tuberculosis. Hoping fresh air would restore her, she went to the Adirondacks where she and Ben had spent such happy vacation times when their children were younger. Mary went along with her to take care of her. Mamie McKee stayed behind to serve as official White House hostess for her father. Carrie Harrison died on October 25, 1892, in the White House, and about two weeks later Ben was defeated in his bid for reelection.

Ben returned to Indianapolis. He was fifty-nine years old, in good health, and able to work, so before many weeks had passed, he became restless. He accepted an offer from Stanford University to give a series of lectures. He then resumed his law practice, but pursued it halfheartedly. Then he tried his hand at writing magazine articles, nine of which were published in *The Ladies' Home Journal*. He also wrote a book entitled *This Country of Ours*, expounding on his views. As he settled more into retirement, Mamie and her family, who had been living with him in Indianapolis, returned to their own home.

It is not certain where Mary Dimmick went to live after the Harrisons left the White House, but it is certain she and Ben kept in touch with each other. Ben accepted a national office in the Presbyterian Church when he returned to Indianapolis, and she may have helped him with the duties of this office. Also he had a collection of many official and unofficial documents covering his years in politics, and she may have helped organize these. At any rate, Mary was still somewhere in the picture.

Ben's friends became aware of a pleasant change in his demeanor in 1895. Republican supporters had been urging him to run for President again, and he had steadfastly refused. These supporters now found him "much more approachable" and hoped this was a good sign for their efforts to get him reelected. Others said his sunny mood was "due to love or something else."

It was love—love for Mary. Carrie had been gone for three years, and Ben felt he wanted to have a home of his own again. When he told his children of his plans to marry their cousin, he was surprised and hurt that they reacted so coolly to the idea. In fact, they stated their outright disapproval. They may have feared gossip would start since Mary had lived at the White House before the death of their mother.

Ben was determined to wed Mary. He had loved Carrie dearly and had grieved deeply and sincerely after her death, but life goes on.

Ben loved Mary and she loved him. That was what was important to him, and he made it plain he intended to carry out his plan despite his children's opposition. In a letter to his son, Russell, on December 3, 1895, Ben said, "It is natural that a man's former children should not be pleased ordinarily with a second marriage. It would not have been possible for me to marry one I did not very highly respect and very warmly love. But my life now, and much more as I grow older, is and will be a very lonely one and I cannot go on as now. A home is life's essential to me and it must be the old home. Neither of my children live here—nor are they likely to do so, and I am sure they will not wish me to live the years that remain to me in solitude."

Ben and Mary announced their engagement formally during the 1895 Christmas season, and were married in April 1896, in St. Thomas Episcopal Church in New York City, far away from the scenes of his old life with Carrie.

Levi P. Morton, who had served as Vice President when Ben was in the White House, attended the wedding, as did most of the former Cabinet members. Ben's best man was Benjamin F. Tracy, his former Secretary of the Navy. Forty guests were present all told.

Mary and Ben went back to Indianapolis to live. Soon they were involved in church activities and social gatherings, and they began receiving dinner invitations from friends. Mary enjoyed music, and Ben found himself attending concerts. He said, "I am not devoted to music but Mrs. Harrison is and I am devoted to her."

Ben and Mary appeared to have a happy marriage. To add to their pleasure, a baby daughter was born on February 21, 1897. They named her Elizabeth for both their mothers. She was one of very few children born to an ex-President.

Mary and Ben also enjoyed vacationing in the Adirondack Mountains, where he built a vacation home for them the summer after their marriage. He named it Berkeley Lodge after the plantation home of his great-grandfather, Governor Benjamin Harrison V, who was one of the signers of the Declaration of Independence. Ben deeded the vacation home to

Mary, explaining, "She has helped me to create this little place, and we have spent many happy days there."

Ben declined invitations to speak at various gatherings which would involve much travel. He wanted to stay close to home with his new family. He did agree to be a trustee at Purdue University.

In May 1899, Ben and Mary traveled to Europe on board the ocean liner *St. Paul*. Ben and his two-year-old daughter, wearing her little red coat, could be seen strolling the deck almost every day.

Their trip combined business and pleasure. Ben had been hired by the government of Venezuela to represent it in a dispute with Great Britain over a boundary line. Ben worked long hours on the case, which culminated in an arbitration hearing before a tribunal in October of that year in Paris, France. Ben's closing argument lasted twenty-five hours.

The tribunal was headed by Baron Frederic de Martens, Russian judge and specialist in international law. The decision, read by de Martens, reaffirmed Great Britain's claim to the disputed area except for a small tract at the mouth of the Orinoco River.

Mary was indignant about the decision. She wrote to her sister, Lizzy Parker, "When England will give up anything she has, the world will end. We are all furious...I never did believe in arbitration, and if such a thing is to be, there should be more than one arbitrator who belongs to another country not involved in the dispute." Even newspaper accounts accused Great Britain of "double dealing."

Mary, Ben and little Elizabeth left Paris immediately, completing their trip with a partial tour of Germany, Belgium and England.

The next year they again spent the summer in the Adirondacks. Ben was moderately active in his law practice, which was now confined to cases heard before the Indiana Supreme Court and the United States Supreme Court.

Ben was showing signs of aging and was wearing out. He had spent a lot of energy in the past few years, and his work had taken its toll. In March 1901, he developed pneumonia and after only a few days' illness, he died on March 13, 1901, in Mary's arms. They had had less than five years together.

Mary survived Ben by forty-seven years. The year he died she completed a compilation of papers he had written, resulting in a book entitled *Views of an Ex-President*. He had been working on the book prior to his illness.

Mary never remarried. She took little Elizabeth to the White House on at least one occasion to visit the staff.

On January 11, 1913, President and Mrs. William Taft invited Mary to be their guest at a dinner given in the White House in honor of Frances Cleveland, widow of former President Grover Cleveland. Mrs. Cleveland had recently announced her engagement to marry Thomas J. Preston, Jr., of Princeton, New Jersey.

The dinner invitation to Mary caused a flurry of gossip in Washington, so to quiet critics, Mrs. Taft accorded Mary no special honor. She was seated as one of the ordinary guests. Since Mary had been involved with protocol during her years of serving as her Aunt Carrie's secretary, she was probably aware of the slight to her, but she made no comment.

Ben left an estate valued at $375,000, so Mary had money for support for herself and her daughter, but she was glad to receive an annual pension of five thousand dollars from the United States government as the widow of an ex–President in 1938.

In 1944 Mary attended former First Lady Lou Hoover's funeral in New York. Four years later Mary died on January 5, 1948, in New York City.

Little Elizabeth grew up and married James Blaine Walker of New York City on April 6, 1921. They had a daughter born to them on November 3, 1929, whom they named Mary Jane Harrison Walker. Mary Jane would later marry Newell Garfield, Jr., great-grandson of former President and Mrs. James A. Garfield, in November 1961. Elizabeth died in 1955 and did not get to see her daughter marry.

26. Ida Saxton McKinley

From the moment of her birth in Canton, Ohio, on June 8, 1847, Ida Saxton was indulged in her whims and desires by her fond parents. Ida had the good fortune to be born into Canton's most prominent family. Her father, James Asbury Saxton, was a banker, and her Grandfather Saxton was founder of *The Repository*, Canton's newspaper. The elder Saxton served as editor of the paper until 1871.

Within a short time, Ida had a little sister born into the family, who was named Mary but always called Pina. The two little girls and their brother, George, had a pleasant, uncomplicated childhood, filled with monetary advantages and much love. They were active members of the local Presbyterian Church, and Ida taught a children's Sunday School class in her teenage years.

The children attended local elementary schools, but when the girls were older, they went to Brooke Hall, a finishing school in Media, Pennsylvania, entering in 1867. At Brooke Hall a tour of Europe was considered desirable to broaden the education of the young lady students. In 1869, Miss Jeanette Alexander, one of the teachers, conducted an eight months' trip to Europe with a group of students including Ida and Pina Saxton.

Pina was considerate and got along well during the trip, but Ida set out to do things her own way. Ida had always been stubborn, even as a youngster, and now she acted like a spoiled child. She conspired with another student to attend the theater in Paris with some men they met casually. She insisted on going her own way when shopping, and in general acted like a pain in the neck.

When Ida got back home and her father heard about her antics in Europe, he decided it was high time Ida went to work. And what better place for her first job than her father's own bank? She started work that year as a cashier.

Ida was a pretty girl. She had thick, luxurious auburn hair and blue eyes. Since money was never a problem for her, she dressed fashionably in clothes suited to her trim figure. She attracted interest among the males in Canton, but she could not seem to find that one special man for life. Pina fell in love early and married Marshall Barber.

Ida McKinley. (Courtesy Library of Congress.)

Ida was still working in the bank when she first became aware of Major William McKinley, a young lawyer in Canton. Major McKinley had served in the Union army during the Civil War. He and Ida fell in love with remarkable speed and were married in an elegant ceremony on January 25, 1871, in the New Presbyterian Church in Ida's hometown.

An old adage says, "Love is blind," and so it proved to be with Major McKinley. Where her family and friends considered Ida to be willful and stubborn, he was overwhelmed by her beauty and her firm opinions. When she was changeable in her ideas, well, he reasoned, a woman had a right to change her mind, didn't she?

William McKinley was a handsome, virile-looking man, and if not possessed with a brilliant intellect, he was a hard worker. His strict Methodist upbringing had a salutary effect on his moral character and personal habits. Ida's family liked William and approved of her choice. Ida's father gave them a house on Market Street for their first home.

The newlyweds settled down quickly in their new life together. Ida exerted herself to be more considerate. They entertained other young couples often and received invitations from their friends. On the first Christmas Day they spent together, their first child, a little girl, was born. They named her Katherine, but she would be called Katie. They both adored their little blonde Christmas gift.

Six months later Ida became pregnant for a second time. When Mrs. Saxton died just before Ida's second child was born, the shock of losing her mother plus a hard labor and the frailty of the newborn child caused Ida to descend into deep depression.

The new baby, named Ida for her mother, died when she was only five months old, and from that time on, Ida began having apparent epileptic seizures. If she had been epileptic previously, it had not been noticed.

The next year Ida and William lost three-year-old Katie, who died from typhoid fever infection. Both parents were devastated by grief with the loss of two little girls within such a short period of time. William worked harder than ever in an attempt to regain his stability. Poor Ida became obsessed by fear for William's safety. In the few short years Ida had been married, she had changed from a pretty, high-spirited, fun-loving young woman into a self-centered, querulous invalid.

Earlier William had helped in the political campaign of General Ulysses Grant for President. Now that his life had been so altered in such a tragic way, William threw himself into the political arena with fervor and announced his own candidacy for Congress in 1876. He had been changed by the personal tragedy in his life into a quieter, less buoyant and more compassionate man than before. The voters liked what they saw, and he won the election.

William and Ida moved to Washington, where they lived at the Ebbitt House in a suite of rooms. They were longtime friends of President and Mrs. Rutherford Hayes, and Ida would always make a special effort to go to the White House when they were invited to attend social functions there. Ida went to lunch on two occasions with Lucy Hayes only. Otherwise, the McKinleys' social contacts were necessarily extremely limited due to Ida's poor health.

President Hayes only served one term. When the Hayes family left Washington, Ida and William's sole remaining recreation was to go riding in their carriage.

Ida's health was such by now that she required a paid attendant to be with her at all times when William was not present. She had become very demanding of William's time and frequently had him called out of important meetings to answer trivial questions.

William never appeared to be upset by Ida's demands or resentful of them. He was patient and loving, and continued to hope for many years that Ida would recover her health. He commented frequently to others about how pretty Ida had been as a girl — "And she is still just as pretty to me," he would say.

William was elected as Ohio's Governor when he was only forty-nine, still in excellent health and appearing younger than his age. He had a golden speaking voice, pleasant and soothing in quality. He enjoyed admiration from his fellow citizens, not lessened by his obvious love for his ailing wife.

During the eight years they lived in Columbus, Ida was a little better. They again lived in a hotel suite, this time at the Chittenden, near the state capital. Here Ida did the best she could to entertain their friends through the use of hired caterers and staff, and William was happier than he had been in years. Their friends brought their children visiting with them, and Ida especially enjoyed seeing them.

Ida was a charming, affable hostess when she felt well, but when her nervous ailment manifested itself, she became irritable and almost like a different person. She always wore dark dresses, coats and shoes, unrelieved except for a small emerald or diamond pin. William gave her jewelry for special occasions, and she tried to please him by wearing it.

The McKinleys' financial condition had never been robust, due in part to the expenses occasioned by Ida's illness and in part to the fact that his salary as a Congressman was low. Now that William was Governor, they enjoyed more affluence than they had ever had before, but in 1893 they suffered a tremendous blow to their pocketbook.

A few years earlier, William had countersigned some notes for a good friend, Robert L. Walker, so Walker could obtain a bank loan. Walker used the money to establish a tin-plate manufacturing business, which failed after several years. Mr. Walker could not repay the loan, and William was liable for the debt, which amounted to a total of one hundred and thirty thousand dollars.

Ida had gone to New York City for medical treatment when William learned of his dilemma. She came rushing back to Columbus and gave him the money and property she had inherited from her father to put on the debt. Friends also came forward with financial assistance, and William's credit remained sound. Today he would probably be saddled with charges of undue influence, but times were different then. Ida and the McKinleys' friends probably saved his political career by their generosity. If William had been forced into bankruptcy he could not have continued his political career. Instead he was reelected to a second term as Governor of Ohio.

Locked into her sedentary existence, complicated by phlebitis in her legs, many hobbies and recreational activities were not feasible for Ida. She learned to crochet, and it became a passion with her. It was reported that she crocheted several thousand bedroom slippers, which she had a servant help her mount on cork soles and lace with ribbon. She gave these indiscriminately and repeatedly to family members, friends and casual acquaintances. She also made black satin neckties for her beloved William. He tied these in large old-fashioned bows at his neck.

William's friends marveled at his long-suffering patience with Ida, and they resented her as a burden on his political career. What they did not understand was that William truly loved Ida with all his heart. His emotions were centered on her and their life together. She represented haven and home to him. She had been instrumental in polishing his manners and social graces, and they suited each other in temperament. Orpha Moore, William's secretary, said Ida was also a more astute judge of people and their capabilities than William.

As William's second gubernatorial term came near the end, rumors made the rounds that he would be nominated for President in 1896. To his friends in Canton, he was a logical choice. He had been a good Governor and would make a good President, in their opinion. But what about Ida, would be their next thought. How could William go to the White House with an invalid wife who would be unable to perform any duties as First Lady?

Ida was a proud woman, and she knew most of what went on. She probably guessed what people said about her. Through her love for William, she was determined to make an effort to stop the gossip and help him become President.

Ida staged a huge, elaborate party to celebrate their twenty-fifth wedding anniversary. This elegant affair would surpass anything the people in Canton had ever seen. One hundred guests were expected, with the caterer standing by with reserve refreshments for a hundred more.

The party, held on a mild February day, was an outstanding success. Ida wore her original wedding gown and received guests standing by William's side for six hours. She wanted to make it clear she planned to allow no one to take her place as hostess in the White House.

William was elected President! The McKinleys would be moving back to Washington to live.

Ida struggled gamely to hold on during William's inauguration and the ball held afterward. She was tastefully dressed in a blue and silver gown. She wore diamond jewelry and a violet corsage and carried a lace fan. She took William's arm proudly as they began to walk slowly around the ballroom. Halfway around, however, her knees buckled, and she was seen no more at the ball.

The White House years were happy ones for Ida, as long as William was with her. His job as President meant he was more often available, except for meetings, and most of his time was spent in his White House home and office.

State receptions became large and unwieldy during William's administration, and something had to be done. Part of the problem had arisen because Ida was not able to take any active part in the planning or execution of the receptions, and everything was left in the hands of an indifferent White House staff. Gate-crashing was common. The Executive Mansion held a thousand people without difficulty, but between three and four thousand were attending. Finally, army engineers warned William such crowds were dangerously straining the safety of the floors. William appointed two new men to his staff, who once again brought order to the receptions in the White House.

Ida stayed in her bedroom or in the conservatories most of the time, still crocheting, except for her appearances as official hostess for William. The Chief Usher at the White House during these years said the McKinleys were distinguished from other Presidential families by their love for flowers. "Their rooms and the Presidential office were always filled with fresh flowers," he said.

As had been foreseen by their neighbors and friends in Canton, Ida's illness posed continuous problems for William, often bordering on nightmarish. She always insisted on sitting beside William at state dinners, completely altering protocol set by previous administrations. In her seat beside him, William could drop a napkin over her face if she had a seizure. A maid or a niece was always on hand to take her to her room if the seizure was severe.

When receiving guests, Ida would often stiffen and stare blankly for several seconds. Moments later she would continue with her gracious remarks. Guests were embarrassed when confronted by her obvious problem, but Ida had made up her mind to be the hostess in the White House, and she was by William's side on most occasions.

The Spanish-American War began in 1898 when the United States battleship *Maine* was sunk in Havana Harbor. Theodore Roosevelt emerged a national hero for his war efforts.

Ida was little affected by national worries as the social season of 1899 began in Washington. She continued to attend public gatherings, where she "was helped in, bowed, smiled, fainted, was helped out," to quote one observer. William continued to ignore the confusion generated on these occasions.

In 1900 William was elected to a second term as President, and would have Theodore Roosevelt serving with him as his new Vice President. Shortly after his inauguration in March, 1901, William and Ida, accompanied by several Cabinet members, left by train on a nationwide tour. William received wide acclaim throughout the Southern states, and Ida seemed to be bearing up well.

By the time the party reached the desert Southwest, however, exhaustion was overtaking Ida. She developed a painful infection on one of her fingers, which then spread throughout her body. This led to acute endocarditis (inflammation of the heart) and she had to be hospitalized in San Francisco. Her condition was critical for several days. After she slowly began to recover she and William decided to spend some time in Canton, Ohio, before they went back to Washington.

William had earlier planned to attend an exposition in Buffalo, New York, before Ida's illness forced a change in his plans. In September she had improved enough for travel, and they left for Buffalo.

On September 5 William made a speech at the exposition, and he was pleased with the public's enthusiasm. The next day Ida was too tired to go with him on his rounds to a luncheon, a side trip to Niagara Falls and back to the Temple of Music where he would be the honor guest at a public reception.

By the middle of the afternoon, thousands of people had filed by to meet and greet William at the reception. Secret Service agents were present, both in William's vicinity and mingling with the crowd.

At about four o'clock that afternoon William extended his hand to the next person in the receiving line, when to his surprise the man knocked his hand down and shot him twice before anyone could make a move. One shot was to his chest, the other to his abdomen.

"Don't let them hurt him," William pleaded with agents who were scuffling with his assailant. His next thought was of Ida. "My wife, be careful how you tell her – oh, be careful," he said.

William lived a week in the hospital before gangrene in his wounds ended his life on September 14, 1901. Ida was by his side. He was taken back to Canton for burial.

The assassin, Leon F. Czolgosz, was a child of Polish immigrants and was considered mentally deranged. He thought if the President were killed, the government in the United States would fall. He had been attending meetings conducted by anarchists, who had advocated the destruction of the government, and he thought this would accomplish their aims.

Ida went sadly back to Canton to live in the house her father had given her when she was a bride. She and William had planned to live there after he retired. Her sister, Pina, came to live with Ida and take care of her. Ida spent her days writing grieving letters to friends on paper edged with heavy black borders, and she visited William's grave almost every day.

Ida lived long enough to see many honors bestowed on William posthumously. A domed tomb ninety-six feet high was erected in his memory in Canton. In front is a bronze statue of William making a speech.

Ida died on May 26, 1907, in Canton. She was sincerely mourned by a nation remembering how the severely afflicted woman stayed proudly by her husband's side and made every effort to share all parts of his life with him.

Ida was buried beside William in the McKinley Memorial Mausoleum, near the graves of their two little daughters.

27. Alice Hathaway Lee Roosevelt

Alice Hathaway Lee was born on July 29, 1861, to wealthy parents, Mr. and Mrs. George Cabot Lee, at Chestnut Hill, Massachusetts. Mr. Lee was a dignified Bostonian, a graduate of Harvard and a partner in a banking and investment firm, Lee, Higginson and Company in Boston. The firm was progressive in its thinking and operations. George was the manager of the first safety deposit vault built in the United States, which was installed in his bank.

Alice spent her childhood in a huge Victorian house of many windows, chimneys, porches and gables. Her days included pony rides, birthday parties, dancing school and trips to the beach as well as longer trips. She led a happy, pleasant, sheltered life.

Theodore Roosevelt entered her life in her teens like an exploding Roman candle. Theodore tended to have that effect on everyone.

The two young people met when Theodore visited Alice's cousin, Dick Saltonstall, who lived next door to the Lees. He and Theodore were classmates and friends at Harvard. Theodore was also a member of a wealthy New York family, with a background similar to Alice's.

Theodore had been a frail, spindly child who suffered severely with asthma. Since he was unable to participate in sports, he devoted his spare time to reading and studying natural history. By the time he enrolled at Harvard, he was quite knowledgeable, having spent much time studying specimens as well as books. Regardless of the subject of interest of the moment — and there were many subjects that interested Theodore — he tended to throw himself heart and soul into learning about it.

His courtship of Alice displayed the same characteristic. Theodore fell madly in love. He could not praise her highly enough, for she was, he said, "an enchanting creature," with superior intelligence, wit and charm. Alice was indeed pretty, a slender honey-blonde with blue, blue eyes, whom others also found beautiful.

Before he met Alice, Theodore had a close friend who was the daughter of family friends, Edith Carow. They wrote each other faithfully when apart, and Edith shared his love for sailing, hiking and natural history pursuits. As far as Theodore was concerned, however, he and Edith

Alice Roosevelt. (Courtesy Library of Congress.)

were just friends. If he had ever entertained romantic thoughts about Edith, they were swept aside in his fascination with enchanting Alice.

Alice proved more elusive than he expected. She was flattered by his open adoration and seemed fond of Theodore. But just as they seemed to be progressing nicely in their relationship, in Theodore's opinion, Alice would back away from any serious or exclusive commitment. At these times Theodore would be plunged into the deepest despair. Quite possibly, his passionate, total involvement in his approach to their relationship scared Alice a little.

Then Alice made her debut and the young men swarmed around her. Theodore was roused almost to frenzy by this new complication.

It must have been painful for Edith Carow to witness all this agony on his part because of another woman. She and Theodore had been considered a couple by their friends until Alice appeared on the scene. She held her tongue for the most part, and tried to be his friend. Her own opinion of Alice differed from Theodore's in that she did not consider her as over-whelmingly intelligent as he did. Since Edith was also friends with Theodore's sisters, she continued to be a part of their family outings and celebrations.

Theodore had finally begun escorting other girls to social events, in-cluding Edith, when Alice came to New York for a week with friends at Christmas of 1879. All his desire for Alice was rekindled, and when she went back home, she consented to an engagement in a letter. Theodore was thrilled beyond words.

Alice was too young to marry at nineteen, although her parents raised no objections to the engagement. They allowed her to announce it officially on February 14, 1880, but her father requested that they wait awhile to marry. Theodore went to visit Alice and her family in the spring, and the couple spent long, blissful hours planning their future together.

When Theodore graduated from Harvard a few weeks later, he de-cided to go with his brother, Elliott, on a hunting trip out West. He and Alice would be married in October. After six weeks he and Elliott returned home in time for the last frantic weeks of preparation for the wedding. Edith generously gave a dinner party in his honor, but she did not ask Alice to attend, instead inviting other girls he had dated in the past.

On October 27, 1880, Alice and Theodore were married in an elaborate church wedding in the Brookline, Massachusetts, Unitarian Church. The lavish reception was held in the Lee mansion. Edith attended the wedding with Theodore's mother and a girlfriend, and Edith admitted she had a marvelous time dancing at the reception.

Theodore said later he thought Alice's father consented to the wedding only because Theodore's mother, Mittie, invited the newlyweds to move in with her after their marriage. They occupied a large apartment on the third floor of her spacious home.

The bride and groom went to Tranquillity, Theodore's family's sum-mer home at Oyster Bay, New York, for a two-week honeymoon. Theodore planned to enter Columbia Law School the next year.

On their return the happy couple was immediately drawn into a so-ciety whirl of dinner parties, theater parties, weddings and other events in-volving the ultrafashionable group with whom they mingled. Edith gave a party in their honor, and this time Alice was invited.

Theodore wrote in his diary that he had never before been so happy. Alice and Mittie became genuinely fond of each other, and Alice willingly shared Theodore with his large family, which endeared her most of all to them. There was no friction anywhere. Alice was a member of the Roosevelt family in every sense of the word.

That same winter Theodore entered the murky world of politics, although he kept it a secret from his family at first. His father had been disillusioned during the time he had served as Customs Collector for the Port of New York, thinking the Republican party meant to honor him for his years of public service. Instead President Rutherford Hayes had used his appointment in an effort to embarrass the corrupt boss of the New York political machine, Senator Roscoe Conkling.

Theodore, Sr., was a decent, honorable man, but he was subjected to delaying tactics by Conkling, who wanted Chester A. Arthur reappointed. The elder Roosevelt, afflicted with cancer, died within a few months after this struggle began. His son felt his death was hastened by all the nervous strain he had endured. Theodore now hoped in some vague way to settle old scores on behalf of his father.

The Roosevelt family was very conscious of their place in society, and they were horrified collectively and individually that Theodore would associate with those they considered of low political classes. They were relieved when school was out and he and Alice left for Europe to spend the summer of 1881.

Having never been abroad before, Alice was extremely seasick about half the way, and Theodore was distraught about her misery. At last the ship entered calmer water, and she began to enjoy the trip. They toured England, France, Italy, Ireland, Austria and Switzerland. Theodore climbed the Matterhorn, a mountain in the Alps nearly fifteen thousand feet high.

Upon their return home, Theodore was nominated to run for New York State Assemblyman from his district. When he won the election, he asked Alice if she wanted to move to Albany, since he would have to be there with the Legislature much of the time. The glittering winter social season in New York City was beginning, and Alice decided to remain in their apartment where all the activity was close at hand. Theodore could come home frequently. They would move in spring.

Theodore was asked by Governor Grover Cleveland to help formulate and push a civil service reform law through the Legislature. This would remove most government positions from political control, and a qualified worker would keep his job no matter which political party was in power. The reform bill passed, and it aided Cleveland greatly in his bid to become President of the United States.

By spring 1883, Alice was pregnant, and Theodore turned his attention to buying land and having a permanent home built for them. Before he could fully formulate his plans, however, he became ill with cholera and asthma.

By August he was feeling better. He and Alice were spending a few weeks in the Catskill Mountains. He decided another trip out West would improve his health. Leaving firm, complete instructions on the building of their new home, to be called Leeholm, he left on a buffalo-hunting trip and was gone for several weeks.

When he returned he was defeated in his bid for nomination as Speaker to the Assembly. Why hadn't they appreciated his efforts? But Alice was secretly glad he had been defeated. She had been lonely without him, and their first child was due to be born momentarily. She was very young, this was a big experience, and she could not possibly travel with Theodore.

On February 13, 1884, Theodore received word where he was serving in the Assembly that Alice had given birth to their daughter the night before. He was overjoyed by the news and made arrangements to leave as soon as possible. Before he left Albany, another telegram arrived advising him to return home at once.

The only transportation he could find was a seat on a milk train. As the train crawled through heavy fog, Theodore was worried and upset about what could be wrong. He wished the train would go faster.

He got home at last — to find his mother dying of typhoid fever and Alice dying of Bright's Disease of the kidneys. His mother died at three o'clock on the morning of February 14, 1884, and Alice died in his arms at noon the same day, four years exactly from the day they had so proudly announced their engagement. She was twenty-two years old.

The baby Alice had given birth to survived and was placed in the care of Theodore's sister, Anna, called Bamie. Theodore named his little daughter Alice Lee for her mother.

Theodore was in a state of profound shock, as anyone else would have been under the circumstances. After mentioning his dear Alice only two more times, he never spoke of her again as long as he lived, not even to little Alice Lee. He wrote in his diary, "The light has gone out of my life."

Alice was buried in Greenwood Cemetery in New York City. Theodore returned to the Legislature in Albany to immerse himself in his work in an effort to ease his extreme anguish.

28. Edith Kermit Carow Roosevelt

Edith Kermit Carow was a neighbor and good friend of Theodore Roosevelt. They played together as children (he named his rowboat for her in his teens). She attended his wedding to his first wife, Alice Lee, and had been an important part of his life long before they married on December 2, 1886, in London, England.

Edith was born in Norwich, Connecticut, on August 6, 1861, but when she was a small child, her family moved to New York City to live. Edith's father and Theodore's father became good friends, and Edith became the best friend of Corinne Roosevelt, one of Theodore's sisters, who was almost the same age as Edith.

Edith watched as young Theodore and his brother, Elliott, boxed with each other and blackened each other's eyes. She knew all about Theodore's asthma and other health problems. They attended the same parties and the same dancing school, read the same books, and sailed together on Oyster Bay, New York. Edith's family spent their summers at Oyster Bay, as did all the Roosevelts.

The Roosevelt and Carow children all were privately tutored in childhood, but Edith also attended Miss Comstock's private school in New York City later.

Theodore made no secret of his admiration for Edith in his teen years, going so far as to remark, "When Edith dresses well and don't frizzle her hair, she is a very pretty girl."

Edith and Theodore had "an understanding" by the time he entered Harvard, and it was assumed by both families and all their friends that they would probably marry someday. Both Edith and Theodore had hot tempers, however, and apparently they had a lovers' spat just before Alice Lee came into his life.

After he met Alice, Theodore was transported into a fantasyland where only he and Alice lived. Alice was his darling, his whole life. Marriage only increased his enthusiastic adoration of her.

He remembered Edith dimly, if at all, during the years he spent with Alice. Edith could only stand by and watch silently.

Then Alice died, tragically and suddenly. Theodore suffered terribly

Edith Roosevelt. (Courtesy Library of Congress.)

from her death, and when he also suffered a resounding defeat at the
Republican Convention in his attempt to get George Edmunds of Vermont
nominated for President, he decided to go out West and live for awhile.

Theodore went to the Elkhorn Ranch he had bought in 1883 and lived
there for the next two years, trying to regain his mental equilibrium. He
worked long, hard days, and slowly his physical strength and frame of
mind improved. He returned home in 1885 to see his little daughter, Alice
Lee, and the rest of his family.

Theodore had only been back for a few days when he accidentally encountered Edith, who was visiting his sister, Corinne. All his old affection
for Edith came flooding back, but Edith was wary and unenthusiastic.

Theodore had treated her badly in his sudden wild infatuation and marriage to Alice. Now, to compound the problem, her family had suffered severe financial setbacks, and Edith felt reluctant to encourage him as he might misunderstand her motives. She told him she and her family were moving to England soon and they would live there indefinitely. She was cool to him.

Poor Theodore! He now found grown-up Edith excitingly attractive, and he remembered the long, happy hours and shared adventures of their early years. Edith was now twenty-four, and she had never found another man to replace Theodore in her affections, but she feared he might hurt her again as he had seven years before.

Theodore became ardent in his pursuit of her now. They were adults instead of children, he pointed out. There was nothing standing in their way. Edith could not resist him, and she finally agreed to marry him, though she felt they should keep their engagement secret to avoid criticism until two years had passed since Alice died.

Theodore decided he would remain in New York for the winter social season. Since he and Edith had been such longtime friends, they caused no comment by being seen together often.

While they waited until the proper time to announce their formal engagement, Theodore decided to return to his ranch in the West. There he found a bitterly cold winter had killed some of his cattle. As he tried to resume his old duties and ranch life, he found his interest was waning. He missed Edith and his family back East, and the life of a cowboy was losing its charm for him.

Edith had gone on with her family to Europe when Theodore headed West, and she was still there. Theodore wrote her long, loving letters about how happy he would be when they were married.

At the end of August 1886, *The New York Times* carried the announcement of the engagement of ex–Assemblyman Theodore Roosevelt to Miss Edith K. Carow of New York City. Surprisingly, on September 9 a retraction appeared in the same newspaper, probably placed there by Theodore's sister Anna, who had the baby Alice Lee in her care.

Theodore was in Medora, North Dakota, when this controversy flared. He wrote Anna immediately that the notice of the engagement was true, but that he intended to allow her to keep the baby if that was what she wanted.

Meanwhile, Theodore held a running debate with his conscience about remarrying. He knew he loved Edith deeply, but he considered his love for her to be a character flaw rather than a blessing. How could he be so faithless to Alice and her memory? He had loved her so much! "I have no constancy!" he said in dismay.

At last he returned to his New York home to get ready for his marriage to Edith. He had been back only a short time when he entered the race for Mayor of New York City. He was defeated, partly because of his youth.

On December 2, 1886, Edith and Theodore were married in St. George's on Hanover Square in London. There was a heavy fog the morning of the wedding. Theodore's sister could not even see Theodore at the altar when she came in the door, as the fog had filled the church. There were few guests at the quiet wedding.

Theodore began to regain his old exuberance and optimism in the fifteen weeks he and Edith spent on their honeymoon. They toured England, France and Italy. From Paris Theodore wrote relatives Edith might be expecting a honeymoon baby, and he was obviously pleased.

They returned home to Sagamore Hill, the new name he had given to Leeholm, the home he had built for Alice. Edith insisted that Anna turn over little Alice Lee to them. After a two-month transfer period during which Anna lived with them, she did so. Despite her earlier efforts to discourage Theodore's remarriage, she had been uncertain about her ability to rear the little girl. However, she loved the baby dearly, and it was with pained reluctance that she left her with Theodore and Edith.

Theodore's sister Corinne found early on that Edith set the rules for Theodore's contacts with his relatives. She found this ironic since she and Edith had always been good friends and she had unfailingly encouraged the couple's interest in each other.

The next year Theodore and Edith added a son, Theodore, Jr., to their household. Baby Alice was now three and a lively, pretty child, the apple of her father's eye. Two years later Kermit Roosevelt was born.

Theodore had not given up on politics, even while he had been engaged in writing a three-volume series of books entitled *The Winning of the West*. President Benjamin Harrison asked him to serve as the United States Civil Service Commissioner, and Theodore accepted.

The Roosevelts would be moving to Washington at the beginning of 1890. Theodore rented them an apartment there, about one-tenth the size of their home at Sagamore Hill.

The Washington social season of 1890 began with President Harrison's reception, followed by suppers, dinners, balls and receptions hosted by other dignitaries. Edith and Theodore went to all the top-drawer gatherings, going out an average of five nights a week. Theodore was thrilled with his beautiful young wife and enjoyed showing her off to his friends.

Edith and Theodore entertained in their small dining room also. They prepared guest lists carefully to include such persons of intelligence, wealth and social position as would make an interesting and noteworthy party.

In his civil service job Theodore uncovered abuses which led to both reform of the system and the defeat of President Harrison in his bid for a second term.

Taking a brief rest from what he called his "warfare with the ungodly," Theodore and Edith enjoyed the spring social season in Washington with their friends.

Theodore was surprised when President Grover Cleveland, who was reentering the White House after being ousted by Harrison for four years, reappointed him to the Civil Service Commission. Cleveland had been shaken by his 1888 defeat by Benjamin Harrison, and he felt Theodore's services would add a bipartisan flavor to his administration.

Theodore resigned the post in April 1895 because he was bored. By now everyone agreed civil service reform was a good thing, and since Theodore thrived on adversity, he lost interest.

In 1891 Ethel Carow Roosevelt was born, and in 1894 another son, Archibald, made his appearance. The small Washington apartment was bursting at the seams. When the Mayor of New York City offered Theodore a job as Police Commissioner, Edith welcomed the news eagerly. At last she could take the children to Sagamore Hill, where there was space for all.

Theodore plunged into his new post with characteristic fervor and intensity. Mayor Strong had been a reform candidate, and Theodore worked hard to bring reforms to the police force of New York City. He uncovered evidence of rampant graft and corruption among police officials as well as payoffs to other officials.

Theodore's great zeal for reforming the New York Police Department caught the attention of William McKinley, currently campaigning for President on the Republican ticket. Theodore working diligently to help McKinley win the election, then made it known through a mutual friend and financial backer of McKinley's that he would like to be named Assistant Secretary of the Navy.

During these years of happiness and contentment for Theodore and Edith, Theodore's brother, Elliott, embarked on a serious effort to drink himself to death. When Theodore reproved him for his actions, he went to Europe to live, where stories of his excesses and deterioration became more and more worrisome.

Elliott had a little daughter, Eleanor, who was about the same age as Alice. Theodore and Edith were fond of Eleanor and often invited her to spend time with them and their family. Theodore served as a surrogate father to the little girl, who missed her own father greatly.

William McKinley was elected President, and he decided he wanted peace for the nation more than anything else. Everyone knew of Theodore's enthusiasm for causes, and before McKinley would name Theodore Assistant Secretary of the Navy, he asked Senator Henry Cabot Lodge for reassurance that Theodore would not cause a war if he were named to that post. Senator Lodge assured President McKinley nothing was further from Theodore's thoughts.

Theodore fooled a lot of people. Secretary of Navy John D. Long wrote in his diary, "Best man for the job," following his first formal conference with Theodore. Long was a slow-moving, laid-back individual and worked hard in only short bursts of energy. His style suited Theodore because it gave him plenty of room to begin a campaign of his own to improve and enlarge the United States Navy.

Theodore planned to liberate oppressed Cuba from Spain as soon as he could gain enough supporters for his ideas. In propaganda speeches at various gatherings, Theodore began to project his ideas.

Secretary Long had been happily vacationing when he found out what Theodore was doing, and he threw a fit! Theodore admitted his superior really told him off.

Theodore was forced to spend a few days at home with Edith when another son, Quentin, was born on November 18, 1897. As soon as he could decently leave her and the new baby, he again began pursuing his plan to engage Spain in war.

Secretary Long was somewhat amused and bewildered by Theodore's enthusiasm to fight Spain. Theodore made it clear he meant to "go to the front" himself, and Long couldn't decide if ridicule or agreement was the best approach. He privately thought Theodore had gone "daft in the matter."

At home Edith had become seriously ill with typhoid fever and had been dangerously ill for nine days. Theodore had barely noticed. He was "exceedingly put out" by having to change his plans to go away, and tried to convince Edith if she would just ignore her illness, it would go away.

Rioting broke out in Cuba against Spanish rule. Theodore was ever more convinced the war must come and that the United States must rescue Cuba.

When somebody sunk the United States battleship *Maine*, Theodore was convinced Spain was to blame. (He was later proved to be correct.) War was subsequently declared on Spain on April 23, 1898, exactly one year after Theodore became Assistant Secretary of the Navy on the promise he would do nothing to cause a war.

Edith felt stunned when Theodore resigned his post with the Department of the Navy to lead soldiers into battle. She questioned his wisdom, and other people questioned his sanity. He felt he had to go to prove his manhood.

Leaving Edith and his six children behind, Theodore went charging into the fray as a lieutenant colonel with the army, leading a regiment known as the Rough Riders. If Theodore's efforts made any real contribution to the defeat of the Spaniards, it is not clear from historical accounts, but Theodore impressed the American public with his bravery and daring. When half or more of the men in his regiment became ill from malaria, yellow fever and other tropical ailments, Theodore sent into Santiago for better and more nourishing food to try to restore their health and paid for it with his own money. The men under his command loved him for his consideration, and they told all their relatives what he had done for them. He came home a hero, as he had always dreamed of being. It was during this time he became better known as "Teddy" Roosevelt, although he never liked the name.

Edith was amazed to see the huge crowd that gathered at Oyster Bay when the family finally got to go back to Sagamore Hill. They grabbed and jostled Theodore, and Edith wondered if the family would ever be allowed to live a quiet life again. Theodore had been elevated to the rank of national hero and she could not change that, so she smiled and stayed calm.

New York Republicans recognized a political asset when they saw one, so they nominated Theodore as their candidate for Governor that year. Theodore was elected and became the Governor of New York in 1898. He embarked on a program of reforms, from closer supervision of power and insurance companies to labor reforms regarding hours worked and working conditions.

Theodore stepped on some important toes with his reforms, and the Republicans decided to silence him by nominating him as Vice President to William McKinley, running for a second term as President. McKinley's Vice President during his first term had died not long before.

Neither McKinley nor Theodore was thrilled with the proposed ticket. Mark Hanna, national chairman of the Republican party, was openly appalled at the idea. "Don't any of you realize there's only one life between this madman and the White House?" he asked. All Theodore's past efforts in government had not gone unnoticed by Hanna.

Less than six months later Theodore became President when President McKinley was shot by an assassin and died September 14, 1901. Mark Hanna was furious that the "damned cowboy" was now President of the United States.

Edith and the children had alternated between living in Washington and Sagamore Hill while Theodore was Vice President. When Theodore moved into the White House, Edith was still closing up the Sagamore Hill house for the winter.

The Roosevelt family with its many children living in the White House closely resembled a three-ring circus with all the rings busy all the time. The children slid down banisters, took animals (including a pony) upstairs in the White House, invited friends in to lunch, had pillow fights with their father and each other, and behaved in general like any other lively children. The newspapers were intrigued by the family and their antics. Through it all Edith maintained a dignified calm, the eye in the center of the storm of energy generated by Theodore and the children.

Edith was fun-loving and often played with the children too. One of her sons said, "When Mother was a little girl, she must have been a boy!"

Alice Lee was now a modern young lady of seventeen who drove her own runabout, dressed in the latest daring fashions and smoked cigarettes, considered shocking behavior in the early 1900s. When a colleague asked Theodore if he could not control Alice, Theodore said he could either control Alice or he could be President, but he could not possibly do both.

As White House hostess, Edith arranged many dinners and receptions for dignitaries, including the highly respected Doctor Booker T. Washington, a noted black scientist and educator. Southern newspapers protested loudly about his invitation to dine at the White House but were ignored by both Roosevelts.

The White House was remodeled under Edith's supervision into a "dignified dwelling for the head of a republic," to quote Theodore. She had a gallery of First Ladies' portraits placed in a new ground floor entry for guests, which still contains such an exhibit. At the end of the Roosevelts' White House term, one Presidential aide would remark that Edith Roosevelt "had spent seven years in the White House without making a mistake."

Having been reared in a wealthy aristocratic atmosphere, Edith felt no hesitation in utilizing her own taste and ideas as White House hostess, which gave an impression of an easier, more relaxed elegance than had been seen in recent years.

Theodore still enjoyed going hunting, and he continued to go on such trips for relaxation. One day in Mississippi some of his hunting guides flushed out a little bear cub, terrified and cowering. They told Theodore to go ahead and shoot. He flatly refused to kill the little bear. The *Washington Post* supported his stand and ran a cartoon of the incident. This led to a "Teddy-bear" craze which swept the country, and the stuffed bears are still loved by children everywhere today. When Theodore complained about the name, Edith told him to "be glad they didn't call it a Theodore-bear."

Theodore retained his keen interest in reforms during his administration. He urged enforcement of antitrust laws to prevent large companies from gaining a monopoly on goods and services. He forced arbitration in a bitter miners' dispute. The Pure Food and Drug Act was passed during his administration. Theodore also had expansionist goals, and the United States acquired the Panama Canal Zone while he was President.

Alice Roosevelt married Congressman Nicholas Longworth of Ohio on February 17, 1906, in the White House. Edith worked diligently to make Alice's wedding a memorable occasion, and it was recognized as the social event of the year. Dignitaries of many other nations attended and sent lavish gifts to the couple. A later social event in the White House family was Ethel Roosevelt's society debut.

A serious stock market downturn in 1907, and the resulting sagging economy, caused Theodore to lose favor with the Republican party bosses. He still retained enough influence to get the nomination for William Taft, his preference to succeed him. Taft was elected.

The night before President Taft was inaugurated, Theodore and Edith invited the Tafts to dine alone with them. To Edith's shocked surprise, Helen Taft remarked that she planned to replace many of the White House servants. Edith felt it was unfair to replace a loyal, competent staff without giving them a trial period, and there was a distinct strain between the ladies the rest of the evening. Fortunately, Theodore's nonstop talking and storytelling saved the dinner from being a disaster.

After leaving the Presidency, Theodore went on a hunting trip to Africa, accompanied by his son Kermit. Theodore killed more than five hundred animals, including seventeen lions.

When he returned home, Theodore found himself in violent disagreement with the policies of the Taft administration. His vocal protests to President Taft brought an end to the long-standing friendship between the two.

Since President Taft was not carrying out Theodore's plans for the government, Theodore's solution was to seek renomination for President himself at the Republican Convention. President Taft was renominated, and Theodore decided to run as a third-party candidate. He named his party the Bull Moose Party and he and Taft split the vote, giving the election to Woodrow Wilson, the Democrats' nominee.

Edith had watched all Theodore's feverish activity with growing concern. Just before Theodore left office several years before he had been permanently blinded in his left eye in a boxing bout. She felt he was pushing himself too hard, and she tried to convince him he should slow down.

Apparently she had some effect. A few weeks after his defeat in his bid to be reelected President, Theodore told a friend sadly he was finished. The friend remarked drily that he was not too worried—he expected the volcano to erupt again.

And the friend was right. The volcano that was Theodore erupted in 1914 when he went on an exploring expedition to Brazil, with a company of twenty-one other people including his son Kermit. Edith thought he was truly demented to set out on such a trip given his age and physical condition. He did have some dangerous experiences, but he loved every minute of it.

World War I started in Europe a few months later, and Theodore wanted to form a volunteer troop division similar to his old Rough Riders. He was dissuaded by his old friend Senator Lodge and flatly refused by President Woodrow Wilson.

The war would inflict a terrible blow on Theodore and Edith through the loss of their son Quentin, who crashed into the German war zone on July 17, 1918.

Abruptly the fun went out of life for Theodore with Quentin's death. He fought to regain his old vigor, but this time he could not. On January 6, 1919, less than six months after Quentin's death, Theodore died in his sleep at Sagamore Hill. He was only sixty years old. He was buried in Young's Memorial Cemetery in Oyster Bay, New York.

Edith was profoundly grieved by the loss of both her son and her husband in such a short space of time. After a period of adjustment she began to count her blessings. She had her other children to add interest to her life, and there were an increasing number of grandchildren, always a blessing. She stayed with her stepdaughter, Alice Longworth, when Alice's daughter, Paulina, was born.

Edith stayed busy in public affairs too. She introduced Herbert Hoover at a Madison Square Garden rally in his second campaign to be elected President. She was now seventy years old. Neither Edith nor her children supported Franklin Delano Roosevelt for President, as they feared he would diminish Theodore's Presidential success. If another Roosevelt became President, they felt it should be Theodore, Jr.

Edith took several trips abroad, but Sagamore Hill was home. She had retained her love for reading through all the hectic years, and she had more time to read now. She stayed active in her church work at Christ Church of Oyster Bay and worked in the Needlework Guild, which provided clothes for needy people. She was fortunately able to continue her outside activities until her death.

Edith died on September 30, 1948, at age eighty-seven and was buried beside Theodore at Oyster Bay. Of her children only Archie and Ethel survived her, plus sixteen grandchildren and fifteen great-grandchildren. Alice Longworth also survived her.

Edith was a reserved person who kept her thoughts to herself, but she was the calming influence Theodore needed in his overly enthusiastic approach to life.

29. Helen Herron Taft

Although she was named Helen at her birth on January 2, 1861, in Cincinnati, Ohio, Helen Herron was always called Nellie by her family and friends.

Nellie's father, John Williamson Herron, was a lawyer in Cincinnati. He served one term in the Ohio State Senate, so Nellie grew up in a political atmosphere.

The Herron family lived in a gray brick row house in a fashionable city neighborhood. Nellie's early education was directed toward the study of literature and languages, but she most enjoyed her music lessons. She spent much of her free time practicing, including scales, so intensely that she said, "I wonder the whole neighborhood did not rebel."

When she was seventeen, Nellie, her parents and other family members were invited to visit President and Mrs. Rutherford B. Hayes in the White House, as President Hayes had been a law partner of Mr. Herron's before becoming President. During the visit Nellie's youngest sister was christened. Nellie was thrilled and excited to feel herself to be a part of Washington and the national political scene, even if for only a week.

The next year Nellie met Will Taft for the first time. It was curious that they had not met during all the intervening years because their fathers were close friends, and their sisters were classmates and frequent visitors with each other. One reason may have been because the Tafts lived in a suburb of Cincinnati known as Mt. Auburn. Also Will was four years older than Nellie, so they socialized with different age groups.

One night when she was eighteen, Nellie and some of her friends went to Mt. Auburn for sledding, and Will joined the group. He and Nellie were immediately attracted to each other, and Will rode her down the hill on his bobsled. After that evening they began dating steadily.

Nellie attended Miss Nourse's Private School in Cincinnati and later went to the University of Cincinnati. During these years Will worked as a court reporter while he attended Cincinnati Law School, but they saw each other regularly at parties at the homes of mutual friends and at practices held for the amateur theatrical productions, in which they were both interested.

Helen Taft. (Courtesy Library of Congress.)

Following college, Nellie got a job teaching school and taught for the next two years. Will took a trip to Europe to visit his parents in Vienna, where his father was serving as United States Minister to Austria-Hungary during President Chester Arthur's administration. Both Nellie and Will knew they had strong affection for each other, but they had not yet decided if their affection was strong enough for marriage.

Will returned from Europe to find that Nellie and two of her women friends had started an intellectual salon, at which members and invited guests would broaden their knowledge by discussions of economics and other intellectual topics. "We were bent on improving our minds," Nellie explained later.

Since Nellie and her friends were still single, Will asked her if this salon was not really run for the purpose of meeting men and matchmaking. Nellie denied it indignantly, although she suspected Will was teasing her. Since, in fact, two marriages did result from the meetings, Will was not entirely mistaken. But Nellie gained a real knowledge of and heightened interest in politics from the salon.

Will's father was now serving as Minister to Russia, and in his absence Will was practicing law in his father's firm. His practice increased steadily, and he was soon earning enough money to marry. He proposed to Nellie, who was the only girl he had ever considered seriously as a future wife.

On June 19, 1886, Nellie and Will were married in their Ohio hometown in the presence of relatives and friends. They went to Europe on their honeymoon, where they happily shopped for accessories for their new home. Nellie bought some beautiful Delft plates, which Will carried by hand during at least half of their trip. When they landed in New York on their return home, they entrusted the plates to a New York Express Company to ship them to Ohio. Every plate was broken by the time they reached Ohio.

Will's father had always emphasized his goal that Will be an outstanding citizen. Where Will's father left off, Nellie now took up the slack, urging Will to rise ever higher.

Will was a heavyset, somewhat easygoing individual, pleasant in manner, but he aimed to please. When his own ambition did not push him forward, there was Nellie in the background providing enough ambition for them both.

In less than a year after they married, Will was named to fill a vacancy as judge for the State Superior Court. He was now thirty years old. In the next election he was elected to the post in his own right.

Nellie's and Will's first child, Robert, was born in September 1889. When Robert was about six months old, Will was asked to be the United States Solicitor General by President Benjamin Harrison. In this job he would represent the Federal government in cases heard before the Supreme Court. The Taft family would have to move to Washington to live.

Will and Nellie lived very simply in the nation's capital with Robert and his little sister, Helen, who was born in 1891. The family's chief recreation was taking Sunday afternoon drives in their horse-drawn carriage around Washington.

Will loved Nellie dearly, but he recognized her bossiness and her drive for him to succeed. He told her on one occasion, "I consider obedience the first virtue of a husband." Another time he said, "You are my dearest and best critic." He always remained calm when she became upset, and he regarded her emotional outbursts as an integral part of her personality.

When Nellie opposed his acceptance of a position as an appeals court judge on a Federal circuit composed of the states of Ohio, Kentucky, Michigan and Tennessee, Will ignored her objections and accepted the appointment. Her argument against the appeals court appointment was that if they moved back to Cincinnati, it would "put an end to all the opportunities...of being thrown with the bigwigs."

Will enjoyed being a judge, and said, "I love courts. They are my ideals, that typify on earth what we shall meet hereafter in Heaven under a just God." So in this matter he did not allow Nellie to rule him, and possibly he did only when her desires suited his own.

Will was an outstanding judge. He was the first to uphold the right of workers to strike against employers, which greatly strengthened the Sherman Antitrust Act, largely ignored previously.

Back in Cincinnati another son, Charles, was born to the Tafts. Nellie involved herself in more than motherhood, however. She organized and managed the Cincinnati Symphony Orchestra Association and became involved in volunteer hospital and kindergarten work as well.

Nellie was a good mother who sincerely loved her children, read to them faithfully and assisted them with learning, but she made their life a contest in which they had to win by being best in each activity they undertook.

In April 1900, the Tafts, with their three children, Nellie's sister, Maria, and a group of other families boarded the transport ship *Hancock* to sail to the Philippines. President William McKinley had asked the men to go to the islands and establish a civilian form of government there.

America had recently assumed control of the Philippines as a part of the settlement of the Spanish-American War. General Douglas MacArthur was in charge of the present military government there. Will and President McKinley agreed a civilian government should be put in place as soon as possible, as there was widespread discontent with American rule among the Filipino people. There had been several bloody uprisings to emphasize their resentment.

Will agreed to head the commission if President McKinley would recommend him to fill the next vacancy on the Supreme Court of the United States. When Will asked Nellie if she wanted to go to the Philippines for a few months, she said, "Yes, of course." Only later did she think to ask why they were going!

Everyone who was involved in any way with the project expected it to take about a year to complete. Instead they would be there about three years.

When the *Hancock* reached the island of Oahu in Hawaii, it remained in dock for four days, and the passengers had an opportunity to acquaint themselves with the tropics. The island of Oahu was enchanting to Nellie with its lush greenery and white sands. She was so enthralled she even attempted surfing in Hawaiian canoes. They were invited to be guests at luaus, or native feasts, and hula dances. All the children loved the sandy beach. They ran up and down happily, glad to be on land for a few days.

The ship went on to Yokohama, Japan, where Will left his family and returned to the Philippines. Robert Taft had contracted diphtheria and was in quarantine, so the family had to stay in Japan for a while. They lived there in a rented bungalow.

Nellie learned that the Emperor and Empress of Japan expected her to have an official audience with them during her stay in their country. She had not brought dresses suitable for such an event, but that fact only slowed Nellie down. It did not stop her. She found a local seamstress to remodel one of the dresses she did bring, giving it a high neckline suitable for an appearance at the Royal Palace.

In the Philippines Will and the other commissioners found their work of establishing a civilian government to be uphill all the way. General MacArthur was resentful because he would be replaced, and between his hostility toward them and native uprisings, life was as sticky as the hot, humid weather. Will, who was very fat, wrote Nellie that their reception by General MacArthur was so cool that he almost stopped sweating!

When Nellie, Maria and the children joined Will in August in Manila, they found a city of contrasts. Many shacks, the homes of extremely poverty-stricken natives, stood shoulder to shoulder with the beautiful cathedrals and elegant mansions which had belonged to the former aristocratic rulers from Spain. Huts were built on stilts, women accompanied by their naked children did their family laundry on the river banks, and outrigger canoes darted about on the water. The streets were clogged with pony-drawn carts, and American soldiers seemed to be everywhere.

Nellie was not one to complain about her surroundings, and she set about making a home for her family. The first house they lived in was large and rambling, overlooking Manila Bay. There was a moat around the house, with a large veranda on all sides, which gave Nellie space for dinner parties. They had native music for entertainment. The Tafts lived here for several months until the Commission decided to appoint Will as civilian Governor of the islands. He was inaugurated as Governor on July 4, 1900. Will then moved his family to a palace at Malacañan, after which the Tafts set off on a tour of all the Philippine Islands. They were fascinated by the many diverse inhabitants.

When they returned to the palace, Nellie began an intensive effort to show Filipinos they had nothing to fear from Americans, that they were the Filipinos' friends. She held an "at home" reception each week at the palace to which homesick Americans, such as United States officials and their wives, missionaries and school teachers, as well as many Filipinos came.

A typhoon struck the Islands while the Tafts lived in the palace, causing heavy flooding. Again, Nellie coped. After all, she was First Lady of the Philippines.

Will worked feverishly in his job as Governor, and the hard work plus the heat, which he hated, undermined his health. Following an attack of dengue fever, he developed a serious abdominal abscess which required two surgeries to correct.

During Will's debilitating illness in the Philippines, Theodore Roosevelt became President of the United States following the assassination of President McKinley, who died on September 14, 1901. Taking advantage of Governor Taft's illness and the change in administrations in the United States, the Filipino opponents of the civilian government in the Islands staged a massacre of United States army officers and soldiers at Balangiga.

Will was forced to come back to the United States that year in December for a rest, even though he worried about the Filipino people and their country. He returned to Manila within a few months, where he remained until 1904. At that time Will was named Secretary of War in President Theodore Roosevelt's Cabinet. In this post he could oversee the government in the Philippines, which he wanted to be able to do.

Nellie had enjoyed much of their stay in Manila. One of her favorite places there was a public park called the Luneta, where band music was played frequently on warm evenings while people strolled and visited with each other freely. She enjoyed the informality and friendliness of the park, and thought it would be nice if Washington had one like it.

Nellie spent several months in California before coming on to Washington in order to rebuild her own health, which had been damaged by Will's serious illness, her mother's sudden death and the recent increased strains of living in a foreign country in the midst of civil unrest.

The Taft children were growing up. Robert was now a student in his uncle Horace Taft's boys' school in Watertown, Connecticut.

Certainly President Roosevelt and Will were good friends and worked together closely. Will had managed to get the Filipinos on the right track with a civilian government. He was then sent by President Roosevelt to expedite work on the Panama Canal, and in 1906 he went to Cuba to arrange a peace treaty with that country.

During one of the Tafts' visits to the White House, President Roosevelt claimed to be clairvoyant. "I see a man weighing three hundred and fifty pounds," the President said. "There is something hanging over his head. I cannot make out what it is. . . . At one time it looks like the Presidency, then again it looks like the Chief Justiceship." He watched the Tafts for their reactions.

Nellie said quickly, "Make it the Presidency."

"Make it the Chief Justiceship," Will urged him.

Theodore Roosevelt decided he wanted Will as his successor to the Presidency, and with his endorsement, Will was elected in 1908. At least Nellie's ambition for Will had been realized, even if it was not his own.

As First Lady, Nellie attended all important political conferences in the White House. She plainly considered herself an active partner in the Presidency, although Will never indicated he shared her belief.

She changed the servants' uniforms to livery and replaced the male steward with a female housekeeper to supervise the other servants. She refurnished many of the rooms with Philippines-style furniture, and had masses of plants and flowers everywhere throughout the White House. Soon Washington wits were calling the White House the Malacañan Palace.

The Tafts had been living in the White House for only a few busy weeks when Nellie suffered a stroke, which essentially robbed her of speech. She was forced to curtail her activities for about eighteen months, while her official hostess duties were assumed by her sisters and her daughter, Helen.

Will rescinded an order of Theodore Roosevelt's which placed large areas of lands in the Northwest under Federal jurisdiction so they could later be used as sources for waterpower. He brought assistant postmasters in the civil service system, and advocated a Constitutional amendment which would allow Federal tax to be levied on income to finance government expenditures.

Theodore Roosevelt was unhappy with Will's actions, and the two friends became estranged. Roosevelt felt Will had betrayed him and his policies by his actions.

As Nellie improved in health, she chose to entertain with receptions which included dancing, and held fewer formal dinners.

She had not forgotten how much she enjoyed the Luneta in Manila, and she decided to create a modified version of the park in Washington in Potomac Park. She had a bandstand built so concerts could be held twice a week, and ordered eighty Japanese cherry tress from various nurseries to be planted along the banks of the Potomac River.

When government officials in Japan learned of Nellie's efforts, they sent three thousand cherry trees as a gift from the city of Tokyo to the city of Washington, D.C. Nellie planted the first tree, and Viscountess Chinda, wife of the Japanese Ambassador, planted the second. There were enough trees to be planted around the Tidal Basin and along Riverside Drive in both East and West Potomac Parks. Today these trees provide a vision of springtime beauty in Washington for all visitors and residents.

Will and Nellie celebrated their silver wedding anniversary on June 19, 1911, at the White House with an elaborate party. The shrubbery around the White House was filled with thousands of tiny twinkling electric lights.

Water fountains were lit by colored lights, and paper lanterns swayed in the trees. The thirty-four hundred guests were served a buffet supper, which featured a giant cake decorated with crystal hearts, turtledoves and tiny American flags. Among the guests were Warren and Flossie Harding, who would one day be residents of the White House themselves. Nellie wore a special gift — a diamond tiara from Will.

Theodore Roosevelt was still angry about Will's actions as President, and decided to campaign against Will in his bid for reelection. Will was hurt and bewildered by Roosevelt's attitude, and the rift between them was never mended.

Will was renominated on the Republican ticket, but since Roosevelt split the Republican vote by running as a third-party candidate, the Democratic nominee, Woodrow Wilson, won the election.

When Will's term ended, he accepted a job as the Kent Professor of Constitutional Law at Yale University. When the Yale officials offered him the Kent chair, Will said he wouldn't fit a chair, but a sofa would be just right!

In 1921 Will finally realized his own lifetime ambition when President Warren Harding offered him the Chief Justiceship of the Supreme Court. Will had always wanted to be a Supreme Court justice more than he wanted to be President.

Robert Taft had graduated from Yale and Harvard and was now a lawyer. He married Martha Wheaton Bowers in October 1914. Helen Taft married Frederick Manning, a Yale history professor, in 1920, and received her own Ph.D. in history in 1924 from Yale. The younger son, Charles, also became a lawyer, and he and Robert opened a law office as partners in 1922.

Nellie was busy and happy during these years, continuing to travel when possible and attending concerts. But Will's health began to fail badly from arteriosclerosis, and he was forced to retire from the Supreme Court in February 1930. He died a few weeks later on March 8, 1930, and was buried in Arlington National Cemetery in Virginia.

Will's death was a severe blow to Nellie, but she was still vigorous and active, and soon began traveling again. She still suffered from speech difficulties, but she did not let her handicap diminish her enjoyment of life.

Will left an estate of four hundred and seventy-five thousand dollars, so Nellie was able to live in comfort until her death. Robert managed her financial affairs for her, and she lived to see him elected a United States Senator from Ohio.

Nellie died in her home in Washington, D.C., on May 22, 1943, and was buried beside Will in Arlington National Cemetery.

30. Ellen Louise Axson Wilson

Ellen Louise Axson was born into a family with a strong tradition of service in Presbyterian church ministries. She was born May 15, 1860, in Savannah, Georgia, just about a year before Georgia seceded from the Union. She was the first child of her parents, Reverend Samuel Edward Axson and Margaret Jane Hoyt Axson, both of whom were also children of Presbyterian ministers.

After the beginning of the Civil War, young Ellen's life and that of her parents were marked by separations, instability and her father's illnesses. Ellen and her mother divided their time alternately between both sets of grandparents while Ellen's father served as chaplain of the First Regiment, Georgia Infantry, in the Confederate army.

In 1866, after the war had ended, Reverend Axson accepted a pastorate in Rome, Georgia. While they lived in Rome, Ellen's brother, Stockton, was born and her Grandmother Hoyt came to live with the family.

There were no public schools in Georgia after the war, so the Axson children were tutored by their well-educated mother. Reverend Axson's church was doing well, and the family's life assumed a more normal pattern.

When she was eleven, Ellen was sent to Rome Female College, which had been closed during the war but reopened in 1871. The school was first established by Presbyterians, and while it had a college department, it also contained departments for primary and preparatory classes for young girls.

A new world of friendship and fun opened to Ellen with her entry to school. She reveled in friendships with fellow students, which she had never before experienced. These friends and others she made later would always be of outstanding importance in her life.

Ellen discovered she possessed artistic talent, and she began to pursue this interest in earnest. After she graduated from the college in 1876, she continued to take art lessons from one of the teachers at the college, Helen F. Fairchild. Miss Fairchild was impressed by Ellen's talent and dedication to art, and she submitted a "drawing of a school scene" to the Paris International Exposition in France where it was awarded a bronze medal.

Ellen wanted to continue her education at Nashville University in

Ellen Wilson. (Courtesy Library of Congress.)

Tennessee, but her father could not afford to send her. She then enrolled in classes in German, French and art at Rome Female College. She also began to earn money by making crayon portraits, and she started daydreaming of going to New York to study art. But another brother, Edward William, had arrived in the Axson family, and Reverend Axson could not afford to send Ellen to New York. Her best friend, Rosalie Anderson, shared the same dream, but her parents felt they were both too young to be in New York alone.

In 1880 Ellen's father suffered the first of many breakdowns when he could not decide which of two pastorates to accept. He decided he would remain at Rome after he recovered.

Although Ellen and her girlfriends had dated various men, each claimed to have not found any special one. Then all at once, it seemed to Ellen, her friends began pairing off and getting married. Ellen wanted a man who enjoyed literature and art, as she did, a man who was intellectual and vitally interested in the world around him, but so far she had not met anyone like that. Would she ever find her ideal?

Ellen was visiting Rosalie Anderson in Sewanee, Tennessee, when her mother gave birth to a fourth child, named Margaret Randolph, on October 10, 1881. The child would be known as Madge. Ellen hurried home to help her mother care for the new baby, and found her mother very ill. Mrs. Axson died on November 4 that year. The fulfillment of Ellen's dreams would have to wait.

Ellen was not thinking about her ambitions then. She was devastated by grief. She and her mother had always enjoyed an especially close relationship since Ellen had been the only daughter. Ellen knew her mother had denied herself many times in order that Ellen's life could be more pleasant.

Ellen's aunt Louisa Hoyt Brown took the baby Madge to rear in her own home, and Ellen assumed the duties of housekeeper, surrogate mother to her two brothers and hostess for her father.

With the death of his wife, Reverend Axson became extremely depressed and less and less able to cope with daily living. His depression was having an adverse effect on Ellen, and by the summer of 1882, Ellen's uncle Will insisted that Ellen visit some of their Hoyt relatives in the New York and New England areas.

Ellen had a wonderful time, and her cousins made a special effort to entertain her with sightseeing trips and dinners at fancy restaurants. When she returned home, she could not help comparing the opulent life in New York with the emotional and financial poverty of her life in Georgia. Her father had collapsed again, and Ellen's grandfather Axson came to stay with the children and assume his son's pastoral duties until he could recover his health.

It was during this emotionally trying time that Ellen met her dream man, Woodrow Wilson, in April 1883. Ellen's father felt well enough to conduct services in his own church that morning, and Woodrow attended the services. Ellen was so pleased with her father's improvement that she was unaware of young Wilson's close scrutiny during the communion service.

Later that same day, the young man called at Ellen's home, where he introduced himself as a nephew of one of the leading families in the church. He had really called hoping to see Ellen again. They had an almost immediate attraction to each other, and their courtship began.

In Woodrow Wilson Ellen found the intellectual, sophisticated, handsome, sensitive man for whom she had been searching. He was employed as a lawyer for an Atlanta firm, and he was also the son of a Presbyterian minister. Ellen lost her heart completely — to the intense amusement and delight of her friends, and to her own amazement.

Woodrow told Ellen he planned to leave his law practice, as he did not like law. He wanted to enter Johns Hopkins University in Maryland, where he would study for advanced degrees in both history and political science so he could teach. Ellen told him her dream of studying art in New York City. Neither felt they should make a commitment just then, but Woodrow drove from Atlanta to Rome almost every weekend to see her and spend some time with her. He had told his mother Ellen would be his wife someday, but he had not yet proposed!

In September 1883, Ellen was waiting for her train in Asheville, North Carolina, when to her surprise she met Woodrow in the depot. She had been visiting an old school friend in nearby Morganton and was on her way back home. Woodrow's mother, sister and younger brother were vacationing in nearby Arden, and he had come into Asheville to catch a train to Baltimore and his new graduate studies.

This was fate! They were both convinced that a higher power had had a hand in their meeting. Woodrow insisted on postponing his plans for a few days while he took her to meet his family. Two days later, when Woodrow finally boarded the train to Baltimore, he and Ellen were engaged.

Ellen and Woodrow then began an ardent correspondence, which they would continue at intervals even after their marriage. Woodrow was busy and happy in his studies and plans for a different direction for his life, while Ellen was becoming more and more concerned about her father's state of mind. One of her brothers was in boarding school, but Eddie was still at home and she had the care and responsibility of him as well as their father.

At Christmas in 1883, the three of them went to live with the Reverend Axson's parents in Savannah, Georgia. On January 13, 1884, Ellen's father was committed to the Georgia State Mental Hospital after he became violent. This necessary move broke Ellen's heart, and she wondered how Woodrow would react to the news. It had been his loving letters that had sustained her during these past awful months.

Woodrow's answer was prompt and reassuring. He left his school and came to Savannah to be with her for a week while she struggled to deal with this horrifying event in her life.

In April he wrote her he had heard about a possible job opening in Arkansas at an industrial school. He told her he was willing to go ahead and take the job if he could get it, so they could be married. He planned to include her two young brothers in their home life, as he knew they had nowhere else to go.

Ellen was sorely tempted because money was a never-ending problem, and after all she loved Woodrow and they had already planned to marry. However, she also knew he might never again have a chance to complete his graduate studies, and in Arkansas research facilities would not be available to complete a book he had already started. She decided another solution to her problem would be to go to work herself.

On May 28, 1884, Ellen's father died in the mental hospital, possibly of a drug overdose. Ellen's grief was so overwhelming she could not even write to Woodrow, but instead asked a friend to write for her. When he came to Georgia to be with her, Ellen offered to break their engagement. Suicide was held to be a mortal sin, and she feared that the manner of her poor father's death might have changed Woodrow's feelings for her. He assured her that nothing could be further from the truth, and their engagement was unbroken.

Ellen's father left an estate of twelve thousand dollars, which today would translate into a financial worth of about one hundred fifty thousand dollars. The money relieved Ellen's anxiety about how to pay for her brothers' educations, and renewed her own dream of studying art in New York.

Stockton, her oldest brother, enrolled in Davidson College in North Carolina, and Eddie went to stay with an uncle in Georgia. Ellen spent four weeks visiting and resting before going to New York. Woodrow went along with her to help her get settled.

Ellen found peace in the big city through her artwork and the many cultural events available to her for the first time in her life. She allowed a young man named Arthur Goodrich to show her the town for a time until Woodrow became jealous because of her frequent mentions of Goodrich. When Goodrich declared he loved her, Ellen realized she had allowed matters to get out of hand and broke off with him. She loved Woodrow!

By the time their school terms had ended in May, Ellen and Woodrow felt they could not endure further separation. He got a job as an associate professor of history at Bryn Mawr College near Philadelphia, a women's college established by Quakers.

Ellen and Woodrow were married in her grandparents' parlor in Savannah on June 23, 1885. Her brother, Eddie, and Woodrow's young nephew, Wilson Howe, chose the occasion to have a fistfight. Ellen was horrified, but Woodrow was amused.

The newlyweds spent a six-week honeymoon in Arden, and when they left for Pennsylvania to begin their new life together, Ellen was pregnant.

Margaret Woodrow Wilson was born on April 16, 1886, and a second daughter, Jessie Woodrow Wilson, was born the next year, altering Woodrow's plans to go to Berlin for a year of study. He was giving lectures at Johns Hopkins to supplement their income as expenses mounted.

Woodrow became dissatisfied with the heavy workload and low pay at Bryn Mawr. He moved on to teach at Wesleyan University in Middletown, Connecticut. Again, within about two years' time, he became restless and hoped to find a more interesting and challenging job. Their third daughter, Eleanor Randolph, was born in Connecticut on October 6, 1889.

During these busy years, Ellen tried to put her own art interests out of her mind, as she seemed to have no hope of furthering her art career. Woodrow's ambitions became hers. Not only did she have a husband to care for, there were the three little girls, as well as her two brothers and various other relatives who came and went constantly, some spending one night, others staying for months.

In 1890 one of Woodrow's dreams came true when he was given a full professorship at Princeton to teach political economy and jurisprudence. Ellen and Woodrow moved to Princeton, where they settled happily. Since both were from families headed by Presbyterian ministers, they felt at home with the many other Presbyterians. They stayed there a total of twenty-three years, the longest they lived anywhere.

They first rented a home, then built their own rambling eleven-room house, where the constant parade of visitors and temporary live-in relatives continued. In the midst of all the confusion, Ellen and Woodrow were content with their life. They took an active part in church activities and the social life of the town.

The Wilsons reared their three little girls in strictest Presbyterian faith, allowing no room for Sunday frivolity. Attendance at religious services, walks or quiet conversations were the only recreations available to them on the Sabbath.

This did not always lead to improvement of their characters, however. The two older girls often joined together in teasing their little sister, Nell. Nell was a pretty child, dark-haired and sensitive by nature. They would call her a "Yankee" since she had been born in Connecticut. Nell was uncertain what a Yankee was, but from the tone they used, she knew she didn't want to be one, and she would cry.

A favorite game they played was "dividing things." They divided among themselves the states, Greek gods and goddesses, household furniture or anything else that occurred to them. Nell always got the worst of this game, and again she would cry.

Ellen and Woodrow went on a vacation trip in 1895, and they attended an art exhibit. Ellen realized how much she had missed being a part of the art world. Since the girls were growing up, she hoped to be able to put in a little time with painting and gradually work her way back.

Meanwhile, Woodrow was suffering from the effects of chronic overwork. He had continued to "moonlight" on the lecture circuit to earn extra money, as well as hold down his full-time job at Princeton. His doctor told him he must get away for a few weeks, and he decided to go to Europe. He had developed pain and numbness in his right hand and arm that was so severe he had to write with his left hand. In view of later events in his life, this may have been the result of a light stroke.

Ellen went with Woodrow to New York, where he sailed for Europe on May 30, 1896. He would be gone for fifteen weeks on a tour of Scotland and England. As soon as she had him settled on board the boat, Ellen went to the Metropolitan Museum of Art. It was the first time she had been back to the museum since she was an art student in the city.

Ellen returned home, where she spent the summer caring for their daughters and visiting relatives. She still found no time to devote to art.

Woodrow returned from his trip in the fall. He was still edgy and easily upset, but he continued teaching at Princeton and lecturing at Johns Hopkins. Gradually his health improved, and he began attracting attention in academic circles.

To his great surprise and delight, on June 2, 1902, he was named president of Princeton University. Neither he nor Ellen had expected him to receive such an honor. He accepted the post gladly, and considered it to be the pinnacle of his success.

Princeton provided a house for its presidents, and the Wilsons moved into it to live. Ellen spent the next several months refurbishing the house and directing extensive landscaping of the grounds. They sold their own home.

It was well that Ellen had a project to occupy her mind, as Woodrow's ailing, elderly, confused father came to live with them for a number of months before his death. Ellen was completely exhausted, mentally and physically, when it was over.

In 1903 Woodrow took Ellen on a trip to Europe on a "second honeymoon" to restore her well-being. They had a wonderful time. She went back the next year with her daughter Jessie and two women friends from New Orleans.

On her return home, Ellen found her relatives were suffering from so many serious problems that she wondered if she were at fault and lacked faith. Her brother Stockton was now in and out of treatment for the same type of mental condition from which their father had suffered; her other brother, Eddie, his wife and young son drowned in an accident; and Woodrow continued to have difficulties with his health.

Ellen had several positive forces in her life during these trying days. Her faith sustained her, she loved to read, she again began painting and their daughters seemed to be doing well in college. Margaret was at Women's College in Baltimore, Jessie was a student there the next year, and Nell entered St. Mary's College in Raleigh, North Carolina, in the fall of 1906.

Ellen and Woodrow had planned a trip to Bermuda in January 1907, but Nell had to have tubercular glands removed from her neck and Ellen could not go. She insisted that Woodrow go on without her.

This trip resulted in the most serious problem they had in their marriage. It was on this trip that Woodrow met Mary Peck.

Woodrow met Mrs. Peck during the last two days he was in Bermuda in 1907. They were both dinner guests at the town mayor's home, and the next evening Mrs. Peck invited Woodrow to dine with her at her vacation home. In a note to her before he returned to Princeton, he said he had rarely met anyone he "could so entirely admire and enjoy."

The next year he returned to Bermuda, again by himself. Stockton was worse, and Ellen did not feel she could leave him as he clung to Ellen for emotional support. Ellen did not realize she was neglecting her husband, but Mrs. Peck lost no time in helping Woodrow come to this conclusion. She set out to cause trouble because she was bored more than anything else. She had had two unhappy marriages of her own; indeed, the second was still in effect, but she too came to Bermuda alone for vacations.

Woodrow was flattered by the attentions she paid him. He wrote Ellen that Mrs. Peck was "fine and dear," rousing a faint warning in Ellen's mind, but no more at the time. When he got back home he continued to write to Mrs. Peck.

Nell began to become aware that her parents were having marital problems, and when Woodrow planned a trip to England the next year, she insisted that her mother go with him. Instead Ellen took her three daughters to vacation near an art colony in Connecticut. Woodrow had been difficult to live with for some time now, and Ellen felt a need to pursue her own interests for awhile.

This period of separation gave each of them time to think. Woodrow began to regret the trouble he had caused Ellen. Ellen decided she had overreacted to his friendship with Mrs. Peck and vowed to try harder to get along.

When he came home, Woodrow wanted Ellen to go with him to visit Mrs. Peck at her home in Pittsfield, Massachusetts. They went, and Ellen found she liked the woman, and some of Ellen's suspicions were laid to rest for the moment. Mr. Peck was present, and it was hard to suspect Mrs. Peck of trying to wreck her marriage when she had her own husband — or so Ellen reasoned. That Mrs. Peck admired Woodrow, there was no doubt, and she did not bother to hide her admiration for Woodrow from her husband.

Woodrow was embroiled in bitter controversy his last year at Princeton because of a disagreement about the site to be used to build a new graduate college. Woodrow felt a site on campus was preferable to an off-campus site chosen by the Dean and some of the trustees, which was about a mile away from the main campus. The controversy soured his feelings about Princeton.

Woodrow continued his frequent correspondence with Mrs. Peck, and asked her advice about the course of action he should take with the Princeton trustees. He also visited her at her home in Massachusetts and at an apartment she rented in New York. It is doubtful Ellen ever knew how many times they were together, but she realized Woodrow was still fascinated by Mary Peck.

Ellen later told her doctor that Woodrow's interest in the other woman was the source of the greatest unhappiness she had during their entire marriage. She had to be careful and not cause any scandal as it would harm Woodrow's career, making it necessary to confide only in her doctor.

When Woodrow turned his attention to politics, Ellen encouraged his new interest, hoping it would lessen Mrs. Peck's hold on his affections. Woodrow's political studies were a normal correlation to his history and political science education, and he began to write articles about political subjects which attracted much favorable attention from the New Jersey Democrats. Woodrow and Ellen were both members of the Democratic party.

When they looked at the Wilsons, the Democrats liked what they saw. Woodrow had an excellent background in studies of government, if not in actual experience, and Ellen was deeply involved with the Princeton Women's Auxiliary, which had recently made substantial improvements to the infirmary there. It looked to the Democratic leaders as if Woodrow might be a good candidate for Governor of the state. They had not won a gubernatorial election in over twenty years.

They nominated Woodrow in 1910, and Woodrow was elected to be Governor of New Jersey. It could not have come at a better time for him, in both his and Ellen's opinion. They had no hesitation in this career change since he felt so much bitterness toward the trustees at Princeton.

As the new Governor, Woodrow rode the crest of a new wave of popularity. In his first year he successfully gained four major legislative triumphs on reform bills he had sponsored. By the end of the year, Democratic leaders at the national level were taking a hard look at Woodrow and his electability to the Presidency.

Ellen was ambitious for Woodrow and reassured the leaders of the party that his health was much improved. She campaigned alongside him in his 1912 bid to be elected President. He won, and Ellen was supremely confident he would be a good President.

Even with the bitter memories of the Princeton graduate school controversy still in their minds, the Wilsons, including the daughters, were tearful when they moved from Princeton. They had lived in the town for such a long time.

At their new home in the White House, Ellen assumed her duties as First Lady with the same ease that Woodrow did his as President. They felt it would be better to not have an inaugural ball, and she kept their entertainments simple.

Former President and Mrs. Taft had made every effort to acquaint Ellen with her duties and responsibilities before they left Washington. President Taft told her money had been appropriated to renovate the third floor. Ellen was glad to hear this as she enjoyed renovating houses. During their first summer, five bedrooms and three bathrooms were installed. She used the money left over to renew and brighten other areas of their living quarters. She chose mountain-crafted rugs, quilts and bedspreads, which had been handmade by women in Tennessee and North Carolina. With the example set by the First Lady, other American women adopted the same style for their homes, and the sale of these handcrafted items boosted the income of the Southern women. Ellen also had the rose garden begun, which endures today. She did not see it completed.

Ellen involved herself to a great extent in cleaning up the slum alleys and areas in Washington. Some of the society ladies in Washington remarked that they felt obliged to talk of alley improvements if they wanted to be invited to the White House.

When Ellen first became ill in June 1913, the White House physician told her she needed to slow down in her extensive activities. She went to Cornish, New Hampshire, with her daughters for a vacation in hopes of feeling better. Mrs. Peck had offered to rent them her Nantucket house, but Woodrow tactfully declined the offer.

Jessie, Ellen's middle daughter, announced her engagement to Francis Bowes Sayre during the vacation. Mr. Sayre was a lawyer in the New York District Attorney's office. They planned to be married in the White House.

Ellen returned from vacation in a happier frame of mind. Woodrow had severed his ties with Mary Peck, and had assured Ellen he had never once stopped loving her. She was looking forward eagerly to helping Jessie with her wedding and having an opportunity to renew old friendships and acquaintances.

Since her vacation in Connecticut near the art colony a couple of years earlier, Ellen had renewed her efforts to manage some time to devote to painting, and she had completed several pieces. In an ironic twist of fate, now that she was swamped by White House and family duties, her art caught on with the critics and the public.

She had hesitantly sent one of her oil paintings to a New York gallery while Woodrow was still Governor of New Jersey. It was accepted, shown and won a prize without the gallery owner knowing the name of the artist, since she had submitted it under another name.

Becoming a little braver, she then sent several works to the gallery in

1912, admitting she had painted them. The owner of the gallery told her the pictures were good, which she had doubted, and he helped her select some to be shown at various galleries in the Northeast. These were praised by critics, and shortly before Woodrow was inaugurated in 1913, Ellen's first one-woman show, consisting of fifty landscapes, opened at a gallery in Philadelphia.

An art critic for The *New York Times* said, "Mrs. Wilson's paintings show her to be a real lover of nature and the possessor of a fine faculty for interpreting it. . . ." But now that Ellen had gained recognition with her work, she was too busy to enjoy her new fame and honor!

Ellen sold a number of her paintings and donated the proceeds to the Berry School near Rome, Georgia. This school had been founded "to educate underprivileged and mountain children." Ellen had earlier established a scholarship at the school in her brother Eddie's name when he and his family were drowned.

Jessie had a beautiful wedding on November 25, 1913, and Ellen felt good about the prospects for the couple's future happiness. Jessie had always been the most down-to-earth and levelheaded of all her daughters. She received over five hundred wedding gifts.

The excitement had buoyed Ellen temporarily, but when it was over, she again felt tired and drained. She wondered if her concern for Margaret was causing it. Margaret had suffered a nervous collapse sometime earlier and had to leave college. She was now launched in a singing career in New York, and was not very successful so far.

Ellen was also concerned about Nell, who had recently fallen in love with her father's Secretary of the Treasury, William G. McAdoo. Mr. McAdoo was twenty-six years older than Nell, had been married before and had six children, some nearly as old as Nell. His wife had died some months earlier.

Ellen and Woodrow were stunned by Nell's choice. They had always liked Mr. McAdoo, but they felt he was an unsuitable husband for Nell. She was only twenty-four.

Nell insisted on marrying Mr. McAdoo in a White House wedding, which took place on May 7, 1914. It was a simple wedding, smaller than her sister's had been as she preferred a family-type wedding. The Wilsons and the White House staff made every effort to stage a gala event for Nell, although Ellen was still moving painfully at times from a fall she had suffered two months earlier when she slipped on the polished floor of her bedroom.

Through sheer determination, Ellen managed to see Nell married. After the wedding was over, her health declined dramatically. In an effort to revive her spirits, Woodrow began making plans for a vacation in New Hampshire. She showed no interest, although she seemed pleased when she received the news that Jessie expected a baby. It was becoming evident to everyone that Ellen was seriously ill.

The White House doctor knew that Ellen was dying from a kidney ailment known as Bright's Disease, but he could not bring himself to tell Woodrow or the Wilson daughters the truth. He knew Woodrow was concerned about events taking place in Europe, and there were fears the United States might be drawn into a war if some settlement could not be reached on the issues.

Woodrow spent every spare moment he had with Ellen, even though he did not know how serious her illness was. The morning Congress passed the "alley bill" for which Ellen had worked so hard, she died. The date was August 6, 1914. She was buried in the Myrtle Hill Cemetery beside her mother and father in East Rome, Georgia.

Woodrow would remarry, and the account of his second wife follows this chapter.

31. Edith Bolling Galt Wilson

Edith Bolling was the daughter of William Holcombe Bolling, a lawyer and circuit court judge, and Sallie White, a Southern beauty with a gentle nature, of Wytheville, Virginia. She was born October 15, 1872, seventh of eleven children in her family. Edith traced her ancestry back to English settlers of before the Revolutionary War era. She also numbered Pocahontas, the Indian princess who married John Rolfe, as one of her ancestors. Edith's Indian heritage was evident in her lovely, dark, glossy hair and high cheekbones. She was a pretty little girl who grew into a beautiful woman.

Mr. Bolling had served in the Confederate army not many years before Edith's birth. He had owned a plantation before the Civil War, but he lost it, and the family moved in with his mother to live at Wytheville.

Edith received most of her education from her Grandmother Bolling, a peppery little woman, who had been severely crippled when she fell from a horse in her childhood. Edith shared a bedroom with her grandmother and was her favorite grandchild.

Mrs. Bolling was an exacting teacher, and Edith was an interested student. From this tiny, strong-minded grandmother, she learned to read, write, do simple arithmetic and speak some French. Mr. Bolling felt it was more important that his sons be formally educated, as he assumed the girls would marry and be provided for, with the result that Edith received no formal schooling until she was fifteen and went to Martha Washington College at Abingdon, Virginia.

Edith had meant to further her music education, but living conditions at the school were so bad, with freezing cold classrooms and inedible, scanty food, she stayed only a short time before her father brought her back home. She had lost weight and was glad to return.

When Mr. Bolling realized some months later that Edith was becoming too fond of a man she was dating, who was twice her age, he sent her to the Powell School in Richmond, a girls' academy. The cost to attend Powell was high, and she did not go back the next year.

Edith's maternal grandmother, Mrs. White, also lived with the family. She was traditionally Southern and elegant in her manner. She read and

Edith Wilson. (Artist: Emile Alexay. Courtesy National Portrait Gallery, Smith-sonian Institution. Gift of Dr. Alan Urdang.)

sang with the children and taught them etiquette. With eleven children in the household, no one had time for bickering, and their life was peaceful.

When she learned she would not return to school in Richmond, Edith decided to visit her sister and brother-in-law, Mr. and Mrs. Alexander Galt, in Washington for a few weeks. She was then eighteen years old and still engrossed in music.

One night she returned from an opera in high spirits, thrilled with the performances she had just seen. Alex's cousin, Norman Galt, was visiting, and when he saw Edith, he was immediately attracted to this lovely, vibrant, enthusiastic young woman. For the next four months he was her constant escort and hoped she would marry him. But Edith liked her life the way it was and did not want any changes, so she refused to consider Norman a serious suitor.

Norman continued his romantic pursuit for four years, until they were finally married on April 30, 1896. He was able to support his bride in luxurious style, as he owned a jewelry and silversmith store, which had been owned and operated by his family in the area since 1802. In addition to jewelry, the store sold fine china, crystal and silverware. All brides in society received wedding gifts from Galt's.

Edith was not in love with Norman, who was nine years her senior, but he loved her deeply. For the next several years they had a happy and exciting life together, with trips to Europe and invitations to Washington social gatherings. They were snubbed by some Washington hostesses, especially by those who had political connections, because the Galts were in "trade." Edith laughed at this absurdity of their attitude, since these same people got their fine fittings for their receptions and balls from Galt's.

Edith's much-beloved father died not many months after her marriage, and when Mrs. Bolling told Edith she could not stay in Wytheville without her husband, Edith brought her mother, sister, and two younger brothers to Washington to live in an apartment she secured for them. One brother, Julian, lived in the house with Norman and Edith while he was a student in a private school.

At age forty-five, Norman was suddenly stricken with a liver ailment and died after a brief illness in 1908. His will left the store to Edith. With the help of valued longtime employees, she continued to operate the store for a number of years, selling it finally to the employees.

Each year after Norman's death, Edith traveled to Europe. The first time she took her sister, Bertha, as a companion. The second time she took a young family friend, Altrude Gordon, whose father had also recently died. The third year, Bertha went with her again. While they were in Paris on this trip, Woodrow Wilson was elected President.

Edith and Bertha had been back in America for a few days when Annie Bolling, Edith's sister-in-law, insisted that Edith go with her to the theatre one night because Woodrow Wilson and his family would be there. Edith, who had never been interested in or impressed with politics, agreed to go because Annie had worked so diligently in Wilson's campaign, and she was amused by Annie's great enthusiasm.

Edith thought Wilson looked tired and bored, but Annie was thrilled that she got to see him in person. A few days after this, Edith and Annie attended a reception at the White House, and they shook hands with Wilson. Edith forgot it promptly, as she and Altrude left almost immediately on another ocean voyage to Europe, where they had a wonderful time.

Upon their return to the United States, Edith had a dinner party for her friends. After dinner they all went off to a barracks dance, at which Edith met Dr. Grayson, Wilson's official physician and friend.

Edith learned that Wilson had been extremely depressed since the death of his wife, Ellen, a few weeks before. Despite the best and loving efforts of his family, friends and doctor, he could not seem to regain his former zest for life. Dr. Grayson explained to Edith how frustrated he felt in dealing with Woodrow as his grief did not seem to lessen.

Edith felt deep sympathy for Woodrow, having lost her own husband a few years earlier, and when she encountered Dr. Grayson and Woodrow accidentally at the White House about six months later, she made an extra effort to be cheerful and entertaining. Helen Bones, cousin of the President and Ellen's former secretary, was a friend of Edith's and had invited her to visit.

Woodrow joined the two friends, and he was enchanted with Edith, as he had always admired good conversationalists. Edith had traveled widely and knew many important people in and out of Washington; best of all, Woodrow and Edith found they had Southern connections through mutual friends and relatives. Woodrow had been extremely lonely without Ellen, and Edith was vibrantly attractive.

Before long, tongues were wagging all over Washington about the President's marked interest in Mrs. Galt. Some of his advisors felt it would be unwise for him to remarry until he had been reelected. Neither Edith nor Woodrow wanted to wait, however, so on December 18, 1915, they were married at her home in a quiet ceremony attended by only fifty people. She wore a black velvet dress, black velvet hat with a feather plume, a diamond brooch and a corsage of lilies of the valley.

After a two-week honeymoon at The Homestead, the Wilsons had to hurry back to Washington because of the worsening conditions in Europe, which threatened to involve the United States in war. They were welcomed back by both families. Woodrow's children, now all adults, were glad their father had found someone to share his life and bring him out of his grief for their mother.

Edith assumed her role as First Lady with grace and dignity. Her chief alterations were to complete Ellen's plans to change the formal garden to a rose garden, and to bring more comfort to their own quarters with fires in the fireplaces, soft cushions, flower arrangements, books and magazines.

Ellen and Woodrow had slept in the same twin beds the Tafts used, but Edith had the large Lincoln bed brought to their bedroom. Edith lavished all her love on Woodrow, and he appeared to be genuinely in love with her. They shared many common interests, and their marriage seemed happy and stable from the beginning.

War clouds in Europe dampened everyone's spirits. Edith devoted herself to keeping Woodrow as happy and cheerful as possible. Altrude married Admiral Grayson in May 1916, and the Wilsons attended the wedding. Edith was glad Altrude had also found someone to love.

Edith's day often began before 5:00 A.M., and both she and Woodrow were busy until late hours. She was very careful to see that they both dressed appropriately and presented a good appearance.

Woodrow was renominated to run for President at the Democratic National Convention in St. Louis in 1916, and was reelected on the slogan, "He kept us out of war."

Woodrow took the oath of office on March 4, 1917, and on April 6, 1917, war was declared against Germany. This declaration was the result of Germany's assertion that they had the right to surround England with submarines and restrict the number of United States ships allowed in the area.

Edith became a Red Cross volunteer and, like other Americans, told various relatives goodbye as they entered the Armed Forces. The year 1917 was a year of much effort and confusion as the United States prepared for a war they had not expected to fight.

The White House doors were closed to the public during the war, and formal entertaining ceased. Edith and Woodrow would slip away for a few days together occasionally on the yacht *Mayflower*. They both worked hard in drives to sell liberty bonds to help finance the war.

Edith was given the task of naming new United States ships, including renaming those captured from the Germans. In some cases it was simple such as changing *Amerika* to *America*; in others she had to be more imaginative. To some ships she gave Indian names.

The war lasted until November 9, 1918, when the Kaiser in Germany abdicated. The German people had rebelled against his rule, and a republic was formed. Two days later, on November 11, 1918, at 11:00 A.M., all hostilities ceased and firing stopped. World War I had ended.

About a month later, Woodrow and Edith were in England, where they visited King George V and Queen Mary. Edith elected to not curtsey to the queen, feeling she was her equal, and wanting Woodrow to be recognized as equal to European heads of state. Queen Mary gave no indication she was displeased, and the visit went well.

From England they went on to Paris, where a Peace Conference would be held. Representatives of nations from all the world attended in an effort to forge a lasting peace.

It was at this meeting that President Wilson first proposed that a League of Nations covenant be included in the Peace Treaty. He got little support for his idea, and he became very upset. Edith soothed his ruffled feelings as best she could, but he would not give up his proposal. March and April of 1919 were trying months for them both as Woodrow campaigned vigorously among the representatives to adopt his League of Nations plan.

On April 3, 1919, Woodrow collapsed with a thrombosis. At about the same time Edith learned that Colonel Edward M. House, Woodrow's aide and good friend, was claiming credit in the peace initiatives. Edith reported her findings to Woodrow, and his friendly relations with House stopped.

On his return to Washington, Woodrow decided to take his idea for a League of Nations to the American people. He and Edith set out on a cross-country train trip in September 1919. Edith was miserable, as she saw how frail Woodrow's health was becoming, and she saw how hard he drove himself as he made speech after speech from Columbus, Ohio, to Portland, Oregon.

When they reached Los Angeles, Woodrow visited with his old friend Mrs. Peck, now Mrs. Hulbert. The meeting was cordial, but not emotional. She spent part of the time bemoaning her bad luck since they had last met.

As they were heading back East, in Salt Lake City, Utah, Woodrow made one of his impassioned speeches to a large crowd in the Mormon Tabernacle, which was stifling hot. Edith even felt faint, and she feared Woodrow would collapse. He made it through, continued on through Cheyenne, Wyoming, and finally collapsed in Denver, Colorado, forcing cancellation of the rest of his campaign. The train traveled nonstop until they at last reached Washington two days later. The word had been given out that President Wilson had flu.

Edith knew in her heart Woodrow was failing, and their lives could never be the same again. So far his illness manifested itself by extreme restlessness, but on October 2, 1919, he suffered a major stroke, which paralyzed his left side and robbed him of speech. Within a few days his bladder became blocked by an enlarged prostate gland.

Through it all, Edith maintained an outward calm and fiercely resisted any effort to have Vice President Thomas Marshall assume the office of President. Instead she elected to make decisions and help Woodrow sign documents based on what she thought he would have done. The whispers began that Mrs. Wilson was now running the government.

Edith allowed no visitors to see Woodrow, and his condition was not fully known by anyone except herself and Dr. Grayson. Finally, two of the Senators decided they would go in person and check on his condition. Edith carefully arranged him in bed so his paralysis was not evident. She put important documents on the bed within reach of his right hand, which he could use. He talked with calmly and sensibly, joked with them and shook their hands when they started to leave. They stated to the newspaper reporters and others that in their opinion he was capable of rational decisions (to the disappointment of Woodrow's and Edith's detractors). The truth, however, was that Woodrow had been having a good day, out of a large number of bad days when he appeared unable to think straight, make decisions or understand what was said to him.

Why did Edith do it? Why would she go to such lengths to deceive not only the American public but the government officials who should have been told the truth? From the beginning, she had been jealous for him of his position and power, and possibly she wanted to protect both as long as possible. Perhaps she even enjoyed the sense of her own power under the circumstances.

She was so successful she even deceived Wilson himself. He began talking of the possibility of being a candidate for a third term so he could continue his push for the adoption of the League of Nations. Dr. Grayson was dismayed at this turn of events. He had a quiet talk with the chairman of the platform committee before the convention and told him Woodrow was unable to serve if elected.

Woodrow did slowly improve, and in time became aware of the lapse of many government functions during his illness. He saw to it that Ambassador appointments which had been held up during his illness were made in 1920. He learned that the American people had lost confidence in his ability to govern.

When his second term ended, he attended Harding's inauguration and then the Wilsons went to their home on S Street to live out their lives. Edith cut out friends of Woodrow's she disliked and refused to let them see him. His understanding and moods changed drastically from one day to the next, and on good days she would invite friends and relatives to visit.

On Armistice Day, 1923, Woodrow insisted he was able to address the nation by radio. It was his last speech, and in it he continued to extol the desirability of the League of Nations.

At Christmas that year, he was able to attend the theater, and on January 16, 1924, they held a reception for the Democratic National Committee. It was breaking Edith's heart to see him so feeble and trying so hard to appear normal. He had become almost completely blind in recent months.

Woodrow Wilson died on February 3, 1924. He had requested a simple funeral service, and Edith chose to have it in their home on S Street.

His daughter, Margaret, still unmarried, and Nell McAdoo, another daughter, were present. His third daughter, Jessie Sayre, was in Siam with her husband and could not be reached.

Nell's husband, William McAdoo, had hoped to receive an endorsement from Woodrow to further his own Presidential ambitions. Near Woodrow's coffin, Nell and he were discussing his chances for the nomination at the convention, and Edith overheard them. She berated the McAdoos so sharply that Nell never forgave her.

Margaret came into the room a short time later mumbling vaguely that death was only an illusion, and Edith angrily ordered her to stop talking nonsense.

Henry Cabot Lodge was chosen as the Senate representative to attend the funeral, but when Edith heard of it, she wrote him a note asking that he not attend. Woodrow had never liked Senator Lodge because he opposed the League of Nations. Lodge responded that he would respect her wishes.

Woodrow was buried in a crypt of the Cathedral of St. Peter and St. Paul, the national cathedral not yet completed.

Edith lived almost forty more years after his death. She continued all the rest of her life to polish Woodrow's image and to promote his ideas. She chose Ray Stannard Baker to write Woodrow's biography, then protested when he wrote how devoted Woodrow was to his first wife, Ellen, even though Baker was quoting from Woodrow's own letters. The work continued, though strained, and Baker completed his book in 1939, for which he won a Pulitzer Prize. Edith did write to congratulate him.

She was often asked to speak or endorse some person or product. She did none of this if it was not connected to her old life with Woodrow. She made numerous trips to Europe and traveled in Asia. In 1939 her autobiography, *My Memoirs*, appeared. In it she was blunt and at times merciless in her opinions and accounts of past events.

Books, statues, plays and portraits continued to be done of Woodrow, few of which Edith liked. She always felt they failed to show his strengths and abilities.

A movie of Woodrow's life premiered in August 1944. Actor Alexander Knox played Woodrow and Geraldine Fitzgerald played Edith. Edith never voiced an opinion of the film, but she was apparently pleased by it. Twentieth Century–Fox offered her $50,000, but she refused any payment for herself, asking that the money be used to further the cause of making a memorial for Woodrow at his birthplace in Staunton, Virginia.

Edith sat with Eleanor Roosevelt on December 8, 1941, the day President Franklin Roosevelt addressed the joint Congress and asked for a declaration of war against Japan for its attack on Pearl Harbor in Hawaii. Edith felt a strong sense of déjà vu, and she seemed again to hear Woodrow's voice making a similar declaration.

Woodrow's daughter Jessie Sayre died unexpectedly in 1933 from complications after surgery, and Margaret died in India in 1944, where she lived for the past four years in Pondicherry as a member of a guru's group. Nell's marriage did break up, as Ellen and Woodrow had feared when she married McAdoo, and he married yet another woman much younger than himself. Nell spent the rest of her life in California, compiling much of the Wilson family history. She died in 1967 at Santa Barbara.

Edith socialized with many Presidents and First Ladies who followed the Wilsons. She was at the charity entertainment with Eleanor Roosevelt when Eleanor received the news of Franklin's death in Warm Springs, Georgia. Bess Truman and Mamie Eisenhower were both friendly with Edith. She rode in the inauguration parade for John F. Kennedy.

In her last years, a heart condition made it unsafe for Edith to live alone. She hired a companion, Margaret Cherricks Brown, called Cherie, who lived with her.

She remained active until her death, and was able to tend flowers, care for birds and write friends.

By Christmas 1961, Edith's health took a turn for the worse, with respiratory symptoms complicating her heart condition. She died on December 28, 1961, on Woodrow's birthday. She was eighty-nine years old.

She was buried in a crypt in St. Joseph's Chapel in Washington beside Woodrow, whose body had been moved from its original placement.

32. Florence Mabel Kling De Wolfe Harding

Florence Kling was born on August 15, 1860, in Marion, Ohio. Her father, Amos Kling, was a merchant and banker. Because of his success in business, he felt he should be in charge of everything and everyone around him. The family lived in a brick mansion where Pa was boss.

Florence was Amos's only daughter, and she was as stubborn and headstrong as he. They never agreed, even when it would have been better for both of them. Amos felt his daughter was a hopeless case of defiant youth, but he paid willingly for her piano lessons and riding lessons.

Florence was an apt pupil, and when she was older she attended the Cincinnati Conservatory of Music. She spent several years in boarding schools, which increased her independent outlook.

When she was at home in summers, she rode her horse, Billy, as skillfully as either of her two brothers, Clifford or Vetallis. She was a little masculine in her appearance, with an ordinary figure and an awkward walk. She knew that she was not very attractive physically. She did date, but many of her escorts were less than dream dates — unpleasant, unambitious, or not of her social standing.

Florence set her sights on the boy next door, Simon "Pete" De Wolfe. Pete's father was a coal dealer, and the family did not have nearly as much money as the Klings. Pete was an amiable young man, too laid-back in temperament to resist Florence, or Flossie, as he called her.

When she discovered she was pregnant, Pete agreed to marry her, and they eloped in March 1880. Six months later their son, Eugene Marshall De Wolfe, was born.

Pete began spending his days and nights drinking and carousing. In his view he had done Flossie a big favor by marrying her, and he had no intention of working to support her and their little son. Pete's father made a valiant effort to keep Pete in jobs, but Pete began to leave town on occasions and would stay gone for weeks at a time.

Mr. De Wolfe felt sorry for his daughter-in-law, and he paid her grocery bills every week. Flossie's mother gave her money and bought

Florence Harding. (Courtesy Library of Congress.)

clothes for both little Marshall and Flossie. Amos Kling was disgusted with Flossie because of the circumstances of her marriage and refused to help her in any way.

Flossie might have been down, but she wasn't out. She borrowed a piano and began giving music lessons to neighborhood children to support herself and her little son. Her father relented slightly in the face of so much courage and told her she could move back to the Kling home if she took back the last name of Kling. Flossie refused.

Flossie was not maternal by nature even if she did have a son. After her divorce from Pete De Wolfe in 1886, she allowed her parents to rear Marshall.

She continued to earn her own living with her piano lessons at fifty cents an hour. One of her pupils was named Charity Harding, called Chat. Through her, Flossie met Chat's brother, Warren Harding.

Warren was a handsome, virile young man who attracted the attention of women all over town. He was the editor of the *Star* newspaper, which he had recently bought. He was flattered by Flossie's obvious admiration, but not overwhelmed.

Flossie had decided he was her man, however, and she went after him with grim determination. She haunted him when he tried to escape her. Once when he returned to town by train after seeing another woman, he got off on the other side of the tracks from where he saw Flossie waiting.

"You needn't try to run away, Warren Harding," she yelled, peering under the train. "I see your big feet!"

All this open pursuit of Warren by Flossie caused amusement among their friends but not with her father. Amos Kling exploded with fury when he learned of their romance. He had a low opinion of Warren and both his parents. Warren's mother and father were both licensed to practice medicine but were not highly regarded in the Ohio town.

Warren decided marriage to Flossie might bring him both money and prestige in Marion, so he began to encourage her instead of running away as he had been doing.

Amos Kling met Warren by accident one day in the courthouse. He let Warren know in a loud voice that he did not approve of him as a future son-in-law. He threatened to shoot Warren and made a pointed reference to Warren's ancestry, which was reported to include some black relatives. Warren's father might be Dr. Tryon Harding, but this cut no ice with Amos.

Flossie calmly ignored her father's tirade, and she and Warren began making their wedding plans. They had a house built together before their marriage, and their vows were spoken in the front hall of their new home on July 8, 1891. Flossie's mother attended the wedding, but left before Flossie saw her. She had given Flossie money to buy furniture for her new house as a wedding present.

Amos Kling did not relent in his opposition to the marriage for the next seven years. He tried in every way possible to ruin Warren and his family financially. He refused even to nod to Flossie when they met on the streets of Marion. Fifteen years would pass before he and Flossie were friendly again.

Flossie's second marriage also began on a sour note because Warren had so many attacks of nervous indigestion. He often called his father to come over to treat him — so often, in fact, that Dr. Harding finally insisted the newlyweds move in with him and his wife. So Flossie and Warren left their new house and went to live with his parents for the next six months.

Flossie nagged Warren as she had a low opinion of his business ability, even though the *Star* was the town's leading newspaper. Warren delegated work to his employees, while Flossie thought he should work alongside them. Her constant carping finally resulted in his suffering a nervous collapse, and he spent a large part of 1894 in Battle Creek Sanitarium, finally recovering his health.

In his absence Flossie marched down to the *Star* offices and organized the business aspect of the newspaper according to her own ideas. "I went down there intending to help out for a few days, and I stayed fourteen years," she was fond of saying. She never intruded into newspaper policy, reporting or editorial comments, however. The big advantage she gained by working for the newspaper was that she could watch Warren.

To be charitable, Flossie might have been driven by a grinding fear of again facing the poverty she had left so recently. The newspaper continued to be successful, but it had been successful even before she took over as circulation manager.

During this same period, her first husband, Pete, drifted in and out of town, reminding her of her former life. But Pete De Wolfe had shortened his life by his alcohol abuse, and he died at age thirty-five.

Warren formed the habit, when he was released from the sanitarium, of traveling to various nearby towns by train and talking with other publishers and politicians. In this way he could at least escape Flossie briefly. He now referred to her as "The Duchess," and not always in a friendly tone.

Harding was convinced by some of his friends that he should enter politics. He decided to run for a seat in the Ohio State Senate, and was elected in 1899. His political career was off to a flying start.

Flossie's son, Marshall De Wolfe, continued living with his Kling grandparents until his grandmother died. After her death, Amos sent him to boarding school for several years, where the young man apparently used the name Marshall Kling. He was still using that name when he graduated from Marion High School later.

Marshall was another apple that didn't fall far from the tree. He was of the same indolent, gambling, hard-drinking nature as his father. When he failed to get money from his Grandfather Kling, he would beg Flossie or Warren for it. He treated Warren with amused condescension. Flossie tried hard to ignore Marshall's existence whenever she could.

Warren served two terms as State Senator, and then was elected Lieutenant Governor of Ohio. Flossie traveled with him as often as possible, but she drove him wild with her petulance and watchfulness.

Part of Flossie's irritating actions may have stemmed from the fact that she was a sick woman. She eventually became seriously ill and had to have a kidney removed.

Jim and Carrie Phillips were probably their best friends. When Jim suffered an emotional breakdown, Warren helped Carrie with business and family matters. Jim was hospitalized in Battle Creek Sanitarium for several months, and Carrie and Warren fell madly in love.

Warren had always been a womanizer, and Flossie's suspicions of him were not without foundation, but this time he was really in love. When Jim got better and Flossie's health improved, the two couples took a trip to Europe together as well as other shorter trips. Neither Jim nor Flossie suspected anything was going on, but Carrie and Warren were in each other's arms at every opportunity.

When Warren was nominated for Governor of Ohio in 1910, Carrie asked him if he planned to divorce Flossie so they could marry. Warren just could not bring himself to do this. He did not love Flossie in the same way he loved Carrie, but she was a familiar fixture in his life. Flossie represented home and stability to him. He was defeated in his race for Governor.

Carrie threatened to move to Germany, where she had felt she would like to live when the two couples had gone to Europe together. With Carrie pushing so hard for marriage, Warren backed away and became romantically involved with an eighteen-year-old girl from Marion named Nan Britton, daughter of another Marion doctor. Nan's father died not long after they met, and Warren once again assumed the role of family adviser.

Nan had had a schoolgirl crush on the handsome politician for some months, and finally their involvement reached Flossie's ears. She promptly arranged a trip to Europe for herself and Warren and insisted that he go.

Earlier that same year Carrie Phillips had made good her threat and had gone to Germany to live for a time. She enrolled her daughter in school there. Warren wrote her long, passionate love letters, but apparently had no chance to visit her while he and Flossie were in Europe.

In 1914 Warren was elected to the United States Senate, and he and Flossie moved to Washington to live. On January 1, 1915, Flossie's son, Marshall, died in Colorado, leaving a widow and two small children. Flossie had no interest in knowing her grandchildren, and was irritated when they all came to Marion to live. Flossie was fifty-four and conscious that she was aging. Warren was younger than she, and he looked it.

Warren was glad to go to Washington and leave Marion. Carrie Phillips had returned, and he did not mind putting distance between them.

Flossie and Warren bought a large brick duplex in Washington for their home. Warren intended to try to behave. He knew a divorce was out of the question if he wanted to continue in politics. At that time no divorced candidate had a chance of being elected to any office.

In Washington Warren soon found a regular seat at poker parties at the Nicholas Longworth home. Longworth had been acquainted with Warren in Ohio, and he hurried to renew their friendship.

Longworth's wife was Alice Lee Roosevelt, Teddy Roosevelt's daughter, and she was less than thrilled with her husband's choice of the Hardings for friends. When the poker parties were in the Longworth's home, Flossie went with Warren, but "Princess Alice" never visited the Hardings while Warren was a Senator. Flossie was aware they were being slighted, but Warren ignored it.

It was at one of the Longworth parties that Flossie and Warren met the rich, eccentric Ned and Evalyn McLean. They became good friends even though they had little in common. It may have started because Evalyn felt sorry for the aging, lonely Flossie at these gatherings.

For whatever reason, when Flossie became seriously ill about ten days later, Evalyn McLean rushed to the Harding home to visit her, and sent flowers as long as Flossie was ill. Every time Evalyn came to call, Flossie asked her what acquaintances in Washington society said about the Hardings.

World War I was brewing in Europe, and Carrie told Warren that if he voted in the Senate to declare war on Germany, she would tell her husband and Flossie about their longtime love affair. Not many days later, Secret Service agents came to visit Carrie and questioned her closely about her loyalty to the United States government. She did not make good her threat to tell either Flossie or Jim, and Warren told Jim he thought Carrie should stay away from Washington.

Nan Britton was now living in New York, and Warren visited her at every opportunity. They were involved in an ardent love affair, but Warren managed somehow to keep it secret from both Flossie and Carrie. Nan finally gave birth to a baby girl she said was Warren's.

Flossie turned her attention to Red Cross work for the war effort and spent much of her time sewing for them. In November 1918 she developed further kidney problems.

Warren's preoccupation with young Nan caused him to bring her to Washington for trysts. They walked together openly on the streets, and he made love to her in his office in the Senate Office Building.

The year of 1920 was a big one for Warren. Nan and her little daughter, Elizabeth Ann, were living in Chicago, and Nan regularly dunned Warren for money. Carrie Phillips had decided Warren never intended to marry her, and she told her husband about the affair in an effort to get revenge. Nothing much came of her confession, as her husband was the forgiving type and the affair was, after all, over.

Warren began campaigning for the Presidential nomination in primary elections around the country. Flossie strongly opposed his candidacy as she feared his health was failing.

In May that year Flossie consulted a clairvoyant, Madame Marcia, who was the Washington fad at that time. Madame Marcia told Flossie the man she mentioned would be elected President but would die in office. The man was, of course, Warren Harding, whom Flossie had identified only by his birthdate.

The Republican Convention was held in Chicago, and Warren managed to elude Flossie long enough to visit Nan. However, he refused to see the little girl Nan claimed was his, who was playing in the park nearby with Nan's sister.

Warren gave Nan a ticket to the convention, and she watched as Warren was nominated. Flossie and Evalyn McLean were also watching in another area of the Convention Hall.

Warren and Flossie returned to their home in Marion after his nomination. There he attempted to take care of unfinished business with the women in his life. He sent money by messenger to Carrie and Jim Phillips to pay for a trip around the world. He had a Secret Service agent deliver eight hundred dollars to Nan so she could take a long vacation.

It had become necessary to get Carrie out of town when Flossie heard of her former involvement with Warren. Flossie reacted violently one night when Carrie passed by their house and spoke to Warren, who was seated on the porch. Flossie came rushing out of the house and threw a feather duster, a wastebasket and finally a piano stool at Carrie. Carrie impudently threw Warren a kiss before she left the scene.

Warren was elected President, and he and Flossie returned to Washington in December before his inauguration on March 4, 1921. Mrs. Woodrow Wilson invited Flossie to the White House and gave her a tour of the Hardings' future home. Flossie promptly informed the housekeeper, Mrs. Jaffray, she would not need her services when the Hardings moved into the White House. Mrs. Wilson left and was gone several hours. When she returned, Flossie was still there talking to the cook.

When President Harding took office, he quickly set out to reward friends and relatives with Cabinet positions and other government jobs. The Hardings brought a new openness to the White House, however. No longer were the iron gates to the grounds locked. Since World War I was over, the lower floors of the White House as well as the grounds were once again open to the public. The annual Easter egg roll for children was reinstated. The Marine Band held concerts on the White House lawn, and an open public reception was held every day around noon.

The general public loved Flossie, but elitist Washington society did not. Her hair was always waved a little too perfectly, and they found her gauche in her gushing manner and remarks.

Flossie relented and kept Mrs. Jaffray as housekeeper. This was a wise decision, as Flossie needed advice and assistance in entertaining matters. Mrs. Jaffray came to regard Flossie with a reluctant fondness in the two years Flossie lived in the White House, though Flossie and Warren had been something of a cultural shock after keeping house for the fastidious President and Mrs. Wilson.

As First Lady, Flossie held many private conversations with administration officials and tried to keep abreast of all political developments. Warren was heard to comment, "Mrs. Harding wants to be the drum major in every band that passes."

President Harding continued with his down-home ways and held private stag dinners for twelve to fifteen men frequently, at which they played poker and ate sauerkraut and wienerwurst. He ordered toothpicks to be kept on the dining room table. Twice a week he held poker parties with Flossie fluttering around and mixing drinks for the guests. Despite the passage of the Eighteenth Amendment, which outlawed alcoholic beverages, liquor was served. Nicholas Longworth always attended Warren's parties, but Alice never did.

Flossie continued to consult fortune-tellers. She would get the White House housekeeper to go with her.

In 1922 Secretary of the Interior Albert Fall leased publicly owned government land in Wyoming to Mammoth Oil Company. The leased area was known as Teapot Dome. Fall and others in the Cabinet made a habit of using the knowledge and privilege gained in their government positions for huge personal profits. Some rumor of all this illegal activity reached President Harding, but he chose to ignore it. And despite Flossie's efforts to make the government's business her own, these activities had gotten by her and she knew nothing about them. The scandal would not reach the ears of the public for two more years. After that some would receive prison sentences, while others would even commit suicide.

Nan Britton had allowed her sister and brother-in-law to adopt Elizabeth Ann and considered making a career for herself in the movies. She had visited President Harding several times in the White House, where they continued their romantic pursuits. These visits ended suddenly when Flossie returned one day unexpectedly and almost caught them. Warren knew his political career would crumble to dust if Flossie left him, so he reluctantly broke off with Nan.

President Harding felt he was not winning the hearts of the general public, and he and Flossie set out on a cross-country "Voyage of Understanding." They left on June 20, 1923, by train with an entourage of sixty-five people, including news reporters and photographers. They traveled through the Midwest and West, with President Harding making speeches in most of the larger cities.

By July 27 they had reached Seattle, where Warren became ill while making a speech. He was rushed back to San Francisco, where he died on August 2, 1923, after either a heart attack or possible cerebral hemorrhage. He was buried in Marion, Ohio.

The bereaved Flossie went to stay temporarily with the McLeans. While staying in their home, she burned many letters and documents of Warren's White House days, removing them forever from history.

Flossie then went on to Marion, where she lived in the home of her personal physician. She continued burning papers there. She explained she wanted to get rid of whatever would "harm his [Warren's] memory."

Flossie died on November 2, 1924, from kidney failure. She had lived only a little more than a year since Warren died. She left all her possessions to the Harding Memorial with nothing going to any relatives. She is buried beside Warren in Marion, Ohio.

33. *Grace Anna Goodhue Coolidge*

Grace Anna Goodhue was the only child of Andrew Isaachar and Lemira Barrett Goodhue. She was born in Burlington, Vermont, on January 3, 1879. She counted old New England settlers among her ancestors. Grace's father worked as a mechanical engineer and steamboat inspector for the Champlain Transportation Company, and always provided a substantial life for his family.

Grace grew up in Burlington, well-loved by her parents and popular with her friends. She was a black-haired beauty, slender and vivacious. She had a slight spinal curvature which troubled her for a time in her teens with pain and discomfort, but which in no way detracted from her appearance.

Mr. and Mrs. Goodhue encouraged Grace to get a good education, and in 1902 she graduated from the University of Vermont with a Bachelor of Philosophy degree. Her best girlfriend, Ivah Gale, lived with Grace and her parents from 1900 until the two girls both graduated from college. Grace and Ivah went bobsledding and attended church activities and school functions together.

While still a young girl, Grace became interested in Clarke School for the Deaf in Northampton, Massachusetts. Her interest was first developed through her father's friend, John Lyman Yale, who lived across the street from the Goodhue home. Mr. Yale's sister, Caroline Ardelia Yale, was principal of the school. Upon graduation from college, Grace got a teaching job at Clarke, where she lived in Baker Hall, a residence dormitory for teachers.

Grace had been teaching at Clarke for more than a year when she first saw Calvin Coolidge. She was watering flowers in the yard at Baker Hall, when she happened to glance at an upstairs window in a neighboring house. At the window a man stood shaving, dressed apparently only in his long underwear, but wearing a hat!

Grace, who had a lively sense of humor, laughed out loud, and the man heard her. She finished with the flowers and went on into Baker Hall, and thought no more about the incident. But the man was impressed with her attractiveness, and her sense of fun. He decided he wanted to meet her and asked his landlord to arrange the meeting.

Grace Coolidge. (Photographer: Clara E. Sipprell. Courtesy National Portrait Gallery, Smithsonian Institution. Bequest of Phyllis Fenner.)

The man, of course, was Calvin Coolidge. After he was introduced to Grace, they found they enjoyed being together, and they began dating frequently. (He explained he wore the hat while shaving to anchor a stubborn lock of hair which fell in his face when he shaved!)

Calvin and Grace were almost complete opposites in personality. Grace was friendly, outgoing and loved being with people. Calvin was dour, unsmiling and talked very little.

Both Grace and Calvin were members of the same Congregational Church, and they discovered they had mutual friends. Grace insisted on going on picnics, attending social and church gatherings, and going skating and dancing on their dates. Calvin hated all these activities, but for her sake he even tried both skating and dancing, though he could do neither well. They both enjoyed sailing.

Despite their different interests and being such opposites, they got along well together. Calvin admired Grace for her good humor and liveliness, while she enjoyed his dry humor and unexpected witty comments, even if they were infrequent. He remarked to a friend that "having taught the deaf to hear, Miss Goodhue might perhaps cause the mute to speak," referring to himself.

In the summer of 1905, Calvin asked Grace's father's permission to marry Grace before he proposed to her. Her father was surprised at this old-fashioned approach, but gave his consent. As time passed, Mr. Goodhue became genuinely fond of Calvin. Grace's mother, however, never liked him.

Grace and Calvin were married on October 4, 1905, despite her mother's protests. The wedding took place in the Goodhue parlor on a rainy day with only fifteen of their friends there.

The newlyweds moved into a rented white frame duplex house in Northampton. They had to be careful and budget their money as Calvin did not yet have much income from his law practice. Grace did all her own housework and cooking. Shortly after they got settled in their new home, Calvin brought her fifty-two pairs of his socks to be darned! She cheerfully darned them neatly, then asked him teasingly if he had married her just so he could get all his socks mended. He said, "No, but I find it mighty handy."

In 1906 Calvin was elected by the Republicans as a State Representative, and he went to Boston to serve, while Grace remained in the duplex in Northampton. He came home every weekend.

In September their first son, John, was born. Just before his birth, Grace bought a book from a door-to-door salesman entitled *Our Family Physician*. It cost eight dollars, which was a lot to pay for a book then, and she hesitated to tell Calvin about it. She just left it lying on a table where he would be sure to see it. A few days later when she looked at the book, she found he had written a note, "Don't see any receipt here for curing suckers! C. Coolidge."

In April 1908, their second son, Calvin, Jr., joined the family. Coolidge was very proud of Grace and his two children, but he seldom mentioned them to anyone. It was Grace who played baseball with the boys in the backyard, but Calvin read to them and went fishing and took them skating. They often went for long, silent walks together.

Calvin was highly critical of Grace's lack of domestic skills and often complained. He said her biscuits thumped when they hit the floor, and her pie crusts were like cement. But for all his caustic comments, he loved her fiercely. Grace was always well-dressed, as Calvin insisted she buy pretty clothes. He even took time from his own duties to shop for her and would buy clothes on his own for her, especially hats.

Also in 1908, Calvin was elected Mayor of Northampton and served until 1912. During these years he was at home every night, but in 1912 he returned to Boston, this time as a State Senator. His family remained in the rented duplex, and he again came home every weekend.

The Coolidges lived very quietly, had few visitors and went out little socially. Grace would go to Boston occasionally to shop with Calvin.

During these years, the Coolidge sons were growing up and attending public schools. Grace involved herself with their school affairs and knitted endless numbers of socks, sweaters and helmets for the Red Cross as well as her own family. She and the boys attended church suppers and other church social events with or without Calvin, but she stayed out of political activities entirely. Calvin preferred it that way.

After he had served three terms as State Senator and three terms as Lieutenant Governor of Massachusetts, Calvin began attracting much political attention. One wealthy Republican supporter, Frank Stearns, urged Calvin to move his family to a historic house in Boston. He said if Calvin could not afford to buy such a house, he could rent. Calvin would not even consider the move. He liked their rented duplex in Northampton.

In 1919 he became Governor of the state, and his family continued to live in the rented duplex. Calvin rented two rooms in the Adams House and came home weekends, as he had always done. Grace devoted her attention to being a good mother to their sons.

Mr. and Mrs. Stearns often entertained the Coolidges in the Stearns mansion, which Calvin always enjoyed. They were generous people and gave lavish gifts to Calvin and his family. Even though he realized these were kindly meant, Calvin began to feel uneasy about accepting these and finally returned a five thousand dollar check.

It was through Frank Stearns's influence that Calvin was chosen to be Warren Harding's running mate on the national Republican party ticket in 1920. When Harding was elected President and Calvin became Vice President, the Coolidges moved to Washington. They took a suite of four rooms at the New Willard Hotel. The suite consisted of two bedrooms, a reception room or parlor and a dining room. They used hotel catering service for entertaining. Their two sons were sent to boarding school at Mercersburg Academy in Pennsylvania.

In Washington Grace continued her lifelong habit of consideration and thoughtfulness of other people. She made every effort to return calls promptly and was unfailingly kind and charming. The simple housewife became a popular member of Washington society, while Calvin, still the silent Puritan, was frequently overlooked at Washington's gala events.

On August 2, 1923, President Harding died relatively suddenly after a brief illness, and Calvin was thrust to center stage. The Coolidge family were visiting Calvin's father when they got the news of Harding's death. The elder Coolidge was a notary public, and Calvin took the oath of office in his father's parlor. Grace was now First Lady. Both were numb with shock.

Calvin worked hard in his job as President, but he never talked about any problems or decisions with Grace. In fact, he still talked as little as possible to everyone, including dinner guests, to Grace's dismay. He also remained blunt-speaking. He refused invitations from anyone in Washington who had not been friendly to him and his family when he was Vice President.

He ordered Grace never to make political comments. He would not allow her to cut her hair or wear slacks, and he expected her to be home by six o'clock every evening.

Grace's charm and tact helped surmount hurdles. She was a sparkling conversationalist, interested in baseball, music, novels and the theater. She was still a good dancer, but Calvin forbade her dancing in public. She was a dignified, unpretentious hostess.

Following the Harding Presidency with its attendant personal and financial scandals, President Coolidge was perceived as a thoroughly honorable, honest man. Alice Roosevelt Longworth, Teddy Roosevelt's daughter, said the White House was different with the Coolidges living there. "The atmosphere was as different as a New England front parlor is from a back room in a speakeasy," she said after a visit there.

Calvin had a completely conservative way of dealing with problems — he usually waited them out. He took no action when the stock market began to show signs of hyperactivity. He felt any regulation of the New York Stock Exchange could be done by the state of New York. He did not see such regulation as a responsibility of the Federal government.

He ordered that aid be given to the Japanese people when an earthquake and typhoon almost destroyed that country a month after he became President. Obviously, he would take action when he saw a good reason to do so.

For all his reticence, President Coolidge loved his family deeply. He teased them in private, and his sons were a source of immense pride to him. They did good work in school and were lively but obedient.

"Ike" Hoover, Chief Usher at the White House, reported that President Coolidge often walked around in the family's section of the White House in his nightshirt, showing his spindly legs and embarrassing the White House staff.

When he first became President, he tried to rock on the front porch of the White House after dinner as he had always done wherever they had lived before. Now he found a large crowd always gathered and watched with interest, so he had to change his habit.

In July 1924, less than a year after Coolidge became President, Calvin, Jr., died after a brief illness at age sixteen. A couple of days before his death, he had played tennis wearing shoes without socks. A blister developed on one of his toes, causing blood poisoning to develop, which led to his death. He was a handsome young man with what had appeared to be a bright future, and the family was devastated with grief. President Coolidge said when Calvin, Jr., died, "the power and the glory of the Presidency went with him."

Grace tried to not let her deep grief interfere with her duties as White House hostess, but it was an intense struggle to appear as usual to guests. Social functions were severely curtailed.

Calvin was persuaded to run for the Presidency in his own right and was elected in 1925. This helped occupy his mind during this troubled period. Also their pets helped them in their grief. Grace had a white collie dog named Roy Roy and a cat named Tige. Calvin often draped Tige around his neck, as he did his own pet raccoon, Rebecca. Rebecca was allowed to run freely in the White House.

As a possible result of his overwhelming grief, Calvin became overly protective of John, their other son. He also became more insistent on complete control of their life's smaller details. He would add or remove names from White House guest lists which Grace had carefully compiled, and would change menus capriciously. He had outbursts of temper with Grace and John, which had not been the case before. Grace kept her cool serenity, sensing his anguish.

Grace was his mainstay. When she was home, Calvin was with her as much as possible. When she was away, he eagerly looked forward to receiving letters from her. She went for visits to her mother's home in Northampton occasionally, and sometimes left seeking relief from a sinus ailment.

Calvin finally took over complete household operations, and Grace would find out her scheduled duties at the last minute. When she tried to explain how difficult it was never to know her own schedule, he said, "Grace, we don't give out that information promiscuously."

To get a change of scenery, Calvin and Grace, accompanied by some of his staff and Secret Service men, took a trip to the Western states. Grace aroused Calvin's jealousy when she and a Secret Service agent took a long hike in the South Dakota hills and got back two hours late. She explained that they had got lost when they took the wrong trail, but Calvin had the Secret Service agent transferred and did not speak to Grace for several days.

Calvin had always had a fear of contracting tuberculosis, and when he began having recurrent nose and throat infections, as well as persistent indigestion, he decided he would not seek reelection. He typically did not tell Grace of his decision, and she learned of it from news reports. It was no surprise to her, since she knew him so well. Earlier she had made a quilt embroidered with his name and the dates of his Presidency: "1923–1929."

Grace was having increasing sinus problems herself in the humid Washington climate and looked forward to getting back home to Massachusetts. Her hostess duties had become burdensome to her and she no longer found pleasure in living in the White House.

Now that Calvin had made his decision to go home, he became more relaxed. He accepted a few invitations to private dinner parties for Grace and himself, which he had never done before while he had been President. Herbert Hoover teased Calvin and told him his decision not to run again was based on the exciting hours spent by Secret Service agents dodging his fly-casts in fishing. Since there were twenty-five million fishermen in the United States, Hoover went on, he knew he would not win.

John Coolidge graduated from Amherst College that year of 1928. He accepted a job with the New York, New Haven and Hartford Railroad.

When his term ended, Grace and Calvin left Washington eagerly and returned to live in the same rented duplex in Northampton where they had begun their life together. Conditions had altered since they had lived there before, and they were soon forced to buy a home to get any privacy.

They bought The Beeches, a twelve-room house on nine acres of land. The property had a tennis court and swimming pool on it. Most important of all, it had a front porch were Calvin could sit and rock in his rocking chair without attracting attention.

They had been home about a year when John married Florence Trumbull, daughter of the Governor of Connecticut, Robert Trumbull. Both Grace and Calvin were pleased with John's choice and warmly welcomed Florence to the family.

In 1929 the Coolidges traveled to Florida, New Orleans and California. William Randolph Hearst, publisher, invited them to visit him at his home, San Simeon. Grace had a marvelous visit, and even Calvin admitted he was impressed with the Hearst estate. The house at San Simeon was constructed in the style of a medieval castle. "The whole experience rivaled Alice in Wonderland," Grace wrote.

In 1931 Grace was voted one of the twelve greatest living American women. The National Institute of Social Sciences awarded her a gold medal for her excellent personal influence while she was First Lady.

In retirement Calvin stayed busy. He wrote magazine articles and a syndicated newspaper column. He felt practicing law again would be improper. The Coolidges did not lack for money to pay their bills as Calvin had always been frugal and made wise investments.

One icy January morning in 1933, Grace went grocery shopping while Calvin worked in his office at home. When she returned she found he had died from a coronary thrombosis. He had died as quietly as he had lived.

Grace chose to not have an official Washington funeral, feeling Calvin would not have wanted it. Instead it was held in the Northampton Church to which they and their children had belonged, where they had attended church the Sunday before his death. Calvin was buried at Plymouth Notch, Vermont.

Grace sold The Beeches a little later, feeling it was too large to live in alone, and bought a smaller house. She entered into new adventures with the same enthusiasm she had always had, taking her first trip to Europe and her first airplane ride.

She devoted her attention to serving as trustee for the Clarke School where she had taught years before and attending baseball games. She also derived much enjoyment from visiting with John, Florence and their two little daughters, Cynthia and Lydia.

Her college friend, Ivah Gale, moved in to live with her and help take care of her as her health failed. Miss Gale was now deaf herself.

John left his railroad job to work for a time at Connecticut Manifold Forms Company of Hartford, which he headed. When he retired in the late 1950s, he assumed the operation of a cheese factory in Plymouth.

Grace kept her sense of fun until her death. She died on July 8, 1957, from heart disease caused by her early childhood spinal curvature. She was buried beside Calvin at Plymouth Notch in Vermont.

34. Lou Henry Hoover

Lou Henry was born in Waterloo, Iowa, on March 28, 1875, but she only spent the first ten years of her life in Iowa. Lou's mother, Florence, became ill with suspected tuberculosis and the family moved to Monterey, California, in an effort to improve the mother's health.

Lou's father, Charles Delano Henry, was a banker, and Lou had few wishes that were not gratified by her proud parents while she was growing up. Mr. Henry took Lou with him on fishing, hunting or camping trips, in his time away from banking. They both enjoyed horseback riding, and Lou was an excellent rider who enjoyed the outdoors as much as her father.

Lou developed into a slender tomboy, but was no roughneck by any means. Her upbringing had been traditional and genteel, and she matured into a tall, glamorous blonde who never had to worry about having an escort to parties or dances.

Lou graduated from college at San Jose State, qualified to teach school. She worked briefly in her father's bank, then got a job teaching third grade in Monterey. After attending a lecture by a noted geologist, she decided to go to Stanford University and study geology, the only girl in the class. She lived in one of the more prestigious sorority houses on campus.

Lou first met Herbert Hoover in her freshman geology class when he was introduced to her by the class professor. Herbert was immediately attracted to beautiful Lou, and he lost no time in offering to help her with her studies. Herbert was a senior and a teaching assistant. Lou accepted his offer gratefully.

During their time together, Lou learned Herbert had lost both his parents before he was eight years old. He made his home with various Quaker relatives and had worked his way through college. He had a capital sum of forty dollars to begin his career as a geologist when he left college. Any future he envisioned for Lou and himself would have to wait until he got a good job.

Herbert was unable to find a job as a geologist after graduation. He was forced to accept a job pushing mining cars in a Nevada gold mine seven days a week on a ten-hour night shift. Even this job gave out, and he began a desperate search for another.

Lou Hoover. (Photograph by Harris and Ewing Studio. Courtesy National Portrait Gallery, Smithsonian Institution. Gift of Ailene Conkey.)

Lou and Herbert kept a lively correspondence during the next three years as she continued her college work. She was elected president of the Stanford Geology Club, replacing Herbert when he graduated.

Herbert found a job in another mine, worked for the United States Geological Survey for sixty dollars a month and earned college credits toward an engineering degree while Lou was at Stanford. A later job he got with Bewick, Moreing and Company took him to Australian gold mines to work.

Lou was again teaching school in California, but she now had a mining engineer's license.

After Herbert had been in Australia for several months, his employer asked Herbert to go to China as their company representative and also to serve as resident chief mining engineer in two provinces for the Chinese government. With the prospect of a decent salary in view, Herbert proposed to Lou by cable.

She accepted his proposal, and they were married on February 10, 1899, in a civil ceremony as no Friends' meeting house was located in their area. Lou had informed her parents of her decision to join Herbert in his religious preference.

Lou and Herbert set sail for China ten days later. Herbert felt gloomy at the prospect of living in Manchuria, but he said it couldn't be any worse than western Australia. Lou set out to learn the Chinese language and made excellent progress. Herbert never learned more than about one hundred words of Chinese in the three years they lived in China. A rented apartment in a Peking compound was Lou's and Herbert's first home.

Not many weeks after their arrival in China, the traditionalists among the Chinese people staged a rebellion against all foreigners in China and the foreigners' Chinese associates. This uprising was called the Boxer Rebellion. The Hoovers were caught in Tientsin, China, and were unable to leave. Lou carried a pistol with her at all times, while Herbert worked to get food brought in for the foreign residents and their refugee friends.

It was a terrible experience, and the Hoovers did all they could to help. They saved the life of one little Chinese girl, who came to Washington many years later as the wife of the Chinese Ambassador to the United States. She thanked them for helping her escape death years before.

While living in China, Lou began a collection of antique Chinese porcelain, blue and white, which dated from the Ming dynasty. It was one of the few pleasant memories she had of their stay.

After they had survived periodic attacks for more than two weeks in the rebellion, Herbert told his employers he had been notified "by way of artillery" that the Chinese government no longer wanted his engineering services. Lou and Herbert then spent five years traveling about, staying only short spaces of time in any one place.

Their first child, Herbert Hoover, Jr., was born in 1903 in London. The baby and his parents had been around the world twice by the time he was two years old! Their headquarters in London was a flat in Kensington, but after the birth of their second son, Allan, they moved to an old eight-room house in London, known as the Red House.

Herbert was now a partner in Bewick, Moreing and Company, and the Hoovers' finances were in better condition. They enjoyed living in the Red House with its lovely rose garden in back, and were glad finally to have room to entertain their American friends. They also rented a country home in Stratford-on-Avon, where Shakespeare had lived, and enjoyed being in a country where the culture was relatively familiar. The whole family enjoyed sailing, and they often spent leisure hours on the water.

The Hoovers were not popular with some of their English neighbors and associates. Herbert considered the British class distinctions silly and thought members of high society were parasites. Lou spent these years quietly caring for their two young sons and enjoying staying in one place for awhile.

In 1907 Lou undertook the direction of building a six-room house in Palo Alto, California, which they would ever after consider their home no matter where jobs took them.

While the family was in California, Herbert and Lou worked to translate an ancient book of metallurgy named *De Re Metallica*, which was written in Latin in 1556. Lou did most of the translation, while Herbert wrote the introduction, contributed his technical expertise in testing formulas, and compiled lengthy footnotes. The limited edition of the book quickly became a collectors' item. Herbert was appointed a trustee at Stanford University after the book appeared in print.

After this publishing success, both Lou and Herbert continued with further such pursuits. Lou wrote a book about a well-known botanist and his plant study, and later one about a seismologist and his study of earthquakes. This last project was especially appropriate for a resident of California.

They were living in London again when World War I began in 1914. There were thousands of terrified American tourists coming into London every day from Mainland Europe trying to get back to the United States. British banks refused to convert American currency to pounds and shillings, and the Americans could not buy steamship tickets.

The American Embassy asked Herbert if he could give them a hand with this problem, as it was too large for their staff to handle. Lou helped him, and they recruited volunteers who helped them set up a gigantic Travelers' Aid for the tourists. They arranged loans with the banks so the Americans could convert their currency and get passage home.

In October of that year, Herbert was asked to head the Belgian Relief

Program. The German army had attacked Belgium earlier and had taken both food and valuables, in addition to destroying crops. The Belgians were literally starving to death, and something had to be done.

Herbert undertook this large task and again recruited able volunteers to help him. None of the workers received any money for their efforts.

Lou took their two sons to California to live and attend school, then she returned to London to be with Herbert. They both missed the boys badly, so at the end of the school year in the spring, Lou went back to the states to retrieve them. She brought them back to England and enrolled them there in a small private school.

Lou stayed as busy as Herbert with relief work for the Belgians, and also worked for the needy in Britain. The Germans were utilizing food as a war weapon, and if the relief organization had not begun when it did, thousands of people all over Europe would have starved to death.

By the time peace finally came in 1918, Herbert was in charge of American food administration. He disagreed sharply with terms of the peace treaty with Germany and predicted there would be another war fought with Germany in a few years.

Lou was again busy in Palo Alto arranging for the construction of their dream home, which would be of Hopi design. The project required about two years to complete. By then Herbert was Secretary of Commerce in President Harding's Cabinet, and the family was living in Washington.

The Hoovers lived in a brick colonial-style house in Washington, a satisfactory home for the time being. The family was contented to be together again, and they had dinner guests almost every night. Their lives were stable again following the war duty years. Herbert was especially happy, as he was always basically a homebody.

Both Hoover sons attended public high school in Washington. Allan kept a variety of pets — from ducks, which were allowed to run around in the yard, to an alligator, which of necessity was confined to a bathtub. In 1931 Herbert, Jr., enrolled at Stanford, and Allan did the same four years later.

Lou stayed out of the public eye, occupying her time working in flower gardens around the house and pursuing scientific projects. The one public activity she engaged in was as honorary President of the Girl Scouts. Under her guidance, Girl Scout membership increased from one hundred thousand to a million girls and their fund-raising efforts brought in two million dollars. For the first time in American history, the Girl Scouts organization became as widely recognized as the Boy Scouts.

Herbert was happy in his job with the Commerce Department. He liked President Harding personally, and said he thought Harding tried to be a good President. President Harding invited Herbert to sit in on one of his famed poker parties, but Herbert attended only one. President

Harding's freewheeling life-style was not to Herbert's taste, and he politely declined further invitations.

President Coolidge took over in 1923. He, along with some of the other leading Republicans, did not like Herbert. Nevertheless, Herbert was nominated to run for President in 1928, and he won the election.

As First Lady, Lou set about making the White House a home for her family, which had always been a special talent of hers wherever they were required to live. She had the study restored in Lincoln's style and it became Herbert's study. The Red Room was restored to look as it had during the Monroes' time, after the disastrous White House fire of 1812. Bookcases were installed down the long White House halls to hold the thousands of books the Hoovers owned.

Lou fed every guest who came to the White House, instead of merely serving tea as had been the custom. The Chief Usher, Ike Hoover, said the Hoovers were difficult to work for because of their constant entertaining, as well as dictatorial demands on the servants. Also he did not approve of the many changes Lou Hoover made in the private family quarters in the White House, even though the Hoovers paid for the changes themselves for the most part.

Elegant formal receptions were limited to about ten each year, but there were numerous unscheduled dinners for distinguished foreign guests. The Hoovers paid for all entertaining from their own private funds.

Lou kept all the White House servants who were working when Herbert became President, only to have Eleanor Roosevelt discharge them all four years later.

Economic storm clouds were gathering when Herbert took office in 1929. After he had been in office about eight months, the stock market crash of 1929 occurred, and most of the world's governments were soon mired in a global depression. The devastation was so complete that American government officials could not agree on methods with which to cope, and many Americans spent from ten to twenty years recovering from the loss of jobs, homes and investments.

The country's economic woes so overshadowed Hoover's Presidency that his accomplishments were unnoticed. For example, he was the first twentieth-century President to address the problems and concerns of the American Indians. Herbert had Indian playmates in his boyhood, and two of his uncles had served as Indian agents.

Herbert encouraged development of a written record of various Indian sign languages. He paid direct Federal aid to Indians to improve health care, schools and hospitals. He authorized payment for forest lands taken by former President Theodore Roosevelt from the Utes.

President Hoover ordered the Department of Agriculture to stop leasing land in the national forests. He had inland waterways built up and was the instigator of the Tennessee Valley Authority project at Muscle Shoals in Alabama, which provided much needed electric power and led to the economic development of that severely depressed Southern region.

President Hoover firmly believed that development of new jobs was the key to ending the economic problems of the nation. He would agree to welfare payment of any kind only on a limited basis. He was severely criticized by the liberal citizens as they felt this welfare restriction showed a lack of compassion on his part. He argued that any other welfare assistance would encourage indolence on the part of those receiving it.

Herbert, Jr., and Allan visited their parents often. When Herbert, Jr., contracted tuberculosis in 1930, his wife, Margaret, and their three children lived in the White House for a year. The oldest grandchild, Peggy Ann, always made sure her grandfather, President Hoover, got to lunch on time. "Come on, you lazy man," she would say, pulling him toward the table. The Hoovers never let the public know of their appealing moments in their family, and guarded their privacy jealously.

As the Depression deepened, President Hoover worked longer and longer hours, trying to find a solution for the nation's anguish. His family and friends wondered, not *if* he would collapse, but *when*. He was often irritable, as nothing seemed to help in his efforts to stimulate the economy.

Lou was often in tears because of harsh criticism from the Democrats. The financial problems were worldwide in scope, but the Democrats preferred to place the blame on Herbert with the hope of defeating him in 1932.

Herbert tried to comfort Lou by telling her to imagine their enemies burning in the fiery Hell they both believed in for sinners. Lou was not amused.

When Herbert was defeated in his bid for reelection by Franklin D. Roosevelt, the Hoovers finally got to go back to Palo Alto to live in their dream house. Lou encouraged Herbert to join her in her old beloved sport of fishing, and they fished long hours for salmon and other game fish, usually accompanied by friends. They enjoyed their first prolonged period of relaxation from public duty in many years. Herbert said leaving office was "an emancipation from a sort of peonage."

Herbert had been too long at the center of political activities, however, and he soon became bored in California. In 1934 they began spending much of their time each year in an apartment in the Waldorf-Astoria in New York City. Herbert's interest in public affairs continued, and now it was his turn to criticize the Roosevelt administration. He especially criticized the powers bestowed on the President by the New Deal.

Lou died from heart failure on January 7, 1944, while World War II raged in full force throughout much of the world. After her death, Herbert learned for the first time that she had helped numerous young people further their education with direct gifts of money and letters of encouragement. She also sent financial aid to their former parlor maid in London during Depression years. She was buried in Palo Alto, California.

Lou did not live, unfortunately, to see the tide of public opinion turn back in Herbert's favor as he again headed food distribution programs this time for the Truman administration, and headed the Hoover Commission for government reform.

Herbert survived her by twenty years, always actively engaged in public service. He died in New York on October 20, 1964. He was buried in West Branch, Iowa, and at his prior request, Lou's body was brought from California to rest beside him on the grounds of the Hoover Presidential Library.

35. Anna Eleanor Roosevelt Roosevelt

Anna Eleanor Roosevelt was born in New York City on October 11, 1884. She was the eldest of Elliott and Anna Hall Roosevelt's three children. The Roosevelt and Hall families were longtime members of elite "old money" society. Some of the later members of the families would have difficulty in holding onto the money, but the prestige and name recognition was always there.

When Eleanor was young, her father was in and out of their home — sometimes on trips to Europe, once on a safari to India. He was Theodore Roosevelt's brother and loved the rugged life of adventures as much as Theodore. Wherever he was, Elliott struggled with the severe problem of alcoholism. When two more children were born, both sons, there was no change in his life-style.

Eleanor doted on her father as she grew up. Possibly because he did come and go so freely and was not required to assume much control over her behavior, he seemed a remote, glamorous, loving figure of whom she never tired. Her mother, Anna, on the other hand, stayed close to her children (she and Eleanor shared a room) and was sometimes forced to discipline them in ways they did not like.

Eleanor's mother was tall and slender, fair-haired, and very pretty. Eleanor admired her mother's clothes and jewelry, but, according to a son of Eleanor's, never mentioned loving her. Anna used her talent to arouse guilt in Eleanor about misdeeds as a way of exercising control over her. Also, Eleanor wrote, her mother "was always a little troubled by my lack of beauty."

As far back as she could remember, Eleanor, her mother and two brothers spent their summers with her Grandfather Hall at Tivoli, the Halls' summer home on the Hudson River. When her mother died when Eleanor was seven, followed closely by one of Eleanor's brothers, Eleanor and the remaining brother went to Tivoli to live permanently. Anna had named her mother guardian of her children in her will, and there was no question about their father assuming their care. Eleanor loved her grandparents and

Eleanor Roosevelt. (Artist: Alta Shore Purdy. Courtesy National Portrait Gallery, Smithsonian Institution.)

enjoyed their summers on the Hudson and their winters in a 37th Street home in New York City.

Both families in Eleanor's background were extremely duty-oriented, with a highly developed social consciousness. Her Grandfather Roosevelt was a trustee for Children's Aid Society for many years and started clubhouses for boys. Her Grandmother Hall took Eleanor with her each year to help decorate a Christmas tree in the baby ward in Post-Graduate Hospital in New York. Eleanor's Aunt Gracie took the young girl with her to visit with patients at Orthopedic Hospital, and Eleanor often sang hymns at the Bowery Mission.

Eleanor was ten years old when her dear father died after long years of extreme alcoholic abuse. Eleanor was completely overcome with grief.

Her Grandmother Hall flatly refused to allow Eleanor to attend her father's funeral because of the reason of his death. The grandparents had fundamentalist religious beliefs, and her grandmother tried to impose her views on Eleanor and Eleanor's brother, as well as her own children.

Eleanor was allowed to visit her father's sister, Auntie Bye, who was severely crippled by a spinal deformity. Auntie Bye was sweet-natured and kind to Eleanor. For a time Eleanor visited frequently with her uncle Theodore Roosevelt and his large family at Sagamore Hill, but these visits were curtailed as Eleanor got older.

Eleanor was given the usual cultural instructions of the little girls of her class in piano and ballet. She also learned to sew, but with servants always available to cook and clean, Eleanor never learned to do household chores for herself.

Eleanor was unusually unattractive, and this concerned all her relatives. After a visit to Sagamore Hill, Theodore's wife, Edith, wrote Auntie Bye, "Poor little soul, she is very plain. Her mouth and teeth seem to have no future. But the ugly duckling may turn out to be a swan." One of her mother's sisters became angry with Eleanor one day and said Eleanor would probably never have a boyfriend.

Poor Eleanor! With all these wondrous beauties passing judgment on her looks, she must have felt like crawling in a hole. It is no wonder she was shy and had little to say.

When she was fifteen, Eleanor was enrolled in an English girls' school, called Allenswood, near London. She remained there for three years, rarely seeing a man other than an occasional traveling cousin. She read and reread her late father's letters as though they were a prayerbook. Death had not changed her love for him.

She returned to Tivoli at age eighteen to find her Grandmother Hall engaged in a valiant attempt to reform her own alcoholic son, Vallie. It evolved into such a futile, full-time effort on the part of her grandmother that Eleanor and her Aunt Corinne moved back to the Hall house in New York City.

Here Eleanor gradually renewed old acquaintances and made a few new friends, while she assumed direction of the running of the household for Aunt Corinne and herself. Her aunt was given to frequent tempestuous love affairs, which occupied most of her time. When the romances were not going well, Corinne shut herself in her room, weeping for hours and refusing to eat.

Eleanor was now a debutante, so she received invitations to various society parties and dances. She frequently encountered her cousin Franklin Roosevelt at these events, as he would come into the city from Harvard, where he was in college. Eleanor and Franklin had always known each other, but had never been close. Now this began to change.

Franklin Roosevelt was an unusually handsome young man, intelligent and personable, and he must have attracted many pretty girls who interested him. Why would he begin a courtship of his "plain Jane" cousin?

One reason could have been that Franklin was very conscious of family and breeding, and he had no intention of becoming seriously involved with a nobody. For another, he was rich, and rich people often have to wonder whether they are loved for themselves or only for the family money. While Eleanor's side of the family had to cut back on spending from time to time, money was always there when needed, and this would not be a problem with her.

Despite Franklin's debonair looks and manners, he was the only son of a doting mother, Sara Roosevelt, and he had probably had less experience with women than other men his age because of his mother's strict eye on his activities. Eleanor had a total lack of sophistication, and her starry-eyed devotion to him must have appealed strongly to Franklin. It would be interesting to show this young, impressionable cousin something of the world. They continued to date each other under the watchful eye of a chaperone.

In 1903 Eleanor looked like a woman, but with the sheltered life she had led, she was still a child in many ways. She had never had to work on a job, worry about money, keep a house or take any responsibility for her own future. She had been working as a volunteer for the Junior League organization, which was just getting started.

When Franklin asked Eleanor to marry him that fall, it seemed the most natural event in the world to her, but not to Franklin's mother. Sara Roosevelt couldn't see any reason why her son would want to marry, and especially why he would want to marry Eleanor. She attempted to end what she considered an infatuation by taking Franklin and his former college roommate on a cruise to the West Indies. The two young men met several pretty fellow passengers, but no love affairs developed. Then Sara asked her friend Joseph Choate, who was Ambassador to England, if Franklin could go back to London with him as his secretary. Ambassador Choate, who had come to the United States for a conference, felt Franklin was too young to fill such an important position, and refused.

On March 17, 1905, Eleanor and Franklin were married in an elaborate ceremony at the brownstone home of one of Eleanor's cousins, Mrs. Henry (Susie) Parish, where Eleanor had been living in recent months.

There were about two hundred guests present for the lovely ceremony and elegant reception. The bride was given away by her Uncle Theodore, who had been inaugurated only two weeks before as President of the United States.

Since Franklin was still a student at Columbia Law School, the newlyweds spent a brief honeymoon at Hyde Park, Franklin's family home. He completed the school year while they lived in a hotel apartment. Eleanor made every effort to win Sara's approval as her daughter-in-law, but she would never succeed.

As soon as the school term ended, Eleanor and Franklin sailed for Europe for a real honeymoon, during which time they visited England, France, Italy, Germany, Scotland and Switzerland. They had a wonderful trip, and by the time they got back to New York, Eleanor was pregnant.

For the first three months of this and all her subsequent pregnancies, Eleanor was violently nauseated. Sara took her to her house to stay while Franklin continued in law school. Sara rented a house three blocks from her own home and outfitted it completely, down to the pots and pans. She hired three servants to work for Franklin and Eleanor, and as soon as Eleanor was up and about, the house became her first real home with Franklin.

Although Sara Roosevelt had always had servants to do her household work for her, she was capable of doing any or most jobs herself. Not only did Eleanor not know how to do housework, she had no desire to learn. She just sat back and let Sara run their household as well as her own.

On May 3, 1906, Eleanor gave birth to their first child, a little girl they named Anna for Eleanor's mother. A son, James, was born the next year in December. Eleanor felt totally inept in caring for the children, and again made no attempt to learn. Her solution was invariably to hire more servants.

Realizing that Eleanor did not mind her running a portion of their lives for them, Sara bought property in a fashionable area of New York City and had large twin homes built on it — one for herself and the other for Franklin and Eleanor. This time, however, Sara had overstepped. Eleanor was most unhappy with this arrangement and their close proximity to his mother, but Franklin made light of her objections.

Franklin became bored with law school and quit, but he still passed his state bar examination. He went to work as an unpaid law clerk at Carter, Ledyard and Milburn, a noted law firm. He worked there for three years and enjoyed it tremendously. For the first time in his life, he encountered people who lived on a different social level than his, and he found them interesting.

When Elliott Roosevelt was born in 1910, Eleanor was getting a little weary from all her rapid childbearing. A three-month-old son had died several months earlier, and it seemed her whole life was becoming an endless round of pregnancy and children.

Eleanor's solution to the problem was to deny her sexual attention to Franklin. She had no one to tell her anything about how to regulate the size of their family, and she was too proud to ask. She admitted years later that she was a complete innocent when it came to sex.

Franklin turned his attention to politics after Elliott's birth. He was nominated by the Democrats to run for the New York State Senate, and he won. A decided boost to his campaign had been the lavish spending by his mother. Sara Roosevelt spent five times more of her own money on Franklin's race than any other candidate spent at all.

Franklin and Eleanor moved their family to Albany to live for the six months while the Legislature sat in session. For the first time in their marriage, Eleanor was far away from Sara and her benevolent tyranny in their lives. Franklin was reelected, which lengthened the time they spent in Albany. Eleanor decided politics was interesting as she learned more about it, and it had certainly done her a favor by removing her from the sphere of her mother-in-law's influence.

In the 1912 election Franklin supported Woodrow Wilson in his campaign for President. To reward Franklin for his efforts, President Wilson appointed Franklin Assistant Secretary of the Navy in his Cabinet.

Eleanor and Franklin's marriage began to show signs of strain caused by his intense devotion to political activities and her enforced domestic ones. It seemed they never had a meeting point any more in their lives. He completely forgot to acknowledge their eighth wedding anniversary.

Franklin may have thought his own efforts would be all important in his political future, but this would not be the case. Eleanor was preparing to enter politics also, and her work would be equally vital to his success.

Since Franklin's duties as Assistant Secretary of the Navy would be in Washington, they would have to move there to live. Eleanor did not look forward to the move. Her shyness made her dread the obligatory calls she would have to make on other officials' wives in the capital. She talked about the problem with Auntie Bye, who advised Eleanor to make life more pleasant in any way she could for the young navy officers' wives. Eleanor listened carefully and heeded the advice.

The next year, after they moved to Washington, Eleanor became pregnant again, and suffered her usual debilitating nausea. This son was named Franklin Delano Roosevelt, Jr. Eleanor's last son, John, was born in 1916.

It was during this period of frequent pregnancies and coping with the other children that Eleanor decided what she needed was a private secretary to help her with letter writing, keeping track of appointments and issuing invitations. She hired Lucy Mercer.

Lucy was very pretty, tall, charming, well-bred and well dressed. For the first few months Eleanor blessed the day she had hired Lucy, who was a tremendous help to her. As time passed, however, Eleanor began to have an uneasy feeling that maybe Lucy and Franklin were becoming a little too friendly with each other.

Eleanor was not mistaken. Franklin was captivated by the beautiful Lucy, and began to talk of her freely with their friends. After finally confronting her husband about his attentions to the younger woman, Eleanor let Lucy go. Lucy then enlisted in the navy in the summer of 1917.

Eleanor heaved a sigh of relief — only to discover a short time later that the navy had assigned Lucy to work in Franklin's office. Franklin was so in love by this time, he decided he would go on active duty in the navy, divorce Eleanor and marry Lucy.

Lucy's charms were not only physical, although she was an outstandingly attractive woman. She was a member of an aristocratic Maryland family, though they had lost their money in recent years through bad investments. Her background and experiences were similar to Franklin's, and she was a distinct threat to Eleanor.

After Eleanor found and read some letters Lucy had written Franklin in 1918, Eleanor gave up. She told Franklin he could have a divorce if he wanted one. She was sick and tired of the whole mess.

Sara Roosevelt, however, viewed the matter differently. Franklin's mother reminded him of the disastrous effect a divorce would have on his political career. During this period no divorced man stood any chance of being elected to any office.

She pointed out he would be separated from his children, and to top everything else, he had no grounds on which to sue for divorce. Eleanor had done nothing wrong. He agreed reluctantly that all her arguments were valid ones, and he said he would give up Lucy.

Eleanor insisted on two conditions for their marriage to continue: Franklin was to forget Lucy, and from that time on he and Eleanor would be married in name only. So far as anyone knows, from that time of their lives — and they were both still young — they were simply friends sharing a house and children. Lucy was out of the picture.

Franklin was much more of a playmate with their children than Eleanor. Eleanor "did her duty" and took good care of them, but she never enjoyed playing with them. Franklin took them sailing and horseback riding in summer, sledding and tobogganing in winter.

Eleanor's already fragile self-esteem had been severely damaged by Franklin's open pursuit of Lucy. In an effort to ease her hurt, Eleanor hurled herself into various civic duties. In her view, with its background of her grandparents' rigid teachings on right and wrong, Franklin did not deserve, and therefore did not receive, forgiveness.

When Lucy married Winthrop Rutherfurd in 1920, Eleanor began cheering up considerably. With a husband, Lucy, who was a Catholic, was out of Franklin's life forever! Eleanor was even more sure the bad days were over when Lucy's little daughter, Barbara, was born the next year.

Franklin was the Vice Presidential nominee on the Democratic ticket with Presidential nominee James M. Cox in 1920. The ticket was defeated when Republican Warren G. Harding won the election.

In August 1921, Franklin developed polio while he and his whole family, accompanied by a party of friends, were on a fishing trip to Campobello, South Carolina. He was dangerously ill for two weeks, and Eleanor rarely left his side. For a short time, he was completely paralyzed. When the viral infection had ended, only his legs remained paralyzed. He would never be able to walk again without aid.

Sara Roosevelt was so demoralized by Franklin's serious disability that she wanted to take him to her Hyde Park home and keep him in an invalid state. But Eleanor loved Franklin enough not to be willing to let him settle for such a barren life as that envisioned by his mother. Eleanor insisted his political career could continue if she picked up the slack and helped him campaign.

Franklin's longtime friend and political advisor Louis Howe agreed with Eleanor. He began giving her instructions as to what actions she should take to win elections. Eleanor had never liked Louis personally, but she had to admit he knew politics.

Louis insisted one of her first moves should be to join the women's division of the New York Democratic Committee. As Eleanor said, "Not that he cared so much for my activities but because he felt they would make it possible for me to bring into the house people who would keep Franklin interested in state politics."

Franklin's recovery moved along at a snail's pace. In 1924 he managed to totter a few steps to the rostrum at the Democratic National Convention to nominate Al Smith for President. Later he headed the Smith campaign for the nomination, but John W. Davis was nominated instead.

One of Franklin's stalwart supporters during these long, tiring days of recovery was his secretary, Marguerite LeHand, called Missy. Franklin and Missy enjoyed each other's company, joking and laughing together, and Missy made Franklin's life her life. According to one of the Roosevelt sons' account of these days, Missy was his father's mistress.

If Eleanor was jealous of Franklin's relationship with Missy, she never gave any indication of it. She liked Missy too, and when Missy's mother died, Eleanor went with her to the funeral.

Franklin was nominated to run for Governor of New York in 1928 by acclamation at the convention. He won the election and was later elected to a second term. Franklin had an excellent speaking voice, mellow and persuasive. His radio campaign speeches were the reason people voted for him.

The Roosevelt family moved to Albany to live when he became Governor. At the same time, Eleanor again was forced to endure the pain of being supplanted in her husband's life by another woman and having the world know of it.

Elliott Roosevelt, then in his teens, said of Franklin's and Missy's closeness, "It was not unusual to enter his sunny corner room and find Missy with him in her nightgown. There was no attempt to conceal their relationship. . . ."

Eleanor had involved herself for some time with fund-raising efforts of the Democratic National Committee, but she would not help Franklin campaign for Governor. She directed her attentions to the candidates at the national level.

Eleanor was "starting to enjoy herself in what is politely called public service, but is more accurately identified as the obtaining and exercise of power. . . . Money spelled power, as she knew from life with Granny," to quote Elliott. Certainly Eleanor was becoming more and more enthusiastic about her role in politics and spent more and more time with political activities.

Elliott also claimed that his grandmother, Sara Roosevelt, spent approximately one million, two hundred thousand dollars in the campaign to bring Franklin into the White House. If so, she got her money's worth, as Franklin was inaugurated President of the United States on March 4, 1933, in the midst of the great Depression.

Franklin went to work immediately to institute relief programs and other projects to stimulate the economy. Some of these programs were effective, some were not. All were somewhat radical to the American mindset of the time, as most had never been tried before in any form.

During Franklin's administrations, the Farm Credit Administration came into being; the gold standard was abandoned for American money; the Social Security Act was passed; the Federal Bank Deposit Insurance Corporation was created; and other regulatory agencies to help stabilize the economy were put into place.

As First Lady, Eleanor became more fashionably dressed and better groomed. She believed women were entitled to play a larger role in society than to serve as their husbands' hostesses. She concerned herself with what she felt to be larger issues and left the entertainment requirements, such as selecting menus, preparing food, arranging flowers, and accommodating guests, to the White House staff. She pursued her own career as an author, lecturer and activist.

In 1936 Eleanor wrote her widely acclaimed autobiography, *This Is My Story*. Even Alice Roosevelt Longworth, Eleanor's cousin, was impressed, and she had never liked Eleanor. She had even encouraged Franklin in his romance with Lucy Mercer by inviting the two of them to dine with her, which she must have known would hurt Eleanor.

By 1939 a Gallup poll indicated 67 percent of Americans approved of Eleanor's conduct as First Lady, even though some critics had complained earlier she had commercialized the role. After six years of living in the

White House, she was now an integral part of the civil rights movement, various youth programs, and poverty programs. She took many trips in connection with these varied interests, and a large part of each year she spent away from the White House.

When World War II began with the Japanese attack at Pearl Harbor, Franklin, Jr., and Elliott entered the armed services. The war became intensely personal for Eleanor with two of her sons engaged in the war effort. The other two would enter later.

Missy LeHand had a stroke in 1940 and had to leave her job at the White House permanently. When she died in July 1944, after many months of invalidism, Eleanor represented the Roosevelt family at the young woman's funeral. Franklin was too busy with the war effort, and was possibly not able to make the trip to attend Missy's funeral.

During World War II Eleanor turned her own attention to Civil defense efforts and nutritional programs that would help Americans eat well during rationing. Eleanor traveled so extensively that jokes appeared about her in the newspapers. The movie star Gary Cooper, while entertaining troops in the South Pacific, was asked by some of the soldiers, "Where's Eleanor?"

Gary said, solemnly, "Well, we saw her tracks in the sand at one of the islands where we stopped — but we couldn't tell which way they were headed!"

Eleanor was opposed to a third term for Franklin, but he was reelected. She was vehement in her objections to a fourth. The war years had taken a heavy toll on his health, which was obvious to the most casual observer. He was gaunt and drawn appearing. Eleanor did not campaign vigorously on this term as she had before. She wrote her son James, "I don't think Pa would really mind defeat."

All the Roosevelt children were now adults. Anna married John Boettiger and lived in Seattle, Washington, prior to their divorce. She had two children, Buzzie and Sistie. James graduated from Boston University Law School and had become active in politics, as did Franklin, Jr. John was a stockbroker, and Elliott entered the literary field as an author of historical books and murder mysteries, as well as working as a television producer.

Following her divorce, Anna and her two children came to live in the White House. Anna assumed the duties as White House hostess and became her father's confidante. Again Eleanor felt displaced in Franklin's affections, but by now it was an old story. At least with Anna there was no involvement beyond companionship.

On April 12, 1945, Franklin had gone to his retreat at Warm Springs, Georgia, and Eleanor held her usual press conference at the White House. Laura Delano, Franklin's cousin, had gone with him to Georgia, and she called Eleanor to tell her Franklin had fainted and had to be put to bed.

Eleanor asked Laura to keep her informed and said she would come to Georgia if he wanted her to be with him.

Since she had previously scheduled a speech to raise money for the Thrift Shop, one of her favorite charities, Eleanor went on to the meeting and made the speech. As soon as she had finished, she was told a message had arrived that she should return to the White House immediately. When she got there, she learned that Franklin had died in Georgia a short while before.

Eleanor then called Vice President Harry Truman to come to her office, where she told him of Franklin's death. Within an hour or so, Truman took the oath of office as President.

All the anguish and bitter memories of long-ago years came flooding back to Eleanor when Laura Delano told her that Lucy Mercer Rutherfurd was with Franklin when he collapsed. Their affair had never ended. Each time he went to Warm Springs, he usually went by to visit her at her home in Aiken, South Carolina. Eleanor also learned that Anna had invited Lucy to be a dinner guest at the White House when Eleanor was away.

Eleanor was stunned. She had always felt married to Franklin. They had children, mutual relatives, mutual goals. She had been a good wife to him. She confronted Anna with Laura's information. How could Anna ever invite Lucy to dine in the White House when she knew how much heartache her mother had suffered because of Lucy? They became estranged as a result of Anna's disloyalty, and they were never really reconciled.

Eleanor said she found herself in a peculiar state before and during the funeral. She said she had "an almost impersonal feeling" then, and in the days following Franklin's death. She was sorry that a President of the United States had died in the same way other Americans were sorry, and she was sorry the young man she had loved so dearly was gone.

The man who died in Georgia was a man she didn't know. This Franklin had deliberately deceived her for many years, and had consistently lied to her about Lucy. She realized his primary concern had been his political career.

Franklin's will left instructions that all Missy's medical bills should be paid from his estate, up to as much as half the total amount of the estate. The other half was left to Eleanor. Franklin was buried at Hyde Park, New York.

President Truman appointed Eleanor to be the first United States Representative on the United Nations Council. She gave distinguished service in this position. She traveled in Europe in connection with the appointment, and she felt that her most important work was what she did for the Human Rights Commission. She took trips to India, Japan, China, Bali and Morocco.

A few years earlier Eleanor had had a cottage a few miles from Hyde

Park remodeled as a personal retreat. She moved to the cottage and made it her permanent home. She actively campaigned in 1956 for Adlai Stevenson, the Democratic nominee for President.

Alone in her cottage, Eleanor had much time for reflection about her past life. Her only companion many times at Val-Kill, as she had named her home, was Franklin's Scotty dog, Fala. She and the little dog were inseparable.

In a burst of compassionate generosity, Eleanor sent a watercolor portrait of Franklin to Lucy Mercer Rutherfurd. The portrait was the work of Lucy's friend Madame Elizabeth Shumatov, who had been working on another portrait of Franklin on the day he died.

Eleanor enjoyed the new freedom she had to speak her mind. No longer did she have to worry about having views distorted and remarks misquoted which might injure Franklin's career.

At age seventy-five, Eleanor became a lecturer at Brandeis University. In addition to this job, she appeared regularly on a television program called "Prospects of Mankind." She continued to write a monthly question-and-answer page for *McCall's* magazine, which she had begun before leaving the White House, and she wrote numerous articles and books. She believed firmly in what she said: "When you cease to make a contribution, you begin to die."

In 1960 Eleanor again campaigned for the Democratic nominee, this time John F. Kennedy. When he was elected President, he invited Eleanor to sit in the Presidential box for his inauguration ceremony. She declined with thanks. If she had accepted she would have had to sit with Joseph Kennedy, President Kennedy's father, and Eleanor had never liked the elder Kennedy at all.

Later in 1961, Eleanor's health began to fail. She developed severe anemia, but she took medicine prescribed and tried to carry on as before. She became so ill she required transfusions of blood, at which time her illness was diagnosed as tuberculosis.

After many months of declining health, she died in a New York City hospital on November 7, 1962. She, too, is buried at Hyde Park, New York.

36. Elizabeth Virginia Wallace Truman

Elizabeth Virginia Wallace, usually known as Bess, was born in Independence, Missouri, on February 13, 1885, the oldest child and only daughter born to David and Madge Gates Wallace. Since she grew up with three younger brothers, Bess was a good baseball player at third base, a marble shooter and a mumblety-peg champion. As she reached her teens, Bess became proficient in tennis, horseback riding and ice-skating.

Bess's maternal grandfather, General Porterfield Gates, was a wealthy man, having made his fortune in milling flour which carried the trade name "Queen of the Pantry." Bess's mother grew up in an atmosphere of luxury and refinement, which led her friends to wonder why she chose to marry David Wallace.

Wallace was a nice person, none better, but he was not very well "fixed for money." He worked valiantly to support his family, but at best they lived in marginal poverty. Mrs. Wallace had an unfortunate tendency to remind him of her background frequently, and was, to quote neighbors, "the queenliest woman Independence ever produced."

The early 1890s, known as the Gay Nineties Era, was a good time to be a child. Bess and her brothers enjoyed their life even if their mother did make them change out of their play clothes and dress for dinner. After summer dinners they would usually walk to the ice-cream parlor on the town square, enjoy the delicious treat and visit with friends.

All this idyllic existence ended abruptly for Bess when her father committed suicide one night after he had been drinking heavily. Bess had adored her father, and she was devastated by the blow. Investigation showed he had large debts he could not pay and apparently he saw no other way out. Like all family members of suicide victims, Bess wondered, "Wasn't there *something* I could have done?"

When Margaret Truman, Bess's daughter, mentioned Mr. Wallace's death in later years, her father Harry reprimanded her sternly and told her she must never hurt her mother that way again. Bess never once spoke of the tragedy to her daughter.

Bess Truman. (Courtesy Library of Congress.)

Bess met Harry Truman when he moved to Independence and entered fifth grade with her. They were in class together until they graduated from high school in 1901.

Bess was a slender, blue-eyed blonde, with long shining hair, and Harry Truman fell in love for life in the fifth grade.

Following graduation, Bess was sent to the fashionable Barstow School for Girls in Kansas City. She was still depressed about her father's death, and her mother and grandparents hoped a change of scenery would help her cope better with her loss. Bess did good work at the school and was popular with girls and boys alike, but there is no record that she had any special boyfriend, other than Harry.

Harry faced a problematic future when he graduated from high school, for he had very little money. He yearned to go to college, but as his family was always in debt, they could not afford to send him. He applied for admission to West Point Academy, but his eyesight was so poor that he was not accepted. There were no student loans or part-time jobs then, and college was beyond Harry's reach.

Harry and Bess dated regularly when they were both at home, to the dismay of Madge Wallace. Madge felt her daughter could find a more promising beau than Harry if she tried. Bess had inherited her father's common sense and despised her mother's pretentious outlook of life and people. She calmly ignored her mother's pointed comments and went on keeping company with Harry.

Harry was having so much trouble getting started financially that any possibility of an early marriage for him and Bess seemed remote. He worked for a while as timekeeper for a railroad construction crew, and later as a bank clerk, but neither job paid very well, and he knew he could not support a family without better wages.

Then World War I began. Harry was a member of the Missouri National Guard, and when war was declared, the National Guard units became a part of the regular army. Harry received a commission as a first lieutenant when he entered, and held the rank of captain when he was discharged.

While Harry was in the army, he and Bess wrote each other every day. Many years later, after he became President, he found Bess burning the letters, which they had saved. He told her she should not burn them. "Think of the history," he said.

"I have!" Bess told him.

When Harry was discharged from the army and returned to Indianapolis, he found Bess now had several other interested suitors. Harry decided his pride, which led him to think he had to have an outstanding job and a large savings account, was not as important to him as Bess. He began insisting that they go ahead and get married.

Bess married Harry on June 28, 1919, in the Trinity Episcopal Church in Independence. Bess wore a beautiful traditional wedding dress, and Harry wore a suit with a checked pattern. Harry had a casual approach to life which resembled that of Bess's late father, and Bess sometimes was irritated by it. After their marriage, they moved in with Bess's mother and grandmother to live in the Gates mansion.

Harry did not have a job yet, and he and an army buddy decided to open a clothing store as a way to earn a living. Within less than two years they were deeply in debt and had to close their business when the value of their inventory dipped sharply. It would be fifteen years before Harry paid off all the debts he had accumulated during the venture.

Harry decided commerce might not be his field, and he decided to run for County Judge. He needed a job, he had many good friends in the county and everybody else was kinfolk. He won the election easily.

Even though Harry and Bess were buoyed by his success, his mother-in-law was not impressed because he had limited powers.

"He can't even marry anybody or sentence a robber!" she said. Madge Wallace was free with such comments, despite the fact that she had never held a job and had inherited her wealth.

Harry's job duties were similar to those of county commissioners in other states. He worked hard and got roads improved, and effected a complete overhaul and update of the local Old Folks' Home when he investigated deplorable conditions there.

Bess took an interest in Harry's budding career and helped him by making suggestions for various improvements she or her friends thought ought to be made.

Despite his intense efforts and family support, Harry was defeated in his bid for reelection when the Republicans swept the state in victories that penetrated even county politics.

Just after Harry lost his job, his and Bess's daughter, Margaret, was born on February 17, 1924. Margaret's parents had not had time to buy a crib, as she was born early. The baby slept in a well-padded dresser drawer until they could buy a crib. All their relatives were delighted that Bess and Harry had such a fine baby, as everyone took an interest in each other's lives.

Harry next went to work selling memberships for the Auto Club of Kansas City. Despite his earlier failure in the clothing business, he proved a good salesman. During one campaign for new members, he sold fifteen hundred memberships.

Democratic party officials urged Harry to run for Presiding Judge of the county court in the 1925 election. He won this time, and served for two successive terms, a total of eight years. In this job Harry was the county's chief executive officer.

Bess was busy with her little daughter and happy and satisfied with the life she lived with Harry. These years would be some of the happiest she would have, living among family and friends in a community she loved.

Neither Bess nor Margaret welcomed a move to Washington when Harry was elected to the United States Senate in 1934. Margaret was now ten years old and hated leaving her friends. Bess found she could not leave her mother, even though Madge Wallace was often contentious and insulting, so Madge moved to Washington to live with the Trumans.

Bess never once complained about living in the small, four-room furnished apartment Harry rented for them in Washington, as she knew it was all he could afford. Margaret and her grandmother shared a bedroom.

Bess went to work for Harry as an assistant in his Senate office, for which she received an annual salary of forty-five hundred dollars. She was widely criticized for this action, but she ignored her critics and kept on working. Even Harry's most dedicated opponent, Roy Roberts, managing editor of the *Kansas City Star*, defended Bess as a hard worker.

Margaret attended a private school, Gunston Hall, in Washington. Both Margaret and Bess took the opportunity to go sightseeing in Washington, but they both missed Missouri and their former life there.

At first the wives of government officials in Washington snubbed Bess at social gatherings, which infuriated Harry. As time went on, however, all the Trumans made many good friends, especially during his second six-year term as Senator. They were beginning to feel as if they really belonged.

As Margaret got older, Bess and her mother often went back to Missouri for long visits, and Mrs. Wallace usually spent her summers in Missouri. Harry missed Bess dreadfully when she was gone and would beg her to come back as soon as she could. Bess never really liked Washington and jumped at the chance to spend her summers in Missouri.

Harry tried to reenlist in the army when the Japanese attacked Pearl Harbor in December, 1941. When he was rejected because he was fifty-seven, he was annoyed. He felt there was plenty of fight in the old boy yet!

The next year Margaret graduated from Gunston Hall. Her father made the address at her commencement exercises. In his speech he told the audience he was glad Margaret had inherited her mother's capabilities in English and Spanish, in which Margaret had taken top honors. Bess blushed in irritation, while Harry grinned.

Harry worked hard as a Senator, as he had in all his other jobs. He was appointed to serve on a Senate committee to investigate defense contractors and their business dealings. He and other committee members uncovered much careless waste and several instances of outright fraud.

The Democrats were impressed by Harry, and as the election in 1944 drew near, rumors were circulated that current Vice President Henry Wallace would be dumped from the ticket, and replaced by Harry as President Roosevelt sought election to a fourth term.

Bess was torn between delight that Harry might be so honored, and dismay when she considered how the Wallace family and the Vice President would view such an event. The Vice President's daughter and Margaret were good friends. Also Bess had lived in Washington long enough to observe the adverse effect on children of being in the political spotlight. She did not want that for Margaret.

Despite Bess's misgivings, Harry was nominated to run for Vice President with President Roosevelt. President Roosevelt told his new running mate that he had enough to do with directing the activities of the armed services while World War II continued, and Harry could run the campaign.

Campaigning was a natural for Harry. He could talk as much as he wanted, about whatever he wanted and just be himself. In North Dakota he performed a war dance with Sioux Indians, and in Minnesota he entered (and lost) a cow-milking contest. When Bess saw news pictures of his antics, she called him and said, "Now, Harry, remember your mother said to behave yourself!"

The American people loved his cornball jokes and his antics. He and President Roosevelt won the election.

When Harry had spoken to President Roosevelt before the election, he had noticed how ill the President appeared. Apparently President Roosevelt was not feeling well. He kept urging Harry not to fly in his campaign trips.

"Don't fly," he begged Harry. "Ride the trains. Can't both of us afford to take chances." Harry's campaign manager asked Harry if he realized he would live in the White House before long.

All the foreboding was justified. President Roosevelt died in Warm Springs, Georgia, on April 12, 1945, and Harry Truman became the thirty-third President of the United States. Harry no doubt served as evidence for the statement, "Behind every successful man stands a surprised mother-in-law."

When they moved into the White House, Bess made it clear she was in charge of the housekeeping. She demanded and got better food from a kitchen staff which had grown indifferent and slack. She was careful with money and watched expenditures closely. She was a considerate supervisor, however, and treated the staff with kindness when they did their job right.

The White House was the first real home the Trumans had ever had, as strange as that may seem. Bess delighted in having it redecorated to her own taste with chintz slipcovers, new drapes and different types of pictures on the walls. It was repainted inside and outside.

On Sundays Harry walked to services at the First Baptist Church and Bess and Margaret went to St. John's Episcopal Church across the square from the White House. Often they attended together, alternating churches.

Bess was well informed politically after all her years with Harry. She did not hesitate to express her own opinions about various issues, but she refused flatly to hold her own news conferences as Mrs. Roosevelt had done. If she had ideas she thought Harry might find helpful, she would tell him, but Harry always handled problems on his own.

Bess soon learned that customs once established in Washington are not easily changed. She was too shy and ill at ease in public appearances to talk with reporters at news conferences, but she delegated the task to either her personal or social secretary after some incorrect information appeared in a news report.

Despite Harry's sometimes unbridled tongue, he was a religious man. He was well informed in both Christian and Jewish history. He felt that the Nazis' atrocities against the Jewish people before and during World War II imposed an obligation on the free world to do something to help ease the Jews' physical and emotional trauma. He knew that for some time Hebrew leaders had longed for a homeland of their own, as the Bible had prophesied they would have someday. Harry thought the time was now.

He met with Jewish political leaders and rabbis to work out their aims. He proposed that the matter of implementation be put in the hands of the United Nations under the sponsorship of the United States government. The Jews were amazed and delighted when they realized Harry was completely serious in his proposal, and the state of Israel came into being. It was officially recognized as an independent entity in May 1945.

The war with Japan continued, and Harry ordered that a newly developed atomic bomb be dropped on the Japanese mainland in an effort to exert pressure on the Japanese to surrender and prevent further losses of American lives. When several bombs were dropped, the Japanese did surrender in August 1945. (Germany and Italy had surrendered some months earlier.) Harry was severely criticized in some quarters for the bombings, but they undeniably brought an end to World War II.

Despite Harry's many worthwhile achievements, Bess's mother never liked Harry. She was even unimpressed that he was now the President of the United States and commented acidly she knew of plenty of men better qualified to be President than Harry. Bess had to walk a fine line when her mother's remarks irritated her husband, but Harry never replied to the older woman. He just walked away. He knew Bess loved him dearly and approved of all his actions, and that was what mattered to Harry.

In the next election Harry ran for President and was elected in his own right, defeating Republican candidate Thomas E. Dewey. The race was so close that the *Chicago Daily Tribune* first editions carried headlines reading "Dewey Defeats Truman." With red faces, the editors issued a corrected version several hours later when final returns showed Harry was the winner.

Margaret had grown up into a young lady during these busy years, had graduated from college, and decided to pursue a career in singing in New York. She got an apartment where she would live alone, but Bess decided her own personal secretary might just as well go with Margaret since Bess took care of her own correspondence.

Shortly after Harry began serving his second term, it was found that the White House was structurally unsafe. Congress authorized extensive repairs and renovation. While this was in progress, the Trumans lived in Blair House across the street. Entertainments were reduced in size and number for a time, and formal state dinners were held at the Carlton Hotel.

In July 1950, North Korean Communist forces invaded the republic of South Korea. General Douglas MacArthur was named commander of the American forces who were sent to defend South Korea under United Nations auspices.

On November 1, 1950, two Puerto Rican nationalists evaded Blair House security in an attempt to assassinate Harry. One attacker was killed and the other was captured. There was violence again in the nation.

Bess was shocked and worried for days after the attack. Her mother was quite ill during this time, and they did not tell the older woman what had happened.

Margaret gave a concert at Constitution Hall on December 4, 1950, which received an unfavorable review from the *Washington Post* critic. For Harry, any criticisms of his daughter were fighting words. He sat down and dashed off the following note:

> I have just read your lousy review in the back pages. You sound like a frustrated man that never made a success, an eight-ulcer man on a four-ulcer job, and all four ulcers working.
>
> I have never met you, but if I do you'll need a new nose and plenty of beefsteak and perhaps a supporter below. . . .

When the *Post* published Harry's rebuttal to the critic in its entirety, Bess was livid. Her own mother had always meddled in Bess's life, and Harry was *not* going to start the same thing with Margaret! Was that *clear*? Harry admitted he had never before seen "The Boss" so angry. House Speaker Sam Rayburn called Bess to ask her why somebody didn't hide the pens from Harry.

Harry set off another explosion in the press when he fired General MacArthur from his command in Korea. The General believed the war should be expanded, and Harry disagreed. After vehement discussions, Harry fired him.

This action brought negative reaction from Harry's mother-in-law as well as the American public. Why did Harry fire that nice man? she wanted to know. The General was a refined gentleman, and she felt sure she would like him. He was not like some people who came from a background of dirt farming!

That was the first and only time anyone ever heard Bess snap at her mother. She told her mother that she did not know all the facts, and she didn't know what she was talking about.

In 1952 Harry could have run again for President since he had served only one term in his own right, but he was tired and wanted to go home to Independence. General MacArthur was called to testify in Congressional hearings about his dismissal by Harry, but he was not reinstated in his command.

Bess's mother died that year, still convinced Bess married beneath her station in life.

Bess and Harry were glad to be home, and they never left again except for short periods. Harry was still more visible to the public than Bess since he took early morning walks each day. They lived quietly and had few visitors.

Margaret Truman married Clifton Daniels, editor of the *New York Times*, on April 21, 1956, in the same church where her parents were married thirty-seven years earlier. As time passed, four handsome Daniels sons were born, and Bess and Harry were enthusiastic grandparents. However, Bess was one grandmother who never wished any of them would be President some day.

On December 26, 1972, Harry died from the debilities of old age, his lifelong love by his side. He had lived a full life, and he would be missed by many people.

Bess lived on for ten more years. She had hoped to be able to stay in her grandfather's fourteen-room mansion as long as she lived, and she did for many years. At age ninety-five Bess was still interested in world events and still enjoyed reading, especially murder mysteries.

Margaret found it was difficult to continue a singing career now that she was a wife and mother, and she tried her hand at writing murder mysteries with a Washington locale. These mysteries have proved to be very popular and are widely read. Harry would have beamed with pride if he could have known of her success in this new field. In an ironic twist of fate, Bess's eyesight became too poor to read any of Margaret's books by the time they were published.

Bess's last year of life was spent in a confused state of mind due to extreme frailty and old age, requiring her to spend time in and out of treatment centers. She died in 1982 at age ninety-seven. She was buried beside Harry in the courtyard of the Harry S Truman Library in Independence, Missouri.

37. Mary Geneva Doud Eisenhower

Mamie Doud was born Mary Geneva Doud in a simple one-story frame house on the outskirts of Boone, Iowa, on November 14, 1896. She was nicknamed Mamie early and always used that name.

Mamie's father, John Sheldon Doud, was descended from English landowners who emigrated to America in 1639 and helped found the town of Guilford, Connecticut. Mr. Doud was a self-employed meat packer. He made enough to support his family, but when Mamie was eight, Mr. Doud sold his packing company and he and his wife moved their family of four daughters to Denver, Colorado. In Denver their home was a three-story brick house.

From early childhood Mamie had servants to do her bidding. The Douds' home projected an aura of wealth, charm and comfort. With four girls in the family, there were frequent parties and visits from friends, especially in summer. Then the Doud girls entertained callers on the porch, which was cheerfully furnished in white wicker furniture with flowering and green plants growing in pots and baskets as accessories.

Mamie Doud was breezy, friendly, petite and very feminine. She loved frilly dresses with ruffles. She liked school, but excelled more in school related activities than in classroom work. She took dancing lessons, her closest approach to athletic interest. On Sundays the Doud family enjoyed going for drives in their Stanley Steamer automobile to City Park or Elitch Gardens in Denver.

With her bubbly personality, Mamie attracted the young males in her vicinity without difficulty. She never lacked an escort for any party or dance. She was pretty, with long brown hair and smiling blue eyes. Her face was often brightened by her infectious grin.

Eleanor Doud, Mamie's sister, was in poor health due to a heart problem, and the Doud family usually spent winters in their second home in San Antonio, Texas. It was while they were in San Antonio that Mamie met Dwight Eisenhower for the first time.

Mamie had recently graduated from a finishing school in Denver, and Dwight, called Ike, had graduated some time before from West Point. He had been assigned to duty in San Antonio in 1915 because of unrest along

Mamie Eisenhower. (Courtesy Library of Congress.)

the Mexican border. He told Mamie he came from a poor Kansas family, and could not have gone to college if he had not received an appointment to West Point.

Ike and Mamie were instantly attracted to each other, but each tried to appear nonchalant. When Ike called Mamie the day after they met to ask for a date, she told him she was busy for the next four weeks, but she usually got home about five o'clock in the afternoons if he wanted to call her.

Ike didn't call—he was on her doorstep the next afternoon when she reached home. From that time their courtship was swift, ardent and conclusive. There was no doubt they loved each other.

The whole Doud family liked Ike, as he had an appealing personality, but Mamie's father had reservations about Ike as a prospective son-in-law when Ike requested permission to ask Mamie to marry him. Even many of Mamie's friends told her they thought she could do better than to marry a poor soldier.

"She has always had a maid to work for her, and she gets a generous allowance now, but you two will be on your own if you marry," Mr. Doud told him.

"Yes, sir. I know that. I expect to support my wife myself," Ike said.

Mr. Doud then turned his discouraging words on Mamie. He told her that life as an army wife would be one of moving frequently, having Ike gone for months at a time, and no longer having much money to spend. Mamie was supremely confident she could handle any and all problems that might arise.

On July 1, 1916, Ike and Mamie were married in the Douds' Denver home. Both the bride and groom wore white — he in tropical summer dress uniform and she in Chantilly lace.

They went to visit Ike's family in Abilene, Kansas, before going on to Fort Sam Houston to live in Ike's three-room apartment in the officer's quarters.

Despite her father's dire warnings, Mamie loved her new life. Both she and Ike enjoyed entertaining, and on an army post that did not require much money. Everyone was about equally poor, and the refreshments ran more to beer and economical uses of ground beef than to gourmet dishes. Entertainment was provided by the guests themselves by singing pop songs, as they gathered around a rented piano which Mamie played.

Mamie was still unafraid of trying something new. Her father gave her a car as a wedding gift, but she rarely drove, preferring to leave the driving to Ike. When Ike was sent to another army base sixty miles away for several weeks in 1917, Mamie decided to drive her car down to see him. She telephoned ahead that she was on her way — fortunately. As she neared the entry gate to the post, Ike was waiting.

"Get on, get on quickly — I don't know how to stop this thing!" Mamie yelled. Ike jumped on and got the car stopped. No doubt Mamie was required to learn how to stop the car before she left for home that day!

Ike and Mamie agreed on the premise that Ike's career was all important, and Mamie felt most of her attention should center on him. Her mother had spent her life catering to Mamie's father, and Mamie considered this way of life to be the norm.

Mamie was not a complainer, if she had been somewhat spoiled as a child. In the army reassignments were usually made annually, and Mamie moved their household cheerfully each time, which further endeared her to Ike.

While Mamie was pregnant with their first child, Ike was reassigned to Fort Oglethorpe, Georgia. Mamie could not be with him and went to San Antonio to stay with her parents until after their baby was born. It was her mother who took Mamie to the hospital for the birth, and it was two days later before Ike learned he had a son.

The new little Eisenhower was named Dwight Doud, but he was called Icky. Ike was enthralled with the wonder of being a father and loved the little boy with a total commitment of his affections. Tragically, little Icky died at age three from scarlet fever. Ike then developed a shell-like defense around his emotions. He was even cold to Mamie for a time, and he worked desperately to get transferred to another post away from memories of their baby. In his request he did not foresee being sent to Panama, but that was his new assignment. He said later that after Icky's death he was "on the ragged edge of a breakdown."

The Eisenhowers arrived in Panama in January 1922. It was far different from living in the United States. Their home was a shanty built on stilts in a cleared area of jungle where snakes and lizards abounded. There were bats around because no one had lived in the house for the past ten years.

Household help was cheap but unreliable. Mamie bought all their groceries herself. She had to closely supervise all cleaning and cooking, which kept her busy, and she gradually found her grief was becoming bearable.

Ike sought peace of mind in hard work. He developed a close friendship with his commanding officer, General Conner. Ike said later that General Conner influenced him more favorably than any other commanding officer he ever had.

After they had been living in Panama for several months, Mamie became pregnant a second time. She again returned to the home of her parents, this time in Denver, so her baby could be born in a hospital and in a more pleasant climate than hot, sticky Panama.

John Sheldon Eisenhower was born on August 3, 1922. Ike and Mamie rejoiced that their new son was normal in every way and hoped he would survive the perils of childhood. They would never forget their firstborn, of course, but they had another child to love and to give their lives meaning again.

After spending two more years in Panama, Ike was transferred to the Command and General Staff School at Fort Leavenworth, Kansas, to learn about tactical operations. He entered with the rank of major and he left with the same rank, although he graduated first in the class. Promotions were slow and hard to get in the army in the late 1920s. There were already a large number of senior officers, and it was felt no more were needed. Only through retirement and deaths did vacancies occur. Since Ike was now thirty-six, time was running out for him to reach the top of his army career.

After Kansas, Ike was assigned to the Washington, D.C., area to aid General John J. Pershing in writing about American battle scenes in Europe. While he assisted General Pershing, the Eisenhowers lived in the Wyoming Apartments near Rock Creek Park, and they stayed on when he was assigned to the Army War College in the same area. The courses at the War College were designed to prepare officers for command at the highest levels.

Following his War College assignment, he was sent to France. The Eisenhowers lived there for the next fifteen months. Mamie was thrilled to have an opportunity to shop in Paris. John was now six years old, and he started school at the McJanet School, which was operated for children of Americans living in Paris. Because of their inability to speak the French language, the Eisenhowers socialized largely with other American service families, but they enjoyed learning about the country and being a part of Europe for a time. They returned to the States in 1929, just after the stock market had crashed.

The crash did not affect them adversely as Ike had a steady income and was in no danger of losing his job. He was now assigned to work with the Assistant Secretary of War to formulate mobilization plans for American industries to follow in the event of a war starting. Ike had never registered to vote for a candidate of any political party, and he was impressed by the leadership demonstrated by President Franklin Roosevelt with his New Deal programs.

General Douglas MacArthur was serving as President Roosevelt's Chief of Staff, and Ike had been assisting him in preparation of budget requests and annual reports for Congress. In 1935 General MacArthur left to serve as military adviser to the new Philippine government in the creation of their own army, and he insisted that Ike go with him.

Mamie was frantic. Their years of living in Panama had given her an acute dislike for living in the tropics. Using John's education as her excuse, she refused to go to live with Ike in the Philippines.

Ike never liked his Philippine tour of duty, but he was a soldier — now with the rank of lieutenant colonel — and went where he was told. He was intensely frustrated with the small amount of money they had to use in equipping and training an army. He also found General MacArthur to be a difficult superior officer.

He missed his family, and he repeatedly begged Mamie to join him. Finally, in June 1936, she and John sailed for Manila.

The Eisenhowers lived three years in Manila, and Mamie hated every single minute she spent there. In the tropical climate, they suffered from heat and extreme humidity most of the time. They had no air conditioning, and Mamie was troubled with frequent stomach disorders, later revealed to be the result of a diseased gall bladder.

John attended the Bishop Brent School on Luzon Island, a boarding school, almost two hundred miles from Manila. The school was in a mountainous area and the climate was cooler. He enjoyed his school days and was a tennis star there. He said the three years he spent in the Philippines were "among the happiest of my life."

At last Ike's tour of duty was over, and they returned to the States. Ike's brother, Edgar, offered to pay for John to attend both college and law school if John would promise to join him later in his law practice. John thanked his Uncle Edgar for his generous offer, but explained he had decided to try to get an appointment to West Point. Ike was surprised and pleased that his son wanted to make the army his career.

John was admitted to West Point in 1940, although he found it surprisingly difficult to get an appointment. He was finally allowed to take a competitive test on which he received the highest score. He got in.

Ike and Mamie celebrated their twenty-fifth wedding anniversary in July 1941. Ike had been promoted to colonel, and his new duty was to be Chief of Staff of the Third Army at Fort Sam Houston in San Antonio. This was where they had first met. Mamie was very excited about living again in familiar surroundings.

This time the Eisenhowers had a fourteen-room red brick house to live in. Their living arrangements were better than they had had in years.

Six months later the naval base at Pearl Harbor in Hawaii was attacked by the Japanese navy, after months of European conflict had been raging, and the United States was at war. Ike was assigned to the War Plans Division of the army in Washington. He left for Washington immediately and rented a two-bedroom apartment at the Wardman Park for his family. Mamie stayed behind in San Antonio to pack their household belongings and get ready to move again. Her stay in San Antonio had been far too short, and she was sorry to have to leave so soon.

An aide of Ike's named Mickey McKeogh was assigned to accompany Mamie to assist her in any way he could. They boarded the train intending to go first to New York, where Mamie would visit John in West Point before going on to Washington. A problem arose when Mamie was seated in a first-class compartment while McKeogh had a coach seat. In Chicago the train divided, with Mamie's car going to Grand Central Station and McKeogh's going to New York's Pennsylvania Station. Neither of them realized what had happened.

McKeogh decided he needed to check with Mamie after they left Chicago, and he walked through the train to the last coach without finding her. The train was shorter by several cars! Mamie's car was gone! For the next twenty hours McKeogh worried with the dilemma. How could he tell Ike he had mislaid Mamie? No one, absolutely no one, loses a General's wife, he thought frantically.

When he finally reached New York, McKeogh rushed from Penn Station to Grand Central. Mamie was standing in the station, surrounded by bags and boxes and steaming mad. "Where were you?" she wanted to know.

Sergeant McKeogh explained what had happened, and she calmed down. For years it was a joke between him and the Eisenhowers about the time he lost Mamie!

In Washington Ike and Mamie settled down to a fairly routine life for the next four months, with Ike at home every night, but in June 1942, he was promoted to brigadier general and sent to London to assume command of all the United States troops in Europe.

John had come home from West Point for a brief visit with his father before he went to Europe. When John started to leave, he turned and saluted Ike. Mamie wept bitter tears when she realized both her men would probably be engaged in battle before long. And indeed, this was the last time the three Eisenhowers would be together until the war ended.

With Ike gone Mamie was more lonely than she had ever been before in her life. She was terrified for Ike's safety, and she wondered if she would ever see him again. She and Ike had been apart in the past, but this was so very different. Mamie moped around their apartment, wouldn't eat, lost weight to the point of emaciation and couldn't sleep.

Mamie's best friend during these days, Ruth Butcher, also had a husband in Europe. He was Lieutenant Commander Harry Butcher, naval aide to Ike. The Eisenhowers were long time friends of the Butchers, and now they were neighbors.

Ruth Butcher was a heavy drinker, and now it became easier and easier for Mamie to join her. Besides worrying herself to death about Ike's safety, there was a new cloud on the horizon. Ike's driver in Europe was a young, pretty English girl named Kay Summersby. It seemed to Mamie that every time Ike's picture appeared in the newspaper, Kay was beside him. She could not look at newsreels without crying, so Mamie never went to movies.

Mamie wrote Ike how lonely she was without him and how fearful she was that Kay or some other woman would come between them. Ike always reassured Mamie that Kay was a friend, his driver and nothing more. He told her he, too, was living for the day when the war would be over and they could be together again.

Mamie made a real effort to pull herself together. She started working as a volunteer in service clubs and for the Red Cross. She even joined a class to learn to speak Spanish — though apparently all this last effort accomplished for any of the students was to provide someone to have lunch with.

Ike came home secretly in January 1944, for twelve days. Mamie was ecstatically happy while he was with her, but then, "I said good-by to him and thought my heart would break," she said.

June 6, 1944, was D-Day in Europe, when a secret invasion of France was planned to establish beachheads for Allied fighting forces. On the same day John graduated from West Point. Mamie was in a daze all day, between worrying about what would happen to Ike during the invasion and trying to be cheerful and happy for John.

She went to John's graduation ceremony with her parents, and they all met for lunch afterward. When John came in to lunch, Mamie saw the sealed orders he was carrying in his hand. She knew what that meant. As an army wife Mamie knew that sealed orders meant combat duty, probably also in Europe.

Only a few short hours later she was waving goodbye to her beloved son as he boarded the European bound troopship. This new anxiety would kill her for sure, Mamie felt.

Her family and friends were concerned about both her physical and mental state for a time. She was well on the way to becoming an alcoholic, which was adding to her other problems. Finally a family member had enough courage to tell Mamie she was using alcohol as a crutch. When Mamie thought about it, she realized that was exactly what she had been doing, and she never again allowed herself more than one drink a day.

At last, at long last, both Johnny and Ike came marching home, and Mamie had her boys with her again. World War II had ended. Perhaps now everyone could get on with their lives.

John had met a girl named Barbara Thompson in Vienna before he returned home from Europe, and wanted to marry her. Barbara wanted them to marry in Europe, but Ike and Mamie pleaded with them to come back to the United States for the wedding. They were married on June 10, 1947, in a chapel at Fort Monroe, Virginia. Barbara was the daughter of an army colonel, so her background meshed well with the Eisenhower beliefs and traditions.

In 1948 Ike's name was being mentioned more and more by politicians and the news media as a possible Presidential candidate. He was considered by some to be a surefire winner because of his heroic war record. Ike flatly refused to consider any such course of action. Instead, he accepted the post of president of Columbia University in New York. Harry Truman was reelected to his second term as President that year.

Mamie and Ike moved to New York to live in the palatial home Columbia University provided for its presidents. Neither of them liked the house or living in New York City, and Ike found he did not really like the job. He was accustomed to making quick decisions followed by immediate actions. With the Columbia officers it was a pattern of discuss, meet in committee, discuss some more, and maybe later take action on the proposal. This type of leisurely approach was alien to Ike's entire background and training.

When he accepted the Columbia University position, he had been assured he would have plenty of free time to pursue his favorite hobby of oil painting and to complete the book he had started about his war experiences. These promises were not kept, as he was extremely busy in the job and had little or no free time.

Ike took some time off anyway, which led to criticism by some of the staff about his absences. After a little more than two years of trying to become the ideal college president, he left Columbia. He had been in the midst of making history too long to be satisfied with academic surroundings.

By this time John and Barbara had two children, David and Barbara Anne. Ike and Mamie both doted on their precious grandchildren. John had also assumed academic duties as an English instructor at West Point.

In 1950 the Eisenhowers bought a farm in Gettysburg, Pennsylvania, for their retirement home. Mamie was delighted. In their entire married life of more than thirty years, they had never before owned a home. They looked forward to remodeling the two-hundred-year-old farmhouse to more nearly fit their lifestyle, but this idea proved to be impractical as the house was in such poor condition. They had it torn down, and had a large white brick and stone house built, which had seven bedrooms in addition to the other usual rooms.

The next year Ike was sent to France by President Truman to be Supreme Commander of the North Atlantic Treaty Organization. Neither Ike nor Mamie wanted to live in Europe, but as a five-star General, Ike was still subject to orders by Commander-in-Chief Truman. Ike anticipated the job itself eagerly, as it would involve the creation of a multinational armed force to serve as a peacekeeping force throughout the Western European area. The nations of Western Europe had become fearful of Communist invasion following the North Korean Communist attack on South Korea's democratic regime.

The French government offered the Eisenhowers a fourteen-room villa called Petit Trianon, which had once been occupied by Marie Antoinette. Mamie considered this offer for a magnificent residence generous on the part of the French, but she declined in favor of a smaller house near Paris in the little town of Marnes-la-Coquette. The Eisenhowers had this house remodeled to their own taste, which they could not have done with the historic villa.

Mamie came to love this house, and they soon felt at home. Ike planted a vegetable garden, and friends and relatives visited frequently.

Ike began whipping the NATO forces into shape, working hard on the project. He insisted that all the nations in the pact should bear a fair share of the expenses and provision of manpower.

Ike's successful efforts in organizing the NATO peacekeepers had not been unnoticed in the United States. Since President Truman did not plan to seek election to a third term, the Democrats hoped to be able to persuade Ike to become their candidate. Ike did become a candidate, but for the Republicans.

Ike was not acquainted with his running mate, Richard Nixon. When the campaign had been under way for only a few weeks, Mr. Nixon was accused of improperly accepting lavish gifts and large sums of money for his personal use from supporters. Ike would not have objected if Nixon had been replaced on the ticket at this time, but more experienced politicians insisted Ike should support Nixon and keep him as his Vice Presidential hopeful.

Ike and Richard Nixon won the election in 1952. Ike was inaugurated as President in January 1953. For the inauguration balls in Ike's honor Mamie wore a pink rhinestone-studded gown designed by Nettie Rosenstein, with all accessories matching the gown. This was a radical departure for Mamie, as she had either bought her clothes by mail order from the States while they lived in France or bought her dresses off the racks of department stores there.

Ike was suitably impressed by the new First Lady's appearance.

"By golly, Mamie, you're beautiful!" he said when he saw her in her new finery. Mamie certainly looked younger than her fifty-six years.

Living at the White House seemed to be a fairy tale come true to Mamie. "I never drove up to the South Portico without a lump coming to my throat," she told an interviewer in 1974.

Otherwise, their life in the White House gradually assumed some of their previous ways. Mamie still enjoyed watching soap operas during the day when she could, and both Ike and Mamie watched variety and comedy television programs at night. Ike enjoyed Western movies particularly, and they had movies shown about twice each week.

Mamie bought some of her dresses from designers now, but she still continued her habit of buying costume jewelry from dime stores for adornment.

Ike said he thought Mamie's outstanding contribution as First Lady was her ability to make the White House a real home and make their visitors feel warmly welcome. To the dismay of Washington socialites, only receptions necessary for the entertainment of visiting statesmen were held by the Eisenhowers.

Another granddaughter, Susan, was born in 1951. Ike and Mamie enjoyed visits with their three grandchildren more than any other social event. When little grandson David first visited his grandparents in the White House, he looked around with his eyes big as saucers and asked, "Mimi, why did you build yourself such a big house?" The children never lacked for babysitters when their parents wanted time to themselves.

Mamie was active in charity drives and causes such as the Heart Fund, but she had no interest in making speeches or holding her own press conferences. "I think Ike speaks well enough for both of us," she said firmly.

Ike respected Mamie's judgment of people more than his own. He frequently asked her opinion about various people with whom he came in contact, but Mamie said they almost never discussed politics or issues in government. "When Ike came home, he came home," she said.

Mamie was firmly in control of housekeeping operations in the White House, according to the Chief Usher, J. B. West. She clipped coupons for the staff to use when shopping to reduce food expenditures. Mr. West said that under her fluffy, exuberant exterior, Mamie "had a spine of steel, forged by years of military discipline."

Ike suffered from several health problems during his Presidency, particularly during his first term, which led Mamie to plead with him not to seek a second term. He insisted he was feeling better, and was reelected. In fact, his health was better during his second four years in the White House.

During Ike's administrations the Korean War ended with an armistice. Senator Joseph McCarthy pursued Communists both in and out of government with a zeal often misplaced. Schools were racially integrated throughout the nation for the first time, and economic conditions remained stable and predictable.

After attending John F. Kennedy's inauguration on January 20, 1961, Ike and Mamie were chauffered by a Secret Service agent to Gettysburg in Mamie's five-year-old car. They stayed there that year, but began spending winters in California later. They always returned to their Gettysburg home in time to see the crocuses bloom in spring.

They enjoyed their retirement years. Ike stayed busy writing his memoirs, while Mamie puttered about the house.

In May 1968, Ike suffered a second major heart attack, and for the next ten months he was hospitalized at Walter Reed Hospital in Washington. Mamie never left the hospital during all that time, except for a few hours occasionally, until Ike's death on March 28, 1969. He was buried on the grounds of the Eisenhower Memorial Library in Abilene, Kansas.

Mamie returned to their home in Gettysburg, spending much of her time in her bedroom suite on the second floor of the big house. She had less income since Ike died, and she allowed financial worries to become too important to her. She had a married couple as household help. She made a trip to Abilene each year to visit Ike's grave on his birthday, but she was never able to walk to the museum because of weakness.

Mamie had suffered for a number of years from inner ear infections as well as reflex strictures in her carotid arteries, both of which caused her to be dizzy and made her stumble. She broke her wrist in a fall in her kitchen when she was eighty-two. John then pleaded with her to come live with him and his family, but she refused. He hired around-the-clock companions for her, and she remained in her home.

During Mamie's later years, a television miniseries aired based on Ike's reputed World War II romance with Kay Summersby. Mamie said she wasn't disturbed by it as Ike had told her he loved only his wife and there had been no truth to the gossip.

Betty Ford, later a First Lady herself, said she always doubted the stories about Ike's romance with Kay. She said when she saw them together at Congressional parties, Ike and Mamie were obviously devoted and loving to each other.

When Mamie spoke at a commencement exercise at Eisenhower College in Seneca Falls, New York, after Ike's death, she said she would always remember Ike's "wonderful hands." She said, "Every knuckle was broken from football or whatever, but I always felt in all the years we were married that I could grab onto them when I felt sick or worried, and nothing was ever going to happen to me."

In telling about this, Betty Ford said, "It isn't a bad testimonial to a marriage."

During the summer of 1979, Mamie did not feel well at all, and she spent days as well as nights in her bed. She lapsed into a stroke-induced coma on September 25 that year, dying on November 1, 1979. She was buried beside Ike and little Icky in Abilene, Kansas.

38. Jacqueline Bouvier Kennedy Onassis

Jacqueline Bouvier was born in 1929 into a fairy-tale world, a modern-day princess. Her mother, Janet Lee, and her father, John Vernou Bouvier III, called Jack, were both attractive, aristocratic members of an elite social group, as both came from wealthy families.

Jackie spent her early years on the Bouvier family estate, Lasata, in East Hampton on Long Island, New York. It was a vast, luxurious and elegant spread with a large staff of servants, riding stables and beautiful gardens tended by gardeners.

Whenever the family tired of Long Island, they could enjoy a change of scene in New York City. There they held a large, well-appointed apartment on Manhattan's Park Avenue.

When Jackie was three months old, the great stock market crash of 1929 occurred, and her life as well as the lives of most other American children were significantly altered by ensuing financial events.

It took time, however, for the Bouviers to realize their world had changed so dramatically, and that there would be no return to the great wealth they had enjoyed previously. At first it was believed good times would return in only a matter of months. They continued to maintain the sumptuous life-style to which they had always been accustomed until almost all their money was gone. Still, they were not actually poor, except by Park Avenue standards.

Jackie's Grandfather Lee offered a rent-free apartment, also on Park Avenue, to daughter Janet for the family to live in while they recouped their losses. Since the Bouvier family had considered themselves to be of higher social standing than the Lees, Jack Bouvier accepted the offer reluctantly.

Jack's reluctance was well-founded. Mr. Lee tended to remind his daughter and her husband frequently of his generosity, and ordered Jack Bouvier to curb his expenses, especially to drop expensive club memberships. All these financial changes and difficulties would put a strain on any marriage, and the Bouviers' was no exception.

Lee Bouvier was born when her sister, Jackie, was about four.

Jacqueline Kennedy Onassis. (Courtesy Library of Congress.)

Following the baby's christening, Jack and Janet held an elaborate reception for over two hundred guests in honor of the event. In that year of 1933 it seemed troubled times might be ending, and they wanted to celebrate.

The Depression was nowhere near over, however, and by 1938 the Bouviers were divorced. Janet was left with a five-year-old and nine-year-old daughter to rear on support payments from their father. Supplemented by occasional extra gifts of money from Grandfather Lee, Janet and the little girls continued to live on Park Avenue with all the luxury that implies, but their income was limited, and the extras from Grandfather Lee were not given with any regularity. Despite the difficulties, Jackie and Lee both attended Miss Chapin's School for Girls, an elite private school.

When he left the Park Avenue apartment, Jack Bouvier moved into the Westbury Hotel, and the two little Bouvier girls became pawns in the endless struggle between their mother and father for their love. On weekends Jack took them to movies, skating, the theater, to the zoo, on pony rides, all of which the girls enjoyed immensely. They had missed having their fun-loving, permissive, expansive father with them, and they began to complain when the weekend was over and they had to go home to their mother.

Jackie credits her father with helping her develop her own fashion sense. He had inherited the French eye for style from his ancestors, apparently, and he took an avid interest in what his daughters wore. He also taught them how to cope with dating problems and gave them a deep understanding of their own worth.

Jackie was quieter and had a stronger artistic bent than Lee. She enjoyed sketching, especially faces, and she liked reading and writing both stories and poetry. Lee was given to sudden passionate enthusiasms for projects of either civic or social worth.

In June 1942, when Jackie was thirteen, Janet Bouvier remarried. Her new husband was Hughdie Auchincloss, also a member of the Social Register. Hughdie was a wealthy man who owned two large estates, Merrywood in McLean, Virginia, and Hammersmith Farm in Newport, Rhode Island. He also owned a New York apartment.

Hughdie was mild-mannered and was genuinely fond of Janet's two daughters. Life in his household was serene and orderly.

As time passed, the Auchinclosses had two children born to them, and this gave Jackie and Lee an interest in staying home they had not had before. They enjoyed caring for and playing with their baby brother and sister. Also, with great wealth a part of their life again, they had stables of horses to ride, parties to attend, clothes to buy and all the other fringe benefits that accrue from having no money worries.

Jackie began receiving invitations to attend sub-debutante parties in New York City, and her father rented an apartment so she could stay with him while she was in the city. She stayed there sometimes, but she had to be careful about not talking too much about the changes and improvements in her life-style. Jack Bouvier viewed the Auchincloss marriage as Janet's way of getting revenge on him, and would hurl insulting, disparaging remarks at Jackie about her mother.

Often they would quarrel, and Jack would again rage about the way he perceived his former wife had treated him. Since Janet had caused neither the stock market crash nor the bad investments Jack made with the money he did have, she was not really to blame for his misfortune, but Jack was a little immature in his thinking.

He began to complain that Jackie did not spend enough time with him in New York. When she decided to attend Miss Porter's Finishing School in Farmington, Connecticut, he was ecstatic. There Jackie would be much closer to him than to her mother and the Auchincloss estates.

Jackie was rapidly leaving her girlhood behind, and one of her developing desires was to support herself and be independent of anyone's financial aid. She studied diligently, made excellent grades and was learning to rise to occasions. She was voted Debutante of the Year in 1947.

Jackie made her debut at the Clambake Club in Newport at a dinner dance hosted by her mother and stepfather, which enraged Jack Bouvier. He could no longer afford such lavish expenditures for his daughter.

That fall, Jackie enrolled at Vassar in Poughkeepsie, New York. She stayed at Vassar for only two years, as she found it was not to her liking. She transferred to Smith in her junior year so she could take advantage of a planned year of study in France, which Smith offered.

Jackie loved living in France and studying at the Sorbonne. She enjoyed the scenery, the language, the literature and the people. It was one of the happiest years she had ever had.

When she returned to the States, Jackie entered Georgetown University in Washington for her senior year. While there, she entered a fashion contest which was sponsored by Vogue magazine. First prize in the contest was six months' employment in the Vogue offices in Paris, followed by another six months' employment in New York. Contestants were required to write four essays on aspects of fashion world events. This was an interest that strongly appealed to Jackie. She threw her energies enthusiastically into the project, and she won the first prize.

Jackie was thrilled and excited, but her mother strongly opposed her acceptance of the prize. Janet felt it was on a level with accepting a scholarship and that only poor people accepted scholarships.

Jackie reluctantly relinquished her fairly won prize. She had worked terribly hard for it, but she found giving it up would be easier than arguing with her mother.

Mr. Auchincloss saw Jackie's keen disappointment, and he arranged an interview for her with Frank Waldrop of the *Washington Times–Herald* newspaper, who was looking for a photographer. Jackie was hired as a photographer and reporter at a starting salary of $42.50 a week.

Her news reports were amusing, provocative and gained a wide audience. One day while making her rounds in the capital, she asked little Julie Nixon, then five years old, if she were allowed to play with Democrats. "What's a Democrat?" the little girl asked with interest.

Jackie first met Congressman Jack Kennedy in May 1952 at a dinner party given by mutual friends. Neither appeared particularly interested in the other at the time. Jackie was now twenty-two; Jack was thirty-five and reported to be a confirmed bachelor.

Jack was involved in a campaign for a Senate seat at the time, and in November he was elected as a Senator from Massachusetts. Shortly afterward, he called the beautiful roving reporter and asked her to go out with him. When Jackie was sent to London six months later to photograph Queen Elizabeth II's coronation, Senator Kennedy called her frequently. During one of the many calls, he proposed to her.

Their wedding was scheduled to take place on September 12, 1953, at the Newport Hammersmith Farm of the Auchinclosses. Perhaps it was the thought of being exposed to the Auchincloss wealth and prestige, especially at the elaborate reception to follow that caused Jackie's father to drink so heavily the night before the wedding that he was unable to attend. Possibly he was also having difficulty dealing with the knowledge that Jackie was now a woman and would visit him only infrequently.

Jackie's stepfather gave her away in the beautiful wedding ceremony at St. Mary's Roman Catholic Church, with Archbishop Cushing presiding. The event was undoubtedly one of the weddings of the year. It had an aura of royalty with eight hundred guests at the wedding and twelve hundred at the reception.

When Jack Bouvier recovered from his binge, he was horrified to realize he had behaved so badly. He wrote Jackie a contrite letter, begging her forgiveness, while the newlyweds honeymooned in Acapulco. Jackie understood better than anyone else the enormous amount of nervous strain her wedding caused her father, and she replied with a loving, forgiving letter.

The newlyweds moved into a house in Georgetown, and Jackie prepared to fulfill her duties as a Senator's wife. She and Jack dutifully attended cocktail parties and dinner parties, as well as hosting their own. Jack was full of ambition to be elected President someday in the future, and he dictated Jackie's every move from what to wear to what to say and to whom.

If the restrictions of her new life chafed at times, at least Jackie had one consolation. They had plenty of money to spend, as the Kennedy family was richer than either the Bouviers or Auchinclosses.

The Kennedy clan, by and large, was an uninhibited brood. They considered it great fun to throw a fully clothed, well-dressed guest into a swimming pool, and Jack's sisters were given to deliberately upsetting loaded tea tables into the laps of guests. Jackie was a little put off by all these merry pranks, but she tried to join in family activities to a degree, except for any that offended her sense of decorum.

Another favorite pasttime for the Kennedys was playing touch football. A Kennedy friend, Ted Sorenson, said Jackie asked him in all seriousness when she made her first attempt to play the game, "Just tell me one thing: when I get the ball, which way do I run?" When her ankle was broken during an overzealous pursuit by some of Ted Kennedy's team-mates, Jackie gladly gave up the sport.

When they married, Jackie knew her husband suffered from Addison's disease, insufficient function of adrenal glands, and he regularly took steroids to control the problem. When he had to have spinal surgery in 1954, Jack almost died, and for the next two years, his health was a matter of deep concern to his family.

During this same period Jackie suffered both a miscarriage and gave birth to a stillborn baby. Jack was away, resting on the French Riviera, when the baby was born, and he flew home as soon as he received the news. He was shocked to learn Jackie had also been near death.

Jackie finally got the baby for which she had prayed for so long when Caroline Kennedy was born in November 1957. It seemed their bad times might be behind her and Jack now as they gladly welcomed the little girl to the family.

Jackie was again pregnant and hopeful for a successful birth when Jack was nominated to run for President on the Democratic ticket in 1960. John Kennedy, Jr., was born on November 25, 1960, only weeks after his father won the election. He was one month premature and his condition at birth was not good, but he did survive and slowly gained strength.

Jack Kennedy was now President-elect, so they would have two children to move with them into the White House.

Jackie was a vision of beauty at the Inaugural Ball, clad in a long gown of white chiffon and wearing her hair arranged in the bouffant fashion, which would later be copied by American women everywhere. She walked with assurance and grace, and the American public fell in love with their real-life princess.

Americans were not the only ones impressed with the regal Jackie. When she and Jack went to France to visit in May 1961, she was loudly ac-claimed by the crowds of people lined up along the motorcade route. Since Jackie had spent time in France earlier in her life and had a French maiden name, the French people felt she was one of their own.

Jack watched all this fervor with amusement. On their last day in France, he drily told the Paris Press Club, "I am the man who accompanied Jacqueline Kennedy to Paris and I have enjoyed it."

Jackie made redecoration of the White House a top priority, and she set out to restore the Executive Mansion to its original beauty as it appeared when it was built in the early 1800s. With many donations of money, antiques and works of art, she accomplished her goal without any tax money being used. She then took fifty-six million Americans on a tour of the White House via television, which was carried by all three of the major networks. In all she spent two million dollars on the renovation.

If Jackie attracted national and world attention as First Lady, her children, Caroline and "John-John," stole the show. They were both beautiful, well-mannered children, and reporters had a field day in recounting their activities. Once when Caroline was asked where her father was, she said he was "sitting upstairs with his shoes and socks off not doing anything."

Jackie had the seating at state dinners changed from the formal seating at long tables to more informal seating with six or eight people to a table. She always included artists at her parties, whether their talents were musical, literary or in the field of painting or sculpture.

In 1962 she went alone on a trip to Asia and the Far East, where she was entertained lavishly and welcomed warmly by the heads of state in various countries. She had an entourage of maids and Secret Service men as well as reporters along, but Jack and the children did not go with her.

Jackie had another son in August 1963, named Patrick, who died after only two and a half days. Jackie was severely shaken by her tragic loss, and when her sister, Lee, invited her to spend some time accompanying her on a yacht owned by Aristotle Onassis touring the Aegean Islands, she accepted gratefully.

It was a pleasant, leisurely trip, lasting six weeks, during which time Jackie rested and regained her strength. Onassis, a Greek shipping magnate and millionaire, was intrigued by the lovely Jackie and made her feel welcome.

Jackie got back to the White House in October 1963, and went shopping for clothes to wear on a trip with Jack to Texas, where he hoped to mend some rifts in the Democrat party. According to White House staff and relatives, there was a strong love and much affection between the Kennedys. They acted reserved and formal in public, but the staff said their life in private was entirely different, and Jackie was as glad to be back home with her family as Jack was to have her back with him.

On November 22, 1963, Jack, with Jackie sitting beside him, was riding in a motorcade in an open car in Dallas, Texas, when he was shot by assassin Lee Harvey Oswald. Jackie held him in her arms all the way to the hospital, but he died a few hours later. She was present when Vice President Lyndon Johnson was sworn in as the new President as the Presidential plane returned to Washington with Jack Kennedy's body on board. She was a pitiful figure in her blood-stained clothes, and her appearance made it obvious that she was in complete shock.

Jack was buried in Arlington National Cemetery, his grave marked with an eternal flame. He was entitled to be buried here by reason of his former navy service and his Presidential role of Commander-in-Chief of the Armed Forces.

Jackie and her two children moved to a New York apartment and tried to get on with their lives. For a time Jackie was so obsessed by death, some of her relatives were worried about her mental stability, but she gradually recovered from her tragic losses. The children were in school, and Bobby Kennedy, Jack's brother, assumed the role of advisor to Jackie and surrogate father to the children.

John Kennedy had attended Harvard University, where he majored in political science. Jackie began working toward the establishment of a John F. Kennedy Memorial Library there.

She was criticized for her perceived paranoia in protecting her privacy and that of her children. When Bobby Kennedy was also assassinated in 1968, the criticism lessened, as it was evident the Kennedys were not safe.

A short time after Bobby's death, Jackie announced her engagement to Aristotle Onassis. Rose Kennedy, Jack's mother, was surprised, but told Jackie to make whatever plans she liked and to carry them out with her best wishes. The elder Mrs. Kennedy had always been fond of Jackie and felt she had been a supportive, good wife for her son.

The public, however, was outraged by the news of Jackie's engagement. She was seen as only a gold digger by some, and as an innocent victim of an old, rich tycoon by others. Ari was twenty years older than Jackie, but Jack Kennedy had been thirteen years older.

Despite the storm of criticism, Jackie married Onassis on October 20, 1968, on the island of Skorpios, off the Greek coast, in a Greek Orthodox ceremony in the Chapel of the Little Virgin.

She continued to maintain her New York apartment, and her children stayed in New York. Ari spent part of his time there, and they spent vacations and holidays in Greece.

Before long, rumors began that Ari continued to visit his former mistress, Maria Callas, the opera star. Also rumors began and persisted that Ari resented Jackie's spending habits.

As a wedding gift, Ari had given Jackie three million dollars in tax-free government bonds. In addition she received thirty-three thousand a month with which to pay her expenses for the New York apartment, servants, clothes and the like. Both Kennedy children received five thousand dollars per month.

All these financial facts do not indicate Jackie charged a price for being Ari's wife. When any man is as wealthy as Ari, all his advisors tell him to spell out any financial arrangements in detail.

Despite additional rumors from time to time that they were separated, actually Jackie and Ari got along well together and enjoyed their marriage.

In fall 1973, Ari and Jackie went to Acapulco for a vacation. It was the twentieth anniversary of Jackie's honeymoon in Acapulco with Jack Kennedy, and ten years since his assassination. She begged Ari to buy a villa in Acapulco to commemorate the occasion, but he flatly refused. Jackie reportedly became very angry and they quarreled bitterly.

On the plane trip back to New York, Ari spent his time writing furiously. Jackie assumed he was working on business affairs, but he was rewriting his will. Under their premarital agreement she was to receive at least one hundred million dollars at his death, as under Greek law she was entitled to one-fourth of his estate. When he finished writing and asked her to sign an amendment to an agreement giving her two hundred thousand a year, she thought this would be in addition to the original amount, but she was mistaken. He was really disinheriting her in effect. When he returned to Greece, he had Greek inheritance laws changed so there would no longer be an automatic inheritance for widows.

The next year Ari developed a condition called myasthenia gravis, a progressive nerve-muscle junction abnormality, which caused profound weakness of muscles. His health declined steadily during the next several months until his death in March 1975. Only his daughter, Christina, was with Ari when he died. Jackie was in New York with her children at the time of his death. She was again criticized, this time for not staying by her husband's side during his final illness.

Jackie was dismayed to learn later how he had tricked her in his financial arrangements with her. She sued his estate for a large amount of money, finally receiving more than twenty million dollars in settlement.

About six months after Ari's death, Jackie was hired to work as an editor for Viking, a publishing company. In 1977 she resigned angrily in a dispute with the company, which had agreed to publish a novel entitled *Shall We Tell the President?* In this fictitious story, Ted Kennedy was elected President and was also assassinated. Jackie felt strongly that the subject matter was inappropriate in view of her own connection with the company.

Jackie has always made a real effort to be a good mother. When she was First Lady she said she considered making her children's lives normal and her husband's life peaceful to be the greatest contribution she could make.

"It doesn't matter what else you do if you don't do that part well, you fail your husband and your children," she told a reporter with firm conviction. She continued, "That really is the role which means the most to me, the one that comes first."

Jackie has been a good mother. Her children have done well in their education, and appear to have matured into responsible, solid citizens. If Jackie sometimes appeared too bossy to her daughter, Caroline, it was because of her strong desire to give Caroline the best possible life. Strong-willed Caroline has adamantly refused to concern herself with fashion or French cuisine, both dear to Jackie's interests. Instead Caroline wears corduroy jeans and sweatshirts, refused to allow Jackie to have a party for her debut, and most enjoys sausage pizza and beer.

One area of Caroline's life pleased Jackie, however. That was her choice of a husband. On July 19, 1986, Caroline married Edwin Schlossberg in Our Lady of Victory Catholic Church on Cape Cod. Caroline's wedding was much simpler than that of her parents years before. Jackie came out of the church escorted by her brother-in-law, Ted Kennedy, smiling radiantly. After taking only a few steps, her face suddenly crumpled into tears. For just a moment, no doubt, Jackie wished Jack could have been there to see his little girl married, the little girl he called "Buttons."

Following her wedding, Caroline entered Columbia University Law School. Mr. Schlossberg owns his own logo design company, which provides designs for colleges, museums and media exhibitions. They now have a daughter.

John Kennedy, Jr., attends New York University Law School. He is not yet married. After graduation he will work as an Assistant Prosecutor for the Manhattan District Attorney.

Jackie now works for Doubleday, another New York publishing house, as an editor. She continues to visit her same longtime hairdresser and often eats lunch at expensive restaurants, but otherwise she tries to conform to the standards of the other employees. She gets her own coffee and makes her own copies at the copying machine. She also eats lunch some days in the company snack bar.

Jackie's frequent escort to social gatherings is Maurice Tempelsman, owner of large interests in African diamond mines, as well as in mines of other minerals. Mr. Tempelsman is Jewish (as is Caroline's husband), and some Kennedy and Bouvier family members have expressed their disapproval.

Jackie will, however, follow her heart as she always has, and will hold her head high, ignoring gossip about her as she has always tried to do in the past.

39. Claudia (Lady Bird) Taylor Johnson

Lady Bird Johnson is a true Southern belle. From the time of her birth on December 22, 1912, in Karnack, Texas, throughout her childhood, college years, marriage and retirement most of her interests and connections have been with the South.

Lady Bird's mother was born Minnie Lee Pattillo, from Evergreen, Alabama. Minnie Lee was a daughter of a wealthy plantation owner and was exposed early to cultural advantages. The Pattillo family was descended from early aristocratic Spanish settlers.

Minnie was out riding a new horse one day when she found she had ridden beyond the plantation boundaries. She dismounted to turn her horse and fell, injuring her leg. A neighbor's son, Thomas Taylor, found Minnie lying where she had fallen. He treated her injury as best he could and took her on to his home nearby. Thomas, or Tommy as he was called, was tall, handsome and well-built. Minnie fell in love with Tommy that day, but they had to conduct their romance secretly for several months.

Tommy Taylor's family also farmed for a living, but they had less land to use, and they were as poor as the Pattillos were wealthy. When Tommy finally insisted on asking Mr. Pattillo for Minnie's hand in marriage, Mr. Pattillo was amused and condescending in his attitude toward Tommy. Mr. Pattillo told the young man he had no money to support a wife and to forget his romance with her.

Tommy was hurt and insulted by Mr. Pattillo's response to his sincere desire to marry Minnie. He left Alabama to try to make enough money so they could get married anyway. He went to Karnack, Texas, where he built and operated a grocery store. After six years, Tommy had made enough money, not only to support a wife, but to buy the biggest house in Karnack. Tommy returned triumphantly to Alabama, married Minnie and took her back to Texas with him to live.

There were two sons born to Minnie and Tommy before their little girl, Claudia, was born. In her little daughter, Minnie found someone to share her love for some of life's finer pleasures, which Mr. Taylor did not.

Lady Bird Johnson. (Courtesy Library of Congress.)

Claudia got her nickname of Lady Bird from a nurse, who commented when she saw the baby, "She's purty as a lady bird."

Minnie Taylor had brought trunkloads of books, magnificently bound, with her to her new home in Karnack. She read to all her children, but it was little Lady Bird who most enjoyed the stories and shared her mother's literary interests.

Minnie also loved opera and "went East" every winter to Chicago during opera season. Her two sons were attending boarding schools in New York, and she visited them while in the area.

Minnie Taylor was a rebel in Southern eyes in her concerns for the poor black people living in Karnack and her support for the right of women to be allowed to vote. She was also a vegetarian.

Minnie died when her fourth child was born (the baby also died), leaving Lady Bird and two little Taylor sons bewildered and motherless. Minnie left Lady Bird a large amount of money and large tracts of farm land in Alabama.

Despite his overwhelming interest in business affairs and making money, Tommy Taylor loved little Lady Bird dearly. He just did not know how he could manage to take care of a little girl without a woman in the house. For a time he kept her with him in his store, T. J. Taylor—Dealer in Everything, a true general store.

When Lady Bird got old enough to go to school, she went to spend part of her time with her mother's sister, Effie, in Alabama. Aunt Effie "opened my spirit to beauty," Lady Bird said, with her love of poetry and literature. Aunt Effie built on the foundation Lady Bird's mother had started.

Lady Bird loved her Aunt Effie, but Aunt Effie was sickly, and Lady Bird wanted to be like her strong, handsome healthy father. At last Aunt Effie agreed to live with Lady Bird in Texas in her father's home there.

Lady Bird's early education was obtained in a one-room schoolhouse with a total student body of twelve to fifteen pupils each year. Her classmates were children of tenant farmers, who moved around frequently, and some children were new to the school each year.

When Lady Bird was thirteen, she and Aunt Effie went to live in Marshall, Texas, where Lady Bird could attend high school. She always made good grades and enjoyed learning, but she was unhappy in high school because she was not accepted socially by the other students. Her chief handicap was her age—Lady Bird was two years younger than her classmates, and she was painfully shy. She avoided any direct contact with boys as much as possible. She graduated from high school at age fifteen.

She went on to a junior college in Dallas, then to the University of Texas. At the university she learned shorthand, typing, and other business subjects, then turned her attention to education courses. She got a Bachelor of Arts degree with honors and a teaching certificate. She continued on to get a degree in journalism. At this particular time in her life, she had no firm career goal in mind, so she tried to prepare herself for several possible career choices.

Lady Bird had left Aunt Effie to live in a boarding house at the edge of the campus while she attended the university. She made several good friends among the other girls living there, and was happier than she had been before. She had a car of her own, dressed well if not always fashionably, and attracted the interest of her fellow students. One of her best friends was a young lady named Eugenia Boehringer, who urged Lady Bird to be more outgoing and friendly, especially with men she met.

Lady Bird was not really very interested in men at the time. She had inherited her father's burning, driving ambition to succeed. She did take a job as a reporter at the *Daily Texan* newspaper in an attempt to overcome her inborn reticence. In this job she was required to interview celebrities at press conferences. She also involved herself in the Intramural Sports Association, volunteering to be the manager of public relations, in an attempt to learn to be more outgoing.

Following her graduation, Lady Bird went to Austin, Texas, to visit her friend Eugenia, who was working there as an aide to the chairman of the Texas Railroad Commission. Eugenia insisted Lady Bird should buy some up-to-date clothes and called her stingy when Lady Bird refused. Lady Bird's father expected his daughter to shop and had opened a charge account for her at Neiman-Marcus.

Lady Bird may have wished a short time later she had gone shopping. At Eugenia's home she met Lyndon Johnson for the first time, and Lyndon was immediately smitten by this shy, proper young friend of Eugenia's. Lyndon was from Texas and was working as a secretary to Texas Congressman Richard Kleberg in Washington, D.C., but was home for a few days vacation.

Lyndon and Lady Bird met for breakfast the next morning, at which time Lyndon gave her a detailed account of his family, what his ambitions were for the future, and even how much insurance he carried! Lady Bird wondered why he felt comfortable giving her all this information when they had just met. While she was puzzling about this, he asked her to marry him!

Lady Bird agreed to meet his family the next day, but since this breakfast date was their first date, she was not considering marrying this rash young man. She was suspicious he might even be joking.

Lady Bird met Lyndon's family and liked them. The Johnsons appeared to approve of her. That same day Lyndon took her on to the King Ranch, home of his employer, Congressman Kleberg. This ranch was like a feudal empire, and Lady Bird was suitably impressed by both its size and beauty. Congressman Kleberg's mother told Lady Bird privately that Lyndon was a fine young man, and she hoped Lady Bird would marry him. Apparently the marriage proposal was no joke.

Lady Bird's father liked Lyndon and raised no objections to any marriage plans they might have, but Aunt Effie begged Lady Bird to give the relationship more time.

Lyndon left to go back to his job in Washington a few days later, and Lady Bird was amazed to feel unaccustomed loneliness. She realized, to her surprise, that she was seriously considering accepting the proposal of a man she barely knew. She was even embarrassed by her feelings.

Lyndon wrote Lady Bird every day or telephoned her from Washington. When he came back to Texas seven weeks later in November, he insisted that they get married as soon as possible.

Lady Bird had not made up her mind completely, but she did agree to drive with him to Austin to buy her an engagement ring. When it was bought, Lyndon said there was no reason not to just go ahead and get married, so they were married on November 17, 1934, in St. Mark's Episcopal Church in San Antonio with only two of their friends present at the wedding. Lyndon bought his new bride a wedding ring at Sears, Roebuck for two dollars and fifty cents!

The newlyweds went to live in a tiny apartment in Washington, D.C. Lyndon had hopes of being Congressman Kleberg's successor, and he began inviting dinner guests who had political connections to increase his chances.

Lady Bird had been surrounded by numerous servants all her life, and she did not know how to cook, clean or do any ordinary household tasks. Necessity is not only the mother of invention but also of learning, and Lady Bird decided to learn to do these things herself as they could not afford to hire people to do the work of entertaining for them. She admired ambition and she loved Lyndon, so it was not long before she began to enjoy these political social gatherings as much as he did. Sam Rayburn, one of the most prominent politicians in Texas, was a frequent guest, and became a close family friend.

As time passed, it became evident Congressman Kleberg had no intention of retiring, so Lyndon turned his attention in other directions. He was not making a large salary in his present job, and he wanted a position with a chance of promotion. When General Electric Corporation offered him a job as a corporate lobbyist in 1935, he considered accepting it even though the salary was ten thousand dollars, the same amount he received from Congressman Kleberg. He thought such a job might lead to better things.

Before he could accept the lobbyist job, President Franklin Roosevelt asked him to become the director of the National Youth Association program in Texas. This was a program designed to train young people for jobs in trades and help alleviate the problems of the Depression years. Lyndon accepted, becoming the youngest NYA director in the United States.

He and Lady Bird moved to Austin, Texas, which would be his headquarters. He worked hard in his job, recruited capable assistants and managed to create or find most of the twelve thousand jobs needed by the young people in Texas. Lyndon wanted to live in Washington, but he wanted to go back there as a member of Congress, and he felt the NYA director's job could help him reach his goal.

In 1937 a vacancy occurred when Texas Congressman James P. Buchanan died. Lyndon felt this might be the chance he needed. Lady Bird and Lyndon talked with former Senator Alvin Wirtz about Lyndon's possible candidacy for the Congressional seat, and they asked him what he thought Lyndon's possibility of being elected might be. Senator Wirtz thought Lyndon would be a candidate with a strong possibility of being elected, but he told Lyndon he would need at least ten thousand dollars to begin the campaign.

Lady Bird called her father and asked him to take ten thousand dollars from her bank account — money she had inherited from her mother — and to deposit it to Lyndon's account. Her father transferred the money as she asked, excited to hear that his son-in-law hoped to be elected to the United States Congress.

With his money problems taken care of temporarily, Lyndon set out on the campaign trail while Lady Bird kept things going at home. Lyndon was not popular with some of the more social group of citizens, but he won all the votes of the poor and disadvantaged. They knew him as their former NYA director. He had visited them in their homes, he had secured jobs for them or members of their families, and most important of all, he had talked with them about their problems. No politician had ever before been interested in what they thought or how they felt.

Lyndon won the election. He and Lady Bird returned to live in an apartment in Washington. As he had dreamed, he was returning as a freshman in Congress.

Lyndon worked long hours trying to get help for the poverty-stricken Texans. He got rural electric power, run by publicly owned companies, and job-skills training centers for the youth. He was instrumental in getting a naval air training base located in Corpus Christi. With all this effort on behalf of Texas, he was reelected in the next campaign.

In 1941 Lyndon campaigned for a seat in the United States Senate, but this time he lost. He then joined the United States Navy and served on active duty with a rank of lieutenant commander. He traveled to the Pacific theater of operations and visited various bases there as a fact-finding envoy for President Roosevelt.

While Lyndon was away from home, Lady Bird took over and ran his Congressional office. She did a good job, as he was reelected in 1942.

The next year Lady Bird decided to put some of her money to work. She bought a radio station in Austin, Texas, with the assigned letters of KTBC, for which she paid forty thousand dollars. The station had been floundering during its entire three-year history, and attitudes as well as business affairs were haphazard and disorganized. Lady Bird whipped the station into a money-making proposition within a short time.

After suffering three miscarriages, Lady Bird gave birth to their first child, Lynda Bird, on March 19, 1944. She was named for both her parents, as they feared she would be their only child. However, in 1947 another daughter was born, whom they named Luci Baines.

Lyndon viewed Lady Bird's radio station as his road to fame, and he made it his duty to gain network affiliation with Columbia Broadcasting System. Later the station was granted a television channel by the Federal Communications Commission, and its success was assured.

As the little Johnson daughters grew, Sam Rayburn, now Speaker of the House of Representatives, was one of their most devoted admirers. Lady Bird had always been cordial when he visited her and Lyndon and made him feel welcome wherever they lived. Each year he gave birthday parties for Luci and Lynda and ten to twelve of their little friends in his apartment, since the Johnsons' living quarters were smaller.

Lady Bird continued to keep a watchful eye on her Texas media stations as she reared Luci and Lynda. Since Lyndon served three consecutive terms as a Senator, she was also required to hostess many dinners and parties.

In 1955 Lyndon suffered a major heart attack, which necessitated a long rest for him. Once again Lady Bird took over and supervised his office staff, keeping everything in order until he recovered. About six months later he was back on the job, now as Majority Leader of the Senate.

Lyndon had been named a member of various important government committees from the earliest days of his political career, which stemmed in large part from his support of President Roosevelt's proposed programs, especially to increase the number of Supreme Court justices. President Roosevelt liked this friendly, expansive Texan and always made sure he received political attention. Lyndon admired President Roosevelt more than any other person in American government, so he was not just buttering up the boss.

When the 1960 Democratic nominating convention was held, Lyndon seemed a good choice as a Presidential candidate. He had long, distinguished years in government service, and he had many friends in high places. However, a younger Senator from Massachusetts, John F. Kennedy, won the nomination and later the election. Lyndon amazed everyone, including Lady Bird, by agreeing to serve as Vice President with President Kennedy.

During the campaign Lady Bird had traveled right alongside Lyndon, partly so she could insist that he get enough rest and not allow the strenuous campaign schedule to trigger another heart attack. During the campaign she traveled some thirty-five thousand miles.

President Kennedy liked his Vice President, and he made sure Lyndon and Lady Bird were invited to all the public and private parties he and Mrs. Kennedy held.

Lyndon was restless in his post as Vice President, but he kept quiet about his dissatisfaction and made it a point never to criticize President Kennedy.

Attorney General Bobby Kennedy, brother of the President, despised Lyndon and urged President Kennedy to dump him when the next campaign drew near. The "next campaign," however, would never take place. On November 22, 1963, President Kennedy was assassinated in Dallas while riding in a motorcade.

Suddenly, Lyndon was President of the United States. He took the oath of office on board the official Presidential plane, Air Force One, as he, Lady Bird and Mrs. Kennedy flew back to Washington with President Kennedy's body also on board the plane.

The Johnson girls were now teenagers. Lynda was a student at the University of Texas in her sophomore year, and Luci, who was now sixteen, attended high school in Washington. When the family moved into the White House, the girls had a third-floor solarium converted into a teenage hideaway where they could entertain friends away from the ever-present Secret Service agents, and the closely watching eyes of their father.

Lady Bird assumed White House duties with a sure hand since she had lived in Washington for so many years and had entertained frequently. Lyndon continued his lavish open-handed entertaining, but now it was on a much larger scale. During the five years the Johnsons lived in the White House they sent invitations to a total of more than two hundred thousand guests.

Lyndon insisted on practicing one economy while President, and that was saving on the huge electric bill. Woe be to anyone, staff member or family member, who left a light burning in an unoccupied room! At times the Executive Mansion was so dark it appeared no one was home. The staff stumbled and crept through the darkened halls at night. Thus Lyndon earned his nickname of "Light-Bulb" Johnson.

Lady Bird was a champion at keeping her cool composure. Lyndon's demands and, at times, rude comments to her would try the patience of a saint, but no one ever saw her ruffled. She had an ability to retreat within herself and emerge in full control.

In her First Lady role in the White House, Lady Bird became more of an individual than ever before in her marriage. She made no attempt to interfere with Lyndon or his duties as President. Instead she developed her own programs and interests. She instituted a beautification program for the nation, especially along the public highways, which required her to travel all over the country to make speeches to civic groups to gain support for the program.

She also began the Head Start program for children as part of Lyndon's dream of a Great Society. This program provided pre-school training to disadvantaged children so they could move ahead faster when they entered school.

Lady Bird was still shy and reticent by nature, but when she was fired with enthusiasm for a project, she could face groups and speak. She spoke to Congress and state legislative bodies about what money would be needed for her various programs. News reporters who accompanied her said she ran them ragged trying to keep up with her.

Lady Bird always found time to entertain effectively, be a charming, kind, welcoming hostess, and provide mature guidance to her two daughters through their teenage years.

Luci worked for a time as a student nurse at Georgetown University Hospital. Then she met a young man named Patrick Nugent one weekend in 1965 at Camp David, the Presidential retreat in Maryland. From that time on, love and marriage occupied most of Luci's thoughts.

On August 6, 1966, Luci and Patrick were married in the Catholic Church Shrine of Immaculate Conception in Washington in a large elaborate wedding. The reception, held at the White House, featured a seven-tier wedding cake in addition to other delectables.

The next June Luci presented her parents with their first grandchild, a little boy named Patrick Lyndon, to be called Lyn. Luci would have three more children before divorcing Patrick Nugent. She is now Mrs. Ian Turpin and lives in Toronto, Canada. Mr. Turpin is head of an international investment firm.

In December 1967, Lynda Bird married Marine Captain Charles Robb in an elegant ceremony held in the White House. They have three daughters.

During President Kennedy's administration military supplies and advisors had been sent by the United States to Vietnam in Southeast Asia in an attempt to prevent a Communist takeover of that nation. President Johnson now decided to send American soldiers, sailors and Marines to shore up the faltering resistance in South Vietnam. He felt the Democrats were perceived by the American public as being soft on Communism and a strong stand was needed.

President Johnson had begun many beneficial social programs in the United States, but the nation forgot all that as they saw American lives being lost in a foreign war. The nation became sharply divided on what course he should have followed and why Americans were fighting there.

Lyndon was very sensitive to public criticism, and he felt it would be unwise to seek a second term. He backed the candidacy of his Vice President, Hubert Humphrey, for President against the Republican nominee, Richard Nixon. He was sorely disappointed when Nixon was elected President.

Lady Bird was glad to get to go back to their Texas ranch. Lyndon had become visibly exhausted from all the agonizing decisions he was forced to make during the Vietnam conflict, and by trying to bring about an honorable end or solution to the war.

Lyndon found to his surprise that he was happier in retirement than he had expected. For the first time in many years his time was his own. He thoroughly enjoyed playing with his grandchildren and visiting his daughters and their families, as well as other relatives and friends.

His and Lady Bird's relationship had grown even closer over the years. Observers saw them exchange many affectionate looks and gestures, and it was evident they loved each other as much as ever.

Lyndon's health had not been really good for several years, and he rested more now. In mid-1972 he had another severe heart attack, from which he suffered pain for the rest of his life. He followed the news from Vietnam avidly as the war continued on through President Nixon's first term in office. There seemed to be no end to the pain, suffering and intense frustration for Americans. Many young American men fled to Canada to live rather than fight in the Vietnamese jungles.

On January 20, 1973, President Nixon was inaugurated for his second term. The next day a cease-fire in Vietnam was arranged, and a new plan was formulated by the Nixon Cabinet for dismantling the poverty relief programs of Lyndon's "Great Society."

All these events occurring in such a short period of time had a profound effect on Lyndon, which no one could have foreseen. One day later, on January 22, 1973, Lyndon died in his bedroom at the Texas ranch from a massive heart attack.

Lady Bird had gone to Austin to a meeting at Lyndon Baines Johnson Library, and no one was with Lyndon when he became ill except Secret Service agents, who tried in vain to revive him.

Lyndon's body was taken to Washington to lie in state in the Capitol rotunda. After funeral services in Washington, his body was returned to Texas for burial in a family graveyard in Stonewall, Texas.

Lady Bird continues to live at their ranch, devoted to Lyndon's memory. She enjoys visits from her children and seven grandchildren. In 1982 she founded the National Wildflower Research Center, still pursuing her interest in and love for environmental beauty. She also serves on the Board of Trustees of the National Geographic Society.

Her autobiography, *A White House Diary*, was published in 1970. A 1981 television documentary, entitled "The First Lady, A Portrait of Lady Bird Johnson," revealed her to be a vital contributor to the Great Society envisioned by her husband's administration.

In 1986 Lady Bird sold her two media stations in Austin, Texas, for twenty-seven million, five hundred thousand dollars, making her the wealthiest living former First Lady. Lady Bird has merited Lyndon's description of her: "A woman of great depth and excellent judgment."

40. Thelma Catherine (Patricia) Ryan Nixon

Thelma Catherine Ryan was born a copper-miner's daughter in Ely, Nevada, on March 16, 1912. Her father, Will Ryan, being a fanciful Irishman, always insisted on celebrating her birthday on March 17, St. Patrick's Day.

Thelma's mother, Katharina Halberstadt, was born in Germany and immigrated to the United States when she was ten years old.

When copper mining began to be less profitable, the Ryan family moved to California to try their luck at truck farming making their home near Artesia. Thelma was one year old.

When war broke out between the United States and Germany in World War I, many Americans' feelings against Germans were very negative. Mrs. Ryan begged her children not to tell anyone of her German background. Thelma's older sister, Neva, and her two brothers, Tom and Bill, promised solemnly. Since Thelma was only five, she was unlikely to mention it, but she would never say anything to upset her mother.

Mrs. Ryan died after a year-long bout with liver cancer when Thelma was only thirteen. Neva had left home the year before, so young Thelma had the main responsibility for taking care of the housework, cooking meals and doing the laundry for her father and two brothers. She raced constantly with the clock, trying to get her work done at home and keep up her school work too.

Somehow, Thelma also found time to be active in drama club and debate team activities. She won the lead female role in the class play in both her junior and senior years of high school. In addition, she maintained a high grade average in all her subjects. Her classmates liked Thelma and admired her courage in keeping the Ryan family together, largely through her own efforts.

All three Ryan children graduated from Excelsior High School in June 1929. By then they all knew their father was dying slowly with tuberculosis. Only one of them could attend college because of their lack of money. Tom received a football scholarship from the University of Southern

Patricia Nixon. (Courtesy Library of Congress.)

California, so he went first. Bill stayed home and operated the truck farm, while Thelma took a stenographic course at night and took care of her sick father during the day.

At last Mr. Ryan's condition worsened and Thelma and her brothers were forced to take him to a Catholic sanitorium in Monrovia, California, where he died in May 1930. He was buried beside his wife in Whittier, California.

When Thelma Ryan enrolled proudly at Fullerton Junior College the next year, she felt she was embarking on a whole new life, and she gave her name as Patricia Ryan. She had never felt the name "Thelma" suited her and she would never use the name again.

These were Depression days, and the Ryans made no profit from their farming efforts. They did well to keep the taxes paid. There was no money to help Patricia in her college studies, so she took a job at Artesia's First National Bank as both a bookkeeper and janitor. One morning when she was sweeping out the bank before business hours began, some of her college classmates passed by and ridiculed her for the job she held. When another person offered to work as janitor for less money than Patricia, she raised no objections, as she was glad to have an excuse to let the job go.

Pat, as she was now called, did not return to Fullerton for a second year. Instead, she opted to spend some time with her father's relatives in New York City. There she got a job working in Seton Hospital, a tuberculosis hospital, operated by the Catholic Church. One of Pat's aunts was a nun who also worked in the hospital.

Pat stayed in New York for two years, and despite her job, she managed to do a fair amount of sightseeing in the area. She toyed with the idea of making New York her permanent home and briefly considered becoming a nun, but homesickness for her brothers and friends in California caused her to forget both possibilities.

Bill Ryan had enrolled at Fullerton and was finding adjustment to college life difficult after working for the past several years. When her brother Tom wrote Pat that it was her turn to go back to college, she jumped at the chance. This would mean a return to California and her brothers.

In 1934 all three Ryan children were students at Southern California University. They shared an apartment, money, hopes and dreams. During the entire three years Pat was a student at Southern Cal, she had never had a special boyfriend. She discouraged any attempts by male acquaintances to get her to commit herself to a long-term relationship. She was too busy getting the education she wanted. At times she worked as a movie extra to help pay expenses, and she worked as a fashion model and salesperson at Bullock's Wilshire in Los Angeles. This particular shop was a favorite of movie stars, where they shopped for clothes for themselves and their children.

Since Tom had entered college first, he graduated first and got a job teaching in high school at Burbank. Bill became a lighting technician at Twentieth Century–Fox movies studio. When Pat graduated, she applied for and got a job teaching commercial subjects, typing, shorthand and accounting, at Whittier High School. Pat's former high school principal was now superintendent of the Whittier School District, and he remembered Pat and recommended her highly for the job.

Whittier was then primarily a Quaker community, and even though it is located only eight miles from Artesia, Pat found it was as different as if it were in another section of the country. The prevailing attitudes here were ones of modesty, high moral standards and a sense of community.

Whittier citizens tended to keep a sharp eye on the teachers of the town children, and Pat somewhat resented the close scrutiny to which she was subjected. She made a practice of going to Los Angeles every weekend to visit her sister, Neva, and her husband. All Pat's dates had to pick her up in Los Angeles for an evening out.

It was during her first year of living in Whittier that Pat joined a Little Theater group and met Richard Nixon, one of Whittier's best-known and most-admired young lawyers.

Richard had graduated from Duke University Law School in Durham, North Carolina, where he had been an honor student and president of the Duke Law School Student Bar Association. He had returned home to join a Whittier law firm.

As Pat got better acquainted with Richard Nixon, she found they had much in common, from Irish backgrounds to lives which had been materially altered by illnesses and deaths of close relatives. Richard had had two young brothers suffer severe illnesses and early deaths, which placed a heavy financial burden on his family. Richard also had to work hard to get his education, and had high ambitions for the future, like Pat.

These similarities did not impress Richard, or Dick as he was better known, so much as Pat's beauty, with her red-gold curls and brown eyes which shaded at times to green. He fell in love with her the first night they met and told her he wanted to marry her, but she refused to consider him seriously for almost two years. On their dates, they often walked along the beach at San Clemente, where they talked about their hopes and dreams.

They were married on June 21, 1940, at Mission Inn in Riverside, California. It was a simple ceremony, attended only by relatives and closest friends. Dick was now a deputy city attorney, and Pat planned to continue her teaching in high school.

World War II was raging in Europe at the time of their marriage, but the war had not yet touched Pat or Dick directly. When Dick was offered an opportunity to help set up a government price control and rationing agency in Washington in 1941, both of them felt this was a positive step that could possibly lead to bigger opportunities.

In January 1942, the Nixons moved to Washington. Dick went to work immediately, but Pat had to job-hunt for several months before she finally got a job as an economist, also with the Office of Price Administration, known as OPA.

Dick became restless in his job, feeling he was accomplishing little with the expenditure of great effort. He decided to join the navy.

His Quaker parents were greatly distressed by his decision. They felt he could serve his country in a non-military way. Pat supported Dick in his decision, and proudly wrote both of her brothers that Dick was entering the navy, as both of them had done previously.

Pat continued to work at the OPA, and Dick was sent to the Southern Pacific Theater of Operations. He was gone overseas for fifteen months, months during which their love letters were their sole contact. They wrote each other daily, but mail service was erratic. One week would see no mail for either of them, while the next might provide three letters a day.

Dick left his navy service with the rank of lieutenant commander after having served for four years. Upon his discharge from the navy, Dick took Pat back to Whittier to live.

In January 1946, Dick decided to run for the United States Congress from his district. One month later the Nixons' first child, a little girl they named Patricia, was born on February 21. She would be called Tricia.

When baby Tricia was three weeks old, Pat left her with Hannah Nixon, Dick's mother, during the day and helped Dick in his campaign for a Congressional seat. The baby slept peacefully all day in the care of her grandmother, and then wanted to party all night when her mother took over her care. Pat felt as if she were sleepwalking at times, as the baby kept her awake so much.

Dick made a habit of speaking from his knowledge of the issues and used no notes. His grasp of government operations must have been apparent to the voters, for he won the election. It was most fortunate that he did win, for they had used all the money they had saved on his campaign.

In Washington Pat found there were few social obligations for the wife of a freshman Congressman, and there were no sources of information about types of dress expected for various social gatherings nor about protocol to be observed. Pat did not let such matters overly concern her. She spent part of her time working in Dick's office and considered herself an important member of his team.

On July 4, 1948, Julie Nixon was born. Hannah Nixon came from the farm she and her husband had recently bought in Pennsylvania to help Pat, but became ill shortly after arriving. Pat was then forced to take over the care of her newborn daughter, two-year-old Tricia and her sick mother-in-law in a townhouse-style apartment, with endless trips up and down stairs.

Finally conditions improved, but for the next several years Pat's days would be filled primarily with child care and housework, all of which she insisted on doing herself.

In 1950 Dick decided to seek a seat in the United States Senate. Despite a ruthless, smear-tactic type of campaign on the part of his opponent, Helene Gahagan Douglas, Dick again won the election. He had gained national attention and won public support for his work as member of the House Committee on Un-American Activity. This committee had uncovered several instances of espionage activity, for which arrests had been made.

That same year the Nixons finally bought a house of their own, a two-story white brick in Spring Valley, a residential area of Washington. Pat decorated her new home in cheerful California style and colors.

In 1952 occasional news articles appeared which speculated on Dick's chances of being nominated for Vice President at the upcoming Republican Convention. General Dwight Eisenhower was nominated to run for President, and he chose Dick to be his running mate. They won the election.

If Pat had considered her duties as a Congressman's wife to be ill-defined, she found them even less defined as the wife of a Vice President. She went with Dick on goodwill tours to the Far East and Central America. The Far East tour lasted more than two months. Both Pat and Dick enjoyed the tours, as they were somewhat like delayed honeymoons, but Pat especially missed their two little daughters, who had to stay home and attend school.

In Central America their visit was marred by demonstrations, particularly in Venezuela. Pat and the foreign minister's wife were riding together in a car in a motorcade when demonstrators began throwing rocks, spitting and beating on the cars in the motorcade with baseball bats. Windows were broken and some members of the entourage were cut by glass fragments. Through all the turmoil, Pat maintained her cool, calm demeanor.

Despite Dick's good service record, President Eisenhower never did like Dick very much. When he chose to seek a second term as President, he suggested that Dick step down to allow the choice of someone else to run for Vice President. Dick and his supporters in the Republican Party prevailed, however, and President Eisenhower and Dick were reelected.

During this term, Pat and Dick went on a goodwill tour to the Soviet Union. Since the days of the Russian Revolution, few American citizens had visited the Soviet Union, and not much was known about their way of life. Khrushchev was Soviet Premier at the time, and he was defensive when he talked to Dick about Soviet military strength.

"We are strong, we can beat you," Khrushchev bragged to Dick.

Dick said quietly, "It seems that in this day and age to argue who is the stronger completely misses the point. . . . If war comes we both lose."

A few weeks later both Premier Khrushchev and Mrs. Khrushchev came to the United States for a return visit. Relations between the two great nations began to improve slowly from this point until now, and the Cold War began to thaw.

In 1960 Dick was nominated by the Republicans to be their Presidential candidate opposing John F. Kennedy, the Democrat. Pat worked loyally alongside her husband, and Stewart Alsop, a political columnist, described her as a major political asset to Dick. However, he lost the election by a very narrow margin — so narrow that Pat refused to agree for him to concede defeat for several hours.

Pat was crushed by Dick's defeat. She had never seriously considered the possibility he might lose. There were many tales of vote fraud in the election, and influential people urged Dick to ask for a recount, but he refused. He elected to return to Los Angeles to resume practicing law.

Pat and the two Nixon daughters remained in Washington so the girls could complete their school term. Tricia was a freshman in high school, and Julie was in the seventh grade. Pat was bitter about Dick's defeat at the polls and refused all Washington social invitations. As the weeks passed, she devoted her time to getting Tricia and Julie ready for their new home in California, and prepared to face the change in the family's life-style.

When Dick was urged to run for Governor of California in 1962, a friend said, "Pat told me that if Dick ran for Governor she was going to take her shoe to him!"

Her chief objection was based on her fear he would not win, and her fear was valid. Dick was defeated, and according to widespread news reports at the time, his political career was finished.

The Nixons were a little shell-shocked by the two defeats in a row, and when Dick decided to go to New York City to practice law, they were all delighted. To get out of California, they would willingly go anywhere!

In New York they found a condominium for their home. It was badly in need of refurbishing, but it was conveniently located and it had ten rooms. Their broker told them she had been hesitant to even show them the place, but Dick reassured her. "Pat can make anything look good," he told her.

In New York, Tricia and Julie both attended Miss Chapin's School for Girls, a private school. Pat enjoyed living in a new area where she was not constantly on display and was not so readily recognized. She also had more time to devote to her daughters and their activities, which she enjoyed.

The family traveled together to Europe, Mexico and the Bahamas, as well as to Florida and other states. Life was much more normal and relaxed for them. Dick campaigned diligently for Barry Goldwater for President in 1964, but Pat was less involved. She worked answering the phone in Dick's law office when he was out of town. She found she had no interest in doing charity work after the excitement of being involved in politics, and admitted to being frequently bored.

Tricia enrolled in Finch College in Manhattan when she graduated from high school, and Julie went to Smith. In her freshman year at Smith, Julie renewed her childhood acquaintance with David Eisenhower, grandson of former President Dwight Eisenhower. They had last seen each other when David's grandfather was inaugurated President and Julie's father inaugurated as Vice President in 1957. Both had grown up into attractive, personable adults, and their relationship quickly became romantic.

Dick again sought the office of President of the United States in 1968, against Pat's firm opposition. She was unhappy about his decision to reenter politics, but she worked long and hard on the campaign trail to help him achieve his goal.

Former President Eisenhower had recently been made an invalid by a third serious heart attack and was now a resident patient in Walter Reed Hospital. Mamie Eisenhower, former First Lady, had a room beside Ike's so she could be with him during his illness, and she campaigned vigorously for Dick among hospital staff and visitors.

This time Dick reached his goal and was elected to be the thirty-seventh President of the United States. The Nixons would return to Washington in triumph.

On December 22, 1968, Julie married David Eisenhower in New York City in the Marble Collegiate Church of Dr. Norman Vincent Peale. It was a small wedding attended only by family and close friends. Both the bride and groom were still in college and would continue their studies.

One month later, on January 20, 1969, Dick was inaugurated as President and Pat became First Lady. Spiro Agnew was inaugurated as Vice President.

One of the first changes Pat made as First Lady was to turn the lights back on in the White House. Former President Lyndon Johnson had preferred much less light, and Pat had floodlights added to outdoor lighting. Crystal chandeliers replaced the Early American style lighting in White House hallways. Servants no longer crept through darkened hallways at night.

The Johnsons had been noted for their large-scale, elaborate entertaining while White House residents. Yet the number of guests entertained by the Nixons averaged forty-five thousand each year, twice the number of the Johnsons' guests.

Pat was a thoughtful, charming hostess, who took time to really talk with visitors and attempted to make everyone feel warmly welcome.

On June 12, 1971, Tricia Nixon was married to Edward Cox in the Rose Garden at the White House, in a lovely summer wedding during which the weather cooperated for a change. There was an elegant, gala reception following the ceremony, at which Pat and Dick danced together, one of the few times they danced while living in the White House.

Tricia had not been happy to be a President's daughter, and she did not adjust well to being under such close scrutiny by the public. She had spent most of her first months in the White House in her bedroom.

Her new husband still had to complete his law school education, so they went to live in Cambridge, Massachusetts. This was a welcome respite for sensitive Tricia.

Despite the high position their father had attained and their own happy marriages, the lives of the Nixon daughters had their dark moments.

Student demonstrations and subsequent turmoil were so out of control that Julie and David had to ask the Nixons to not attend their college graduations. When the Vietnam War finally ended, the turbulence gradually subsided.

Following his graduation from college, David Eisenhower joined the navy. Julie, more bubbly and outgoing than her sister, cheerfully involved herself in various charitable activities while David was on sea duty. Mamie Eisenhower, David's grandmother, begged Julie to stay as near David as she could, for Mamie knew from experience how important a wife was to a man in military service.

Pat had been a do-it-yourselfer all her life, and in her first months in the White House she undertook to read all the letters she received and to dictate replies to the letters. In the avalanche of mail, she could not keep up, and was soon forced to seek some assistance.

First Ladies are expected to have projects, and Pat chose to lend most of her time and talents to promoting volunteer work. Pat had rolled bandages for the Red Cross during World War II days, and she knew how much many agencies depended on volunteers. She also worked to help organize community self-help groups in various locations.

Pat was convinced that women have greater capabilities than had been utilized in American government, and she urged Dick to appoint a woman justice to the Supreme Court in 1971. He requested a list of qualified women nominees, but instead appointed Lewis Powell and William Rehnquist. Pat was also an ardent supporter of the Equal Rights Amendment, which was never ratified by the states.

Pat and Dick went to China while he was President. This trip led to trade agreements between the two nations for the first time since China had become a Communist nation, and a normalization of relations. The Nixons also paid another visit to the Soviet Union.

Dick was reelected to a second term as President in 1972, but was forced to resign on August 9, 1974, in the aftermath of a scandal involving, among other things, the arrest of several members of Dick's reelection committee for breaking into the Democratic headquarters at the Watergate hotel and attempting to tap telephones there. Dick and Pat sadly left the White House for a life in retirement in their home at San Clemente, where years before a young Dick and Pat had loved to walk on the beach.

When Betty Ford, the incoming First Lady, commented to Pat about the red carpet being rolled out for the Nixons to go to the helicopter to leave the White House, Pat said, "Well, Betty, you'll see many of these red carpets, and you'll get so you hate 'em."

Pat never really enjoyed living in the White House; she had just tried to make the best of it. She was relieved now that they were out of the public eye and the charges and countercharges had ended. Her only concern was that Dick had been crucified on the cross of politics, and she was sorry his Presidency had ended the way it did.

Within a month after their return to California, Dick was hospitalized in serious condition with phlebitis (blood clots) in his legs.

Both Nixon girls were living back East, Tricia and Ed in New York and Julie and David in Washington, where David was in law school. Pat had good friends drop by to console her during these anxious days, but no close relatives. Dick recovered slowly over the next year, and Pat began to breathe easier.

In May 1975, Pat was honored by having a school in her old hometown named for her. The Patricia Nixon Elementary School was located in Cerritos, the new name of the town of Artesia.

Other than this one brief public appearance, Pat spent her days flower-gardening and reading. By 1976 authors all over the United States were writing scurrilous books claiming the Nixons had a troubled, loveless marriage and that Pat had become a heavy drinker.

All these new insults were too much for Pat. She collapsed on July 7, 1976, with a paralytic stroke. For the first time in her life, imperturbable Pat was discouraged and frightened. "I'm beat. I'm through," she was heard to say to one of her nurses. She spent many pain-filled months recovering.

The births of Nixon grandchildren helped Pat regain her strength and her old zest for living. Jennie Elizabeth Eisenhower was born on August 15, 1978, and Christopher Nixon Cox was born on March 14, 1979. With the children now an important part of their lives, Pat and Dick decided to leave San Clemente and move back to New York. They moved back East in 1980.

Pat's health continued to decline, and the next year she and Dick moved to New Jersey where she could get outdoors more. She suffered another stroke in 1983 and has been hospitalized several times since with respiratory problems.

Julie and David now have two more children, Alex and Melanie, who brighten the days for both Pat and Dick when they visit.

Dick continues to maintain his interest in both domestic and foreign political affairs. He has written several books about political matters.

Despite physical problems, Pat is happy now in their retirement years and is getting a well-deserved rest.

41. Elizabeth Ann (Betty) Bloomer Warren Ford

Betty Bloomer was born in Chicago, Illinois, on April 8, 1918. Her parents moved to Grand Rapids, Michigan, when the little girl was only two, so she remembers nothing of having lived in Chicago.

Betty's father, William Stephenson Bloomer, sold conveyor belts to factories in his job with the Royal Rubber Company. His job required him to travel extensively, and Betty, who missed him very much when he was away, vowed she would never marry a man whose job involved travel.

Betty had a happy childhood. Her father loved his little daughter and missed her, too, when he was traveling, so he would bring her little gifts when he came home. Betty was close to her mother, but her mother insisted that Betty observe her rules on modesty and table manners. Betty's two brothers were tolerant of their little sister when she dogged their footsteps and begged to be allowed to play ice hockey and football with them and their friends.

Betty greatly enjoyed the dancing lessons she began taking when she was eight. Her dancing teacher held the usual annual recital for her students, which Betty's mother attended. Mrs. Bloomer may have wondered if her little daughter would ever make the grade as a dancer when Betty dropped a metal flower basket with a loud clang into the footlights! The audience enjoyed Betty's clumsiness and thought it was appealing, even if her mother did not.

Betty persevered, however, as she really enjoyed dancing, in addition to the boys she met along the way. She dreamed of going on to ballet school someday until she saw modern dance. Modern dance intrigued Betty because of its relaxed style and freedom of movement.

Betty's early years were also Depression years, so at age fourteen, she began working as a model for a local department store, as well as giving dancing lessons to younger children. She rented a basement room from a neighbor for a dollar a week and hired a boy to play piano for another dollar. It was a successful venture, despite her youth, and Betty's students learned to dance the usual dances, including the waltz.

Betty Ford. (Courtesy Library of Congress.)

When she was sixteen, Betty's father died, leaving her deeply grieved. Her father had been a most important person in her life. Betty's grief served to bring her even closer to her mother.

When Betty graduated from high school two years later, she wanted to go to New York and get a job as a dancer. Her mother felt Betty was too young to be on her own so far away, so they compromised. For the next two summers, Betty studied dance at Bennington College in Vermont.

Betty loved Bennington. She danced every day until her leg muscles were so tight that she could not walk downstairs in the evening. If an occasion arose that required her to go down stairs, she had to sit and slide down one step at a time.

Betty was impressed with Martha Graham when Martha performed at the Vermont dance school. Betty asked Martha if she could join her dance troupe in New York, and could hardly believe her good fortune when Martha told her she could.

Betty's roommate at Bennington, Natalie Harris, also joined the Martha Graham Company. They rented an apartment together near the Graham Studio, and Betty felt confident she was on her way to stardom. She worked as a model for the Powers Model Agency during the day to pay her bills. She received only ten dollars per performance when she danced.

To be a dancer with the leading group required total dedication. After Betty's mother came to New York to visit, she became concerned that Betty was letting her youth slip away with no interests other than her dance career. Betty had been living in New York for two years, and dancing had been her life.

Mrs. Bloomer urged Betty to return with her to Grand Rapids for six months to rest and think about her future. Back home, Betty found she had missed all her friends and her old way of life, so she did not return to New York. Instead she began teaching dancing again.

Betty had not been back long before she began a serious romance with Bill Warren, a good friend of her brother. Betty's mother had remarried, and Betty felt it was time to settle down herself, as many of her friends were already married and had started families. World War II was raging fiercely, and it sometimes seemed life could never be normal again.

Bill was a diabetic and was rejected for military service. He worked with his father in an insurance agency, and Betty was sure he was the man for her. They were married at her mother's new home in the spring of 1942. They spent their honeymoon in a cottage on Lake Michigan.

Before long Bill left his father's insurance firm and took a job selling insurance in Maumee, Ohio. Betty taught dancing at the university there and worked in a department store.

Bill then decided he wanted to get into another career field and got a job with Continental Can Company in Syracuse, New York, necessitating another move. Betty put up no arguments, and she took a job in Syracuse on the production line of a frozen food processing plant. Before many months passed, however, Bill was tired of his job and quit again.

Betty and Bill returned to Grand Rapids, where he went to work as a furniture salesman for a furniture manufacturer. He had the whole East Coast as his territory, which meant he would be away from home most of the time. Betty had done what she had vowed she would not do — she had married a traveling salesman who would be home very little. At least, she consoled herself, she was living again in familiar surroundings with her friends and relatives.

Betty decided it would be better if she kept busy while Bill was away, so she took a job as a fashion coordinator with the same department store where she had worked as a model when she was in high school.

Whenever Bill was at home, it was party time! He was determined to have a good time and wanted to hit all the night spots with their friends. This was not the kind of life Betty had in mind when she married him, and she decided if he had not changed by now, he never would. After he left on his next selling trip, she wrote him a letter telling him she wanted a divorce.

Before she could mail the letter, she had a phone call from Bill's boss in Boston. Bill was in a hospital there in a diabetic coma and in critical condition. One side of his face was paralyzed.

Dumbfounded by the news, Betty tore up the letter. She went to Boston and stayed with Bill almost constantly for six weeks until he was able to be moved by train to the home of his parents in Grand Rapids.

Back in Grand Rapids, Betty worked at her department store job by day and helped take care of Bill at night. The paralysis had spread into his legs. Later his doctor sent him to a hospital, where Betty visited him every night. His illness continued much the same for the next two years. Betty felt trapped by the circumstances. She did not still love Bill, but she felt she could not possibly leave a sick man.

Bill grimly fought his way back and eventually went back to work. As soon as Betty saw he was able to care for himself again, she filed suit for divorce. Bill did not contest the action and the divorce was final on September 22, 1947. Betty was certain she would never marry again.

About the time her divorce would be final, a girlfriend called Betty at work one night to ask if Betty would go with her, her husband and a friend named Jerry Ford for a drink. Betty explained her divorce was still in process, but Jerry got on the phone and insisted she go with them. Betty had known Jerry by sight for years, but he was four years older than she, and they had been just acquaintances.

After that evening they began having occasional dates, but they both also continued to see other people. Jerry was carrying a large torch for a New York model, and he announced marriage was not in his plans either. His romance with the model had ended when he told her he planned to live in Grand Rapids and practice law there. She wanted to stay in New York where the lights were brighter.

At Christmas of 1947, Jerry went to Sun Valley, Idaho, for three weeks to ski. He had invited Betty to go with him, but she could not. She had to go to New York just after Christmas to attend fashion shows. As fashion coordinator, she had to keep up with fashion trends and give the buyers her opinions.

Both Jerry and Betty found themselves unhappy apart. Just after he returned home, Jerry proposed to Betty, who quickly accepted. They were married on October 15, 1948, in the Grace Episcopal Church in Grand Rapids in a small wedding.

Before they married Jerry had entered the campaign as a United States Congressman from Michigan, and he went campaigning the day of the wedding! He did not arrive on time and came rushing in a few minutes late. His mother had been weepy at the thought of her last son at home marrying and leaving the nest. Then she saw to her horror that Jerry was still wearing muddy shoes he had forgotten to change. She forgot her tears and gave him a motherly lecture after the ceremony.

About three weeks after their marriage, Jerry was elected to serve in the United States Congress. By then he had dashed in and out of their apartment so many times, always in a rush to be somewhere else to campaign, Betty had begun to wonder why in the world they had married. They never seemed to be together. Perhaps now, with the election over, they could live like married couples should.

But first they had to move to Washington, D. C. As Betty said in her autobiography, "We came to Washington for two years and stayed for twenty-eight."

Betty's mother died unexpectedly while Betty and Jerry were on their way to Washington. Betty was deeply saddened to lose her mother, who did not live to see Jerry sworn in as Congressman.

As a new Congressman in town, Jerry was invited to social gatherings without Betty, at first. After Betty got that changed, she entered into political life with enthusiasm. She joined the Congressional Club, a bipartisan group of wives of government officials, and was active in their various projects. She met Lady Bird Johnson and Bess Truman, who both impressed Betty favorably with their friendliness and lack of pretensions. She and Jerry were later invited to Jackie Kennedy's elaborate party at Mount Vernon, which Betty considered one of the most elegant parties ever held in Washington.

During these busy years, Betty also gave birth to three sons and a daughter. She says she could have never kept up with everything if it had not been for a wonderful housekeeper named Clara Powell, who also cooked and helped Betty with the children. Clara was always one of the Ford family's best friends. Jerry says if Clara had not been on the scene, he could have never served in Congress as long as he did.

With growing children, Betty was involved with many activities. She taught Sunday School, she served as den mother for a Scout troop, she cared for endless pets and she visited the emergency room of the nearest hospital with a monotonous regularity. If one of the children wasn't drinking some potentially poisonous substance, then another one had broken a bone. Jerry was usually away from home, and all the care and burden was on Betty's shoulders.

Despite the dismal possibility of more broken bones, the entire Ford family went on skiing trips together. All the children ski well, as does Jerry. When Jerry received an award as "America's Number One Skier," his children teased him that it should have noted, "for his age."

In 1964 Betty developed spinal arthritis with a pinched nerve as a complication. She could no longer dance at all. The pain, unbelievably intense at times, never stopped. She tried to carry on as usual, but instead she had a breakdown and had to visit a psychiatrist regularly for awhile.

In 1972 Betty and Jerry went to China as a part of his role as Minority Leader of the House of Representatives, a trip they both enjoyed greatly.

The next year was full of surprises for the Fords. Jerry became Vice President of the United States when Spiro Agnew, who had been elected Vice President when President Richard Nixon was elected, resigned his office as Vice President. Betty was stunned. She just could not believe Jerry could possibly be Vice President. His highest ambition had been to be a Majority Leader in the House! But more surprises were in store. Within less than a year, President Nixon had also resigned because of political scandal, and Jerry became President.

When Jerry was inaugurated on August 9, 1974, he said the Marine Band couldn't decide what to play at the ceremony — "Hail to the Chief" or "You've Come a Long Way, Baby"!

In addition to having the head of the family become the head of the government, the Ford family also had to become accustomed to having Secret Service agents and newspaper reporters become a part of their daily lives. So many major changes in such a short space of time were dizzying.

The Fords' daughter, Susan, was attending boarding school at Holton Arms in Virginia. One weekend Susan's life was threatened by a radical group of terrorists, which brought Secret Service to her school to stay around the clock.

Betty said she had known Jerry would be a good President, but she really worried about how she would be perceived as First Lady. She is an open, frank, honest woman, and indeed she has found herself in trouble with the American public on more than one occasion. On a talk show she said she thought abortions should be performed in hospitals instead of in the backwoods, and she received a flood of protesting letters. This worried her. On another television talk show, she said she would counsel Susan if Susan were having an affair, meaning she wouldn't throw her daughter out of the house even if Betty strongly disapproved of such conduct.

(Later, news reporters asked Jimmy Carter, the Democrat nominee opposing Jerry in his bid to be elected President in his own right, how he would feel if he found out his daughter were having an affair. Jimmy Carter said, "Shocked and overwhelmed!" Then he grinned and added, "But my daughter is only seven years old!")

The Ford family loved the luxury of having so many servants at their beck and call while they lived in the White House. Betty planned to keep some of Pat Nixon's secretaries to work for her, but when she heard too many protests of "but-we-always-did-it-this-way," she let them go and hired her own.

Jerry had been President for only about a month when he set off a major controversy of his own. He pardoned former President Nixon for any wrongs he might have committed in the Watergate cover-up scandal. He felt this was a logical first step to take in an effort to get the country back to normal, but the reporters went after Jerry in full cry.

Jerry ignored them. He was President, he owed nobody any favors, he felt it was a good move for the country, and he saw no possibility of President Nixon ever receiving a fair trial. Two years later, however, he would come to feel that the pardon cost him election in his own right.

Betty developed breast cancer while she was First Lady and had to have her right breast removed. Fortunately the tumor had been found during a routine checkup and had not metastasized. In her usual forthright fashion, Betty gave honest reports about her reactions to her bout with cancer and urged all American women to be alert for symptoms.

When Betty came out in support of the Equal Rights Amendment, which would guarantee equal rights to women in all matters, particularly in the field of pay scales, she set off the fireworks again among the women opposed to the Equal Rights Amendment. Many of the opponents had secure lives with no need to support themselves or their children with meager earnings, but Betty had not always lived a charmed life, and she could sympathize with women who found themselves suddenly playing the role as breadwinner.

Betty decided surely no one could object if she supported research for diseases, so she got involved with the Heart Association, Easter Seals and the Multiple Sclerosis Foundation.

Betty and Jerry enjoyed entertaining both dignitaries and private citizens during their years in the White House. Betty compiled guest lists carefully and chose menu items and appropriate entertainment. She made sure citizens involved in the arts were included frequently so they would feel welcome in the President's home.

Since they had lived in Washington for so many years while Jerry was a Congressman, they had many personal friends there. Betty said these friendships certainly made life easier and more pleasant for her. She knew some First Ladies had never spent any time in Washington prior to their coming to live in the White House.

In 1975, within a three-week period, Jerry was twice a victim of unsuccessful assassination attempts. Both times his assailants were women, and each woman received a lifetime prison sentence.

Jerry was nominated by the Republicans to run for President in 1976, but he lost the election to Jimmy Carter, the Democratic nominee.

Both Betty and Jerry were sad to leave the White House, but most of all they were sorry to be leaving Washington, which had been their home for so many years. All four children had been born there, went to school and grew up there. They had been happy most of the time.

The Fords smiled and waved to the television cameras and the crowd as they boarded the helicopter which would take them to their home in Virginia. Later, as Betty watched the scene on the news, she decided she had put on a good act, and was relieved.

Betty's arthritis had not improved significantly, so she and Jerry decided to move to Rancho Mirage in California, where the climate is hot and dry. They built a new home there and hoped Betty might find improvement in her condition.

Jerry might not be President any more, but he had not really retired. He continued to take part in national and local political activities and was a member of various boards and committees.

Jerry loves to play golf, and he had a chance to play much more often. He joked that if Arnold Palmer's fans were called Arnie's Army, his were Ford's Few!

Betty found herself staying home with her arthritis pills and martinis. Susas was living at home and dating Chuck Vance, a Secret Service agent assigned to protect the Ford family. Susan watched daily as her mother slipped further and further into an alcoholic haze. Finally, Chuck told Susan, "You've got to do something about your mother."

Finally, Betty had a painful confrontation with her whole family. Each told her of occasions they had witnessed when Betty was unaware of events taking place around her. Betty then agreed to enter Long Beach Naval Hospital for treatment of her alcoholism.

She stayed there for four weeks, returned home cold sober and has never drunk any alcoholic beverage since that time in 1979. When Betty's recovery was assured, Susan married Chuck Vance in Palm Desert, California.

Betty became a leader in alcohol abuse treatment and is now president of the Betty Ford Center, which opened on October 3, 1982, for patients suffering from either drug or alcohol abuse. They receive treatment in a hospital-like setting which is an adjunct of the Eisenhower Medical Center.

Betty is the author of two books, entitled *The Times of My Life* and *Betty – A Glad Awakening*.

In November 1987, Betty underwent quadruple heart bypass surgery, and suffered some complications several weeks later. She is back home now, recovering, and given her determination and courage, she will make a full recovery.

The Ford children are all successful, responsible adults. Michael Gerald graduated from theological seminary and is a minister; John Gardner works in publishing. John recently acquired part interest in *The Del Mar Press* newspaper in Del Mar, California. Steven Meigs is an actor, and has starred in the daily television program "The Young and the Restless." Steve is now studying animal science in college. As mentioned before, Susan is married and has her own home. They are proud of their mother and her courage and honesty, and she is much loved by all of them. Can any woman ask for more than to gain the admiration of all those nearest and dearest to her?

42. Rosalynn Smith Carter

Rosalynn Smith was born August 18, 1927, in Plains, Georgia, a small country town with a population of about six hundred. Her family lived in the typical rural Southern style of the times. Her mother cooked their meals on a wood-fueled cookstove, made most of her children's clothes and kept a few pigs and chickens, as well as a milk cow. Her father, Wilburn Edgar Smith, farmed part-time, drove a school bus and owned a car repair garage.

Rosalynn grew up during the Depression years, and she remembered she and her family felt fortunate because they always had a car to use. Her father could coax service out of the most dilapidated jalopy. The family farm supplied most of their food, so the Smith children were not aware of financial hardship. All their neighbors and friends lived about the same way, so no one felt deprived.

As a little girl Rosalynn loved playing with dolls. When not playing with her two younger brothers, she cut paper dolls and clothes for them from old Sears, Roebuck catalogs. She was obliged to help her mother with household chores, so she learned to run a home, but she didn't learn to cook.

Rosalynn was a good student in school and made excellent grades. Her parents were proud of her, as they were of all their children, but they were strict disciplinarians.

Three miles down the road from Plains was the home of the Earl Carter family. A Carter daughter, Ruth, was two years younger than Rosalynn, but they became friends. Ruth often intimidated Rosalynn with her blunt remarks, but Rosalynn learned to ignore them for the most part.

Ruth's mother, called Miss Lillian by all her family and acquaintances, was a registered nurse. She worked for the health department and took care of anyone who was sick, regardless of race. This led to some disagreement between Miss Lillian and her husband, Mr. Earl. She calmly ignored his prejudices and taught her children to respect black people as well as white.

Rosalynn set her heart on going to summer camp at about age ten, and when she was twelve, she was finally allowed to go. She was excited by her opportunity and enjoyed her days at camp thoroughly. Tragically, when

Rosalynn Smith Carter. (Courtesy Library of Congress.)

she returned home she found her father critically ill with leukemia. Miss
Lillian came every day to give him pain shots, and his condition grew
steadily worse. When his illness was nearing the end, Miss Lillian insisted
that Rosalynn spend the night with Ruth. Rosalynn's father died that night.

Rosalynn felt like the bottom had dropped out of her world when her
father died. In addition to the two younger brothers, there was now
another little Smith daughter who was only four years old. Rosalynn's
grandparents, Mama and Papa Murray, did all they could to help their
daughter and her family, but within a year Mama Murray also died.
Rosalynn worried whether she had done something wrong and God was
punishing her by taking all her loved ones.

Papa Murray left his farm and moved in with his daughter and her children. Mrs. Smith had little money to support the family, and she started sewing for people. They received some farm income and eighteen dollars a month from Rosalynn's father's insurance.

Rosalynn felt her father's influence as strongly after his death as she had while he lived. She tried hard to do everything as she thought he would have wanted and behave as he had taught her. The whole family were active church members, and Rosalynn found her religion to be her greatest source of strength in these troubled days.

When Rosalynn was in the ninth grade she had her first intimation of the differences in education in the "separate but equal" schools for the black and white children. A black woman who lived in Plains asked Rosalynn to type the thesis she had completed for graduation from a black college. As Rosalynn typed, she was startled to see the work was written at about a sixth or seventh grade level. She began then to realize the lack of opportunity black students suffered, but since this was in Georgia before integration, she knew of no way the situation could be changed.

Money continued to be tight for the Smith family, and when Rosalynn was in high school, she gave shampoos at a local beauty shop to earn spending money. She graduated as valedictorian of her class.

With little or no financial backing in view, she decided to attend Georgia Southwestern College in Americus, Georgia. It was a junior college, and she commuted daily. She had only four dollars and fifty cents a week to spend for bus tickets and lunches. If she skipped lunch, she could attend a movie with some of her girlfriends, where they squealed and swooned as Frank Sinatra sang.

That same year Rosalynn fell in love with a picture of Jimmy Carter. Jimmy was in school at the Naval Academy in Annapolis, and he sent his family a picture of himself in uniform. Even though he had grown up in Plains and she saw him often, Rosalynn felt as if she were seeing him for the first time.

Jimmy was a brother to Ruth Carter, and Ruth was terribly excited by this turn of events. She and Rosalynn spent hours fantasizing a great romance between Jimmy and Rosalynn. However, Rosalynn always backed out of any face-to-face meeting with him when he was home on leave. When Ruth called her with a trumped-up reason for Rosalynn to visit her immediately, Rosalynn found an excuse to keep from going to the Carters'.

Finally, after much maneuvering on Ruth's part, Rosalynn agreed to go with Ruth and Jimmy on a picnic a few miles out of town. It was the summer of 1945, and Rosalynn was seventeen. She felt that twenty-year-old Jimmy considered her a kid of the same caliber as Ruth because he teased them both all day.

That evening Rosalynn was attending a youth meeting at the church when Jimmy came by in his car and asked her to double-date for a movie with Ruth and her date. Rosalynn was so surprised and pleased, she left the youth meeting to go with him.

Just after Jimmy returned to Annapolis, the atomic bomb was dropped on Japan. Not many days later, World War II ended, and Rosalynn found she was very thankful Jimmy would not be fighting in a war. He was sent on sea duty, however, and they had to be content with writing each other.

When he came back home at Christmas in 1945, they dated frequently. Before time for him to return to duty, he proposed. Rosalynn had planned to complete four years of college, so she turned him down reluctantly. When she visited him, accompanied by his parents, at Annapolis a few weeks later, he repeated his proposal. Rosalynn was floating on a cloud of love by this time and accepted his proposal.

Jimmy's father, Mr. Earl, complained he hardly saw Jimmy while they visited him in Annapolis, and was even more disgruntled to learn how serious the romance was between Jimmy and Rosalynn. He envisioned great happenings in Jimmy's life, and Rosalynn had never been part of the picture. Even though Ruth had helped Jimmy and Rosalynn get together, now she was jealous of the closeness they felt for each other and their marriage plans. Ruth and Jimmy had always been especially close, and she felt Rosalynn was displacing her in his affections. Miss Lillian, who rooted for the underdog in any situation, was heartily in favor of the match. She had always been fond of Rosalynn.

So Rosalynn and Jimmy were married on July 7, 1946, in a small private church ceremony with no attendants. No invitations had been sent, but the church was packed with neighbors, friends and relatives.

The rosy haze that had enveloped Rosalynn through the wedding evaporated abruptly in Norfolk, Virginia, where Jimmy was stationed. He was at sea for days at a time, and Rosalynn tried to cope with learning to cook, dealing with landlords and repairmen, and doing the family banking. She was a shy Southern girl and felt she was forced to be too forward on some of these occasions.

Almost exactly a year later, on July 3, their first child, John William Carter, was born. Rosalynn spent their first wedding anniversary in the hospital.

Rosalynn found she was utterly charmed by motherhood and their wonderful baby, but with Jimmy gone so much, she found she was completely tied down. For six months she was forced to carry little Jack, as the baby was called, in her arms on a bus to buy groceries several miles away, as there were no stores nearby. At last a grocery store opened in their neighborhood and life became a little less hectic. However, Rosalynn was happy and contented in her new life, however frantic it might have been.

After two years of marriage, Jimmy was moved to a submarine base in New London, Connecticut. Rosalynn found many other service wives living nearby with whom she could visit, and the Carters settled into their new assignment gladly. They both studied art and Spanish since Jimmy was home nights now.

Jimmy's next assignment was to Hawaii, and here their second child, James Earl Carter III, was born. Rosalynn was thrilled with the beauty and climate of Hawaii and thoroughly enjoyed the eighteen months they spent there.

There were few thrills in San Diego, the locale of Jimmy's next assignment. The city was overcrowded, and the only apartment they could afford was located in an extremely rough neighborhood. Rosalynn was often afraid to go to sleep when Jimmy was away.

Their landlady in San Diego had fig trees growing in her yard. Each day she gathered the figs which had fallen to the ground and distributed them to her tenants. If she learned they had not used them, she lectured them about wastefulness. Rosalynn spent most of a week making fig preserves until she and another wife hit on the idea of mashing the figs and flushing them down the toilet!

They spent a brief time in Massachusetts before Jimmy was returned to New London where their third son, Jeff, was born. There he was notified Mr. Earl was dying from cancer. He returned immediately to Plains, and a few weeks later, resigned from the navy and moved his family back to Georgia to live.

Rosalynn was stunned. She had enjoyed their life as a navy family, and could not imagine any other way of life now. For one thing Jimmy had had a fairly good, steady income as a naval officer, and after a lifetime of money struggles, this had seemed like a luxury to her. She felt that their return to Plains was regression, not progression. Rosalynn described her reaction to Jimmy's decision in her autobiography: "I argued, I cried, I even screamed at him." But Jimmy had made up his mind. The family business needed his management skills, and back to Plains they went.

After they had settled in, Rosalynn felt as if she had really gone back to the old days. They had almost no money and were forced to live for a time in government housing. During their first year back there was severe drought in Georgia, and the family business cleared less than two hundred dollars. She held herself aloof from her former friends and neighbors and silently bemoaned her fate.

One day when her mother was visiting, she mentioned one of Rosalynn's neighbors said Rosalynn stayed in the house all the time. Her mother was tactful enough not to say she was acting strangely, but Rosalynn got the message. She decided she would rejoin life in Plains.

She found it was pleasant after all to be able to visit her mother and sister any time she wanted. Before many months had passed, Jimmy asked her to help him in the warehouse by working in the office. From that time on, Rosalynn became more contented with their life in Plains.

Their financial situation improved, and they rented a large antebellum house at the edge of town. Their sons had plenty of play space and room for pets in this location, which made them happier.

Miss Lillian had become increasingly restless since Mr. Earl's death. She heard of a job vacancy at Auburn University as housemother in a fraternity house. She got the job, and stayed there for seven years.

Jimmy and Rosalynn again began taking an active part in their church. They taught Sunday School, and Jimmy served as a deacon and directed a club for young boys in the church.

Jimmy was serving as a member of the local school board in 1954 when the U. S. Supreme Court ordered integration in all public schools. Jimmy had been strongly influenced by his mother's views and by his life in the navy, and he felt integration was an idea whose time had come. He urged the local board to comply with the new interpretation of the law. Many citizens in Plains were upset by Jimmy's viewpoint. They hurled insults at him and his family and even brought insulting placards to school board meetings. White Citizens Council members urged him to join them.

Jimmy lost any influence he might have had with the other board members, and when he was defeated on a school consolidation proposal, he resigned. He had been a member of the board for seven years.

Jimmy decided to enter the race for Georgia State Senator in 1962. He won the election but was not seated until after a long court battle over his opponent illegally stuffing ballot boxes with votes. He easily won reelection two years later.

During these political activities, Rosalynn ran their home and business, aided by Jimmy's brother, Billy, and his wife, Sybil. The Carters' sons were in school, and when Jimmy was not serving in the Legislature, the family attended sports events and went on short trips together. It was a busy, happy life, and Rosalynn wondered why she ever thought she did not want to live again in Plains.

In 1966 Jimmy ran for Governor of Georgia. Rosalynn loyally helped him campaign, but he lost the election to Lester Maddox, an avowed segregationist.

Jimmy turned his attention more fully to religion for the next several years. He made evangelistic campaigns throughout Southern states. Their daughter, Amy, was born October 19, 1967, so Rosalynn could travel with him only occasionally.

Miss Lillian had decided her nursing education and experience could be used by the Peace Corps. She joined the Corps at age sixty-eight and was sent to India.

When Jimmy again entered the race for Governor in 1970, his whole family and many friends worked feverishly to help him. Rosalynn and he went in different directions so they could speak to and shake hands with twice as many people. This time he won.

Until she went there to live, Rosalynn had never been in the Governor's Mansion. She felt somewhat overwhelmed, but she tried not to show it. At a Governor's meeting in North Carolina, just after Jimmy took office, she saw fingerbowls for the first time at a formal dinner. She thought that was what they were, but just to be sure, she waited until she saw another guest use one.

Money was still very tight for the Carters. Rosalynn and her sons' wives — two of her sons were married now — and one of the wives' mothers pooled their formal dresses. Fortunately all wore the same size, and Rosalynn got first choice. It would not do for her to appear in the same dress time after time.

Nothing in Rosalynn's past had prepared her for the job of running an Executive Mansion and training servants. Some of the servants were honor prisoners from the Georgia State Prison. At last she got a competent staff trained, and she was free to turn her attention to other matters.

Rosalynn chose to work for the mentally ill and handicapped citizens as her special project. She had long felt this was a segment of the population who had been badly neglected.

This was not her only interest. When Lady Bird Johnson, then First Lady, came to Georgia with her roadside beautification plans, Rosalynn became a sincere supporter and assistant. When First Lady Betty Ford later began her project of movable art museums, Rosalynn worked to get the advantages of the museums for Georgia citizens.

From working directly with honor prisoners and having them in her home daily, Rosalynn became interested in improving prison conditions. She devoted many hours to this cause, and was the prime mover in the establishment of work release centers for women prisoners.

When the Equal Rights Amendment was proposed by feminists, Rosalynn threw her support behind it. Jimmy was dismayed by this turn of events and felt she should have given it more time and thought, but he knew Rosalynn made up her own mind.

Jimmy proved to be a good Governor. He brought about great reduction in racial tensions in the state. He also brought reform to the state's budget program by scrapping all previous allotments for funds. Prior to this time only new requests for funds had to be justified. Now all requests for all departments had to come under scrutiny. His method saved the state of Georgia a substantial amount of money and provided the Georgia State Treasury with a surplus of two hundred million dollars.

Since Jimmy could not, by law, succeed himself as Governor, at the end of his term in 1976 he decided to run for President of the United States.

For eighteen long months Jimmy and Rosalynn traveled over the United States, speaking to people, shaking hands and making themselves known. It became a blur of faces, questions, interviews and polls for them both. It was reminiscent of his campaign for Governor, but on a huge scale.

Jimmy won the election, and the Carters moved to the White House. Two of their grown sons, Jeff and Chip, with their wives, and Amy, the ten-year old Carter daughter, went to live with them. Jeff attended George Washington University, Chip worked for the Democratic National Committee, and Amy enrolled in elementary school. The other Carter son, Jack, continued with his law practice in Calhoun, Georgia.

Rosalynn was an active partner with Jimmy in the Presidency and, in interviews, was frequently asked questions pertaining to Jimmy's plans and policy-making decisions. He acknowledged publicly that she was an equal partner, which was the first time any President had included his wife in his official group.

Rosalynn had her own office, where she worked faithfully every day. Jimmy sent her on a tour of Latin America as his official representative. There she visited seven different countries and held discussions with the various heads of state. They discussed important political issues in their own countries, as well as how the present United States government policies affected them.

As First Lady, Rosalynn preferred less formal, more modest social entertainments. Guest lists usually included at least one classical musician or other artist. These artists were not always American but were well-known in their own fields of the performing arts. Rosalynn tended to give the White House staff more authority for the details of these events than other First Ladies had done, as she did not view herself primarily as a hostess.

One of Jimmy's crowning achievements as President was the signing of the Camp David accord in September 1978. Jimmy and Rosalynn went to Camp David, the Presidential retreat in Maryland, to meet with President Anwar al-Sadat and Mrs. Sadat of Egypt and Israel's Prime Minister Menachem Begin and Mrs. Begin in an attempt to bring peace to the Middle East. When the accord was reached, it lead to the signing of a peace treaty in March the next year between Egypt and Israel. The treaty brought an end to a state of war between the two countries that had existed for the past thirty-one years.

Jimmy and Rosalynn were proud of his success with the Middle East problem, but they did not get to enjoy it long. In November 1979, the Khomeini government in Iran ordered the seizure of the American Embassy and staff in Teheran. Khomeini had recently seized control of Iran when the reigning Shah had become ill with cancer and come to the United States for treatment. President Carter felt it would be inhumane to refuse the dying man medical treatment, and he stood resolutely by his decision despite Iranian threats of retaliation.

A total of fifty-two American citizens were held hostage for four hundred and forty-four days in Iran. This situation was still unresolved when Jimmy sought reelection, and it led to his defeat in 1980. When Iranian officials learned that President Carter was leaving the White House, they loaded the hostages on planes to return them to America but did not allow the planes to take off until President Ronald Reagan had been inaugurated.

This time Rosalynn did not dread her return to Plains to live. During all the hectic campaigning for Jimmy's second term and frustration about the hostage crisis she had come to view Plains as a refuge. Her only concern was whether they would be bored when they left the intensity and political action of Washington.

Shortly after their return, both Miss Lillian and Jimmy's sister, Ruth, died. Jimmy and Rosalynn were glad they got to visit with both.

Back home now in Georgia, Rosalynn and Jimmy report their lives are as full as ever. There has been no time for boredom.

Rosalynn readily admits that Jimmy's defeat at the polls was a bitter blow to them both. After being married for forty-one years, they share disappointments and joys on the same level. The distinction between his work and her work is still blurred. Jimmy helps with cooking and other household tasks and Rosalynn handles family finances.

Jimmy placed the family peanut business in a blind trust when he became President. Sadly, the business had collapsed during their absence and they owed more than a million dollars. They managed to sell the warehouse in Plains and paid off most of their debt.

The Carters have written books, both individually and together. When they were co-authoring *Everything to Gain*, they would become so annoyed with each other that they would stop speaking for several days. To communicate, they would leave messages on their word processor. As soon as the book was finished, their hostility ended.

They are still intensely family-oriented, visiting frequently with their children, grandchildren and other relatives.

Daughter Amy, in college at Brown University, was arrested for demonstrating against apartheid in South Africa and again in November 1986 when protesting CIA recruitment on college campuses. Later it was reported she was expelled from Brown. Amy is obviously a free thinker along the lines of Miss Lillian.

In summers Jimmy and Rosalynn spend weeks helping build homes for the poor in various American cities. They are a part of Habitat for Humanity, a volunteer project.

Jimmy has always enjoyed woodworking, and he saws, nails and planes lumber for the houses, progressing to the finish work such as cabinets, etc. Rosalynn sands, paints or generally serves as a helper. Other volunteers who have worked with them say they work harder than anyone else.

Jeff is a computer consultant, Jack is now a stock-market analyst and James Earl III (Chip) is a political and business consultant. All three live in Georgia now.

Jimmy and Rosalynn have traveled more since they left Washington, most recently to the Soviet Union. In March 1987, they went to Syria and Israel to try to effect the release of American hostages currently being held there by terrorists, but they were not successful. As Rosalynn said in a recent magazine article, "Our lives are just nonstop now."

Both Jimmy and Rosalynn appear younger than their years. As they have said often, no matter what trials they face in the future, they will find comfort in their strong religious faith.

43. Sarah Jane Fulks Wyman (Reagan)

Actress Jane Wyman has the distinction of being the first living ex-wife of a President of the United States. She and President Reagan were married for eight years before they were divorced in 1949.

Jane was born Sarah Jane Fulks in St. Joseph, Missouri, on January 14, 1914. There have been some published reports that she was an adopted child, but she has never confirmed these.

Jane's father, Richard D. Fulks, was Chief of Detectives in St. Joseph. When Jane was born her brother and sister were already teenagers.

Jane was a pretty little girl with chestnut-brown curls who took dancing lessons for years. Her mother hoped Jane might someday be in movies.

When Jane was fifteen, her father died. Her brother was now a doctor. Her sister, Elsie, also a college graduate, lived and worked in Los Angeles. Jane and her mother went to California to live, and Jane graduated from Los Angeles High School.

The years of Depression began just about the time Jane was ready to go to work, and the best-paying job she could find was dancing in movies. Her mother was right when she had thought little Jane had talent.

In her various dancing jobs as a chorus girl, Jane learned of actress roles available, and she started going to auditions. She had her hair bleached to platinum blonde, and she frequently overdressed in sequinned dresses and costume jewelry, until Hollywood gossip columnist Louella Parsons told Jane she looked like a walking Christmas tree!

Jane's career muddled along for several years. She worked steadily and was highly regarded by directors and the other people with whom she worked, but starring roles eluded her.

Ronald Reagan was starring in movies when Jane first met him. She could not believe how naive and straitlaced he was, considering where he was working, but she enjoyed his obvious sincerity.

They were married on January 26, 1940, in a formal wedding ceremony. Members of both families and many friends were present. Jane had been married once previously, but this was Ronald's first marriage.

Jane Wyman. (Photo: Culver Pictures.)

The newlyweds tried to settle down to a normal life, but they had many demands on their time. They were both very popular in Hollywood, had many friends and continued to get steady acting jobs in movies.

Their little daughter, Maureen, was born January 4, 1941, and life seemed to be going smoothly for them. They were both excited about their new real-life roles as parents.

After the United States entered the war following the Japanese attack on Pearl Harbor, Ronald knew he would probably enter the armed services during World War II. Because the Reagans had such a happy, stable marriage, they became the symbols of the ideal war couple, with Ronald in the

Army Air Corps and Jane staying home working and doing all she could for the war effort.

All this favorable publicity helped the careers of both Ronald and Jane. Ronald spent much of his time in the Air Corps helping to make training films for the armed forces and doing clerical work in one of the movie studios in Hollywood. This was his assigned duty by his commanding officer since he was in the Special Services Division.

The movie, *Kings Row,* was released about the middle of 1942, having been filmed before Ronald went into service. It gave his career new dimensions as a serious actor, and he expected to receive bigger roles and a larger salary when the war ended.

Jane did her part for the war effort by going on bond-selling tours and entertaining at army camps. She continued to act in her usual roles as a dumb, amusing blonde. This typecasting was getting monotonous to her, and she longed for a dramatic part in which she could display her acting ability to advantage. There were a lot of glamour girls in Hollywood, many of whom were as talented as Jane, and competition for roles was fierce.

In 1943 Ronald began taking an interest in the activities of the actors' union, Screen Actors Guild. This interest led, in turn, to an interest in the wider world of national politics. He began to talk with Jane and friends for hours at a time on political subjects. He appeared to have less and less interest in Jane's Hollywood world.

Jane finally got the dramatic role for which she had yearned as the co-star in *Lost Weekend.* Just as she began to feel somewhat better about her acting career, however, the studio decided not to release the film. The subject matter concerned alcoholism, and the studio yielded to intense lobbying efforts by the liquor industry.

Jane's hopes of getting a better deal from her studio plunged to a new low. She made a mysterious trip out of town — and came back with a baby boy just a few days old. She and Ronald had adopted the little boy and named him Michael Edward Reagan. Jane has always said she never considered Michael any less her child than Maureen. He is her son, and that, she has said, settles that.

Lost Weekend was released after all about the same time Ronald came home from the Air Corps to stay. Hollywood acclaimed Jane's work in the picture, and she got an offer to co-star in an upcoming film, *The Yearling,* almost immediately.

Ronald got a role in *Stallion Road,* and since this film concerned horses and horse farms, Ronald and Jane bought a ranch in the San Fernando Valley and named it Yearling Row. Ronald discovered he had an intense interest in horses. He enjoyed doing the ranch work himself as a release for nervous tension, but Jane was less enthused.

Ronald continued to become more and more politically aware. His friends noticed his deepening interest in politics. Ginger Rogers, who co-starred with Ronald in a movie, said that he talked politics all during their lunch breaks. Meanwhile, Jane was becoming bored with Ronald's political talk.

Jane suffered a miscarriage not long after Ronald's return home, and in an attempt to ease her depression, she plunged headlong into her starring role in *Johnny Belinda*, in which she played a deaf-mute. The role required her to cry at times, and the director said his problem with Jane was getting her to stop crying.

Ronald brought their two children to visit her on the movie set when he could. He was by now deeply involved with Screen Actors Guild. He made trips to Washington to testify before Congress in behalf of the guild concerning possible Communist infiltration of the union.

In December 1947, Jane told the world and Ronald, via news reports, that their marriage was over. Ronald refused to believe it, and told everyone who asked him about it that he felt sure they could work out their problems. Despite a few reconciliation tries, however, Jane filed suit for divorce in May 1948, and the divorce was final on July 18, 1949.

Jane won an Academy Award for her *Johnny Belinda* role. She continued to work steadily through the years in movies—some outstanding, some losers.

Jane and Ronald stayed on friendly terms, and they cooperated with each other about the care of their children. Both children officially lived with Jane, but they spent much time with Ronald.

Today, Michael Reagan is married, has two children and works as a sales representative. Maureen entered the world of politics as her father did. She was most recently a candidate for United States Senator from California, a race she lost.

Jane remarried, as did Ronald. She married the same man twice and lives now in Beverly Hills, California. Her last husband is deceased.

Jane is presently the star in the weekly television series "Falcon Crest," in which she plays the matriarch of a large wealthy family. She receives more than one hundred thousand dollars per episode, making her the highest-paid television actress in the industry. She won the Golden Globe award in 1984 for her portrayal of Angela Channing in "Falcon Crest."

In the real world, Jane donates time to make fund-raising speeches for Catholic charities, as well as visiting with and taking an interest in her children and grandchildren.

Jane reminds anyone who asks her about her former marriage to Ronald Reagan that the marriage ended thirty-eight years ago and has no bearing on, or relevance to, her life today.

44. Nancy Davis (Anne Frances Robbins) Reagan

Nancy Davis Reagan was born Anne Frances Robbins on July 6, 1921, in Manhattan, New York. Her father, Kenneth Robbins, was an automobile salesman, and her mother, Edith Luckett, had been an actress on the stage in New York and with traveling companies. Mr. Robbins had no great enthusiasm for being either a good husband to Edith or a good father to his little daughter, so before Anne Frances had reached her second birthday, her parents were divorced.

Finding a need to support her child and herself, Mrs. Robbins returned to working as an actress. She got a job with a touring company, and it was next to impossible to take the baby with her. So Anne Frances, age two, went to live with an aunt, uncle and cousin in Bethesda, Maryland.

Anne Frances — who began to be called Nancy about this time — loved her aunt and uncle and was treated well by them. She has said she would have been happy there if her mother had been there too. She missed her mother badly and got to see her only when the touring company was playing in the area or when her mother would have a job playing a role in New York productions. Then Nancy would spend several days with her mother.

Nancy was taken to see her mother act in one play in which the character she was playing was severely mistreated. Nancy became hysterical, thinking her mother was really suffering. She went backstage after the show and would not speak to any of the other performers because she thought they had been mean to her mother.

When Nancy was seven, her mother remarried, and Nancy's whole life changed. She could live with her mother all the time. Nancy's new stepfather was Dr. Loyal Davis, a neurosurgeon in Chicago. Nancy felt as if a dream had come true. She had a whole family now with two parents.

Nancy and Dr. Davis always loved each other. No doubt he had great sympathy for the little girl who had never had a real home of her own, and he made every effort to reassure her she had one now. Nancy always thought he was wonderful in every way, and never once stopped loving him until his death in 1982.

Nancy Reagan. (Courtesy Library of Congress.)

In Dr. Davis's home, Nancy lived on a much higher social scale than before. She had beautiful clothes to wear, servants to do the work and friends who invited her to join them at parties and other fun gatherings. When Nancy was fourteen, Dr. Davis adopted her, and she took the last name of Davis. Dr. Davis had a son, Richard, so Nancy gained a new brother.

She went to the Girls' Latin School, a prestigious day school in Chicago, operated for daughters of the elite in Chicago society. After graduating there, she went on to Smith College. She had a debutante party to launch her in society.

Nancy studied drama at Smith, planning to follow in her mother's footsteps and become an actress. When she graduated from college, she went to Hollywood and was hired by Metro-Goldwyn-Meyer Studios. She appeared in a total of eleven movies, the last of which was *Hellcats of the Navy*, also starring Ronald Reagan, in 1957.

Nancy first met Ronald Reagan in Hollywood in 1951 when she discovered her name was appearing on Communist mailing lists. Since Ronald was President of the Screen Actors Guild, she went to him and asked if he could help her get her name taken off the mailing lists. She was not a Communist and had no idea why such a mistake had been made. She had no desire to receive Communist propaganda.

Ronald promised to take care of the problem — and asked her for a date! He had been divorced from his first wife, Jane Wyman, for about two years. With his good looks and winning personality, he got dates easily. He was no tightwad on dates either, often spending as much as seven hundred and fifty dollars a week in nightclubs.

But Ronald was lonely. He was not really looking for another casual date — he was hoping to find another wife. He didn't tell Nancy that, of course, and it was good he didn't. She would have thought he was rushing her.

Their romance did develop into a real love, and they were married on March 4, 1952, with actor Bill Holden serving as best man, and Ardis Holden, Bill's wife, as Nancy's matron of honor.

Ronald had been a member of the armed forces during World War II, and he had found it more difficult to get good movie roles since he had been discharged. Competition was keener. For a brief period he appeared at a nightclub called The Last Frontier in Las Vegas, Nevada, but he was not a nightclub performer by choice, and he kept looking for another job.

General Electric Corporation hired him to host the company's new weekly television program, called "G. E. Theatre." He was also to appear in a few of the plays and to work for the company in public relations. He worked for General Electric until 1962. His job involved making as many as fourteen speeches in one day at times, and this served to greatly enhance his skills as a public speaker. He found these skills handy as his involvement in politics continued to grow.

Ronald tried to stay involved in the lives of his two children from his first marriage. Both Maureen, his daughter, and Michael, his son, spent weeks each year with Ronald and Nancy in their Pacific Palisades home. Later Michael lived with them for two years. Ronald and Nancy also had children together: Patricia Ann Reagan, called Patti, was born on October 22, 1953, and Ronald Prescott Reagan, called Ron, arrived on May 28, 1958.

Even though Nancy was a successful movie actress, she decided to relinquish her career to stay home with her children. She admitted she was always far more family-oriented than career-minded.

Maureen Reagan said Nancy was offered a choice television role after her marriage, but she declined with thanks.

Nancy embraced motherhood enthusiastically, as she had her marriage commitment to Ronald. When her children were growing up, she helped with school fairs by manning a hot dog booth at John Thomas Dye School, the private school in Bel Air that both Patti and Ron attended. She involved herself in other school activities also, and helped establish a home for unwed mothers called The Colleagues. It evolved into a shelter for abused children and is now an adjunct of Los Angeles Children's Hospital.

In 1962 General Electric felt Ronald's increasing political involvement was not in keeping with company policy, and they canceled their business relationship with him. Ronald then went to work hosting "Death Valley Days" on television for the Borateem Company.

In 1964 Ronald campaigned vigorously for Presidential candidate Barry Goldwater. Mr. Goldwater did not win the election, but Ronald demonstrated his own ability as a persuasive speaker and political fund raiser. Republican party leaders began to notice Ronald Reagan.

In 1966 Ronald decided to enter the race for Governor of the state of California on the Republican ticket. Despite a bitter, vituperative campaign waged by incumbent Pat Brown, Ronald won the election. As Ronald said after he won, "I am part of the government now (a funny thing happened to me on the way to Death Valley...)."

Nancy and Ronald went to Sacramento, California, the state capital, to make arrangements to live there while he served as Governor. Nancy found the official Governor's Mansion was not at all suitable. She said the mansion was nothing but a firetrap, and she refused to live in it. She was not alone in her assessment of the safety of the mansion — the Sacramento Fire Department Chief said the Reagans would never get out of the building in time if there should be a fire. It was also located on an extremely busy one-way street near the State Capitol Building. The mansion has since been made into a museum.

The Reagans rented a private mansion from one of the town councilmen for their new residence instead. It was located in an elite neighborhood, was of Tudor design and had a swimming pool on the grounds. Here the children were near schools (Patti was now in junior high school and Ron in elementary). Nancy was severely criticized for refusing to live in the Governor's Mansion, which had no schools nearby, but she felt she took a stand any caring mother would take.

When a new Governor's Mansion was being planned, Nancy organized a statewide request for donations of antiques or old California furniture owned by private citizens to be used to furnish the new mansion for the Governor. The opposition newspapers again criticized her for her efforts.

Nancy became angry at last. She called her one and only press conference the next day and let remarks fly at the man who had been most critical. There were no more smart remarks directed at California's First Lady from that point on.

The response to Nancy's request for donations to furnish the mansion was tremendous. She completely furnished the new house with donated items, and there was no cost to taxpayers.

While living in Sacramento, Nancy often returned to Los Angeles by plane for a few days. On one trip she heard two men, who were sitting behind her, talking about Ronald and making disparaging remarks. As the comments became more and more insulting, she turned around in her seat to face them and said, "That's my husband you're talking about, and every bit of information that you two are exchanging is wrong and incorrect. I would like the chance to correct you."

The two men were, by now, red-faced and squirming. She turned back around, and heard no more insults to Ronald.

Nancy was not happy living in Sacramento. She missed being in their own home, socializing with her own friends and keeping up with local events and gossip. However, Ronald wanted to be Governor, so Nancy made the best of it. He was reelected, but was defeated in 1974 after the Watergate scandal in Washington cast a pall on Republican races nationwide.

Most of the hurtful remarks made about Nancy during these years were made by women reporters. Nancy does not often win admiration from other women, and does not seek it. She had been ridiculed for the way she fastens her eyes and total attention on her husband when he is speaking. Her detractors refer to this as "The Gaze." She looks at him this way because he is always at the center of her attention, and she is totally devoted to him.

There was no doubt in anyone's mind that Ronald wanted to be the Republican nominee for President in 1976. However, incumbent President Gerald Ford decided to seek election in his own right, so that settled the matter, with Ford narrowly defeating Ronald for the nomination. The Democratic nominee, Jimmy Carter, won the election, so the Republicans were out of power for a while.

For the next four years Ronald continued to make radio speeches as he had since 1975, and in other ways he made it plain he hoped the nomination would come his way in 1980. When not traveling and making speeches, he and Nancy worked on the ranch they had bought in the Santa Barbara area and generally stayed busy.

Their six hundred and eighty-eight acre ranch is named Rancho del Ceilo, and they paid more than a half million dollars for it. The Reagans became millionaires when Ronald sold land he owned to Twentieth Century–Fox studios during his first term as Governor of California.

The Spanish-style, stuccoed adobe brick ranch house on their ranch was built more than one hundred years ago. They have had some remodeling done, and have done some of the work themselves. When they go to California, they usually go to the ranch. As Nancy said, "Presidents don't get vacations. You just get a change of scenery." They still own their home in Pacific Palisades as well.

Stuart Spencer, a political consultant who has helped Ronald during various campaigns, insists Ronald would not have been elected President of the United States in 1980 if he had not had Nancy by his side. He says her support and drive made the difference.

Ronald Reagan was inaugurated as President on January 20, 1981, and Nancy became First Lady.

Nancy Reagan set off critics almost immediately when she proposed having the family living quarters in the White House redecorated and repainted. This has been a long-standing custom since Dolley Madison had things cleaned up for President Thomas Jefferson after he succeeded President John Adams. To hear some of the reporters tell it, Nancy was embarked on a project that would bankrupt America.

The simple fact was that the White House walls were dirty and cracked, and they badly needed painting. The floors had not been refinished since Bess Truman had them done. There was not even a good complete set of White House china, due to the regrettable habit of guests taking pieces for souvenirs.

Nancy asked friends for donations for her fix-up project. Again the familiar uproar began. But as Lyn Nofziger, Presidential assistant and political advisor, pointed out, the criticism was unfair, since private donations (such as the new dishes, which were contributed by a foundation) meant taxpayers' money was not used.

Nancy was then castigated for spending too much money for her clothes. But she was defended by those close to her. Letitia Baldrige, social advisor to both Jacqueline Kennedy and Nancy, said that because the First Lady represented American fashion, the public wanted her to be well dressed. Nancy's son, Ron, said that his mother was just trying to put the Presidency in a good light by being careful about her appearance.

Ronald had been President only a little more than two months when an attempt was made to assassinate him on March 30, 1981. His assailant was a young mental patient, John Hinckley, Jr. Ronald was seriously wounded in the attempt, and James Brady, Ronald's Press Secretary, was permanently paralyzed by the attack.

Nancy was devastated by the attack. Of course, she had known assassination was a possibility for any President, but she had not felt

Ronald had done or said anything to seriously offend anyone. She spent endless hours with her husband in the hospital. She couldn't eat or sleep, and she lost weight. Nancy is petite and slender naturally, and she could ill afford to lose any weight at all. By this time she must have questioned the wisdom of Ronald's seeking the Presidency in the first place.

Ronald tried to reassure her and the nation about his condition by throwing out one-line jokes, as when he told her, "Honey, I forgot to duck!"

As surgeons prepared to remove a bullet from his chest, President Reagan said, "I hope all you fellows are Republicans!"

It was a long, slow road to improvement in his health, but he did recover. Nancy felt better about him as time passed.

Her background before marriage and the years she spent as the wife of California's Governor gave her valuable preparation for her duties as First Lady. The Reagans entertained elegantly and tastefully. The biggest problem Nancy found in the area of entertainment was the suddenness of some of the luncheons and receptions she had to arrange. On one occasion she told her stepdaughter, Maureen, that she had just found out twenty minutes beforehand about a luncheon she was to host the next day — her fourth in two days.

Nancy Reagan has never been a supporter of the Equal Rights Amendment, nor has President Reagan. She says she and Ronald are both in favor of equal rights for the sexes but do not favor an amendment to the Constitution for that purpose.

As a former career woman, Nancy had been presumed to be in favor of the amendment at first. However, she had said on numerous occasions she was not career-oriented, and she felt women should stay home when possible and care for their own children. Betty Friedan, one of the feminist leaders, told Nancy she had an obligation to support the feminist movement. Nancy refused.

In an effort to improve her image with news reporters, Nancy agreed to appear at a Gridiron dinner. There were prestigious writers present from all over the country. A loaded dress rack was rolled on stage, and Nancy stepped out from among the dresses, in an outfit that could be only described as the ultimate in tacky. She sang a song, which poked fun at herself, then threw a china plate on the floor. The newsmen loved it!

President Reagan was present and almost fell off his chair in surprise. He had not known she planned to appear.

Nancy has received no criticism from any source in her ongoing crusades against the use of drugs and alcohol. Her "Just Say No" campaign has proved to be both popular and effective. As a California citizen and wife of the Governor of California during the turbulent 1960s, Nancy knows firsthand how insidious drugs and alcohol can be in taking over people's lives. She has traveled many thousands of miles and spent many long hours speaking and counseling, in her efforts to help young people keep their lives on track, or turn their lives around if they have been drug or alcohol abusers.

In his 1988 State of the Union Address on January 25, President Reagan gave his wife special recognition for her anti-drug program. He said the use of both cocaine and marijuana among young people is now decreasing.

Nancy is also still involved in her original Foster Grandparents Program, in which senior citizens are encouraged to "adopt" a child in day-care or an institution and serve as a surrogate grandparent. This has proved beneficial to both the children and the elderly people involved.

Both of the younger Reagan children married while their father was President. Patti married Paul Grilley, a yoga instructor, in a private wedding, and Ron married Doria Palmieri on November 24, 1980, in New York in a simple wedding. Both children are multi-talented. Patti has worked as an actress and wrote a book entitled *The Home Front*, a novel about the family of a President, said by some to be a thinly veiled account of her own life. Patti has never acknowledged the truth of this allegation, however. Ron has worked for several years as a professional dancer with the Joffrey Ballet, has written magazine articles and presently works as a feature producer for the American Broadcasting Company's news show "Good Morning, America."

Nancy's life was filled with trouble during her White House years. In addition to the horrifying assassination attempt on his life, President Reagan had colon cancer surgery, as well as treatment for skin cancer. Both Nancy's parents died during those years, and Nancy herself had a modified radical mastectomy to remove a cancerous breast. The cancer was discovered during a routine physical and had not spread. She recovered satisfactorily.

Nancy insists she did not get involved in official government affairs. She only protected her husband from people she felt were not sincere in their dealings with him. She said being First Lady was more work for her than she had expected, but she enjoyed it. She says she thinks her husband enjoyed being President, and that was what was important to Nancy.

She continued to be subjected to criticism by the media during the last few months of the Reagan administration. It was learned she consulted an astrologer on occasions, something she said began after the assassination attempt on her husband. Some reporters, as well as former White House Chief of Staff Don Regan, said she altered the date of a summit meeting between President Reagan and Soviet leader Mikhail Gorbachev based on astrological readings. They claimed she consulted the stars about the most favorable time for other appointments as well. Don Regan said her involvement with altering dates amounted to "a shadowy distaff presidency."

Nancy admitted she is interested in astrology, but said such claims by her critics were ridiculous. President Reagan, angry with Nancy's detractors, said he doesn't "look too kindly" on people who criticize her.

Both the President and Nancy were teary-eyed on the day they left the White House, with the President wandering around looking at his office one last time. He said they had known this day had to come, but he would miss being a part of the national scene.

"We have not attended church as regularly as we used to before Ronnie became President, and it's something we miss a great deal," Nancy said in a recent interview in the *Ladies' Home Journal*. Their first Sunday back in California found them worshipping in the Bel Air Presbyterian Church, where they received a standing ovation from other members of the congregation. A smiling minister cautioned them not to expect such a hearty reception every Sunday.

Nancy said her New Year's resolutions for 1989 included never giving up her fight against drug and alcohol abuse. Realizing she will not have access to the same publicity in her efforts, she said she will have the same amount of determination.

She is pleased with her husband's accomplishments, mentioning control of inflation and interest rates, a growing economy, low unemployment rates and improved relations with the Soviet Union. As she told *Ladies' Home Journal*, "These are tremendous achievements. Ronald Reagan has restored pride in America, and I am very proud to be Mrs. Ronald Reagan."

Smiling, she told the magazine interviewer that the Reagans were looking forward to returning to California. "We are going home," she said. And for Nancy that's even better than living in the White House.

Bibliography

Books

Akers, Charles W. *Abigail Adams: An American Woman*. Boston: Little Brown, 1980.

Allen, Gary. *Richard Nixon: The Man Behind the Mask*. Belmont, Mass.: Western Islands, 1971.

Ambrose, Stephen. *Eisenhower: Soldier, General of the Army, President-Elect (1890–1952)*. New York: Simon and Schuster, 1983.

Ammon, Harry. *James Monroe: The Quest for National Identity*. New York: McGraw-Hill, 1971.

Barnard, Harry. *Rutherford B. Hayes and His America*. Indianapolis: Bobbs-Merrill, 1954.

Bent, Silas, and Silas B. McKinley. *Old Rough and Ready*. New York: Vanguard, 1946.

Birmingham, Stephen. *Jacqueline Bouvier Kennedy Onassis*. New York: Grossett and Dunlap, 1978.

Bourne, Miriam Anne. *First Family: George Washington and His Intimate Relations*. New York: Norton, 1982.

Bowers, Claude G. *The Young Jefferson*. Boston: Houghton Mifflin, 1945.

Brant, Irving. *The Fourth President: A Life of James Madison*. New York and Indianapolis: Bobbs-Merrill, 1970.

Brodie, Fawn M. *Thomas Jefferson: An Intimate History*. New York: Norton, 1974.

————. *Richard Nixon: The Shaping of His Character*. New York and London: Norton, 1981.

Brough, James. *Princess Alice: A Biography of Alice Roosevelt Longworth*. Boston: Little, Brown, 1975.

Burner, David. *Herbert Hoover: A Public Life*. New York: Knopf, 1979.

Burns, James MacGregor. *Roosevelt, the Soldier of Freedom*. New York: Harcourt Brace Jovanovich, 1970.

Butler, Nicholas Murray. *Across the Busy Years: Recollections and Reflections*. New York: Scribner's, 1939.

Butterfield, L. H., Marc Friedlaender, and Mary Jo Kline. *The Book of Abigail and John: Selected Letters of the Adams Family, 1762–1784*. Cambridge, Mass.: Harvard University Press, 1975.

Cannon, Lou. *Reagan*. New York: Putnam, 1982.

Caro, Robert A. *The Path to Power: The Years of Lyndon Johnson*. New York: Knopf, 1982.

Carter, Jimmy. *Why Not the Best?* Nashville, Tenn.: Broadman, 1973.

Carter, Rosalynn. *First Lady from Plains*. Boston: Houghton Mifflin, 1984.

Cleaves, Freeman. *Old Tippecanoe*. New York: Scribner's, 1939.

Cresson, W. P. *James Monroe*. Chapel Hill: Univ. of North Carolina Press, 1946.

Daniels, Josephus. *The Life of Woodrow Wilson*. Charlotte, N.C.: C. H. Robinson, 1924.

Dugger, Ronnie. *On Reagan, the Man and His Presidency*. New York: McGraw-Hill, 1983.

Ehrlichman, John. *Witness to Power: The Nixon Years*. New York: Pocket/Simon and Schuster, 1982.

Eisenhower, Julie Nixon. *Pat Nixon: The Untold Story*. New York: Simon and Schuster, 1986.

Fleming, Thomas. *The Man from Monticello*. New York: Morrow, 1969.

Flexner, James Thomas. *Washington: The Indispensable Man*. Boston: Little, Brown, 1974.

Ford, Betty, with Chris Case. *The Times of My Life*. New York: Harper and Row, 1978.

Ford, Gerald. *A Time to Heal*. New York: Harper and Row, 1979.

Geer, Emily Apt. *First Lady: The Life of Lucy Webb Hayes*. Kent, Oh.: Kent State University Press, 1984.

Goodrich, Frederick E. *The Life and Public Services of Grover Cleveland*. Augusta, Me.: True, 1888.

Grant, Mrs. Ulysses S. *The Personal Memoirs of Julia Dent Grant*. New York: Putnam, 1975.

Hagedorn, Hermann. *The Roosevelt Family of Sagamore Hill*. New York: Macmillan, 1954.

Hamilton, Holman. *Zachary Taylor: Soldier in the White House*. New York: Bobbs-Merrill, 1951.

Handlin, Oscar and Lilian. *Abraham Lincoln and the Union*. Boston: Little, Brown, 1980.

Harwell, Richard. *Washington*. New York: Scribner's, 1968.

Hoover, Irwin Hood (Ike). *Forty-Two Years in the White House*. Westport, Conn.: Greenwood, 1974.

Howe, George Frederick. *Chester A. Arthur: A Quarter-Century of Machine Politics*. New York: Dodd, Mead, 1965.

Hoyt, Edwin P. *William McKinley*. Chicago: Reilly and Lee, 1967.

_____. *John Tyler*. New York: Abelard-Schuman, 1969.

James, Marquis. *Andrew Jackson: Portrait of a President*. New York: Grossett and Dunlap, 1937.

Johnson, Lady Bird. *A White House Diary*. New York: Holt, Rinehart and Winston, 1970.

Kane, Joseph Nathan. *Facts About the Presidents*. New York: Wilson, 1981.

Kearns, Doris. *Lyndon Johnson and the American Dream*. New York: Harper and Row, 1976.

Kennedy, Rose Fitzgerald. *Times to Remember*. Garden City, N.Y.: Doubleday, 1974.

Ketcham, Ralph. *James Madison: A Biography*. New York: Macmillan, 1971.

Klapthor, Margaret Brown. *The First Ladies*. Washington, D.C.: White House Historical Assn., with the cooperation of the National Geographic Society, 1985.

Lash, Joseph P. *Eleanor: The Years Alone*. New York: Norton, 1972.

Leech, Margaret. *In the Days of McKinley*. New York: Harper and Brothers, 1959.

_____, and Harry J. Brown. *The Garfield Orbit*. New York: Harper and Row, 1978.

Lomask, Milton. *Andrew Johnson: President on Trial*. New York: Farrar, Straus and Giroux, 1960.

Lyons, Eugene. *Herbert Hoover: A Biography*. Garden City, N.Y.: Doubleday, 1964.

McCormac, Eugene Irving. *James K. Polk*. New York: Russell and Russell, 1965.

McCoy, Donald R. *Calvin Coolidge: The Quiet President*. New York: Macmillan, 1967.

McCullough, David. *Mornings on Horseback*. New York: Simon and Schuster, 1981.

McFeely, William S. *Grant: A Biography*. New York: Norton, 1981.

Malone, Dumas. *Jefferson, the Virginian*. Boston: Little, Brown, 1948.

Mazlish, Bruce, and Edwin Diamond. *Jimmy Carter: An Interpretive Biography*. New York: Simon and Schuster, 1979.

Mellow, James R. *Nathaniel Hawthorne, in His Times*. Boston: Houghton Mifflin, 1980.

Miller, Merle. *Plain Speaking: An Oral Biography of Harry S Truman*. New York: Berkley, 1974.

————. *Lyndon, an Oral Biography*. New York: Random House, 1980.

Mollenhoff, Clark R. *The President Who Failed: Carter Out of Control*. New York: Macmillan, 1980.

Morella, Joe, and Edward P. Epstein. *Jane Wyman: A Biography*. New York: Delacorte, 1986.

Morgan, George. *The Life of James Monroe*. Boston: Small, Maynard, 1921.

Morgan, H. Wayne. *William McKinley and His America*. Syracuse, N.Y.: Syracuse University Press, 1963.

Morrel, Martha McBride. *Young Hickory*. New York: Dutton, 1949.

Morris, Edmund. *The Rise of Theodore Roosevelt*. New York: Coward, McCann and Geoghegan, 1979.

Moses, John B., M.D., and Wilbur Cross. *Presidential Courage*. New York and London: Norton, 1980.

Murray, Robert K. *The Harding Era: Warren G. Harding and His Administration*. Minneapolis: University of Minnesota Press, 1969.

Myers, Elisabeth P. *Benjamin Harrison*. Chicago: Reilly and Lee/Henry Regnery, 1969.

Nash, George H. *The Life of Herbert Hoover*. New York: Norton, 1983.

Neal, Steve. *The Eisenhowers: Reluctant Dynasty*. Garden City, N.Y.: Doubleday, 1978.

Nelson, Anson and Fanny. *Memorials of Sarah Childress Polk*. New York: 1892.

Nevins, Allan. *Grover Cleveland: A Study in Courage*. New York: Dodd, Mead, 1932.

Nichols, Roy Franklin. *Young Hickory of the Granite Hills*. Philadelphia: University of Pennsylvania Press, 1958.

Oates, Stephen B. *With Malice Toward None*. New York: Harper and Row, 1977.

Parmet, Herbert S. *Jack: The Struggles of John F. Kennedy*. New York: Dial, 1980.

Patterson, James T. *Mr. Republican: A Biography of Robert A. Taft*. Boston: Houghton Mifflin, 1972.

Prindiville, Kathleen. *First Ladies*. New York: Macmillan, 1941.

Rayback, Robert J. *Millard Fillmore*. Buffalo, N.Y.: Stewart, 1959.

Reeves, Thomas C. *Gentleman Boss: The Life of Chester Alan Arthur*. New York: Knopf, 1975.

Remini, Robert V. *Martin Van Buren and the Making of the Democratic Party*.

New York: Norton Library, by arrangement with Columbia University Press, 1970.

_____. *The Revolutionary Age of Andrew Jackson*. New York: Harper and Row, 1976.

_____. *Andrew Jackson*. Vol. I: *And the Course of the American Empire 1767 – 1821*. Vol. II: *And the Course of the American Empire 1822 – 1832*. New York: Harper and Row, 1977.

Robbins, Jhan. *Bess and Harry: An American Love Story*. New York: Putnam, 1980.

Roosevelt, Eleanor. *The Autobiography of Eleanor Roosevelt*. New York: Harper and Brothers, 1961.

Roosevelt, Elliott, and James Brough. *An Untold Story: The Roosevelts of Hyde Park*. New York: Putnam, 1973.

_____, and _____. *Mother R.: Eleanor Roosevelt's Untold Story*. New York: Putnam, 1977.

Ross, Ishbel. *Grace Coolidge and Her Era*. New York: Dodd, Mead, 1962.

_____. *The President's Wife, Mary Todd Lincoln*. New York: Putnam, 1973.

Russell, Francis. *The Shadow of Blooming Grove*. New York: McGraw-Hill, 1968.

Saunders, Frances Wright. *Ellen Axson Wilson*. Chapel Hill: University of North Carolina Press, 1985.

Seager, Robert II. *And Tyler Too*. New York: McGraw-Hill, 1963.

Sefton, James E. *Andrew Johnson and the Uses of Constitutional Power*. Boston: Little, Brown, 1980.

Severn, Bill. *Frontier President, James K. Polk*. New York: Ives Washburn, 1965.

Shachtman, Tom. *Edith and Woodrow: A Presidential Romance*. Thorndike, Me.: Thorndike, 1981.

Shepherd, Jack. *Cannibals of the Heart*. New York: McGraw-Hill, 1980.

Sievers, Harry J. *Benjamin Harrison: Hoosier Statesman*. New York: University, 1959.

_____. *Benjamin Harrison: Hoosier Warrior*. New York: University, 1960.

_____. *Benjamin Harrison: Hoosier President*. New York: Bobbs-Merrill, 1968.

Taft, Mrs. William Howard. *Recollections of Full Years*. New York: Dodd, Mead, 1914.

Taylor, John M. *Garfield of Ohio: The Available Man*. New York: Norton, 1970.

Ter Horst, J. F. *Gerald Ford and the Future of the Presidency*. New York: Okpaku, 1974.

Thomas, Helen. *Dateline: White House*. New York: Macmillan, 1975.

Thomas, Lately. *The First President Johnson*. New York: Morrow, 1968.

Truman, Margaret. *Bess W. Truman*. New York: Macmillan, 1986.

Tugwell, Rexford G. *Grover Cleveland*. New York: Macmillan, 1968.

Tully, Andrew. *When They Burned the White House*. New York: Simon and Schuster, 1961.

Wallace, Chris. *First Lady: A Portrait of Nancy Reagan*. New York: St. Martin's, 1986.

Warren, Harris Gaylord. *Herbert Hoover and the Great Depression*. New York: Oxford University Press, 1959.

Wead, Doug, and Bill Wead. *Reagan, In Pursuit of the Presidency*. Plainfield, N.J.: Haven, 1980.

West, J. B. *Upstairs at the White House*. New York: Coward, McCann and Geoghegan, 1973.

White, William Allen. *Puritan in Babylon: The Story of Calvin Coolidge*. New York: Macmillan, 1958.

Whitney, David C. *The American Presidents*. Garden City, N.Y.: Doubleday, 1985.

Withey, Lynne. *Dearest Friend*. New York: Free Press/Macmillan, 1981.

Articles

Batelle, Phyllis. "Jimmy and Rosalynn: Living Well Is the Best Revenge." *Woman's Day* (June 16, 1987).

Hall, Jane. "Presidential Pillow Talk." *Women's Day* (Oct. 25, 1988).

"James Madison, Architect of the Constitution." *National Geographic* **172**, no. 3 (Sept. 1987).

Littwin, Susan. "Why Betty Ford Decided to Share Her Most Painful Moments." *TV Guide* (Feb. 28, 1987).

Morganthau, Tom, with Thomas M. DeFrank and Mary Hager. "Let's Just Hold Hands." *Newsweek* (Oct. 26, 1986).

"Our Last White House Christmas." (Interview with Nancy Reagan.) *Ladies' Home Journal* (December 1988).

Plaskin, Glenn. "Christmas with the First Family." *Family Circle* (Dec. 2, 1986).

Shearer, Lloyd. "Intelligence Report." *Parade, the Sunday Newspaper Magazine* (November 30, 1986; Sept. 19, 1987; and Jan. 4, 1988).

U.S. News and World Report (May 11, 1970).

Weinhouse, Beth. "Nancy Reagan, Traditional First Lady." *Ladies' Home Journal* (May 1985).

Weiss, Michael J. "Nancy Reagan Gets Tough." *Ladies' Home Journal* (August 1987).

Other Sources

"ABC Evening News." Television broadcast. Jan. 22, 1989.

American Heritage Editors. *Books of the Presidents and Other Famous Americans*. 12 vols. New York: Dell, 1967.

Index